Global Media Coverage of the Palestinian-Israeli Conflict

SOAS PALESTINE STUDIES

This book series aims at promoting innovative research in the study of Palestine, Palestinians and the Israel-Palestine conflict as a crucial component of Middle Eastern and world politics. The first ever Western academic series entirely dedicated to this topic, SOAS Palestine Studies draws from a variety of disciplinary fields, including history, politics, media, visual arts, social anthropology and development studies. The series is published under the academic direction of the Centre for Palestine Studies (CPS) at the London Middle East Institute (LMEI) of SOAS, University of London.

Series Editor:

Dina Matar, PhD, Chair, Centre for Palestine Studies, and Reader in Political
Communication, Centre for Global Media and Communications, SOAS
Adam Hanieh, PhD, Reader in Development Studies and Advisory Committee
Member for Centre for Palestine Studies, SOAS

Board Advisor:

Hassan Hakimian, Director of the London Middle East Institute at SOAS

Current and Forthcoming Titles:

Global Media Coverage of the Palestinian-Israeli Conflict

Reporting the Sheikh Jarrah Evictions

Edited by
Noureddine Miladi

I.B. TAURIS

LONDON • NEW YORK • OXFORD • NEW DELHI • SYDNEY

I.B. TAURIS
Bloomsbury Publishing Plc
50 Bedford Square, London, WC1B 3DP, UK
1385 Broadway, New York, NY 10018, USA
29 Earlsfort Terrace, Dublin 2, Ireland

BLOOMSBURY, I.B. TAURIS and the I.B. Tauris logo are trademarks of Bloomsbury
Publishing Plc

First published in Great Britain 2023
This paperback edition published 2025

A catalogue record for this book is available from the British Library.

A catalog record for this book is available from the Library of Congress.

ISBN: HB: 978-0-7556-4989-1
PB: 978-0-7556-4993-8
ePDF: 978-0-7556-4990-7
eBook: 978-0-7556-4991-4

Typeset by Newgen KnowledgeWorks Pvt. Ltd., Chennai, India

To find out more about our authors and books visit www.bloomsbury.com
and sign up for our newsletters.

To my family

Contents

Contributors

Konstantin Aal is a PhD student and research associate in the Department for Information Systems and New Media at the University of Siegen, Germany. Currently his main research focus is on fall prevention with older adults (iStoppFalls) and the use of social media during the Arab Spring (Arabellion). He is also part of a research project which founded several computer clubs for children and their parents in Germany and the Westbank.

Shadi Abu-Ayyash obtained a doctoral degree in Digital Arts and Humanities from the National University of Ireland Galway. He is an assistant professor at the Faculty of Graduate Studies, Arab American University. His research interests include mediatization studies, new media and media management.

Ali M. Abushbak is pursuing PhD at AJK Mass Communication Research Centre, Jamia Milia Islamia, New Delhi, India, in new media studies. He has worked as a journalist in Gaza city, Palestine. His expertise includes broadcast journalism, conflict reporting and social media research. His area of interest includes new media, social media analytics, Israel-Palestine conflict and peace journalism.

Hussein AlAhmad holds a doctorate in Middle East Politics from the University of Exeter, UK. He is Assistant Professor in Political Communication at the Faculty of Graduate Studies, Arab American University. His ongoing research focuses on Middle East's politics and mediatized conflicts through the lens of mediatization. His key research emphasis is on pan-Arab media and its influence on Arab public sphere.

Mazhar Al-Zo'by is Associate Professor of Culture and Politics in the Department of International Affairs, College of Arts and Science at Qatar University. His interests, both in research and teaching, focus principally on the politics of representation, identity and social change in the context of globalization. While his work is comparative in nature, his area of focus is the Muslim world in general and the Arab world in particular. Among the critical issues on which his teaching and writing have concentrated are the role of culture in the production of hegemony, media and identity, social movements, colonial discourse and the world system.

Yusuf Devran is a professor at the Faculty of Communication, Marmara University, Turkey. His main research interests are in media studies, media language and political communication. Devran is the author of seven books and scores of scientific papers in English and Turkish.

Rania El-Malky is a professor of practice at the Journalism Program of the Doha Institute for Graduate Studies, where she teaches video journalism, news writing, multimedia storytelling and documentary production. She holds a Master of Fine Arts (MFA) degree in Documentary Production and Studies from the University of North Texas. El-Malky also holds a master's degree in journalism (International) with distinction from London's Westminster University, which she attended as a Chevening scholar. Her transition to documentary film-making and higher education followed a long career as a reporter and editor, which culminated in a six-year tenure as editor-in-chief of the Cairo-based *Daily News Egypt*, then the local publishing partner of the *International Herald Tribune*.

Zaina Erhaim is a communication and gender expert working with a couple of international organizations in the Middle East and North Africa region. Zaina contributed to three books related to journalism and women including 'Our Women on the Ground'. She worked with IWPR as communications manager for eight years. Before that, she was a journalist with BBC. She writes for different outlets such as Newslines Magazines, Open Democracy and Al Modon, amongst others. Zaina has an MA in International Journalism from City University of London.

José Luis Gordillo has a PhD in Law from the University of Barcelona, Spain. He is an associate professor in the Department of Political Science, Constitutional Law and Legal Theory. He has published six books and more than thirty articles on subjects such as civil disobedience, pacifism, ecology and law, the constitutional role of the monarchy and the war on terrorism. He is also a senior researcher at the Delàs Centre for Peace Studies.

Loreley Hahn-Herrera holds a PhD in Media from SOAS, University of London, where she is currently a lecturer at the Centre for Global Media and Communications. Her work and research interests focus on the use of ICTs and the implementation of discursive practices by state and non-state actors.

Kelly Lewis is a research fellow in the Australian Research Council Centre of Excellence for Automated Decision-Making and Society (ADM+S) and the Emerging Technologies Lab at Monash University. Her interdisciplinary research focuses on the social, political and cultural implications of digital media technologies and platforms, as well as new and innovative digital methods and critical approaches for studying them, with an emphasis on social justice, visual politics, power and violence. Kelly holds a PhD in Digital Media and Communication from Queensland University of Technology (2020), an MSc in Media Psychology from the University of Salford, a Graduate Diploma in Journalism and a BA in Visual Art (photography) from the University of South Australia.

Sherouk Maher is a UAE-based journalist and multimedia producer with more than eight years in media and public affairs. She holds a Bachelor of Arts in Mass Communication and Journalism, with high distinction from the American University of Sharjah, and is currently pursuing an MA in Global Media and Digital Cultures at

SOAS University of London. Previously, she was part of the communications team at the UAE Government Media Office under the Ministry of Cabinet Affairs. Some of the stories she reported throughout her tenure as a journalist have been quoted in the *Guardian*, the *Independent* and *BBC*.

Dounia Mahlouly lectures for SOAS Centre for Global Media and Communications, where she convenes the postgraduate programme 'Global Digital Cultures' and 'International Political Communication'. She designed the 2021 course entitled 'Prejudice, Conspiracy and Misinformation', which explores contemporary academic debates about 'post-truth' from a critical perspective and beyond the Eurocentric framework of Western neoliberal democracies. Her work focuses on the interplay between state and non-state actors' communication strategies in post-2011 North Africa. She completed her PhD at the University of Glasgow in partnership with the American University in Cairo in 2015. She is the founder of the Middle East Research Hub, a non-profit association, which promotes the work of young analysts from across the Middle East and North Africa and carries out fundraising activities to support research capacity programmes in the region.

Tawseef Majeed has a practice-based PhD in documentary studies from AJK Mass Communication Research Centre, Jamia Milia Islamia, New Delhi, India, with a precise focus on memory, violence and trauma. He worked as a video journalist and later became engaged with documentary film production. He explores novel possibilities of non-fiction animation to contribute to the practice of narrative and film journalism. His areas of research include animation, documentary, journalism, Kashmir, Palestine, press freedom, memory, representation and media psychology.

Dina Matar is a professor at the School of Oriental and African Studies (SOAS), University of London. She is also Chair of the Centre of Palestine Studies. Dina works on narrative politics, media and conflict, political communication, cultural politics, memory, oral history and Islamist movements in the Arab World and its diaspora. Dina was co-founder and co-editor of the *Middle East Journal of Culture and Communication*. She is also co-editor of the journal *War, Media and Conflict*. Her publications include *What It Means to Be Palestinian*; *The Hizbullah Phenomenon*; *Narrating Conflict in the Middle East: Discourse, Image and Communication Practices in Lebanon and Palestine* and *Gaza as Metaphor*.

Aaya Miladi studies Politics and International Relations at the University of Leeds, UK, and is a researcher on the project 'Media Coverage of the Palestinian-Israeli Conflict'. Being half Tunisian in origin, she is naturally invested in the Arab world and Middle Eastern politics. More specifically, she is interested in studying the power dynamics at play in a post-colonial world, especially with regard to the role of media representation and discourse creation in the formation of narratives concerning the Global South.

Karima Miladi has a Bachelors in Linguistics and Literature from Queen Mary University of London and an MPhil in Anglo-Saxon, Norse and Celtic Studies from the University of Cambridge. Her research interests lie in the study of languages, discourse, historical archives and film analysis.

Noureddine Miladi is a professor of media and communication and former Head of the Department of Mass Communication at Qatar University. He is the editor of *Global Media Ethics and the Digital Revolution* (2022) and co-editor of *Routledge Handbook on Arab Media* (2021). He is currently working on a research project, 'Media and Social Change in the GCC Countries'. Miladi supervises MA and PhD researchers in social media and social change, media and democracy, Arab/Middle Eastern media systems and media ethics.

Aspriadis Neofytos is a research affiliate at the Center for Information, Technology and Public Life of the University of North Carolina at Chapel Hill. He worked before as a visiting research fellow at the Department of Political Science and International Relations of the University of Peloponnese, conducting research on strategic communication in international crises with a focus on domestic home front management. He got a PhD with a scholarship from the State Scholarship Foundation of Greece (IKY) from the Department of International and European Studies of the University of Piraeus. His research interests are in strategic communication, crisis communications, public diplomacy, information warfare, psychological operations, fake news, disinformation, character assassination and rhetoric.

Sarah Rüller holds a degree in Media Science (BA) and in Human Computer Interaction (MSc) from the University of Siegen. Since January 2020, Sarah Rüller has been working as a research associate in the Department of Information Systems and New Media. She continues to work in subproject B04 of the Collaborative Research Center 1187 – Media of Cooperation. Her research interests are Ethnography in HCI, Intercultural Learning Settings and Community Cooperation and Innovation.

Ruth Sanz Sabido is Reader in Media and Social Inequality at Canterbury Christ Church University and Director of the Centre for Research on Communities and Cultures. She has authored two monographs: *The Israeli-Palestinian Conflict in the British Press* (2019) and *Memories of the Spanish Civil War: Conflict and Community in Rural Spain* (2016) and edited *Representing Communities: Discourse and Contexts* (2017). Her research interests include media discourse, memory studies, war and conflict, violence against women and social movements.

Peter Tolmie is an ethnographer and ethnomethodologist who has worked on a wide range of HCI-related projects since 1997. He previously worked at Xerox Research Centre Europe and the Mixed Reality Lab at the University of Nottingham and is now the principal research scientist in the Department of Information Systems and New Media at the University of Siegen. He has conducted ethnographic studies across numerous settings, including: retail banking; small businesses; home environments; journalism; museums; and film, TV and music production.

Christopher David Tulloch is Associate Professor of International Journalism and Global Communication at the Pompeu Fabra University in Barcelona. He has published various books and articles in journals such as *Media, Culture and Society, Journalism Studies, Journal of Communication Inquiry* and *Journal of Mass Communication Education* on subjects such as the role of the press in political transitions, foreign correspondents and armed conflicts, communication and crisis, press coverage of terrorism, climate change in the media, journalism innovation and media ethics. He is also associate professor at the Peace University of the United Nations in Costa Rica.

Volker Wulf is Professor of Information Systems and New Media at the University of Siegen. He is also the Managing Director of the School of Media and Information (iSchool) at the University of Siegen. In addition, he heads a research group at the Fraunhofer Institute for Applied Information Technology (FhG-FIT) in Sankt Augustin. His research interests lie primarily in the area of Socio-Informatics, taking a practice-based approach to the design of IT systems in real-world settings. This includes the development of innovative applications in the areas of cooperation systems, knowledge management and community support

Muhammad Jameel Yusha'u is Edward S Mason Fellow at the John F. Kennedy School of Government and candidate for the Mid-Career Masters in Public Administration at Harvard University, USA. He is editor-in-chief of *Africa Policy Journal* at Harvard Kennedy School and the author of *Regional Parallelism and Corruption Scandals in Nigeria*; and co-editor of the *Palgrave Handbook of International Communication and Sustainable Development*. He worked as a journalist for the BBC World Service, London, and was Senior Lecturer in Media and Politics at Northumbria University, Newcastle-upon-Tyne, UK. He also taught Global Journalism at the University of Sheffield and Mass Communications at Bayero University, Kano, Nigeria. Dr Yusha'u holds a PhD in Journalism Studies and MA in Political Communication from the University of Sheffield, MBA from IE Business School and Bachelor's Degree in Mass Communication from Bayero University, Kano, Nigeria.

Introduction

Noureddine Miladi

This edited volume discusses the complexity of the media war that took place in Palestine/Israel during May 2021. Various international news media organizations covered the outbreak of the dramatic events at the time, which started with the forced eviction attempts of Palestinian residents in Sheikh Jarrah area in East Jerusalem by the Israeli army and Israeli settlers. Covering the Arab-Israeli conflict remains one of the hot yet contentious issues on the international news agenda. It has generated more attention as well as complaints about the discrepancies in news reporting than any other conflicts in other parts of the world. The region has one of the highest concentrations of journalists in the world, reflecting the intense worldwide interest in the conflict. But how have local, regional and global media outlets been covering the ongoing conflict? To what extent have citizen journalists challenged the propaganda war? What competing narratives emerge about the conflict due to the explosion in digital technology widely available to activists on both sides?

This edited book attempts to unpack the media management of this war by the different players in this crisis. It looks at the stance Israeli as well as Western media have taken in covering the conflict as compared to the Palestinian, Arab and other world media. What alternative news have social media networks been providing in reporting this war as compared to global media channels supportive of the Israeli narrative? In sum, the book argues that the media war, which previously used to take place on TV screens, radio airwaves and newspapers, is nowadays mostly conducted on virtual platforms. Social media sites have become the new sophisticated battlegrounds of activism where the war narratives are reported and challenged at the same time.

Book outline

Part One of the book presents a cross-country perspective on the media coverage of the Sheikh Jarrah events in Jerusalem during May 2021. Contributions are concerned here about the discrepancies on how the conflict was reported, and what distinguished one narrative from another.

Chapter 1 titled 'Digital Media and the War of Narratives in Reporting the Palestinian-Israeli Conflict' introduces the debate about the media coverage of the conflict in light of the modern technological changes. Noureddine Miladi and Aaya Miladi argue that the media war, which ignited in May 2021, revealed yet again a complex picture in relation to how the Palestinian-Israeli conflict was told by various actors. The chapter highlights the growing presence of social media platforms as tools employed to counter balance fake news, and whitewashing attempts to duck the Palestinian narrative about what takes place on the ground. The chapter also furnishes the reader with background context on the history of the conflict and the continuous occupation as key reasons for Palestinians' growing tension.

In Chapter 2, 'Gaza 2021: Newsworthiness and Context in the Spanish News Coverage of the Israeli-Palestinian Conflict', Ruth Sanz Sabido employs a Critical Discourse Analysis of 369 articles published by the online version of 3 mainstream Spanish newspapers (*El País*, *El Mundo* and *La Vanguardia*) and three alternative native online newspapers (*El Español*, *El Confidencial* and *OK Diario*) as a way of comparing the media coverage of the Sheikh Jarrah events. Her chapter explores two main aspects of the coverage: the newsworthiness of this conflict in the Spanish press and the contextualization of the May 2021 clashes in relation to the past and contemporary events. The analysis indicates that the newsworthiness of the conflict increases when new violent clashes erupt, and violence tends to be represented as retaliatory. There is a significant focus on the resulting humanitarian crisis and, above all, proper historical contextualization is mostly lacking. The chapter argues that this contextual gap should be addressed in order to challenge the reductionist views that emphasize the religious and violent nature of the conflict and minimize its political and territorial aspects.

Chapter 3, titled 'Counter-Hegemonic Global Media Narratives on the Palestine–Israel Conflict: The Sheikh Jarrah Protests on CGTN, RT, France 24 and TeleSUR' by Christopher D. Tulloch and Jose Luis Gordillo, presents an original perspective on the media coverage of the conflict by examining the news production on the websites of four counter-hegemonic state-funded television channels during the conflict in Gaza and Israel following the forced evictions of Palestinian families in the Sheikh Jarrah neighbourhood of East Jerusalem in May 2021. The case study features the global media platforms of three permanent members of the UN Security Council – China, Russia and France – along with those financed by three Latin American governments – namely Venezuela, Cuba and Nicaragua – and identifies a divergent news narrative on this story compared to the dominant version of events offered by the Anglo-American media. A qualitative content analysis of the main stories produced and a detailed consideration of the discursive frames, visual aspects, sourcing techniques and semantic structures deployed by them allowed the authors to discover common lines of argument as well as some specific elements in their media discourse regarding the Israel–Palestine story. As well as highlighting the most salient of these shared narrative elements, this analysis points out how in each case the official media outlets of each country instrumentalized the story to fit their wider ideological interests.

Chapter 4, titled 'Media Coverage of the Palestinian-Israeli Conflict, Comparing Al Jazeera English and i24News' by Noureddine Miladi, Ranya El-Malky and Karima Miladi, analyses what the authors consider manifest discrepancies between the news coverage of Israeli TV channel i24News and Al Jazeera English (AJE) satellite TV of the Sheikh Jarrah events and the violent conflict between the Palestinians and the Israelis in May 2021. The chapter discusses the news agenda and editorial line of i24News and AJE by analysing language uses, news sources, framing and the historical narrative each network advances. Based on recordings from two weeks of the conflict, Miladi, El-Malky and Miladi analyse news values of each network, especially issues related to objectivity and impartiality, and identify the extent to which each of the two channels covers the news objectively.

In Chapter 5, 'SDG16 in the News: Digital News Coverage of Sheikh Jarrah in Nigerian Newspapers', Muhammad Jameel Yusha'u posits that the news coverage of the Sheikh Jarrah quarter in the Israeli/Palestinian conflict has generated strong interest in the global and local news media organizations. While news media organizations pay attention to news about conflicts, the coverage of Sheikh Jarrah is unique in many ways. It took place during the Covid-19 pandemic when the lockdown placed a heavy toll on the local population. Most importantly, it took place in the so-called decade of action (2020–30) when the UN's Sustainable Development Goals (SDGs) are supposed to be accelerated. SDG16 focuses on peace, justice and strong institutions. In this chapter, Yusha'u asks how is it possible to achieve SDG16 by 2030 without resolving the Israeli/ Palestinian conflict? Do news organizations reflect the targets of SDG16 on peace, justice and strong institutions in their coverage of Sheikh Jarrah? How do Nigerian newspapers report the Sheikh Jarrah eviction, and is SDG16 a factor in the reporting?

Chapter 6, titled 'Reporting the Sheikh Jarrah Evictions on TRT World's Twitter Account' by Yusuf Devran, discusses how TRT World covered the conflict, in which Israeli forces attempted to evacuate Palestinians from their homes in early May 2021. Both in traditional media and on internet platforms, the events covered gained great interest. In this study, content published on TRT World Twitter account between 14 and 20 May 2021 about the above-mentioned events in Palestine is analysed. The language, words, sentence structures, cause-and-effect relations, news sources, experts' opinions, background information and all rhetorical dimensions of TRT World Twitter account have been examined. Through this analytical method, the study discusses whether TRT has objectively presented the case to its global audience. It is anticipated that this work will contribute to both the readers and media professionals towards helping them analyse TRT World's social media reporting on the current conflict and other issues in the Middle East.

Part Two of this book moves to address the social media management by various players in an attempt to influence both local and international public opinion.

It starts with Chapter 7 titled 'Digital Activism and the Politics of Protest: Palestine and the Struggle for Global Popular Representation' by Mazhar Al-Zo'by, who argues that the tragic limit of reporting the Palestinian plight in global media persists in its denial of the Palestinian self-narration and the writing of its own collective communal identity into history. However, the dramatic evolution of the global public sphere has ushered in alternative and shifting forms and features in social advocacy and political mobilization in many contemporary societies. During the Israeli military assault on Gaza and East Jerusalem in the summer of 2021, it was amply clear that alternative social media as well as global mass-mediated digital discourse played a vital and transformative role in the coverage and representation of the Palestinian struggle, experiences and realities under occupation. Within this digital-political ecology, this chapter argues that celebrities as public figures have assumed a critical role in advocacy communication strategies as well as the mobilization of discursive tactics in mass-media politics. In order to analyse the critical features of this form of celebrity powered activism related to Palestine, this chapter, argues Al Zo'by, revisits the Gramscian notion of the 'organic intellectual' as *dirigenti,* where the public figure assumes a 'directive' role to guide and frame public and popular discourse for transformative collective action and political change. By analysing celebrity social media discourse and narratives, this chapter contends that celebrity social media platforms critically challenged the hegemonic capacity of conventional media narratives to manage and regulate the production, framing and dissemination of mass communications and information related to the war.

Then, Chapter 8 titled 'The Orchestration of Activist Events: Making Protests Heard (and Seen)' by Konstantin Aal, Sarah Rüller, Peter Tolmie and Volker Wulf draws upon a detailed longitudinal ethnographic study of an activist in a village in Palestine. It examines the rhythm and routine of the demonstrations he was involved in and the well-oiled division of labour that enabled them to be orchestrated across time. The authors argue that as demonstrations in the village changed over time, their focus also changed, with a shift away from physical demonstrations and towards virtual and online demonstrations. They illustrate how the multi-modal, multi-party character of demonstrations and their orchestration demands a wide variety of ICT-based cooperative practices and articulation work. Through this, the authors offer a variety of new insights about what it takes to make protests happen and the role ICT plays within that.

In Chapter 9 titled '#PalDigiplomacy: Palestinian Online Public Diplomacy during Israel's 2021 Attacks', Loreley Hahn-Herrera examines the online content production of the Palestinian Ministry of Foreign Affairs (PMoFA) on Twitter (@pmofa and @MofaPPD) and Instagram (@palestine.mofa) during Israel's military campaign against the Gaza Strip between 6 and 21 May 2021. The chapter focuses on the main frames used by the Palestinian Ministry of Foreign Affairs to articulate strategic narratives through its digital diplomatic practice. Conducting a frame analysis of 286 tweets and 18 Instagram postings reveals that the frames articulated by the PMoFA were emotion and affection, settler colonialism, violence, human rights, and solidarity and internationalization. Findings show how the PMoFA articulates its institutional voice during a highly contested time by using these frames in an overlapping way. This serves, argues Hahn-Herrera, as a storytelling mechanism that aims to construct knowledge, bypass negative mainstream media coverage and improve Palestine's international standing by aiding its overall soft power strategy and the creation of online affective publics. The digital diplomatic practice of the PMoFA constructs and portrays a national identity that makes visible and legitimizes the history of the Palestinian struggle for justice and self-determination.

In Chapter 10, titled 'Social Media, Activism and Mass Protest: Framed Narratives of the May 2021 Sheikh Jarrah's Events', Shadi Abu-Ayyash and Hussein AlAhmad examine the Palestinian narrative on social media platforms during May 2021, in which the Sheikh Jarrah neighbourhood was at the centre of political and media attention. The study follows contents of social media accounts of renowned activists, politicians, academics, celebrities and solidarity groups in Palestine and its diaspora, examining how collective narratives were framed. The authors applied narrative segmentation, framing analysis and binary opposition analysis to digital content. Using the hashtag #SaveSheikhJarrah as a key word for searching content, the chapter found two dominant frames in the narratives: colonial policies frame and resistance frame.

Findings indicate that intervention of social media platforms by acts of censorship and deleting activists' accounts play a role in the mediatized conflict's dynamics. Meanwhile, the high engagement of Palestinian youth on social media provided very rich visual contents, which contributed to the notion that, in mediatized conflicts, social media actors who are at the centre of events play a significant role in enriching conflict digital content, amplifying events and framing their own narratives.

Chapter 11, 'Palestinian War Narrative and Social Media: Ethnographic Account of the Victims of Israel–Palestine War during May 2021' by Tawseef Majeed and Ali M. Abushbak, takes a comprehensive look at the victims, who are also social media users, and offers perspectives on documenting, disseminating and archiving personal war memories using social media as means and space. The main arguments reflect on structures of space on social media as an alternative stage, facilitated by media accessibility, immediacy, lesser censorship and wider reach.

Contextualizing the Israel–Palestine conflict, the key prospects of the chapter explore the shift from the physical spaces of memories and experiences to the virtual space on social media, especially peoples' memories and emotional associations with (what becomes) the past/history. The victim–user perceptions towards their personally recorded evidence evoke possible degrees of emotional interaction and a participatory approach to witnessing the war. Looking through the produsage theory (Bruns, 2007) and the theory of reasoned action (Fishbein and Ajzen, 2010) lenses, the current section tries to understand the specific behaviour of the war victims (users) to record and share their intimate (war) memories, and how that (changed) behaviour affects the broader narrative of resistance literature and journalism. By employing an ethnographic approach, the chapter uses phenomenology and in-depth interviews with the victim-users as a comprehensive methodological pattern to manifest their testimonies. It aims to have an inclusive understanding of their behaviour to (personally) portray the war narratives as their individual experiences and perception. Besides, the methodological design also ensures an evocative conception of the socio-politico-technological aspects of the narratives. Keeping in view the narratological portrayal of the war memories facilitated by social media, the chapter comprehends embedded motivations, behavioural changes and spaces of war memories in the context of social media usage during the recent Israel–Palestine war in May 2021.

Part Three of this book, titled 'Social Media Management and Public Opinion Control', brings in various contributions about the way various actors on social media attempt to manage the dissemination of information on the conflict.

Chapter 12, titled 'Comparative Analysis of Israeli and PLO Diplomacy Practices during the May 2021 Israeli Attacks against Gaza' by Sherouk Maher and Dina Matar, offers a comparative analysis of the public diplomacy practices of Israel and the Palestine Liberation Organization (PLO). By employing a thematic analysis of the contents of the official Twitter accounts of the Israeli prime minister's office and that of the PLO during the May 2021 armed violence in Gaza, in which 240 Palestinians and 12 Israelis were killed, the chapter addresses the different modes of delivery that the two entities used to communicate their messages to the intended recipients. Based on the analysis of tweets published by the official Twitter accounts of the Israeli prime minister (@IsraeliPM) and the PLO (@nadplo), the authors discuss how state and non-state actors consistently seek to maintain what may be called effective strategic public diplomacy that adapts to the rapidly expanding technologies. The chapter suggests that public diplomacy practices are determined by socio-political contexts and, in this case, the nature of the ongoing asymmetric conflict between Israel and the Palestinians. It also suggests the challenges to these practices by grassroots activists and ordinary people using digital platforms to tell alternative narratives of lived experiences and events, thus underscoring the complex and fluid dynamics between media, politics and diplomacy in the twenty-first century.

In Chapter 13, titled 'Platform Necropolitics: Content Moderation and Censoring of Pro-Palestinian Voices on Social Media', Kelly Lewis posits that the violence of the May 2021 Israeli-Palestinian conflict revealed the significance of social media platforms as spaces for Palestinians to publicize instances of human rights violations, conflict and dispossession. It also highlighted the implications of asymmetrical content moderation processes and platform policies that led to the removal of this content and re-obscured the Palestinian struggle. Lewis develops the notion of *platform necropolitics* and demonstrates its theoretical resourcefulness through an examination of pro-Palestinian censorship during the May 2021 Israeli-Palestinian conflict. Platform necropolitics manifests through the corporate and sovereign logics of platforms that violently police the boundaries of speech and space – determining who has the right to speak and who has the right to appear as a legitimate digital citizen, and who does not – and that take as their object the articulations of digital subjects and enact their 'right to kill or let live'. Exploring the tensions of digital media technologies as spaces that we live *with*, *in* and *through*, considering platforms as *political* and *material* actors that determine and condition the social, political and material (in)existence of digital subjects, the author examines how platforms enact forms of necropolitical power though corporate and machinic logics that simultaneously extend and reproduce the necropolitical power of the Israeli state.

In Chapter 14, titled 'Pro-Palestinian Activism: Resisting the Digital Occupation', Dounia Mahlouly and Zaina Erhaim draw on a case study of the gatekeeping processes that precluded biased media coverage of the events leading to the destruction of Gaza's al-Jalaa tower by Israeli forces in May 2021. They start by examining how recent experiences of Palestinian online activism feature in the history of surveillance and censorship imposed on the occupied territories of Gaza and the West Bank. By referring to these long-lived experiences of 'digital occupation', the authors argue that corporate and military control over Palestinian communication networks extends far beyond the region. Mahlouly and Erhaim's case study specifically explores the challenges faced by transnational networks of pro-Palestinian activists, who worked collaboratively to relay Palestinian voices during the crisis of May 2021. The chapter highlights different forms of systemic control over technological infrastructures that resulted in a lack of impartiality and inclusiveness on the part of international media outlets.

Finally, in Chapter 15, titled 'The Media War in the Palestinian-Israeli Conflict: Examining Interstate Character Assassination in International Media', Aspriadis Neofytos examines the presence of character assassination in international media regarding the coverage of the conflict. Neofytos argues that this would expand the hypothesis of character assassination in international relations and shows that such strategies could affect or be used by international news media. In addition, it would add to the existing literature on the Israel–Palestine conflict coverage proposing another explanation for the bias observed. Character assassination is the deliberate destruction of a person's reputation or credibility through character attacks. Such attacks may be used against collective targets like groups, states or nations. This is common among political elites of a country and the media. Data analysis in this work was conducted on three major news media networks, CNN, The Times of Israel and Al Jazeera English. The author aims, through this investigation, to examine the mediated character assassination in interstate conflicts based on the formation of images of the countries in conflict.

Bibliography

Bruns, A. (2007), 'Produsage: Towards a Broader Framework for User-Led Content Creation', *Proceedings of 6th ACM SIGCHI Conference on Creativity and Cognition 2007*, presented at the 6th ACM SIGCHI Conference on Creativity and Cognition 2007, Association for Computing Machinery, New York, 13–15 June 2007, 99–105.

Fishbein, M., and I. Ajzen (2010), *Predicting and Changing Behavior: The Reasoned Action Approach*, New York: Psychology Press.

Part One

Mediating the Conflict:
Cross-Country Perspectives

1

Digital media and the war of narratives in reporting the Palestinian-Israeli conflict

Noureddine Miladi and Aaya Miladi

Background to the conflict: The blockade of Gaza, occupation of Palestinian land and the expansion of Israeli settlements

The Palestinian-Israeli conflict is among the longest witnessed in modern history. Origins of the conflict date back to the British Mandate for Palestine (1918–48), marked by a period of consolidation of imperial rule and exploitation of Palestinian land in favour of waves of Jewish settlers coming from Europe and the United States. A landmark historical turn was the forced eviction of hundreds of thousands of Palestinians, which began on 14 May 1948 and coincided with the declaration of the state of Israel (Khalidi, 2019). As a result, the first war of many broke out between Palestinians and Jewish groups armed by the British colonial power. This led to what is called the 'Nakba', the violent expulsion of 750,000 Palestinians from their homeland. Most of the expelled Palestinians eventually sought refuge in other parts of Palestine or migrated to various neighbouring Arab countries (Khalidi, 2019). As for the historical Palestine as a country which existed prior to that date, it was split into Israel, the West Bank (of the Jordan River) and the Gaza Strip.

Relations with neighbouring Egypt, Jordan and Syria were not smooth over the following decades with the new Jewish state. The 1956 Suez crisis was the start of a series of major wars after Israel's invasion of the Sinai Peninsula. The next major clash was during the 1967 war, where Israel attacked Syrian and Egyptian air forces, preventing any attempts at retaliation by the Egyptian army led by President Gamal Abdel Nasser. The Camp David Accords signed between Egypt and Israel in 1979 paved the way for a long-term peace treaty but did not serve justice to Palestinians, as it delayed them gaining the right to self-determination and self-rule. Palestinians had to wait until 1993, for the Oslo Accord, to earn a form of unprotected sovereignty on Gaza and the West Bank. The Palestinian Authority (PA), headed by the late Yasser Arafat, was then formed, which became the political umbrella for Palestinians' mediation with the state of Israel as well as the outside world.

Over the decades, the Israeli government has been very reluctant to address the underlying issues of the occupation, hence tensions escalate again and again, following a seemingly determined cycle. For instance, the second 'Intifada' was sparked in 2000 due to the deterioration of Palestinians' living conditions, coupled with Prime Minister Ariel Sharon's invasion of the al-Aqsa mosque in Jerusalem sheltered by hundreds of armed Israeli police. Israel's landmark decision to build a separation wall around the West Bank in 2002 further worsened the occupation's ongoing stifling of Palestinian lives by confiscating more and more Palestinian lands. The Apartheid Wall (as called by Palestinians), deemed illegal by the International Court of Justice, has kept Palestinians and Palestinian land in total isolation from each other. Occupied Palestinian areas have also remained under very strict restrictions on the movement of goods and people. Various civil society organizations have warned Israel and the international community against the drastic repercussions on Palestinian lives due to this wall. The UN Office for the Coordination of Humanitarian Affairs (OCHA) affirmed in 2002 that the wall would restrict

> Palestinian freedom of movement, Palestinian livelihoods and Palestinian access to land – a wall, which divides upon ethnic, national and religious identity. The apartheid wall involves the illegal annexation of some of the most fertile lands in the West Bank and water sources, while pushing Palestinians further into Bantustans, cantons and enclaves, where Israel can ensure maximum control over Palestinian lives and land. (OCHA, 2002)

The ensuing years evidently witnessed an ebb and flow of violent events between the Israeli occupation forces and Palestinians, including armed groups like Hamas, Palestinian Islamic Jihad, Popular Front for the Liberation of Palestine and Democratic Front for the Liberation of Palestine. On 8 July 2014, the Israeli army launched what it called 'Operation Protective Edge', an attack on Gaza ostensibly targeting Hamas's infrastructure. About 2,256 Palestinians were killed during the offensive, 70 per cent of whom were civilians, as recorded by the United Nations Relief and Works Agency for Palestinian Refugees in the Near East (UNRWA). The cumulative death on the Israeli side was seventy people, of whom sixty-six were Israeli Defense Force (IDF) soldiers (UNRWA, 2014). Joronen (2016: 337) studied the Israeli government discourse during Operation Protective Edge and attempted to analyse 'the argument used to morally justify killing on the calculative basis of causing only the minimum necessary collateral damage'. Joronen contends that the military aggression, which resulted in the death of 2,256 Palestinians in Gaza was ethically justified by the Israeli army through various 'warning techniques which range from roof knocking to cautionary phone calls, text messages and air-dropped flyers' (Joronen, 2016: 337).

House demolition and land confiscation by Israel

There are limited statistics on demolitions during the first few years of Israeli occupation since 1967; however the UN documented information on demolitions as early as 1971, reporting on the destruction of thousands of houses and at least eleven entire villages (UN Special Committee, 1971: Chapter III. Section C). The Israeli Committee Against House Demolitions (ICAHD), in combining information from various organizations,[1] estimates that 54,000 Palestinian homes have been demolished in the occupied territories, including Gaza, from 1967 to 2018 (Halper, 2018: 58). This is not including the estimated 52,000 demolished within Israel during the first Nakba of 1947–48.

Demolitions come in three types: punitive (as punishment for specific people who live in the inhabitations), administrative (for homes without building permits, which are near impossible for Palestinians to acquire) and military/land-clearing (Halper, 2018: 58). The vast majority, 66 per cent, are military demolitions, with 20 per cent administrative (Halper, 2018: 58). Between 1967 and 1969, a period known as the second Nakba, when the West Bank and East Jerusalem became Israeli-occupied territories, 7,554 homes were demolished. After 1971, the numbers of demolitions per year drastically decreased, nevertheless in the first decade from 1967, 10,308 homes were destroyed (Halper, 2018: 59).

Israeli demolition of Palestinian homes continued under various pretexts over the decades in a systematic manner. From 1977 to 1986, the total was 216, but by the third decade (1987–97) demolitions increased again, on an average, 284 a year, and so totalling 2,841 homes. In the early 2000s, the rate only increased further, totaling 6,747 from 1998 to 2007. In the last decade that ICAHD recorded, 2008–18, the total comes to a staggering 27,861 homes (Halper, 2018: 59).[2] This includes the 18,000 destroyed in the Gaza Strip during the war on Gaza in 2014 (B'Tselem, 2019).

Moreover, according to OCHA, in the six years from 2009 to 2015, 3,784 Palestinian buildings in the West Bank were demolished or confiscated, leaving a total of 6,305 people displaced (OCHA, 2017: 3).[3] This means that their primary place of residence was taken from them. The above figure does not include the many more Palestinians affected by other forms of property seizing/demolition (OCHA, 2017: 2). Vitally, the vast majority of buildings that Israel targets get demolished, either fully or partly. From 2009 to 2022, 932 buildings in the West Bank were confiscated, sealed or had people evicted from them. Yet in comparison, 7,733 were demolished in the same period (OCHA, 2022b). From 2016 to June 2022, 4,755 Palestinian buildings in the West Bank were demolished or confiscated by Israel, which resulted in displacing more than 6,300 people (OCHA, 2022a: 3). The year 2016 proved to be the worst, with 1,094 buildings targeted – on an average, 91 a month (OCHA, 2022a: 3). This included houses and other structures in East Jerusalem, in Areas A, B and C (OCHA, 2022a: 3). From 2009 to 2022, 26.6 per cent of the total 8,665 targeted structures were inhabited homes.

Israeli settlements built on confiscated Palestinian land

Another significant factor which leads to the renewal of tension between the Israeli government and Palestinians is the incessant and blatant confiscation of Palestinian land/properties. Every plot of land seized by force from its Palestinian owners becomes a new settlement project for Israeli Jewish settlers. From 1967 to 1997, the number of Israeli illegal settlements in the West Bank and East Jerusalem has been growing steadily on confiscated Palestinian land. OCHA's dataset, based on 139 of the 149 settlements that existed by 2005, shows that in the first ten years from 1967 to 1977, 48 illegal settlements were built on Palestinian land (OCHA, 2007: 16). By 2017, the total number rose to at least 250 (OCHA, 2017). It is important to factor in the land mass covered by settlements. For example, in 1987, 128 illegal settlements spanned 4,127 hectares of land. By 2005, the number of illegal settlements had increased to 149, but the *land* they covered increased by nearly 400 per cent to 16,375 hectares (OCHA, 2007: 18).

Between 1987 and 2004, despite new settlement building slowing down, the settler population still increased by nearly 150 per cent – from 169,200 to 421,669 people (OCHA, 2007: 16, 20). This is an average growth of 5.5 per cent per year. From 1993 to 2004, illegal settler population increased by 63 per cent (an increase of more than 163,000 settlers). It is relevant to note that the settlement population growth rate is much larger than the rate inside Israel. Between 2003 and 2004, for example, the settler population increased by 4.6 per cent, compared with 1.8 per cent in Israel (OCHA, 2007: 16). By 2007, the UN reported that 460,000 Israeli settlers lived in the occupied West Bank and East Jerusalem. At this time, 40 per cent of this occupied land was privately owned by Palestinians (Dugard, 2007: 2). Furthermore, in the twelve years from 2005 to 2017, around 100 new illegal settlements were built, with a total of about 250. With a population of 611,000 people, this was an increase of 151,000 in ten years. Two-thirds of the settlers live in Area C of the West Bank, and one-third in East Jerusalem (OCHA, 2017).

As of 2020, B'Tselem[4] reported that settler population increased to 662,000 in the West Bank and East Jerusalem, with about 280 illegal settlements, 138 of which are officially recognized by Israel (B'Tselem, 2020: 9). The other 150 or so are unofficial outposts, which usually contain Jewish farms that illegally take up extensive Palestinian farming land. These tend to be retroactively approved of later by the Israeli government. By the end of 2020, the population of the two largest settlements, Modi'in Illit and Beitar Illit, made up nearly a third of all settlers in the West Bank (B'Tselem, 2020: 9). While little information is available after 2020, the EU and Peace Now report a trend of ever-increasing settlement house plans and tenders, particularly in East Jerusalem (EU, 2022: 1). As of 2021, plans for 14,000 more settler housing units are approved of, to be built in and around East Jerusalem. This is double the units compared to 2020 (EU, 2022: 2).

Sheikh Jarrah evictions and the war on Gaza, May 2021

Israel's attempt to violently evict Palestinian residents of the Sheikh Jarrah quarter in East Jerusalem, back in May 2021, was another phase of the systematic policy of confiscating Palestinian land and properties as cited earlier. The new wave of violent clashes on 8 May 2021 in Jerusalem and the Palestinian territories was evidently a result of the simmering tension between Palestinians and Israelis due to the ongoing occupation. At the time, the upcoming Israeli Supreme Court ruling on 6 May 2021, regarding the eviction of nineteen Palestinian families from their homes, was the catalyst that led to the escalation of events. Palestinians held anti-eviction protests in Palestinian cities across the West Bank and Jerusalem in support of families in Sheikh Jarrah. Violence further escalated due to the Israeli military's assault on Gaza, which led to twenty-one Palestinian deaths (PRC, 2022).

Moreover, the situation worsened because of continuous assaults by small groups of Jewish settlers who repeatedly invaded the Al-Aqsa Mosque, followed by the Israeli police's violent intervention and dispersing of Palestinian worshippers in the mosque during the holy month of Ramadan. This marked the start of the Palestinians' intense protests and violent retaliation from Hamas and other Palestinian factions by launching hundreds of missiles towards Tel Aviv. The ensuing events led to the Israeli army's brutal bombardment of Gaza, which lasted eleven days and resulted in the killing of 248 Palestinians and colossal destruction of Palestinian infrastructure.

Silencing the witnesses

Over the years, international journalists reporting on the Palestinian-Israeli conflict experienced continuous harassment and deterrence from covering conflict zones (Saraste, 2021). A report by the Palestinian Centre for Human Rights (PCHR) documented systematic persecution of scores of journalists from various international media outlets, aiming to impede their normal work of reporting events, especially during military assaults. The report reveals that

> Israeli occupation forces' grave violations against journalists include threats to their personal safety and attack on their equipment with live and rubber bullets, physical and emotional assault, restrictions on the freedom of movement, bombardment of their office and other violations demonstrating a well-planned scheme to isolate the oPt from the rest of the world and to provide cover-up for crimes against civilians, and impose a narrative opposite to the reality on the ground. (PCHR, 2020)

Violations that aim to silence the Palestinian story are complex and multi-layered, as reported by the PCHR (2020). Attempts to obstruct journalists from reporting events on the ground include detaining a crew of journalists, physical assault and verbal abuse. When journalists insist on defying the Israeli army's harassment, they may face attacks or are simply blocked from having any further access to conflict zones. Jevara Albudiri (Al Jazeera's correspondent in Jerusalem) reported on the Israeli media's misinformation about her arrest by the Israeli army while covering events in Sheikh Jarrah (East Jerusalem) in early May 2021. In a one-on-one interview with her on Al Jazeera, Albudiri argues that the Israeli newspapers and TV channels simply sided with the Israeli army's narrative. They 'claimed that she was a Qatari journalist who attacked an Israeli soldier' (Albudiri, 2021). Another notorious case of the Israeli army's violent assault and cold-blooded killing is that of Rachel Corrie, an American diarist and activist from Washington. On 16 March 2003, she was crushed to death by an Israeli army bulldozer when she was documenting the demolition of Palestinian homes in the Gaza Strip. The Israeli troops, according to Corrie's attorney, 'acted in violation of both Israeli and international law prohibiting the targeting of civilians, and the disproportionate use of force against non-violent protest with blatant disregard to human lives' (Macintyre, 2010).

During the war on Gaza in May 2021, and in an attempt to silence critical voices seen as exposing the Israeli assaults, the Israeli army bombarded the tower hosting the Al-Jazeera, Associated Press offices and scores of other media organizations in Gaza. The Israeli army claimed that the building was hosting Hamas intelligence services, but they have never provided any proof for this claim.

The assassination of Al Jazeera's journalist, Shireen Abu Akleh, on 11 May 2022 marked the worst bloodstained attack on Palestinian journalists. Stefani Dekker reported from occupied East Jerusalem on her funeral (Al Jazeera English, 2022). Even in her death, Dekker argued, Shireen wanted to highlight what the occupation means. No Palestinian flags were allowed, and no chanting during her funeral procession (Al Jazeera English, live broadcasting, Friday 4:10 pm). Shireen went to every household. She died while reporting from Jenin Camp, documenting what happened almost on a daily basis. She was the voice of Palestinians when they were muted. On the same morning, Israeli prime minster Naftali Benet circulated a fabricated video claiming that Abu Akleh was killed by Palestinian gunmen. Following international condemnation, Benet withdrew the video and agreed that her death was suspicious. Subsequently four narratives about her killing were sketched by the Israeli government. None of them reflected the truth.

Global media coverage of the ongoing conflict

It is not a contention to claim that global media outlets have their own news agendas when reporting on world affairs (Hall, 2018; Hochberg, 2015). Reporting the Palestinian-Israeli conflict is not an exception. Across various countries, there exist blatant discrepancies in the narrative related to the history of the conflict and its ongoing dramatic facets (Matar and Harb, 2013; Said, 1981; Tawil-Souri, 2015 among others). Academic research on scores of Western media outlets reveals a clear imbalance in reporting the Palestinian-Israeli conflict. Numerous academic studies have analysed the problematic reporting of various media outlets in relation to the conflict. The passivity of the language, play on words and choice of specific terminologies to downplay atrocities inflicted on Palestinians by Israeli soldiers are all common practice.

For instance, Wearing (2021) describes the evidently unreasonable reporting by a few American media outlets of the war on Gaza in May 2021, stating that the 'Western media's continued use of the word "conflict" perpetrates the idea that the occupier and occupied are equals, possessing the same amount of weapons, resources, and international support at their disposal.' The obvious double standards of how victims from both sides are reported on raises big questions. Wearing (2021) further argues that Reuters states, 'More than 67 Palestinians, including 16 children, have died.' When the narrative switches to cover the damage in Israel, however, they are 'killed'. This is evident in another article by the *New York Times*: 'The rockets fired by Hamas and its Islamist ally, Islamic Jihad, killed at least six Israeli civilians.' In another headline of a Reuters' article, the destruction of a Gaza residential building has not resulted from Israeli air strikes – it was not 'destroyed'. Instead, it collapsed after the strikes ended (Wearing, 2021).

Other Western media outlets have also been criticized for using subtle language in support of the Israeli occupation. Most of the time when it comes to describing the illegal settlements, news headlines are often vague, terms used to describe events are elusive and do not come near to condemnation. For instance, during the last days of the fasting month of Ramadhan (May 2021), Israeli police began an onslaught on Palestinian worshippers in Al-Aqsa mosque in Jerusalem. The Organization for World Peace (OWP) argues in an analysis of the CNN coverage of the war on Gaza during that time that 'Under the guise of objectivity, U.S. media outlets' choice to support its national ally Israel is reflected in the language they use to describe the occupation in debates and articles.' The analysis goes on to state that

> An internal CNN memo was leaked on 19 May. The email, addressed to the CNN superdesk, outlined the need for reporters to refer to Gaza's Ministry of Health as the Hamas-run Ministry of Health when reporting on casualty numbers. This word choice sanitized CNN's coverage of the conflict, implying that the Ministry of Health in Palestine is a part of an 'opposing side' or 'threat' to Israel. (OWP, 2021)

Furthermore, other news reports show that the official Israeli narrative mainly paints the war on Gaza as having higher purposes. The sanctioned discourse describes the purposes of the lethal violent attacks of F16 war jets using quasi high-purpose language such as 'offensives', 'strategies', 'operations', 'campaigns' and 'targets' and calls these military offensives names such as 'Guardian of the Walls'. In addition, an analysis of the language of the media coverage implies that Palestinian civilians and Israeli soldiers are on equal footing; what's more, that Palestinians from Sheikh Jarrah or other occupied territories have the same advantages or rights as the Israeli settlers. Such language does not in fact help viewers who are not familiar with the conflict to grasp the truth about the ongoing conflict.

The BBC and the Palestinian story

Criticism of Western media coverage of the conflict has also been directed to well-reputed international broadcasters such as the British Broadcasting Corporation (BBC). Concerns about biased reporting of the Palestinian-Israeli conflict by the BBC is a well-documented and thoroughly discussed topic (Amer, 2022; Barkho, 2008, 2011; De Rooij, 2002; Fisk, 1990; Philo and Berry, 2004, Downey et al., 2019). In a critical analysis of the BBC's coverage of the war on Gaza in May 2021, Annabelle Lukin writes that BBC reporters have accepted the language of the Israeli army by calling the bombardment simply an 'operation'. She further explains

An obvious and often conscious effect of this style is to treat two sides as if they are equal participants in this violence. This is the effect of journalistic shorthand, such as the 'Israel Gaza conflict'... These formulations avoid allocating blame to one side or the other. The BBC report shows a scrupulous formulation so that 'rockets and air strikes' appear side by side, even when the syntax of this formulation doesn't make sense. In their phrase 'rockets and air strikes have continued', while 'airstrikes' can continue, 'rockets' themselves cannot. And 'they said while the others said' structure keeps up the illusion that this violence is symmetrical. (Lukin, 2021)

Contextual issues

Various studies also which analysed the BBC's reporting of the Palestinian-Israeli conflict generally find the BBC's English service lacking context and historical explanation (Llewellyn, 2004; Philo and Berry, 2004), and have a tendency to mislead audiences about the nature and actions of perpetrators in the conflict (Amer, 2022; Barkho, 2007, 2008, 2011). Greg Philo and Mike Berry's seminal book on this topic, *Bad News from Israel* (2004), in its analysis of BBC coverage and viewer perceptions on the conflict, finds rampant inadequacies and inaccuracies in reporting on events in the Occupied Territories. Participants, including that of former Middle Eastern correspondent Tim Llewellyn, perceived the news as neglecting historical and causal explanations and instead focusing on shock factor, to capture the alleged twenty-second attention spans of audiences. As a result, most participants in their study had a remote understanding of the origin of the conflict, and the vast majority had no knowledge of the occupation (Philo and Berry, 2004: 212). They found viewers to have vague understandings of refugees, bombings and land issues – but not the essentials of who, what, when or why – the UN resolutions that established Israel on Palestinian land, nor the forced expulsion of hundreds of thousands of Palestinians from their homes by Israeli military forces and state-sanctioned settler groups. Neither, crucially, that their actions are illegal under International Humanitarian Law, and have resulted in the creation of the largest refugee population in modern history (Barghouti, 2018). Philo and Berry (2004) attribute this to the 'simply absent' Palestinian view in mainstream news (Philo and Berry, 2004: 398) and the BBC's policy of 'balance', which is typically manifested in images of Palestinian casualties 'balanced' by an Israeli perspective on the cause of conflict, resulting in the misunderstanding, or omission, of a Palestinian perspective.

Their updated book, *More Bad News from Israel* (2011), which analyses the BBC's footage and bulletins following the 2008–9 Israeli blitz on Gaza, found that the Israeli viewpoint was widely accepted by the BBC and conveyed as fact. The justification for raining fire onto Gazan civilians was described as a 'response' to Palestinian rockets. Meanwhile the Palestinian view, that Israel violated the almost five-month-long ceasefire, and that Gazans had been pushed to inhumane limits after years of siege and blockade, was scarcely mentioned, if at all. Similarly preventing a holistic understanding was a neglect to mention proposals of a ceasefire by Hamas in the coverage at all. As such, Philo and Berry argue that these inadequacies in mainstream news directly correlate to participants' confusion and lack of understanding surrounding the Palestinian-Israeli conflict.

Llewellyn agrees with the above conclusions, asserting that while the BBC claims a policy of balance and impartiality, its coverage of Israel and Palestine is 'replete with imbalance and distortion' and systematically fails to contextualize the nature of the conflict as one between a military occupier and a people occupied (Llewellyn, 2011). He finds that the BBC, through its obsession over 'balance' and failure to explain historical context, disingenuously paints Palestine (an occupied land with homemade bombs and rockets) and Israel (possessing a lethal army bankrolled in the billions by friends of Israel such as the United States) as two 'equally strong and culpable forces in a "difficult" dispute' (Llewellyn, 2004). Suicide bombings in Israel, for example, are reported using very emotive language, whilst rarely providing context – whether that be a Palestinian reaction to Israeli death squads or the burden of decades of military occupation (Llewellyn, 2004). The conflict is thus misconstrued by the public as one that could be resolved if only the two could see eye to eye, a woeful miss of the mark.

Barkho's (2008) critical discourse analysis of the BBC similarly found that in its attempts at balance, the corporation treads a 'lexical tightrope', which risks them violating their own principles. This tightrope – including a glossary solely created for Israel-Palestine reporting – reflects the inequalities in power and control between the two actors; he found discrepancies in description between reporting Palestinian versus Israeli casualties, and major syntactic differences between Arabic and English services.

Both services, he found, had syntactic patterns which failed to explain context (Barkho, 2008: 291–2). The English service generally possessed four features affecting context: the ample explanation of the Israeli perspective through adverbial clauses; giving the Israeli point of view a high position/priority in the story, often in the first four paragraphs; conveying the Israeli point of view unattributed to anyone, inferring that the BBC by default agrees; where the Palestinian view is mentioned, giving it a lower position/priority in the story, and mostly attributed to officials. These combined to venerate Israel's view and undermine the Palestinian view. For example, one article from 21 May 2007, regarding Israeli air strikes on Jabaliya Refugee camp, provides the Israeli explanation unattributed to anyone in the third paragraph, as an attack targeting Gazan 'militants' firing rockets into Israel, while Hamas's explanation, that Israel in fact killed Palestinian civilians, is given in the sixteenth paragraph, as though irrelevant (Barkho, 2008: 290).

Conversely, the Arabic service is provided more editorial freedom, having a tendency to mention context which aids understanding of the Palestinian perspective. Their reporting on the same event, for example, mentioned the fact that many Palestinians were stranded at the border of Egypt in the heat without food or housing. Barkho thus finds a general theme of the Arabic service catering more to Arabic/Muslim audiences by relying more on Palestinian sources and providing context behind why Palestinians resort to violence. Mohammed Mosheer Amer's (2022) critical discourse analysis of BBC coverage of the Israeli onslaught on Gaza in May 2021 similarly found that the context of 'Israel's occupation, siege, brutalities and violations, colonization and ethnic cleansing were largely missing in the reportage', and that lexical and quotation patterns adopted were mostly favouring Israel, at the expense of a Palestinian or international legal perspective regarding their actions (Amer, 2022: 15).

The BBC is under pressure from multiple sides to satisfy, firstly from the government, since it is largely state-funded, and thus Israeli lobbyists within the government, and secondly a liberal British audience with (presumably) short attention spans and a dislike for long articles and heavy topics. Flood and others (2011) highlight that this forces the BBC to compromise – the demand for context is overridden by the need for marketability, and so its 'impartiality' is skewed since they report in a way that tiptoes Western liberal values and customs. As Foucault (1984) emphasizes, discourse is never neutral and always has power implications for the subjects in question, framed in a way which implores that what is reported is fact and truth. Thus, when editors and journalists, who have a large influence on context, choose to omit essential information, they help minimize the Palestinian voice and reinforce the power inequalities between Israel and Palestine. The essence of this for Palestine is to deny that they have been under systematic apartheid occupation for the past fifty-five years, according to the United Nations (UN Human Rights, 2022).

Israel's media machine and discourse manufacturing

It has been argued by various scholars that Western media plays a large role in constructing and moulding discourse, controlling the flow of information audiences receive and therefore influencing their attitudes and beliefs regarding different actors (Fowler, 1991; Poole, 2004; Rezaei and Salami, 2019; Said, 1984). The neglect in providing accurate and elaborate historical context regarding this conflict, corresponding to a deeply under-educated British public on this topic (see Philo and Berry, 2004), suggests general reluctance by Western media to paint Israel as a 'villain'. Furthermore, the overwhelmingly negative Islam-related news coverage Philo and Berry analysed across two years of BBC recordings, and neglecting to counterbalance with positive stories on Islam, cumulatively helps reinforce violent stereotypes that Western media have a tendency of propagating (Poole, 2004: 47).

It is argued that the Israeli media machine has immense influence over the BBC's reporting (Llewellyn, 2004). Llewellyn quotes a BBC reporter, who describes how after the second Intifada, producers would ring the Jerusalem office with ideas directly from the Israeli embassy, and that the Israeli version of events would be the 'prevailing wisdom in London ... Israel amended the very *language of reporting the crisis*' (Llewellyn, 2004: 4). This comes in various forms, such as dilution of language – the concrete fact of occupation becoming mere 'claims', illegal settlements becoming 'neighbourhoods'; nullifying Israeli agency through passive discourse yet illustrating Palestinians as having full agency; denigrating Arab lives by naming Israelis and not dead Arabs, and lastly, employing inflammatory stereotypes such as 'terrorist' for Palestinians, but not for Israelis (Llewellyn, 2004: 4). Robert Fisk (1990), a frontline reporter on Middle Eastern affairs for many years, argued that the word terrorist is a mere 'political contrivance' reserved for 'those using violence against the side that is *using the word*' (Fisk, 1990: 441) – alleging that Israel will consider anyone who opposes them terrorists, and Britain, as a long-standing Israeli ally, will therefore do the same. De Rooij (2002) similarly asserts that BBC news coverage favours Israel due to intense pressure and lobbying from the UK Foreign Office, which partly controls news coverage, key staff and even budget (De Rooij, 2002). Furthermore, the previous BBC's senior editorial advisor, Malcolm Balen, was appointed in 2003 after meetings involving 'Israeli officials, figures from the British Jewish community, and top BBC representatives', much to the dismay of Pro-Palestinian lobbies (Barkho, 2008: 282). The history surrounding BBC's transparency has also been under question; the Balen report on bias in BBC coverage of the Palestinian-Israeli conflict was fought extensively in court to be kept secret, at very high public cost – allegedly £200,000 in legal fees (McSmith, 2007).

The Israel media machine – structural and cultural advantages

The systematic structural barriers inhibiting a well-funded, organized, independent press presence in Palestine compared with the well-oiled media machine of Israel is another factor affecting BBC coverage. Robert Fisk, during his interview with Philo and Berry (2004), asserted that Israel is able to provide well-organized documents and fluent English speakers dressed smartly to provide an Israeli perspective in a well-lit studio, which naturally appeals to BBC presenters and a British audience. Judith Brown, a journalist previously on the Arab Media Watch executive committee, who visited Palestine as part of her PhD research on 'Imagery of Arabs in the British Media', describes the imbalance. She unveils how Western journalists are extensively catered for by Israeli officials, have a handler and even live with Israelis in Jerusalem and therefore share their fears of suicide bombs and rockets (Brown, 2004).

This equivalent is infrastructurally impossible for Palestine – territories are suffocatingly obstructed by armed checkpoints, dozens of roadblocks or random superfluous inspections that make reaching a studio in Jerusalem for Palestinians extremely hard – where they may also be easily rejected. This also makes it very difficult – but not impossible – for journalists to reach Palestinian territory to report on their viewpoint accurately and empathetically. Western channels such as the BBC, with vested interests in Israel, also do not invest resources into sustaining a news team in the occupied territories, which stifles the Palestinian story at the source. Exacerbating this is also the neglect by journalists to explain why Palestine is disadvantaged in the first instance, which could be a saving grace.

Culturally, as Llewellyn (2004) notes, Israel has an advantage; it is 'more relatable' to see an Israeli casualty with a mall or Walmart in shot, as opposed to an Arab man with a strong accent amongst the rubble; BBC presenters are more inclined to listen to a statesman in a smart suit than a representative wearing a militia uniform, and maybe a 'kuffiyeh', a symbol proudly defending their national identity, who is all but seen as a foreign 'militant' with poor English back in the UK (Llewellyn, 2004: 6). It is therefore easy for Israel to take advantage of Islamophobic and xenophobic stereotypes and cultural norms by juxtaposing this with well-trained, professional, easily understood figures. Llewellyn argues that cultural biases are no excuse – the BBC still neglects to put in effort to provide platforms for the many eager, articulate Palestinian voices in Britain or other Arab experts who would present the Palestinian case accurately (Llewellyn, 2004: 6). They fail in their ability to describe the Palestinian struggle as apartheid, even though it is not dissimilar to the suffering seen in India or South Africa; they fail in their lack of effort to place reporters on Palestinian ground in the West bank or Gaza who can truly empathize with the life of constant occupation, when they so readily did so for Baghdad or the front lines of Ukraine and they fail through their dilution of the Palestinian narrative, which is masqueraded as 'balance'.

Marginalizing the Palestinian narrative

In this conflict like many others around the world, global media outlets work within strict rules of selectivity which marginalize the Palestinian version of events (Miladi, 2006). Like other contexts addressed vis-à-vis media and conflict by Cees Hamelink, 'selective articulation is inherent in the "media logic"' (Hamelink, 2011: 32). This entails that most of the time, the media put focus on certain conflicts more than others. It may also give more prominence to certain people, or voices than others. Also, a driving mode of media coverage of local as well as global events is systematic selectivity of events. Media providers, argues Hamelink, '… make choices … and emphasize differently according to a convergence of factors, such political pressures, economic drivers, personal preferences, professional styles, and mechanisms of human perception' (Hamelink, 2011: 32).

Hassan (2022) summarizes the angle through which Palestinians are usually portrayed in Western media:

> Palestinians usually get mainstream Western media coverage when they are either protesting or physically confronting Israeli aggression, with their outcry broadly coloured as 'escalation of violence'. Historically, however, there seemed to be no escalation of violence when Israel increases night raids on Palestinian homes or Israeli settlers attack Palestinian farmers … 'Gaza militants' firing rockets followed by Israeli retaliation, masking the Palestinian struggle behind Hamas' broad veil of violence.

Moreover, Western media have always been accused of whitewashing Israeli occupation. The Israeli state-sanctioned violence goes mostly unchecked. The blame for the escalation would normally be put on Palestinians, quite often in a subtle way. In a study by El Damanhoury and Saleh comparing CNN's and Al Jazeera America's coverage of the war on Gaza in 2014, it was argued that in the CNN coverage there was a 'legitimation of the Israeli discourse and vilifying of Palestinians by downplaying the victims' (El Damanhoury and Saleh, 2017: 98). The death toll, which exceeded 2,000 on the Palestinian side, was reported as mainly including armed people from Hamas and other Palestinian groups. Al Jazeera's coverage, however, highlights what the UN reports confirmed at the time, that more than 70 per cent of the casualties were civilians. Marzano (2011: 64) also concluded in his study on the Italian press coverage of the war on Gaza in December 2008 and January 2009 that most of the newspapers 'portrayed the Gaza war as part of the wider attack "Islam" was carrying out against "the West"'. The main zoom lens through which the war was portrayed was an Islamophobic prism. The Italian newspapers, he further concludes, 'exploited Islamophobic stereotypes to address 'global Islam', i.e. the Gaza war, in order to portray 'local Islam' (Marzano, 2011: 64).

War of narratives on social media networks

As much as support for Palestinians took place in various capitals around the world denouncing the continuous Israeli aggression, online protests also grew exponentially on social media. During the tense May 2021 conflict, Palestinians plentifully documented the bloody events of Sheikh Jarrah, Al Quds and the war on Gaza. Hashtags such as #SavePalestine, #GazaUnderAttack, #SaveSheikhJarrah and #FreePalestine turned into effective online platforms for sharing day-to-day accounts of the events in a multimedia format. The *New York Times* (2021) reported that social media platforms became new spheres of 'the Mass Protest'. A video recording showing a Palestinian woman in the East Jerusalem neighbourhood of Sheikh Jarrah shouting at a Jewish settler, telling him, 'You are stealing my house' went viral around the world. The newspaper reported that the video 'travelled at 4G speed, leapfrogging across international borders'. The reply which came from the settler, 'If I don't steal it, someone else will steal it', accordingly received shock and dismay from tens of thousands of people on social media platforms (*New York Times*, 2021).

The above example is a glimpse from scores of others that demonstrate the war of narratives taking place on social media platforms during the renewed conflict of May 2021. Both Israelis as well as Palestinians have become aware of the power of social media networks in taking their voices to the world. Social media activism has become synonymous with a digital war waged through smartphones instead of sophisticated weaponry. As much as rocket launching and heavy artillery bombardment was taking place, another war was also happening in the digital sphere. The narrative and counter narrative on the dramatic day-to-day events found their way onto hundreds of social media outlets, posted about by people on both sides of the conflict, including armies of supporters on online platforms.

In an example highlighted by Frenkel (2021), relating to how disinformation gets immediately challenged via social media networks, she argues that one of the justifications posted by Israeli officials for bombing civilians in Gaza was that Hamas militants kept launching rockets from densely populated civilian areas. This was claimed in a video posted on Twitter, TikTok, Facebook and WhatsApp containing 'false information' that 'included videos, photos and clips of text purported to be from government officials in the region'. The Israeli government spokesman at the time, Ofir Gendelman, explained the reason behind the attacks. Immediately after, the *New York Times* revealed that the video found on '... YouTube channels and other video-hosting sites, was from 2018. And according to captions on older versions of the video, it showed militants firing rockets not from Gaza but from Syria or Libya' (Frenkel, 2021).

The above war of narratives also meant pressure on Palestinian content on social media platforms. Sada Social, a watchdog journalism Palestinian Center specializing in protecting Palestinian content on social media platforms, documented more than 770 violations of content during May 2021, the highest figure documented in years. Violations varied between a complete ban and suspension of specific features, complete closure of accounts and pages, and the restriction of a publications' access to the public. Violations against Palestinian content increased remarkably by the beginning of the Sheikh Jarrah events. Facebook topped the list with 350 violations, followed by Twitter with 250, Instagram with 100, TikTok with 50, WhatsApp with 20 and 10 on YouTube (Sada Social, 2021).

At the height of international solidarity with the residents of Sheikh Jarrah in May 2021, Instagram restricted the account of Mona Al-Kurd, a media activist and resident of the same neighbourhood, as well as blocking and restricting access to the 'Al-Aqsa' hashtag, one of the most popular when events escalated in Al-Aqsa Mosque during the holy month of Ramadan. In addition, the application deleted publications and stories, restricted accounts and banned live broadcasts for a number of Palestinian journalists and activists, in conjunction with the intensity of publishing to follow up on field events and the Israeli occupation's assault on Jerusalem and Al-Aqsa Mosque, and the military offensive on Gaza.

Meanwhile, YouTube restricted access to the live broadcast of the Al Jazeera channel at the height of Israeli aggression on the Gaza Strip, while deleting various media clips and materials published on different Palestinian channels. Turkish and Arab users documented that the automatic version of the language translation on the site translated the word 'Palestinians' to 'Terrorists' for a video from a Turkish media platform. Twitter, in turn, deleted hundreds of Palestinian and Arab accounts after they published materials and messages of solidarity with the Palestinian people, the most prominent of which was the pursuit of material published about the Sheikh Jarrah neighborhood in Jerusalem, and others about the crimes of the Israeli army in Gaza.

For its part, the TikTok application also deleted many accounts of Palestinian and Arab journalists as well as various media organizations, foremost of which were the accounts of the Quds Network and the Safa Agency, just hours after the Israeli Minister of Justice, Benny Gates, met with the site's administration (Sada Social, 2021). The Palestinian Journalists Syndicate (JSC) also reported in May 2021 that social networking sites were 'partners in incitement and crimes against the Palestinian people'. More than five hundred violations of freedom of opinion and expression and blocking of Palestinian content took place during the same period (JSC, 2021). According to the same report, the centre monitored a campaign to mobilize groups of settlers via WhatsApp and Telegram platforms, which included violent and inciting speech against Palestinians, without any reaction from the administrations of these sites. The impact of these online assaults extended to the ground, through physical attacks on Palestinians in the occupied territories.

In the online environment, pressure was also placed on celebrities who supported the Palestinian cause on social media. Actress Emma Watson for instance was verbally attacked online by a pro-Israeli lobby when she posted a message in solidarity with Palestinians on her Instagram. After she posted a picture from a demonstration in London which read 'Solidarity is a Verb', a reply immediately came from former Israeli

Ambassador in the UN, Danny Danon, accusing her of anti-Semitism by saying: '10 points from Gryffindor for being an anti-Semite' (Abdullah 2022).

Conclusion

While this chapter was being completed, a new cycle of Israeli assaults on Palestinians began again. On 5 August 2022, the Israeli army unexpectedly launched air missile attacks on a civilian residential tower block in Gaza, killing ten Palestinians including a baby. The target was a leader of the Islamic Jihad group, Tayseer Al-Jaabari. The assault came with no prior warning and was not preceded by any Palestinian provocations. It became obvious in the following days that this was the new routine practice by the Israeli government – to start military campaigns whenever they see fit. As argued by political and military analysts, the military operation in Gaza – which the Israeli army called 'the truthful dawn' – came in the context of the competition for the Knesset elections and the crisis of governance in Israel, in an attempt by the acting prime minister at the time, Yair Lapid and Defense Minister Benny Gantz, to search for a form of victory that precedes the election expected in October 2022. Israeli affairs analyst, Antoine Shalhat, asserted that the main motive for the military campaign against Gaza at the time were the Knesset elections and the political crisis the Israeli government was facing. Lapid (Shalhat argues), who did not come from a security background, aimed to appear as a strong politician who can protect the interests of Israelis. Alongside Gantz, he wishes to be viewed by Israeli voters as a 'successful security leader' (Al Jazeera, 2022).

Notes

1. See Halper, 2018: 58 for the following full list of sources they use for their statistics: Israeli Ministry of Interior, the Jerusalem Municipality, the Civil Administration, OCHA and other UN sources, Palestinian and Israeli human rights organizations, Amnesty International, Human Rights Watch, ICAHD's field work and others.
2. This in fact only includes data up to February 2018.
3. OCHA's statistics do not include Gaza.
4. B'Tselem is an Israeli human rights non-profit organization that provides information on the occupation.

References

Abdullah, F. (2022), 'Emma Watson Stands in Solidarity with the Palestinian Cause in a Post That Provokes Israeli Outrage', Al Jazeera, 1 April, https://www.aljazeera.net/news (accessed 4 August 2022).

Al Jazeera (2022), 'Al-Fajr Al-Sadiq Is Another Face of "The Guardian of the Fence". Gaza Pays the Price of the Crisis of Governance in Israel', 5 August, https://www.aljazeera.net/news/ (accessed 5 August 2022).

Al Jazeera English (2022), Live broadcasting news programme, Friday 13 May 2022, 4:10 pm.

Albudiri, J. (2021), 'From Washington', a one-on-one current affairs programme on Al Jazeera Arabic, Al Jazeera, 12 June, https://www.youtube.com/watch?v=bRnuR9WY C98 (accessed 28 October 2021).

Amer, M. M. (2022), 'BBC and New York Times' Coverage of the May 2021 Israeli Onslaught on Gaza: A Critical Discourse Analysis', *International Journal of English Linguistics*, 12(5): 1–18, https://ccsenet.org/journal/index.php/ijel/article/view/0/47455 (accessed 28 August 2022).

B'Tselem (2019), '4.5 Years after Israel Destroyed Thousands of Homes in Operation Protective Edge: 13,000 Gazans Still Homeless', https://www.btselem.org/gaza_st rip/20190303_13000_gazans_homelsess_since_2014_war (accessed 28 August 2022).

B'Tselem (2020), 'This Is Ours – and This, Too: Israel's Settlement Policy in the West Bank', https://www.btselem.org/sites/default/files/publications/202103_this_is_ours_and_t his_too_eng.pdf (accessed 28 August 2022).

Barghouti, A. S. (2018), 'Palestinians Make Up World's Largest Refugee Population', AA, 20 June, https://www.aa.com.tr/en/middle-east/palestinians-make-up-world-s-largest-refugee-population/1179770 (accessed 28 August 2022).

Barkho, L. (2007), 'Unpacking the Discursive and Social Links in BBC, CNN and Al-Jazeera's Middle East Reporting', *Journal of Arab and Muslim Media Research*, 1(1): 11–29, doi: 10.1386/jammr.1.1.11/1 (accessed 28 August 2022).

Barkho, L. (2008), 'The BBC's Discursive Strategy vis-a-vis the Palestinian-Israeli Conflict', *Journalism Studies*, 9(2): 278–94, doi: https://doi.org/10.1080/14616700701848337 (accessed 28 August 2022).

Barkho, L. (2011), 'The Discursive and Social Paradigm of Al-Jazeera English in Comparison and Parallel with the BBC', *Communication Studies*, 62(1): 23–40.

Brown, J. (2004), 'The Imagery of Arabs', Counter Punch, 4 February, https://www.count erpunch.org/2004/02/04/the-imagery-of-arabs/ (accessed 28 August 2022).

De Rooij, P. (2002), 'Worse Than CNN? BBC and the Mideast', Counter Punch; Indymedia, 2 June, https://www.indymedia.org.uk/en/2002/06/32892.html (accessed 28 August 2022).

Downey, J., D. Deacon, P. Golding, B. Oldfield and D. Wring (2019), 'The BBC's Reporting of the Israeli-Palestinian Conflict', Communications Research Centre, Loughborough University (UK), https://hdl.handle.net/2134/3158 (accessed 29 October 2021).

Dugard, J. (2007), 'Report of the Special Rapporteur on the Situation of Human Rights in the Palestinian Territories Occupied since 1967', A/HRC/4/17, 29 January, https://dig itallibrary.un.org/record/593075?ln=en (accessed 28 August 2022).

El Damanhoury, K., and F. Saleh (2017), 'Is It the Same Fight? Comparative Analysis of CNN and Al Jazeera America's Online Coverage of the 2014 Gaza War', *Journal of Arab & Muslim Media Research*, 10(1): 3–23, doi: 10.1386/jammr.10.1.3_1 (accessed 28 August 2022).

EU: The Office of the European Union Representative (West Bank and Gaza Strip, UNRWA) (2022), '2021 Report on Israeli Settlements in the Occupied West Bank, Including East Jerusalem: Reporting period January–December 2021', https://www.eeas.europa.eu/delegations/palestine-occupied-palestinian-territory-west-bank-an d-gaza-strip/2021-report-israeli_en (accessed 28 August 2022).

Fisk, R. (1990), *Pity the Nation*, Oxford: Oxford University Press.

Flood, C., S. Hutchings, G. Miazhevich and H. Nickels (2011), 'Between Impartiality and Ideology: The BBC's Paradoxical Remit and the Case of Islam-Related Television News',

Journalism Studies, 12(2): 221–38, doi: https://www.tandfonline.com/action/showCit Formats?doi=10.1080/1461670X.2010.507934 (accessed 28 August 2022).

Foucault, M. (1984), 'The Order of Discourse', in Michael J. Shapiro (ed.), *Language and Politics*, Oxford: Blackwell, pp. 108–38.

Fowler, R. (1991), *Language in the News: Discourse and Ideology in the Press*, London: Routledge.

Frenkel, S. (2021), 'Lies on Social Media Inflame Israeli-Palestinian Conflict', *The New York Times*, 14 May, https://www.nytimes.com/2021/05/14/ (accessed 27 June 2021).

Hall, S. (2018), 'Encoding/Decoding'. In J. Bardzell, S. Bardzel and M. Blythe, *Critical Theory and Interaction Design*, Cambridge, MA: MIT Press, 187–97.

Halper, J. (2018), 'ICAHD – Obstacles to Peace: A Reframing of the Israeli-Palestinian Conflict', ICAHD, https://icahd.org/wp-content/uploads/sites/1/2018/07/Obstac les-10-May-2018.pdf (accessed 28 August 2022).

Hamelink, C. (2011), *Media and Conflict: Escalating Evil*, London: Paradigm Publishers.

Hassan, A. (2022), 'The Problem with Mainstream Western Media's Coverage of Palestine', *The Daily Star*, 29 July, https://www.thedailystar.net/middle-east/ (accessed 29 July 2022).

Hochberg, G. (2015), *Visual Occupations: Violence and Visibility in a Conflict Zone*, Durham: Duke University Press.

Joronen, M. (2016), 'Death Comes Knocking on the Roof: Thanatopolitics of Ethical Killing during Operation Protective Edge in Gaza', *Antipode*, 48(2): 336–54, doi: 10.1111/anti.12178 (accessed 28 August 2022).

JSC (2021), 'Social Networking Sites Are Partners in Incitement and Crimes against the Palestinian People', 22 May, https://www.journalistsupport.net/article.php?id=376866 (accessed 4 August 2022).

Khalidi, R. (2019), *The Hundred Years' War on Palestine: A History of Settler Colonialism and Resistance, 1917-2017*, New York: Metropolitan Books.

Llewellyn, T. (2004), 'Why the BBC Ducks the Palestinian Story', *The Electronic Intifada*, 6 February.

Llewellyn, T. (2011), 'BBC Is "Confusing Cause and Effect" in Its Israeli Coverage', *The Guardian*, 23 May.

Lukin, A. (2021), 'When It Comes to Media Reporting on Israel-Palestine, There Is Nowhere to Hide', *The Conversation*, 19 May, https://theconversation.com/ (accessed 27 June 2021).

Macintyre, D. (2010), 'I Saw Israeli Bulldozer Kill Rachel Corrie', *The Independent*, 11 March, https://www.independent.co.uk/news (accessed 23 July 2022).

Marzano, A. (2011), 'Reading the Israeli-Palestinian Conflict through an Islamophobic Prism: The Italian Press and the Gaza War', *Journal of Arab & Muslim Media Research*, 4(1): 63–78, doi: 10.1386/jammr.4.1.63_1.

Matar, D., and Z. Harb (2013), *Narrating Conflict in the Middle East. Discourse, Image and Communications Practices in Lebanon and Palestine*, London: I.B. Tauris.

McSmith, A. (2007), 'BBC Fights to Suppress Internal Report into Allegations of Bias against Israel', *The Independent*, 28 March.

Miladi, N. (2006), 'Satellite TV News and the Arab Diaspora in Britain: Comparing Al-Jazeera, the BBC and CNN', *Journal of Ethnic and Migration Studies (JEMS)*, 32(6): 947–60, https://doi.org/10.1080/13691830600761552 (accessed 28 August 2022).

OCHA (2002), 'Israel's Apartheid Wall: We Are Here and They Are There', 13 November, https://reliefweb.int/report/israel/israels-apartheid-wall-we-are-here-and-the y-are-there (accessed 10 August 2022).

OCHA (2007), 'The Humanitarian Impact on Palestinians of Israeli Settlements and Other Infrastructure in the West Bank', https://www.ochaopt.org/content/humanitarian-imp act-palestinians-israeli-settlements-and-other-infrastructure-west-bank (accessed 28 August 2022).

OCHA (2017), 'West Bank: The Humanitarian Impact of Israeli Settlement Activities', https://www.ochaopt.org/content/west-bank-humanitarian-impact-israeli-settlement-activities (accessed 28 August 2022).

OCHA (2022a), 'West Bank Demolitions and Displacement: An Overview – June 2022', https://reliefweb.int/report/occupied-palestinian-territory/west-bank-demoliti ons-and-displacement-overview-june-2022 (accessed 28 August 2022).

OCHA (2022b), 'Data on Demolition and Displacement in the West Bank: August 2022', https://www.ochaopt.org/data/demolition (accessed 28 August 2022).

OWP (2021), 'Western Media's Impact on the War between Israel and Palestine', Organization of World Peace, 16 June 2021, https://theowp.org/reports/ (accessed 28 October 2021).

Palestinian Return Centre (2022), 'Sheikh Jarrah, Occupied East Jerusalem', https://prc. org.uk/upload/library/files/Shiekh_Jarrah_Factsheet.pdf (accessed 3 August 2022).

PCHR (2020), 'Silencing the Press: Israeli Occupation Forces Attacks on Journalists', Palestinian Centre for Human Rights, https://reliefweb.int/sites/reliefweb.int/files/ resources/prees-report-engliesh-2020.pdf (accessed 28 October 2021).

Philo, G., and M. Berry (2004), *Bad News from Israel*, Glasgow: Pluto Press.

Philo, G., and M. Berry (2011), *More Bad News from Israel*, Glasgow: Pluto Press.

Poole, E. (2002), *Reporting Islam: Media Representations of British Muslims*, London: I.B. Tauris.

Rezaei, S., and A. Salami (2019), 'The Portrayal of Islam and Muslims in Western Media: A Critical Discourse Analysis', *International Journal of Philosophy of Culture and Axiology*, 16(2): 55–67.

Sada Social (2021), 'SadaSocial: 770 Violations during the Month of May, and the Center Is Suing Facebook', 2 June, https://sada.social/ (accessed 3 August 2022).

Said, E. (1981), *Covering Islam: How the Media and the Experts Determine How We See the Rest of the World*, New York: Pantheon Books.

Said, E. (1984), 'Permission to Narrate', *Journal of Palestine Studies*, 13(3): 27–48.

Saraste, A. (2021), 'Media Regulation and Censorship in Occupied Palestine', ICAHD Finland, https://icahd.fi/wp-content/uploads/2010/05/media_regulation_and_cens orship_in_palestine.pdf (accessed 28 October 2022).

'Social Media Is the Mass Protest: Solidarity with Palestinians Grows Online', 18 May, https://www.nytimes.com/ (accessed 4 August 2022).

Tawil-Souri, H. (2015), 'Media, Globalization, and the (Un)Making of the Palestinian Cause', *Popular Communication*, 13(2): 145–57.

UN Human Rights (2022), 'Israel's 55-Year Occupation of Palestinian Territory Is Apartheid – UN Human Rights Expert', 25 March, https://www.ohchr.org/en/ press-releases/2022/03/israels-55-year-occupation-palestinian-territory-aparth eid-un-human-rights (accessed January 2022).

UN Special Committee (1971), 'Report of the Special Committee to Investigate Israeli Practices Affecting the Human Rights of the Population of the Occupied Territories', Chapter III: Section C, 5 October, https://www.un.org/unispal/document/auto-insert-188614/ (accessed 28 August 2022).

UNRWA (2014), 'Gaza Situation Report 68', United Nations Relief and Works Agency, 6 November, http://www.unrwa.org/newsroom/emergency-reports/gaza-situation-report-68 (accessed 29 July 2022).

Wearing, G. (2021), 'Western Media's Impact on the War between Israel and Palestine', OWP, 16 June 2021, https://theowp.org/reports/ (accessed 16 May 2022).

2

Gaza 2021: Newsworthiness and context in the Spanish news coverage of the Israeli-Palestinian conflict

Ruth Sanz Sabido

Introduction

The period between 29 March and 4 July 2021 epitomizes, in an interval of just fourteen weeks, the nature and trajectory of the Israeli-Palestinian conflict: the application of divisive Israeli policies, the organization of Palestinian and pro-Palestinian protests against Israel's oppressive practices, the use of force against Palestinian civilians, the launching of rockets into Israel by Hamas and a new campaign of Israeli air strikes targeting the Gaza Strip, all of which was interspersed with days of apparent quietude and with the involvement of other actors whose role consists, in the main, of expressing their opinions on the conflict from afar. On this particular occasion, a series of incidents took place in the area: on 22 April, hundreds of far-right Jewish Israelis marched in Jerusalem chanting 'death to Arabs' during the Muslim holy month of Ramadan. Following night-time prayer, Palestinians tried to gather on the steps near Damascus Gate in the Old City, but were prevented from doing so by metal barriers erected by the Israeli authorities. Hamas responded to these actions by launching rockets into Israel. In return, Israel deployed fighter jets and attack helicopters.

A few days later, the anticipated decision of Israel's Supreme Court – to evict dozens of Palestinians from their homes in Sheikh Jarrah – led to a number of protests in East Jerusalem on 6 May. The following day, Israeli police forces stormed the al-Aqsa Mosque compound. Between 10 and 21 May, Hamas launched rockets into Israel, while Israel targeted the Gaza Strip with air strikes. These air strikes killed 260 Palestinians, including 66 children, and injured 2,200 Palestinians, including 685 children (United Nations Office for the Coordination of Humanitarian Affairs, 2021). Despite the ceasefire that was reached on 21 May, fighting resumed in June after Hamas launched incendiary balloons into Israel, to which the Israeli Air Force again responded with air strikes. Other key developments took place during this period: Naftali Bennett replaced Benjamin Netanyahu as Israel's prime minister, Mahmoud Abbas postponed the Palestinian Authority elections in the West Bank and concerns were also raised about the rise in a 'civil war' climate in areas that contained a mixed Israeli and Palestinian population.

This analysis of the Israeli-Palestinian conflict between 29 March and 4 July 2021 focuses on three of the most read mainstream Spanish newspapers and three 'alternative' or native online sources. Firstly, the chapter offers an overview of previous studies into the news coverage of this conflict by the Spanish news media. This is followed by an outline of the methodological design applied for this analysis, including details of the sample that was examined. The findings are discussed in the third section, which explores two main aspects of the coverage: the newsworthiness of the Israeli-Palestinian conflict in the Spanish press and the contextualization of the latest clashes in relation to past and contemporary events. Finally, the chapter draws conclusions about the importance of contextualizing new clashes historically so as to provide a more nuanced coverage of the conflict and, as noted earlier, to challenge the reductionist views about it, which emphasize its religious and violent nature while minimizing the political and territorial aspects that remain at its core.

The Israeli-Palestinian conflict in the Spanish press

In Spain, as in other Western countries, the Israeli-Palestinian conflict becomes newsworthy when there are dramatic events that meet the logic of the media in terms of newsworthiness (Galtung and Ruge, 1965; Harcup and O'Neill, 2001; Harcup and O'Neill, 2017). As such, the conflict is perceived as an important, complex and long-standing one, but it is also distant, in the sense that there are no direct political, geographic or geostrategic factors to consider between Israel and Spain. The extent of any relationship between the two countries is partly defined by Spain's historical connection with Arab countries, which was especially salient during Franco's dictatorship. After the Spanish Civil War (1936–9), Franco sought support from Arab countries during the international isolation that Spain experienced after the war, a stance that Franco continued to defend throughout the dictatorship. When Franco died in 1975, King Juan Carlos continued to forge personal friendships with Arab kings and sheikhs, which continue to this day. Meanwhile, Israel identified Spain with the Nazi-fascist axis, based on the military support the nationalists received from Hitler and Mussolini during the civil war, and the nature of the dictatorship that followed (Hernández Córdoba, 2011). Consequently, Spain did not establish any diplomatic connections with Israel until 1986, when Spain joined the European Economic Community (Rodríguez Esperanza and Humanes, 2017).

The fact that Franco sided with Arabs effectively meant that his opposition – the exiled Left – took the opposite perspective by celebrating the creation of Israel in 1948 (Córdoba Hernández, 2011). However, this support for the new state deteriorated over the years. The Six Day War in 1967 and the Yom Kippur War in 1973 clashed with the Left's pacifist stance, particularly in the anti-Vietnam War context of the 1970s. The support of the United States towards Israel further helped to consolidate the Left's perception that the struggle against the United States and Israel was one and the same (Córdoba Hernández, 2011). Therefore, the Left began to support the Palestinian cause as an example of an oppressed people that fought for its liberation (Baer, 2007; Córdoba Hernández, 2011).

This was also the stance that was taken by the pro-Arab government led by the Spanish Socialist Party (PSOE) throughout the 1980s, and later on by the conservative Partido Popular (PP). However, in the post-September 11 context, PP's prime minister Jose María Aznar's alliance with George W. Bush led him to support Spain's involvement in the wars in Afghanistan and Iraq. Then, from a national perspective, the train bombings of 11 March 2004 in Madrid exacerbated the increasing rupture with the previous pro-Arab stances (Portero, 2008). These developments also need to be understood in the context of Spain's struggle with ETA's (Basque separatist organization) terrorism: for PP, taking a strong position against terrorism during the 1990s was their way of emphasizing their democratic credentials. In terms of the Israeli-Palestinian conflict, this meant that the Spanish Right became increasingly critical of the Palestinian cause and their actions, which they described as terrorist and as a threat to democracy.

Spain's contemporary position in relation to the Israeli-Palestinian conflict is also partly determined by its membership of the European Union, an institution that has not been able to formulate a firm stance towards the conflict and its actors. For example, while Hamas is clearly defined as a terrorist organization in the eyes of the United States (given their uncompromising support for Israel), the EU has shifted its position in this regard throughout the years. Moreno Mercado (2018) reminds us that the European Court of Justice declared, in 2014, that Hamas could not be considered a terrorist organization. However, it backtracked on this decision in 2017, after several member states appealed against it. In this context, the news coverage of Hamas is particularly controversial in the EU. In Spain, Moreno Mercado found, in his analysis of the 2014 Gaza war, that *El País* and *El Mundo* often – but not always – tended to avoid any particular description when they mention Hamas, and when they do include any labels, they tend to choose 'Islamist' over 'terrorist'.

Previous studies examining the coverage of the Israeli-Palestinian conflict in the Western media – including the media of the United States, Britain, Italy and Germany, amongst other countries – have pointed out that representations of this conflict often show imbalances of power, usually seen in the choice of news sources that are used to define the events. For example, Nicolás Gavilán (2013) found that official government sources are the most frequently used in the news coverage of this conflict. In the specific context of Israel and Palestine, the journalistic practice of relying on official sources effectively means that there is a pre-determined preference for Israeli sources over Palestinian ones, since it is the former that constitutes a widely recognized state in the first place.

The coverage tends to take more or less obvious pro-Israeli perspectives, even when it appears to critique the disproportionately violent attacks on Palestinians, while in-depth explanations of the history of the conflict tend to be absent from the news discourse (Muravchik, 2003; Noakes and Wilkins, 2002; Philo and Berry, 2004; Philo and Berry, 2011; Sanz Sabido, 2019; Zaharna, 1997). In keeping with these international perspectives, the Spanish news media also presents a tendency to frame the conflict episodically rather than thematically (Iyengar, 1996). Iyengar defines 'episodic' framing as the depiction of issues focusing on specific instances, while 'thematic' framing depicts, by contrast, 'political issues more broadly and abstractly by placing them in some appropriate context – historical, geographical, or otherwise' (Iyengar, 1996: 62). This means that, with the frequent use of episodic framing, the latest incidents often appear divorced from their historical background, which remains unclear to the average reader. Rodríguez Esperanza and Humanes (2017) point out that this lack of clarity is reinforced by the frequent repetition of stereotypes over time, such as the characterization of the conflict as a primarily religious one, which has the effect of discursively erasing its political nature. Moreover, the erasure of key historical events and actions from contemporary discourse has another important effect: the consequences of those actions – namely a legacy of suffering for the Palestinian people – appear unexplained and easy to recontextualize in light of more recent cycles of violence and retaliation. This discursive strategy favours those who were originally responsible for those actions, as their erasure ensures that they are no longer held to account.

Methodology

The chapter is based on the analysis of articles published by a selection of Spanish national newspapers for fourteen weeks, between 29 March and 4 July 2021. In order to sample the articles, publications were selected on the basis of a report published in May 2021 by Comscore, the agency that monitors news readership in Spain. According to this report (EE, 2021), the top eight of the most read Spanish newspapers online were ranked as follows (in millions of unique visitors): *LaVanguardia.com* (23,394), *ElMundo.es* (22,817), *ElEspanol.com* (21,062), *ElPais.com* (20,333), *ElConfidencial.com* (19,111), *20Minutos.es* (19,030), *ElPeriodico.com* (13,771) and *OKDiario.com* (11,474). In order to keep an equal balance of mainstream newspapers and native digital newspapers, the top three of each type were selected: the digital version of three mainstream newspapers (*La Vanguardia*, *El Mundo* and *El País*) and three native digital newspapers (*El Español*, *El Confidencial* and *OK Diario*).

The term 'Gaza' was searched on the websites of the six news outlets, focusing on the fourteen-week period mentioned earlier, in order to monitor the newsworthiness of the conflict before, during and after the military intervention that took place from 10 to 21 May. After removing duplicate and irrelevant articles, the final sample consisted of 369 pieces with the following distribution: *El País* (159), *La Vanguardia* (105), *El Mundo* (35), *El Confidencial* (34), *El Español* (22) and *OK Diario* (14). Using Critical Discourse Analysis (Wodak and Meyer, 2009), the study explores two main aspects of the coverage: (1) the newsworthiness of the Israeli-Palestinian conflict in the Spanish press and (2) the contextualization of the latest clashes in relation to past and contemporary events.

Findings

Newsworthiness and the Spanish connection

Despite the apparent limited connection between Spain and the Israeli-Palestinian conflict, on this particular occasion a link was established between the military intervention in Gaza and Spanish politics: Ceuta, a Spanish autonomous city on the north coast of Africa, bordered by Morocco, was at the centre of the news coverage in Spain while Gaza was being attacked, due to the sudden arrival of thousands of people (most of whom were children and young adults) who tried to make their way into mainland Spain. Some articles made a point of connecting the situation in Palestine with Spain's relationship with Morocco and the migrant crisis in Ceuta (Vives, 2021). For example, Juliana (2021) states in *La Vanguardia* that

> there is an invisible thread that links Gaza with Ceuta. The United States currently needs all the support they can get from the Arab world to cool down the hostilities between Israelis and Palestinians. Morocco, a country that has an excellent relationship with Israel, is a key piece in the US' diplomatic machine. In this context, border controls in Ceuta have relaxed, leading to an avalanche of more than eight thousand people heading towards Spanish and European territory within a few hours. (my translation)

Along similar lines, Peregil and Sánchez-Vallejo (2021) report in *El País* that Anthony Blinken, US secretary of state, had celebrated Morocco's role in helping to maintain stability in the Middle East, with particular reference to the escalation of violence in Gaza, and had also offered his support to find a solution to the resulting crisis between Spain and Morocco in relation to Ceuta.

From a different perspective, some articles report on the ninety-eight Spanish people who live in the Gaza Strip and who refuse to be evacuated (Alamillos, 2021), and on the case of Juana Ruiz who, according to the description in *El Español*, is a Spanish aid worker who was arrested on 13 April by Israeli soldiers (Susanna, 2021). Despite these links, it is still correct to argue, as others have pointed out (Córdoba Hernández, 2011; Moreno Mercado, 2018), that any connections between Spain and the Israeli-Palestinian conflict are indirect and limited to specific circumstances. Consequently, the Spanish news media coverage of the conflict is mainly episodic, as it increases when new clashes or key developments take place. As shown in Graph 2.1, the number of articles mentioning Gaza during the fourteen-week period between 29 March and 4 July 2021 indicate some clear differences attending to two key factors: on the one hand, the type of publication covering the events and, on the other hand, the dates of publication.

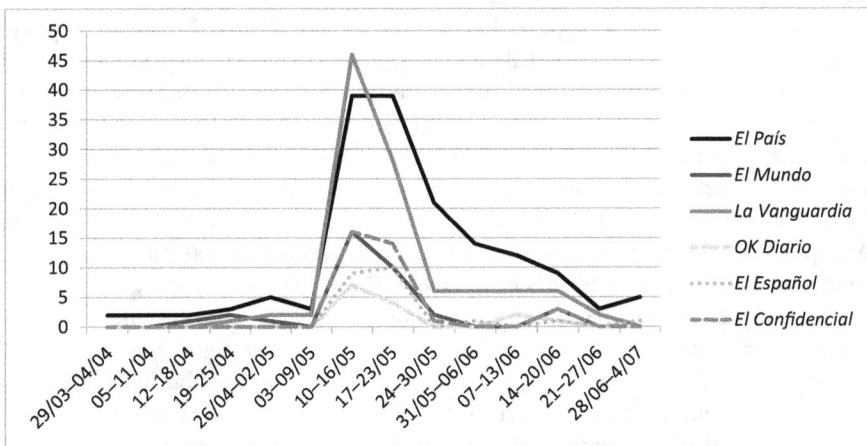

Graph 2.1. Number of articles mentioning Gaza during the fourteen-week period between 29 March and 4 July 2021

Firstly, in terms of the amount of coverage presented by the mainstream and alternative newspapers, the sample of articles published in mainstream publications (*El País*: 159; *La Vanguardia*: 105; *El Mundo*: 35) – a combined total of 299 articles – was significantly higher than those published in the alternative ones (*El Confidencial*: 34; *El Español*: 22; *OK Diario*: 14), with a combined total of 70 articles. The sample consists of one publication (*El País*) that takes a centre-left perspective, four publications that operate broadly at the centre-right (one of which – *La Vanguardia* – is Catalanist) and one publication (*OK Diario*) that sits more firmly on the conservative side.

Secondly, in terms of publication dates, as shown in Graph 2.1, the news coverage peaked during the week of 10–16 May, and was still high the following week, between 17 and 23 May, coinciding with Israel's air strikes on the Gaza Strip between 10 and 21 May. According to this, the sampled period can be divided into three phases: (i) a six-week pre-air-strikes phase, from 29 March until 9 May; (ii) a two-week air-strikes phase, from 10 to 24 May, by the end of which a ceasefire had been reached and (iii) a six-week post-air-strikes phase, from 25 May to 4 July.

(i)   The pre-air-strikes phase

Even though some relevant developments had taken place in the weeks prior to the air strikes, the coverage during the first phase, from 29 March until 9 May, was minimal: only twenty-six articles were sampled for that period, all of which were published by the three mainstream newspapers (*El País*: 17; *El Mundo*: 4; *La Vanguardia*: 5). Eight of those articles were published during the week between 26 April and 2 May. One of the key developments that became newsworthy during that week consisted of the publication of a report by Human Rights Watch (HRW) (2021) condemning Israel's practices and policies against Palestinians in the West Bank, Gaza and East Jerusalem, accusing Israel of committing 'crimes against humanity and persecution' and describing them as an apartheid state. All three mainstream newspapers dedicated articles to discuss HRW's report.

Other key themes that appeared across the sample during this six-week phase included: the suspension of the Palestinian Authority elections; the clashes that had taken place in Jerusalem on 22 April, when Palestinians were prevented from gathering on the steps near Damascus Gate in the Old City by metal barriers erected by Israeli authorities and the clashes that developed between 6 and 9 May in relation to the eviction of Palestinian families from their homes in Sheikh Jarrah and the storming of Israeli forces in the al-Aqsa Mosque compound. For example, in relation to the al-Aqsa Mosque incidents, *La Vanguardia* highlighted that 'more than 200 Palestinians were injured in the clashes with Israelis in Jerusalem' (EFE, 2021a).

Referring to the clashes on 22 April, Emergui (2021) described that week as the most tense in recent times, and stated that the 'hottest night' had ended with a 'Jew being violently attacked by several Palestinians who later burnt his car' (my translation). From this point, the article describes a succession of retaliatory violence from both sides of the conflict, alluding to events that had taken place before and after that specific episode. The article contextualizes these clashes, on the one hand, in relation to the Palestinian Authority elections, which were – at that point – likely to be postponed if Israel did not allow them to hold elections in East Jerusalem. On the other hand, the article also contextualizes the emergence of these clashes in relation to the deep political crisis in Israel, caused by the politicians' inability to form a stable government after holding four elections in the space of two years.

Though important to understand how the conflict continues to unfold on a day-by-day basis, these events received comparatively little attention when they originally took place, although they were mentioned again later throughout the sample in order to provide some context to the ensuing military intervention, once the conflict had already escalated and become visibly violent.

(ii) The air-strikes phase

During the eleven-day air strikes, which occupied a majority of the two-week period from 10 May to 23 May, the sample adds up to a combined total of 238 articles: 60 of those were published by the alternative press (*El Confidencial*: 30; *El Español*: 19; *OK Diario*: 11). The mainstream press, with a combined total of 178 articles, dedicated a comparatively higher amount of attention to the conflict (*La Vanguardia*: 74; *El País*: 78; *El Mundo*: 26). The distribution of news articles throughout the sampled period therefore suggests that it is the escalation of violence, with the increasing death tolls and the images of war and destruction, that draws the attention of the Spanish news media, which is in keeping with other Western media outlets (Philo and Berry, 2011).

A wide variety of themes emerged during this phase, but mainly focused on: descriptions of the bombings and the destruction of infrastructure; the victims, including frequent mentions to children; the asymmetric use of violence and resources; arguments in favour of Israel's right to self-defence; international reactions to the conflict, including those of the United States, the UN and the EU; references to international media, including the destruction of the building that hosted Al Jazeera and other media organizations; the pro-Palestinian demonstrations that were held in multiple cities internationally; the meaning of the air strikes in the context of Netanyahu's political position at the time; references to the intensification of violence; calls to reach a ceasefire and, eventually, news about the ceasefire itself.

For example, a piece published in *El Confidencial* (AA, 2021) provides an overview of several of these themes. The article indicates that Israel has destroyed the building where Al Jazeera, Associated Press and other media offices were located. It includes Israel's justification for targeting this building, but it also quotes from an interview with Palestinian political analyst Hani Habib, who argued that this was not Israel's battle, but Netanyahu's personal battle to hold on to power. It provides some context to the air strikes by briefly referring to the clashes in the al-Aqsa compound, before stating that, up to 15 May, 145 Palestinians had died (including 41 children and 26 women) and 1,100 had been injured. In Israel, by contrast, 10 people had died and more than 250 were injured. The article explains that pressure on Gaza hospitals had quickly escalated, and a Palestinian doctor is quoted describing the harshness of the situation, having to treat the wounds of his own neighbours and friends, while fearing that the next patient might be one of his own family members.

Having established that the ongoing conflict becomes particularly newsworthy when the violence escalates, it is unsurprising that much of the news coverage focuses precisely on describing the latest episodes with a particular focus on the victims (and especially children, women and families). Meanwhile, the attribution of responsibility for the violence and resulting victims presents a mixed picture. There are two main aspects to highlight in this regard: first, the 'asymmetric war' between Israel and Hamas is often mentioned, frequently taking a critical stance against Israel for the vast military resources they use to respond to the rockets launched by Hamas; secondly, the juxtaposition of violent actions perpetrated by both agents builds a discourse of episodic retaliatory violence within each article and over time, which ends up blurring the original causes of the fight and the attribution of responsibility.

(iii)   The post-air-strikes phase

Once a ceasefire was reached, the news coverage of the conflict began, once again, to decline. During the six-week period between 24 May (when the truce had already been reached) and 4 July, the three mainstream newspapers published a combined total of 95 articles (*El País*: 64; *La Vanguardia*: 26; *El Mundo*: 5), while the alternative press published a total of 10 articles (*El Confidencial*: 4; *OK Diario*: 3; *El Español*: 3). More specifically, the news coverage reduced abruptly during the week commencing 24 May, and only remained comparatively high in *El País* during that particular week. Nevertheless, the coverage of Gaza was more frequent in the immediate aftermath of the air strikes than it was before the escalation of violence.

Some of the main themes covered during this phase include: the consequences of the conflict for the Palestinian population, with a particular focus on children, their fears and losses, and the impact of the conflict on new generations; the stance of the EU in relation to the conflict; the latest developments for Benjamin Netanyahu and Naftali Bennett; the distribution of vaccines in the context of the Covid-19 pandemic; discussions about the existence of anti-Semitism; accusations of war crimes; reactions to the death of a Palestinian dissident; the role of Egypt in the conflict; discussions about an autocracy in Palestine and further allegations about the media building that was destroyed by Israel.

The humanitarian consequences of the conflict are frequently reported, usually focusing on victims who 'have died' or 'have been killed' or injured. It is comparatively rare to find references to people who have been displaced. An exception is found in an article published on 21 May, which points out that 90,000 people had been displaced due to the latest military intervention (Deiros Bronte, 2021a). The impact on infrastructure is also described often, including 'schools, hospitals and shops that are on the verge of collapse in Gaza', and the subsequent deterioration of the social and economic fabric in the Gaza Strip as a consequence of the blockade imposed by Israel and the succession of wars endured by Palestinians in Gaza (Deiros Bronte, 2021b). Children are frequently highlighted in news reports. For example, a piece published in *El País* on 23 May, titled 'The hell of being a child in Gaza' (Sanz, 2021a, my translation) quotes a Red Cross representative stating that children live in fear to the extent that 'they do not want to go to the bathroom, they are scared of everything', and parents are not sure 'whether they should sleep with all of their children, for the family to die together at once, or whether they should divide into groups, so at least part of the family might survive' (Sanz, 2021a, my translation).

A prior article, published on 16 May also in *El País*, points out that 'more than 40% of the inhabitants of Gaza were born after Hamas started governing the Strip and they have lived three wars' (Lecumberri, 2021, my translation). This article also discusses the inability of families to feed and provide opportunities for their children, and denounces the fact that women are denied access to life-saving medical treatment in a patriarchal and increasingly isolated society. Lecumberri puts the blame primarily on the Israeli blockade, but also on the internal divisions between Hamas and Mahmoud Abbas' Palestinian Authority, and on the inaction of the international community.

Retaliatory violence, human loss and the importance of context

As discussed earlier, the Spanish coverage of the conflict tends to present a context of episodic retaliatory violence, consisting of cycles in which one agent attacked the other because they had attacked first. The violence is often placed in relation to the events that have developed in the last few days or weeks, leading to the description of a succession of strikes and victims where the original cause of the violence is lost. This factor, combined with the long history of the conflict, leads to the progressive loss of historical context in favour of the more immediate one. This, in turn, facilitates the emergence of reductionist narratives, for example, by reducing the conflict to a religious one while erasing its other key aspects. For example, expressions that are sometimes used to describe the violence in the news discourse, such as 'sectarian violence between Arabs and Jews' (see, e.g. Sanz, 2021b), have precisely that effect of emphasizing the religious aspect of the conflict at the expense of its political and territorial nature.

An article published in *El Mundo* mentions that an Israeli strike had killed ten members of the same family: eight children and two women who 'were safe at home, they were not carrying weapons, they did not throw any rockets' (Agencias, 2021, my translation). Meanwhile, the Israel Defence Forces emphasize that they have killed 'hundreds' of members of Hamas. The violence is described as escalating and further states that – at that point – 'at least 126 Palestinians had lost their lives, including 31 children, and 950 had been wounded'. It also mentions that 'more than 2000 rockets had been launched from the Gaza Strip against Israel, killing nine people, including one child and one soldier, and have wounded 560 people'. After describing the latest attack that had caused an Israeli casualty, Hamas is said to have taken responsibility for it, stating that this was their response to the Israeli attack on the Al Shati refugee camp. As we read through this succession of events, the retaliatory element is very clear within the article, as is the asymmetric nature of the attacks, not only in the Gaza Strip but also in the West Bank: 'Palestinians throw stones, Molotov cocktails and other projectiles against Israeli forces, who respond with rubber bullets and sometimes with real munition. These clashes resulted in 11 Palestinian deaths and some 250 wounded' (Agencias, 2021, my translation).

The description of the violence as retaliatory and as asymmetric is frequent across the sample. However, this particular article is noteworthy because it makes references to two key historical moments in the conflict which feature quite rarely in the sample: first, it mentions the territories that were occupied by Israel in 1967, specifying, later on, that the al-Aqsa Mosque compound was located in East Jerusalem, 'a Palestinian area that had been occupied by Israel since 1967'; secondly, the article also explains that every 15 May, Palestinians commemorate Nakba, the 'catastrophe' caused by the creation of Israel in 1948 (Agencias, 2021, my translation). These historical references are connected to the recent clashes following the threat to evict some Palestinian families from Sheikh Jarrah. These historical references are rare even though the time period covered by this particular sample includes two key commemorations: precisely, the anniversary of the creation of Israel on 15 May 1948 and the Israeli celebration of the occupation of East Jerusalem during the Six Day War in 1967. Even when historical references appear, as they do here, they remain largely decontextualized. In the example given earlier, the reference to 1967 misses the broader context and consequences that the Six Day War had for Palestinians. Meanwhile, the allusion to 1948, while useful to a certain extent, excludes the context and chain of events that led to the creation of Israel, shaping the entire conflict from that point.

Another example is found in *OK Diario*, which mentions the Six Day War twice within the same article, stating that the escalation of violence was closely related to the clashes that developed in East Jerusalem just before the military intervention. East Jerusalem is, the article explains, where 'Zionists' and 'far-right sympathisers' celebrate Jerusalem Day to commemorate the occupation of this area during the Six Day War (*OK Diario*, 2021). Even though the latter reference to 1967 provides slightly more information than the one mentioned earlier, it still misses the opportunity to provide more context. On other occasions, 1948 is mentioned in relation to the evictions in Sheikh Jarrah, as the law allows Jews to claim properties that they owned before 1948 (EFE, 2021b). Of course, it is not expected that news articles should provide comprehensive history lectures, but a brief paragraph would suffice to maintain the historical roots of the conflict present in contemporary discourse, so that the true nature and roots of the conflict can be understood. The chronic lack of this approach over the seventy-three years that have elapsed since the creation of Israel has, precisely, served to leave the original conditions of its creation progressively further behind.

Newspapers sometimes publish articles that intend to cover this gap. For example, *El País* published one such article on 13 May. Titled 'What's happening between Palestine and Israel? The key to understanding the conflict' (El País, 2021, my translation). It is structured around seven sections, each focusing on a specific theme or question: the cause of the conflict; the connection between the conflict and holy places; the evictions in Sheikh Jarrah; who is currently fighting; damages caused by the current conflict; likelihood of a ceasefire and possible scenarios for the next few days. The article explains the significance of holy places, like the al-Aqsa Mosque, in the development of the clashes on Jerusalem Day. Later, when discussing the evictions in Sheikh Jarrah, the article explains that 'groups of settlers linked to the Israeli far-right use property titles which, according to them, they acquired from Jewish owners before the creation of the state of Israel, in 1948' (*El País*, 2021, my translation). Apart from these brief historical references, which resemble those occasionally found in other articles, there is no other attempt to situate the conflict in a historical context, despite the prospects that the article heading might elicit. It can be argued that, even when articles aim to address the context of the conflict with the initial promise of a thematic perspective, the explanations that are provided continue to focus on the latest episodes, with only some brief, decontextualized references to past events.

Conclusions

Even a conflict as visible as the one between Israel and Palestine, which appears frequently in the news media, receives unequal amounts of attention throughout time and across publications. This chapter has shown that there are some differences between mainstream and alternative Spanish news publications in terms of the number of articles they published during the sampled period. However, they tend to reproduce similar patterns in the coverage: the conflict becomes more newsworthy when new violent clashes develop, the violence is often represented as retaliatory and asymmetric, there is a strong focus on the humanitarian crisis and, above all, there is a lack of proper historical contextualization to understand the background of the conflict.

The Israeli-Palestinian conflict is one of the most newsworthy ongoing conflicts in the world, yet it remains a largely misunderstood one, as the background information that would help audiences to understand its evolution is largely missing from the news discourse. The legacy of key historical actions and events that have shaped the lives of Palestinians over the past seven decades still determines the conditions in which Palestinians live today. Without this background information, new developments are susceptible to being recontextualized by omitting details of decisions that were made and actions that were taken, which ultimately has the effect of erasing responsibilities and reshaping the face of the conflict. As shown in previous studies (e.g. Philo and Berry, 2011), this analysis also points at the lack of key contextual information which, in turn, adds to the development of a narrative about the Palestinian story that erases the origins of their plight, even when the focus is placed on their suffering. Despite the newsworthiness of the conflict and the attention given to the humanitarian crisis in the Spanish press, it remains unclear who is responsible for the conditions that Palestinians are living in and how they have ended up in that position. It is striking how Palestinians and their history continue to remain largely invisible within the news discourse. In its place, Palestinians are depicted in reductionist ways, such as being passive recipients of Israeli violence, living under the rule of Hamas, or being stuck in a conflict situation that seems to have become accepted as part of their natural identity.

Despite the indirect link that was established between Spain and the conflict on this occasion – due to Morocco's role in supporting Israel and the subsequent crisis in Ceuta – this chapter has shown that, with some exceptions, the Spanish press presented a broadly neutral coverage of the conflict, with an inclination to sympathize for the losses – understood in every possible way – suffered by Palestinians. The neutral stance is observed, for instance, in the use of a variety of sources that serve to advance different viewpoints, from Israel's statements justifying their actions, to Hamas explaining why they had engaged in an attack, to Palestinian civilians describing their experiences. Death tolls are also provided for both sides of the conflict, although it is more frequent to see details of Palestinian victims, often specifying how many of them were children. This is not strange considering the objective fact that the numbers of dead and wounded Palestinians were significantly higher than those of Israeli casualties. Based on this, one might think that the sympathetic coverage of Palestinian victims and condemnations of Israeli violence automatically constitutes a pro-Palestinian discourse. However, I argue that this is not necessarily the case, and the news coverage of this conflict in the Spanish press requires a more nuanced analysis that considers the complexities involved.

Indeed, these findings must be considered in conjunction with the ways in which the conflict is contextualized. As discussed earlier, conflict is most often framed episodically, as news articles focus on reporting the details of the latest events. While episodic framing is necessary to understand the immediate context of the most recent developments, thematic framing is essential to comprehend the broader nature of the conflict, which can help to view the conflict critically and to see beyond the discourses based on death tolls and descriptions of violence and suffering. For example, in Spain, the news discourse is mainly based on depictions of the conflict as one that consists of endless retaliatory violence. From this perspective, it would be easy to perceive the conflict as a mindless one where different agents are ready to fight again as soon as the opportunity sparks. Similarly, there is a tendency in the Spanish press to represent the conflict as a religious one. Notwithstanding the fact that there is a religious element to the conflict, the point of contention is not related to religious beliefs, but to a fundamental political and territorial disagreement over the land, a problem that has become exponentially complex over the years. Proper contextualization of the origins of the conflict, with reference to Zionism and the chain of events that led to the creation of Israel in 1948, is largely missing from the sampled articles but would help to put the conflict into perspective.

In order to avoid the reproduction of reductionist views of the conflict, I argue that it is important to address this contextual gap by offering a stronger thematic approach that provides a more nuanced coverage of the conflict and helps to understand what is happening in the present time. This thematic approach would also help to acknowledge Palestinians as a people who are resisting a legacy of material conditions caused by a long chain of events that have spanned many decades.

References

AA (2021), 'Israel destruye las oficinas de Al Yazira y AP y la casa del "segundo" de Hamas en Gaza', *El Confidencial*, 15 May, https://www.elconfidencial.com/mundo/2021-05-15/ultima-hora-gaza-israel_3081136/ (accessed 10 November 2021).

Agencias (2021), 'Israel descarga 500 toneladas de bombas sobre Gaza y ataca edificios donde trabaja la prensa internacional', *El Mundo*, 15 May, https://www.elmundo.es/internacional/2021/05/15/609f73a421efa0df188b461f.html (accessed 12 November 2021).

Alamillos, A. (2021), 'Los españoles que no quieren ser evacuados de Gaza: "Aquí está nuestra vida"', *El Confidencial*, 19 May, https://www.elconfidencial.com/mundo/2021-05-19/espanoles-evacuacion-gaza-se-quedaran_3082816/ (accessed 28 October 2021).

Baer, A. (2007), 'Tanques contra piedras: la imagen de Israel en España', *Análisis del Real Instituto Elcano*, https://www.realinstitutoelcano.org/analisis/tanques-contra-pied ras-la-imagen-de-israel-en-espana-ari/ (accessed 5 November 2021).

Córdoba Hernández, A. M. (2011), 'El conflicto palestino-israelí visto desde España: oscilaciones y tendencias de la opinión pública', *Ámbitos: Revista Andaluza de Comunicación*, 20: 149–74.

Deiros Bronte, T. (2021a), 'La ofensiva contra Gaza deja más de 90.000 desplazados', *El País*, 22 May, https://elpais.com/internacional/2021-05-22/la-ofensiva-con tra-gaza-deja-mas-de-90000-desplazados.html (accessed 5 November 2021).

Deiros Bronte, T. (2021b), 'Escuelas, hospitales y comercios al borde del colapso en Gaza', *El País*, 18 May, https://elpais.com/internacional/2021-05-18/un-triple-golpe-a-las-fabricas-las-escuelas-y-los-hospitales.html (accessed 5 November 2021).

EE (2021), 'El Español se mantiene por cuarto mes consecutivo en el podio de la prensa española', *El Español*, 21 June, https://www.elespanol.com/invertia/medios/20210621/espanol-mantiene-cuarto-consecutivo-podio-prensa-espanola/589941563_0.html (accessed 29 September 2021).

EFE (2021a), 'Más de 200 palestinos heridos en los disturbios con israelíes en Jerusalén', *La Vanguardia*, 8 May, https://www.lavanguardia.com/internacional/20210508/7438 668/paletinos-heridos-disturbios-jerusalen-judios-extremistas.html (accessed 10 November 2021).

EFE (2021b), 'Benjamin Netanyahu dice que Israel "no permitirá protestas violentas" en Jerusalén', *El Mundo*, 9 May, https://www.elmundo.es/internacional/2021/05/09/60981 94ffc6c83e0418b4586.html (accessed 10 October 2021).

El País (2021), '¿Qué está pasando entre Palestina e Israel? Las claves para entender el conflicto', *El País*, 13 May, https://elpais.com/internacional/2021-05-17/que-esta-pasa ndo-entre-palestina-e-israel-en-la-actualidad-las-claves-para-entender-el-confli cto-hoy.html (accessed 14 October 2021).

Emergui, S. (2021), 'El fanatismo, el vandalismo y las redes sociales alientan la violencia en Jerusalén', *El Mundo*, 24 April, https://www.elmundo.es/internacio nal/2021/04/23/6082e6bf21efa0bb348b45b6.html (accessed 8 October 2021).

Galtung, J., and M. Ruge (1965), 'The Structure of Foreign News: The Presentation of the Congo, Cuba and Cyprus Crises in Four Norwegian Newspapers', *Journal of International Peace Research*, 2: 64–90.

Harcup, T., and D. O'Neill (2001), 'What Is News? Galtung and Ruge Revisited', *Journalism Studies*, 2(2): 261–80.

Harcup, T., and D. O'Neill (2017), 'What Is News? News Values Revisited (Again)', *Journalism Studies*, 18(12): 1470–88.

Human Rights Watch (2021), 'A Threshold Crossed: Israeli Authorities and the Crimes of Apartheid and Persecution', *Human Rights Watch*, 27 April, https://www.hrw.org/rep ort/2021/04/27/threshold-crossed/israeli-authorities-and-crimes-apartheid-and-pers ecution (accessed 5 October 2021).

Iyengar, S. (1996), 'Framing Responsibility for Political Issues', *Annals of the American Academy of Political and Social Science*, 546: 59–70.

Juliana, E. (2021), 'Marruecos pone en jaque a Ceuta y a Sánchez, con el Sáhara de fondo', *La Vanguardia*, 19 May, https://www.lavanguardia.com/politica/20210

519/7464697/marruecos-pone-jaque-ceuta-sanchez-sahara-fondo.html (accessed 10 November 2021).

Lecumberri, B. (2021), 'Solo víctimas', *El País*, 16 May, https://elpais.com/internacio nal/2021-05-16/solo-victimas.html (accessed 15 October 2021).

Moreno Mercado, J. M. (2018), 'La prensa española ante el conflicto en Gaza', *Revista Ensayos Militares*, 4(1): 77–93.

Muravchik, J. (2003), *Covering the Intifada: How the Media Reported the Palestinian Uprising*, Washington, DC: Washington Institute for Near East Policy.

Nicolás Gavilán, M. T. (2013), 'El conflicto Israel-Palestino en la mira. Análisis de las noticias de los corresponsales de prensa española (2007–2008)', *Frontera Norte*, 25(50): 65–95, http://www.redalyc.org/articulo.oa?id=13628944003 (accessed 14 October 2021).

Noakes, J. A., and K. G. Wilkins (2002), 'Shifting Frames of the Palestinian Movement in US News', *Media, Culture & Society*, 24(5): 649–71.

OK Diario (2021), 'Al menos 24 palestinos muertos en Gaza por los bombardeos israelíes y 700 heridos en Jerusalén', *OK Diario*, 11 May, https://okdiario.com/internacional/ menos-21-palestinos-muertos-gaza-bombardeos-israelies-700-heridos-jerusalen-7209 014 (accessed 10 October 2021).

Peregil, F., and M. A. Sánchez-Vallejo (2021), 'EE UU insta a España y Marruecos a trabajar juntos para resolver la crisis migratoria en Ceuta', *El País*, 19 May, https://elp ais.com/espana/2021-05-19/eeuu-alaba-la-estabilidad-que-aporta-marruecos-en- oriente-proximo-el-segundo-dia-de-la-llegada-masiva-de-migrantes-a-ceuta.html (accessed 8 November 2021).

Philo, G., and M. Berry (2004), *Bad News from Israel*, London: Pluto.

Philo, G., and M. Berry (2011), *More Bad News from Israel*, London: Pluto.

Portero, F. (2008), 'Las relaciones hispano-israelíes', *Araucaria: Revista Iberoamericana de Filosofía, Política y Humanidades*, 10(19): 179–96.

Rodríguez Esperanza, M. S., and M. L. Humanes (2017), 'El conflicto Palestino-Israelí en la prensa española. La cobertura de la Operación Margen Protector en *ABC* y *La Vanguardia*', *Observatorio*, 11(4): 154–80.

Sanz, J. C. (2021a), 'El infierno de ser un niño en Gaza', *El País*, 23 May, https://elpais.com/ internacional/2021-05-23/hijos-de-una-guerra-sin-nombre-en-gaza.html (accessed 15 October 2021).

Sanz, J. C. (2021b), 'Israel intensifica sus ataques sobre Gaza y destruye un edificio que alberga medios internacionales', *El País*, 15 May, https://elpais.com/internacio nal/2021-05-15/israel-y-hamas-se-enzarzan-en-la-guerra-mientras-se-abre-paso-la- mediacion-internacional.html (accessed 10 October 2021).

Sanz Sabido, R. (2019), *The Israeli-Palestinian Conflict in the British Press*, Basingstoke: Palgrave Macmillan.

Susanna, J. (2021), 'El calvario de Juana Ruiz, la madrileña casada con un palestino: encarcelada sin juicio en Israel', *El Español*, 24 May, https://www.elespanol.com/reporta jes/20210524/juana-ruiz-madrilena-palestino-encarcelada-sin-israel/582943242_0. html (accessed 14 November 2021).

United Nations Office for the Coordination of Humanitarian Affairs (2021), 'Occupied Palestinian Territory (oPt): Response to the Escalation in the oPt', *United Nations Office for the Coordination of Humanitarian Affairs. Situation Report*, 7: 2–7 July 2021, https://reliefweb.int/report/occupied-palestinian-territory/occupied-palestinian-territ ory-opt-response-escalation-opt-4 (accessed 5 October 2021).

Vives, J. (2021), 'Crisis migratoria en Ceuta', *La Vanguardia*, 19 May, https://www.lavan guardia.com/vida/junior-report/20210519/7463725/crisis-migratoria-ceuta.html (accessed 10 November 2021).

Wodak, R., and M. Meyer (eds) (2009), *Methods for Critical Discourse Analysis*, London: Sage.

Zaharna, R. S. (1997), 'The Palestinian Leadership and the American Media: Changing Images, Conflicting Results'. In Y. R. Kamalipour (ed.), *The U. S. Media and the Middle East: Image and Perception*, Westport: Greenwood, 37–49.

3

Counter-hegemonic global media narratives on the Palestine–Israel conflict: The Sheikh Jarrah protests on CGTN, RT, France 24 and TeleSUR

Christopher D. Tulloch and Jose Luis Gordillo

Introduction

Academic literature on the coverage of the Palestine–Israel conflict has traditionally been limited to the representation of their conflicting perspectives in the Western elite media (Alkalliny, 2017; Ruigrok, Atteveldt and Takens, 2013). However, the mediation of this story as projected on prominent non-Anglo-American global media platforms can widen our options when analysing the international reporting of the Middle East in general given that they offer an alternative news discourse regarding events like those in Gaza in May 2021. In this sense, this chapter analyses the coverage of the Sheikh Jarrah protests in East Jerusalem on the digital platforms of three permanent members of the UN Security Council (UNSC), namely the China Global Television Network – a country which exercised the presidency of the UNSC during the events under analysis – the Kremlin-sponsored Russia Today and the global operation France 24 – along with the South American channel TeleSUR.

The chapter begins by presenting the revamped global television landscape, considers the 'soft power' dimension and public diplomatic role of these digital platforms and offers a brief introduction to the idiosyncrasies of the four channels under discussion. The text then moves to the case study at hand by presenting relevant background information on the Sheikh Jarrah protests, an explanation of the methodology employed, the presentation of comparative results and some concluding comments which aim to interpret both common transnational findings and discrepancies in their coverage.

The counter-hegemonic global television landscape

The West may have the biggest stalls in the world's media bazaar but it is not the only player. Globalization isn't merely another word for Americanization. (*Newsweek*, 28 February 2000)

International communication scholars often point to four key moments in post-war audiovisual journalism. The first refers to the West–East information flow during the Cold War led by organizations such as Radio Free Europe or Voice of America, media dynamics denounced as 'cultural imperialism' by MacBride in his Unesco report of 1980 (Macbride, 1980). The second is the 'CNN decade' of the 1980s when the channel brought us defining events such as the student protests in Tiananmen Square or the fall of the Berlin Wall. The third is the rapid expansion throughout the 1990s of Western European channels as a response to this US global television dominance. However, it is during the first decade of the twenty-first century when the satellite television landscape was definitively transformed with the arrival of counter-hegemonic platforms including France 24, Russia Today, TeleSUR, CGTN, Al Jazeera English or Iran's Press TV (Painter, 2007). These channels constituted a response to the MacBride-era petition for a 'non-Western' perspective on international news and are symbolized by marketing slogans in which CGTN invites viewers to 'See the Difference', RT asks us to 'Question More', France 24 encourages us to go 'Beyond the Headlines' and TeleSUR announces that 'Our North is the South.'

This transformation provoked considerable academic debate (Rai and Cottle, 2007; Thussu, 2006; Tunstall, 2008) as theorists welcomed (i) the consolidation of a 'global public sphere' (Chalaby, 2003); (ii) greater cosmopolitanism and global citizenship (Voltmer, 2003); (iii) 'deterritorialization' and the transcending of geographical barriers thanks to affordable satellite technology and (iv) an end to the centre-versus-periphery dynamics, the emergence of information counterflows and the consolidation of 'south–south communication'.

While they may differ significantly in terms of professionalism, news agenda priorities and ideological profile, the public nature of their funding remains the most significant common denominator of these channels. France 24 is owned by the government via its holding company France Médias Monde, the China Global Television Network (CGTN) is controlled by the Propaganda Department of the Chinese Communist Party, RT is funded by the federal tax budget of the Russian government and TeleSUR is financed by the governments of Venezuela, Cuba and Nicaragua. The state funding of such news organizations has inevitably led to controversies surrounding 'paradiplomatic journalism' (Cull, 2008; Seib, 2010), 'soft power' issues (Nye, 2008) and persuasive discourse techniques and state propaganda (Freedman, 2020) as well as ethnographic studies concerning the 'legitimization narratives' adopted by journalists to defend their professional autonomy (Wright, Scott and Bunce, 2020). Research regarding the blurred boundaries between mediated diplomacy and journalistic independence has often appeared in studies of such news operations, particularly regarding CGTN and RT.

China Global Television Network (CGTN)

China's commitment to a multilingual global television network dates to the year 2000 when the Communist Party launched the all-English channel 'CCTV International'. At the end of 2016, the five non-Chinese language channels – English, Spanish, French, Russian and Arabic – were definitively relaunched as 'CGTN', a rebrand described as the 'latest push to develop an international broadcast infrastructure allowing China to advance its messages and flex its "discourse power"' (Bandurski, 2017). While its headquarters are in Beijing, CGTN operates from three production hubs in Nairobi, Washington and London. These news centres distribute content to more than 150 million users in 160 countries through CGTN.com – the platform analysed here – and its mobile apps and social media platforms ranging from Weibo to Western-based social media. At a time when Western news media are making major cutbacks in their foreign news operations, the multibillion-dollar investment in its overseas media activities – including the Xinhua news agency or Radio China International – proves that Beijing firmly believes that 'the intangibles of public diplomacy can be converted via communication and international broadcasting into tangible foreign policy benefits' (Rawnsley, 2015: 275).

Often faced with accusations of a lack of objectivity, the channel defends itself by claiming to adhere to the principles of 'rationality and balance in reporting [and to] endeavour to present information from diverse perspectives' ('About Us', CGTN.com) by deploying Western style news formats, by using foreign anchors and presenters in an attempt to reinforce its credibility, by a lively presence on Twitter and by reminding critics that some of its footage is used by prestigious media like the BBC or CNN. Despite this, CGTN has been targeted by UK regulator OfCom and NGO Reporters Without Borders as being a vehicle for government propaganda.

Russia Today (RT)

Russia Today was launched in 2005 with the intention to 'stem the flow of negative and non-objective' information about Russia in the 'global information space' (Yablokov, 2015: 304). Thanks to a ten-fold budget increase between 2005 and 2015, it now consists of three global news channels in English, Spanish and Arabic while multimedia content and Twitter feeds are offered in French and German. Later rebranded as 'RT' in an attempt to distance itself from the state, the channel has twenty-two bureaus in nineteen countries. No reliable data are available to corroborate the extravagant claims made on the channel's Linkedin account of 150 million monthly visits or a global reach of 650 million viewers. That said, some authors do fix RT's YouTube viewership rate at almost 3 billion views (Elswah and Howard, 2020: 624).

According to editor-in-chief Margarita Simonyan, RT's audience consists of people 'who understand that the whole truth cannot be told by Anglo-Saxon television channels' (Yablokov, 2015: 305). This counterhegemonic standpoint has led to constant accusations from the Western media establishment that the channel is the televisual extension of Putin's aggressive foreign policy, a generator of conspiracy theories and a professional malpractitioner. In this sense, RT was blocked in Europe from March 2022 for its coverage of the invasion of Ukraine. To counter such accusations, RT employs respected Western reporters to increase its credibility and widely promotes the television awards it has received. It does not shy away from admitting that it is embroiled in an 'information war' with the West and given the nature of the case study at hand, the 'Truman Pledge' to Israel guarantees criticism from the channel.

France 24.com

France 24 emerged on the scene in late 2006 in an attempt to offer a non-Anglo European take on contemporary world events. With channels available in French, English, Arabic and Spanish, it has a government-funded annual budget of 100 million euros, a roster of 430 Paris-based journalists and 160 correspondent bureaus worldwide. The corporate website claims that the four channels have a 'combined weekly viewership of 61 million viewers' and that France 24 is 'the first international news channel in the Maghreb and in the French-speaking African countries'. Available to more than 300 million TV households, its online media platforms receive more than 16 million visits a month while the channel has close to 40 million followers on Twitter and Facebook. The official tagline 'Liberté, Egalité, Actualité' ('Freedom, Equality, News') is not only a play on words on the French national motto but also responds to what the channel considers a 'desire for something other than the Anglo-Saxon or Pan-Arab news channels which has incited many countries around the world to open up their "screen space" to us' (F24 Press kit).

TeleSUR

Founded in Caracas in 2005 and funded by the governments of Venezuela, Cuba and Nicaragua, TeleSUR considers itself a 'Latin American multimedia platform oriented towards leading and promoting the unification of the peoples of the South'. The 'South' here is understood as a 'geopolitical concept that promotes the struggle of peoples for peace, self-determination, respect for Human Rights and Social Justice'. This self-definition was further outlined by Venezuelan lawyer Eva Golinger while declaring that 'the main aim is to counter the images, the politics and the media manipulation from channels such as CNN. We find ourselves in an incredible situation according to which ... South American people see themselves through the prism of US news agencies ... TeleSur will be the manner in which greater balance can be brought to this media war' (*Democracy Now*, 26 July 2005).

Initially launched exclusively in Spanish, TeleSUR unveiled its English version in 2014. Its satellite coverage claims to reach 65 million viewers in Latin America and an additional 5 million worldwide via cable. As with CGTN and RT, the channel has been subject to constant attacks from the Western media. It has been referred to as 'Al Bolivar TV' or even as 'Al-Chavezeera' after the channel signed a content exchange deal with Al Jazeera in 2006 and has been accused of creating a South–South information axis and for limiting informative plurality in favour of a 'Socialist bias' (Calderón, 2005: 45; Maihold, 2014: 185). The channel defends itself by reminding critics that its consultive council includes Nobel winner Adolfo Perez Esquivel and Ignacio Ramonet, editor of the respected political journal *Le Monde Diplomatique*.

Background to the Sheikh Jarrah protests

The image and legitimacy of the state of Israel has benefited over time from its close ties to the United States and other Western powers given that it has traditionally been considered as a 'wall of containment from the radical Islam world and a spearhead of democratic values in the Middle East' (Nicolás Galván, 2014: 185). This situation has heavily influenced the news treatment it has received from the Anglo-American media which treat any armed offensive by the *Tsahal* as the exercise of its democratic right to legitimate self-defence. From this perspective, the Nakba – the expulsion in 1948 of more than 750,000 Palestinians (Pappe, 2008b: 28) from their homes and lands – along with subsequent forced evacuations are overlooked or justified as unfortunate but necessary *collateral damage* in the process of the construction of a safe homeland for the Jewish people after the genocide perpetrated against them by Nazi Germany.

Academic debate has evolved over the last 30 years with respect to the nature of the state of Israel in which many analysts oppose its self-presentation as a democratic state eternally threatened by barbarians and terrorists and characterize it as a colonial state (Pappé, 2008a: 611–33), which practises a form of *settler-colonialism* when creating a new homeland for the colonists by eliminating or expelling the native population (Pappé, 2020). This colonial state logic proposes that Israeli leaders do not aim to exploit the Palestinian work force but rather expel them from their lands in order to widen their territory in a process which, according to Israeli historian Shlomo Sand (Sand, 2013: 35), is a danger both to its neighbours and the international community because there is no apparent end in sight. While Israel defines itself as a *democratic Jewish State* – automatically discriminating against those Palestinians in the Occupied Territories and the 2 million Arab-Israelis, which make up 21 per cent of the official population of the country – the authorities promote the expulsion of Palestinians and the creation of Jewish settlements in the West Bank.

This is crucial in the case of East Jerusalem and explains the escalation of violence which occurred between 10 and 22 May 2021 due to the eviction of various Palestinian families in the neighbourhood of Sheikh Jarrah. Widespread protests against this measure led to disturbances involving those attending Friday prayers at the Al-Aqsa mosque. As a response to the violent suppression of these protests, Hamas and other Palestinian militia launched missiles at various Israeli cities, an action which was met with a prolonged wave of Israeli bombings of the Gaza Strip until a ceasefire was reached.

Methodology

In order to carry out a qualitative content study of news content on the websites of these four channels, a time frame was first established. Although disturbances can be traced to 6 May in anticipation of the Israeli Supreme Court decision regarding the eviction of six Palestinian families from the Sheikh Jarrah neighbourhood, the decision was made to study the coverage of the global television channels from 10 May onwards – when the level of violence attracted widespread international media attention – until 22 May, twenty-four hours after the ceasefire came into effect.

The news items which compose the sample refer to the static texts of the websites including headlines, sub-headings, photo captions and main text. Video links were not activated. Minor hourly updates were excluded. The content of each article was then entered into a coding sheet featuring the date, headline, typology of news producer, sources, language and vocabulary deployed, photographs and framing techniques. Once the data were collected, the authors carried out a dual analysis: a transmedia comparison of three elements of news coverage – discursive frames, visual/iconic elements and an overview of the sources employed – and the identification of the more specific aspects of their news coverage. To unify criteria when faced with four contrasting languages, the decision was made to examine the English language version of the websites.

While France 24 produced more than one hundred articles throughout the period under analysis, many of them constituted statistical updates or minor variations on a theme. Only those articles which covered a different angle or represented a major narrative step forward were included. That said, the thirty-five articles analysed here represent an average of three a day, testimony to the importance lent to the story by the channel. In a similar vein, CGTN produced two to three articles every day throughout the conflict (*n*=28) while TeleSUR offered almost identical figures (*n*=36). RT was the exception in the sample. Prodigious in its news coverage (*n*=70), it offered an average of five–six stories a day even while excluding repetitive pieces and minor updates. An aggregate count of the sample leads therefore to a total of 169 news items among the four channels over the twelve-day period.

Results: Media narrative and discursive framing – common aspects

A transversal analysis of the discursive framing across all four channels revealed significant common traits in their news coverage of the events in Gaza in May 2021. In this case, the authors identified six lines of argument present on all the channels:

(i) US 'obstructionism' hinders peace process

This leitmotif runs throughout the CGTN coverage as in headlines such as 'China Accuses U.S. of *Obstructing* UN Operation on Israeli-Palestinian Conflict" (14 May) or 'U.S. *Blocks* Friday UN Security Council Meeting on Gaza, Israel' (15 May). As for RT, the Russians lose no time in denouncing the US administration for 'dragging its feet' regarding an end to hostilities. This can be seen in headlines such as 'UN Middle East Envoy Warns of "Full-Scale War" in Gaza as Diplomats Claim the "US Is *Holding Up* Security Council Statement"' (12 May) or 'Israeli Airstrikes on Gaza Resume as Tel Aviv Thanks Biden Administration for *Blocking* UN Statement Calling for Ceasefire' (18 May).

France 24 covers Macron's proposal for an immediate ceasefire before the UNSC and highlights his disappointment at the US veto of the proposal (19 May). TeleSUR goes a step further regarding what it considers as the US hindrance of the ceasefire by criticizing Biden's refusal to condemn Israeli military action, pressurizing Netanyahu into ceasing hostilities against the Palestinian population as can be seen in the headline 'The US Does Not Urge Immediate Halt to Israel Attacks in Gaza' (16 May) and by publishing a story on the US government's approval of a 735 million-dollar project with Israel to develop 'precision-guided munitions' in the midst of escalating violence (17 May).

(ii) *Israel, the main aggressor*

CGTN presents Israel as a ruthless and inflexible opponent which 'limits the movements' of Palestinians, 'hinders their access' to Jerusalem and meets protests with 'violent crackdowns'. The vocabulary adopted allows us to see its political positioning: Israel fires at 'worshippers' not people; Israel bombs people's 'homes' not their houses and we are told that 'Israeli forces, *saying they were responding* to stones thrown towards the Western Wall, stormed Al-Aqsa mosque three times'. The use of the word 'saying' undermines the validity of their actions and is open to question.

As for RT, while some articles do mention the victims of Hamas air strikes, an overwhelming majority of articles refer to incessant Israeli aggression – 'Israel *continues to pound* Gaza with airstrikes' – to its responsibility for the escalation of violence –'Netanyahu to *step up* "might and frequency" of Israeli attacks' – and to ruthless tactics as can be seen in headlines such as 'IDF Will Fight until There Is Complete Silence' or 'Israeli Strikes on Gaza Hit Red Crescent Building Killing, 2 Aid Group Says' (17 May). For its part, TeleSUR implicitly signals Israel as the aggressor in headlines such as 'Netanyahu Pledges More Violence Over Palestine' (12 May) 'Israel Does Not Plan to End Its Military Assaults on Gaza' (19 May) or 'Israel Shells Southern Lebanon and Blames Palestinians for It' 19 May). France 24 shows greater reservation when it comes to identifying Israel as the belligerent party. While criticism is made of specific military actions by IDF armed forces, this does not translate into the automatic categorization of Israel as the main culprit of the conflict.

(iii) *Peace-brokers*

As part of their public diplomacy mandate, all channels portrayed their respective political leaders as peace-brokers during the conflict. As China occupied the UN Security Council Chair during the events in Gaza, CGTN emphasized the negotiating capacity of Beijing during the hostilities. The channel continuously refers to Foreign Minister Wang Li's calls for a ceasefire and his plea to Israel to 'fulfill its obligations under international treaties and guarantee the safety and rights of civilians in the occupied Palestinian territories' (17 May). It also covers China's frustration at the 'wanton' use of its veto power by the United States to obstruct Security Council joint statements (18 May), the UN's call for a 'humanitarian pause in violence' (19 May) as well as China's offer to host direct negotiations (20 May).

Through RT, Russia also presents its candidacy as a peace-broker. Just three days after fighting broke out, the channel reports that 'Russia calls on Israel to "immediately end settlement of Palestinian territories and maintain peace at Jerusalem's sacred sites"' (13 May) and later explains that the Russian foreign minister condemned the attacks 'pledging Moscow will help begin peace negotiations' (17 May). France 24 informs its viewers of all the diplomatic efforts made by the French government to put an end to hostilities and how Macron and Egyptian president Abdel Fattah al-Sisi made a call to end the violence from Paris (17 May).

(iv) *Journalists as Israeli targets*

CGTN focused heavily on the threat to journalists posed by Israeli air strikes. The 15 May article entitled "Building Used by International Media in Gaza Destroyed by Airstrike' explains how the Al-Jalaa Tower used by Associated Press and Al Jazeera was destroyed and how the AP bureau chief told CGTN Europe 'we are shocked and horrified by what happened and we are heartbroken because this building, this office, was our home in Gaza'. This story carries across all channels. RT dedicates considerable space to what it considers as deliberate attacks by Israel on the international media in Gaza 'to cover up the war crimes that will follow' and widens its coverage by reporting that US Republicans openly welcomed it ('American Conservatives Celebrate Israeli Bombing of AP & Al Jazeera Offices') and that the United Nations is 'deeply disturbed by IDF bombing of Gaza media building' (16 May). TeleSUR also denounces this attack in its article titled 'Israel Bombs Attempt to Silence International Media in Gaza' (16 May) as does France 24, which publishes a piece entitled 'Israel Air Strike Flattens Gaza Building Housing AP, Al-Jazeera as Violence Spirals'.

(v) *Palestinians, victims of incompliance to international law*

On CGTN, journalist Omar Elwafai refers to Palestinians as being 'kicked out' of their homes by Israeli courts in Sheikh Jarrah and informs readers that 'Israeli courts have no legal authority in occupied East Jerusalem, under international law' (13 May). Another commentator laments the disregard for UN resolution 37/43 which 'stipulates the Palestinian right to armed resistance' (16 May). RT also shows interest in the legal ramifications of the hostilities when headlining that 'War Crimes Courts Monitoring Events in West Bank: ICC Prosecutor Registers "Great Concern"' (12 May). TeleSUR considers the IDF actions to be illegal as can be seen in the headline 'Israel Uses Disproportionate Force against Palestinians' (11 May) whilst also publishing the story that the 'ICC Prosecutor Warns against Crimes in Recent Gaza Conflict' (13 May).

(vi) *Hamas dominates, 'Palestine' sidelined*

A common trait in all four channels' coverage is the displacement of Fatah and the framing of the armed conflict as a direct confrontation between the IDF and Hamas. On CGTN, the latter is referred to as a 'resistance organization in control of Gaza' while Gaza itself is seen as a 'Hamas-run enclave' and the ceasefire itself as a 'Gaza–Israel deal'. France 24 also presents the conflict as a clash between Israel and Gaza ('Dozen Dead as Israel and Hamas Hurtle Towards "Full-Scale War"', 12 May) while Hamas is presented as an organization which instrumentalizes the conflict to increase electoral support ('"The Political Calculation behind Hamas' Escalating Conflict with Israel' – 12 May). That said, Hamas has no faces and no names in the France 24 texts.

TeleSUR operates along the same lines: references to Gaza/Hamas double those to Palestine and the ceasefire is signed with Hamas (20 May).

Media narrative and discursive framing – specific aspects

CGTN: The 'human rights factor'

CGTN uses the Gazan predicament to shed light on the 'blatant hypocrisy' surrounding US 'disregard' for Palestinian human rights compared to the fierce criticism Beijing receives for human rights' abuses in the Northwestern Muslim province of Xinjiang. The Foreign Ministry claims that 'the United States has been indifferent to the suffering of the Palestinians ... and has ganged up with Germany, the UK, and a few of its allies hoping to host some "meaningless" meeting under the UN banner on the so-called Xinjiang issues'. In reference to what she considers the 'contradictory approach to China versus Palestine', commentator Fiona Sim claims that the political agenda of the United States 'is not one concerned with morality and upholding human rights but one that relies on a U.S.-based, unipolar world order in which it decides who lives and who dies based on its allegiances' (16 May). Two days later, CGTN urges the United States 'to drop its rhetoric on the rights and dignity of the (Chinese) Muslims and to act to protect the rights and dignity of the Palestinians'. Haider Rifaat of the *South China Morning Post* widens the comparison when declaring that 'while the U.S. champions human rights at large, supporting movements like the Black Lives Matter, it conveniently dismisses gross human rights violations against Palestinians, who are suffering far worse than racial violence'. Unsurprisingly, the article is titled 'Palestinian Lives Matter' (18 May).

RT: Semantic bias and non-neutrality

A defining aspect of the Russian coverage is the partiality in the journalistic language employed. The suffixes used to describe the protagonists are clearly opposed. While the nouns 'Palestine'/'Palestinians' receive collates such as 'protesters', 'injured', 'killed', 'demonstrators' or 'rally', – all of which denote a passive/victim frame – Israel(i) suffixes include 'bombs', 'air strikes', 'attacks', 'rockets', 'kills' or 'pounds' reflecting adjectival intent and a certain predisposition towards the plight of the Palestinians. For example, a news story entitled '20 Palestinians Killed in Israeli Air Strikes, *Including 9 Kids*' (10 May) predisposes the reader in two ways: we are told that half of the victims are children – a tragedy in itself – and the use of the word 'kids' adds an extra element of empathy. In other examples, RT tells us that the Israeli armed forces declared ' "Our Intel Is Better": IDF *Brags* about Killing Top Hamas Spies' (12 May) and that it '*celebrates* levelling Gaza residential block', adjectives which induce the reader to adopt a critical posture towards Israeli military action. RT makes it clear that neutrality is unsustainable and covers Iran's denouncement of 'unacceptable neutrality' as it calls upon the international community 'to stop Israeli "aggression" against Palestine' (17 May).

FRANCE 24: *Equidistance and concern for 'civil war'*

In general terms, the coverage by France 24 highlights the government's customary caution on the issue. A Macron speech ('Macron Speaks with Netanyahu, Urges Return to Peace in Gaza', 14 May) reaffirming Israel's 'right to self-defense' from the Hamas attacks was immediately followed by another covering his 'concern' for Gaza's civilian population and his plea for a ceasefire. Neither the IDF nor the Palestinian militias are presented through an 'aggressor/victim' dichotomy and no space is dedicated to debating whether Israel or Palestine has the right to legitimate defence. Coverage is focused on satisfying all the parties involved along with their sympathizers and international allies. Unlike the other channels, France 24 carries out exhaustive coverage of violence on *both* sides including attacks on Israel from Lebanon and intercommunity violence in 'mixed cities' combining Jewish residents and Arab-Israeli locals.

A second focus of interest for France 24 was the possibility of 'civil war' between Jews and Muslims in Israel and its possible 'export' to the streets of France. Clashes between Jews and Arab-Israelis in 'mixed cities' such as Lod – where a 'state of emergency' was declared – proved irresistible to the channel which broadcast thirteen news stories between 13 and 16 May. These were followed by two additional stories – 'Hospital in Israel City of Haifa a Model of Harmony' and 'Against Backdrop of Gaza Violence, Israel`s Jews and Arabs Join Forces for Peace' – which refer to local efforts to combat a 'deadly spiral' and what was referred to as fear of 'civil war'. This heightened sensitivity seems to respond to domestic issues and the concern that something similar could happen in France especially when, on 15 May, the prefecture of Paris prohibited a pro-Palestine rally leading to clashes and detentions.

TELESUR: *The destruction of Gaza*

The defining characteristic of the South American channel is its day-to-day coverage of the annihilation of the Gaza Strip. Users are continually informed of the rising Gazan death tolls and the destruction of schools, homes and logistical infrastructures. More than half of the news items analysed (twenty out of thirty-six) focus on the destruction of buildings in the Gaza Strip and the aggregate figures of deaths and injured as a result of Israeli bombings. The channel also heavily covers the casualties among Palestinians on the West Bank – the channel refers to it as a 'massacre' – when they go on strike or protest in solidarity with Gaza.

Results: Photography

A transversal analysis of the photographic elements across all the channels allows for their division into three main groups. The first – and the largest – reflects the structural and property damage carried out by Israeli air strikes and offers numerous photos of buildings on the Gaza Strip raised to the ground by IDF air strikes and a general trail of destruction, ruins and rubble. This is particularly prevalent on CGTN where shots abound of destroyed residential tower blocs such as the missile attack on the

Al-Sharouk Tower in the Gaza Strip or the Al-Jalaa tower, home to AP and Al Jazeera and targeted by Israeli air strikes. As for TeleSUR, 60 per cent of their photographs portray buildings destroyed by Israeli bombings on the Gaza Strip. Many come from short videos and Twitter captures supplied by Palestinian sympathizers. Meanwhile, France 24 is the only channel which offers images of the after-effects of rocket launches by Hamas missiles on Israeli buildings

The second group of images corresponds to the human tragedy – almost exclusively Palestinian – behind the conflict. CGTN showed no images of Israeli victims but did heavily cover Gazans in desperate circumstances inspecting the wreckage of their former homes, street vendors shifting rubble on the barren streets or young internees at refugee camps such as Jabalia or Maghazi.

On RT, Gazans are photographed alongside ambulances, on stretchers and wrapped in Palestinian flags in a state of despair. TeleSUR viewers are shown photos of Gaza Strip funerals and Palestinian parents with their deceased or injured children in their arms. On this issue, France 24 differs from the others by offering images of a civilian population seeking medical assistance both in Israel *and* Gaza. While the Israeli images reflect concern, they do not project desperation. On the Gazan side, those photographed cry, shout out and express their rage and sense of helplessness.

The third group of images refers to the photographic presence across all channels of world leaders such as Erdogan, Biden, Trump, Netanyahu or former Israeli prime minister Ehud Olmert. No such photos of Palestinian leaders –whether from Hamas or Fatah – were found. Palestine is, therefore, denied a visual projection of order, structure, leadership and is deprived of agency.

Results: Sources

Unlike the identification of shared discursive frames and photographic criteria, the divergent professional practices regarding the use and attribution of sources led the authors to adopt a case-by-case approach.

CGTN

This channel draws its information (and opinion) from five main groups: (i) international news agencies (Reuters and AFP); (ii) the Chinese national agency Xinhua; (iii) International desk editors; (iv) foreign correspondents and (v) 'experts' or freelancers used to offer a critical voice and controversial opinion but who 'do not represent the views of CGTN'. The extended use of the first three groups means that articles are often peppered with establishment sources such as army spokespersons, Israeli government leaders, members of Hamas, US representatives, Chinese UN officials or Foreign Ministry press releases. Foreign correspondents offer a more colourful narrative and introduce voices such as university professors or liberal Israeli observers who are, in general, empathetic towards those under attack in Gaza. It is in the outsourcing of articles to freelancers – who under the guise of 'experts' provide the reader with highly charged copy and a clear ideological bias – that CGTN shows its hand.

RT

Tracing the news sources adopted by the Russian channel is an elusive task. To begin with, no texts are authored, limiting the accountability of those responsible for them. Secondly, indirect formulas are employed through the citing of other – mostly Western – media outlets. Interestingly enough, most of the sources are Israeli (Haaretz, Channel 12, The Times of Israel). Thirdly, there is evidence of the 'official sources syndrome' (Tulloch, 2004) where vague generic references are made to 'IDF sources', 'Hamas leaders' or the Hamas 'military branch'. The voices of the victims of air strikes on both sides are conspicuously absent.

France 24

In general, the information on F24 comes from Western news agencies – AFP, AP or Reuters – from the channel's correspondents in Jerusalem and Washington and from special envoys sent to cover the conflict. While all these journalists covered the declarations made by Western leaders, Netanyahu and the IDF, it barely transmitted those comments made by Palestinian militias or those leaders allied with Palestine (Iran, e.g.). Throughout the twelve-day sample, such comments are limited to just two or three phrases and only on two occasions are members of Hamas referred to by their own names. Analysis and interpretation are left to the anchor journalists at the international desk while interviews and debates are frequently broadcast about different aspects of the conflict featuring academics, scholars, journalists and activists.

Telesur

The South American channel presents an interesting case study when it comes to sourcing not only because it employs a wider range of voices than its northern hemisphere counterparts but also because it clearly positions itself through the very nature of the sources it references. By way of example, TeleSUR cites the Gaza Ministry of Health along with the UNRWA (United Nations Relief and Works Agency for Palestine refugees), UNICEF and the WHO for information about the destruction in Gaza. When informing of the consequences in Israeli cities of the rockets launched by Hamas and other Palestinian militia, it does so by referring to alternative sources such as the Spanish news agency EFE, the Chinese agency Xinhua or Al Mayadeen, the Arab satellite news network based in Beirut. Within this context, rocket launches from the Gaza Strip are presented as part of the 'Palestine resistance', a term regularly used by TeleSUR when referring to Palestinian militia.

Discussion of key findings

The advantage of submitting to academic analysis one intense episode of the Palestine–Israel conflict from the standpoint of the news platforms representing three of the five permanent members of the UN Security Council – an organ which very often has to publicly position itself on this issue – not only consists in pointing to wider issues such as the discovery of a counter-hegemonic discourse regarding events in the region or the 'soft power' dimension and public diplomatic role of these global channels but also to specific aspects regarding the media projection of the protagonists and the depiction of the legitimacy of their respective positions.

In this sense, four main key findings can be detected. To begin with, all these global channels (with nuances in the case of France 24) adopt a hostile posture towards what they consider as US obstructionism, the disproportionate aggression from the Israeli military and the incompliance with international public law regarding the plight of Palestine.

A second finding reveals how each of these state-sponsored media strive to benefit from the tensions aroused by 'peak' moments such as the Sheikh Jarrah evictions as a 'Trojan horse' discursive vehicle to counter criticism and further their specific political goals. In this sense, China overtly uses Palestine as a smokescreen for its own human rights issues, Russia aims to counterbalance a growing international image as an aggressor within global politics by framing Israeli attacks on Gaza as part of a US-sponsored initiative while France, through self-styled equidistance, aims to project itself in the media as a global peace-broker.

A third finding concerns the visual projection of all involved. In somewhat ironic fashion – given the *counter-hegemonic* nature of their respective news operations – all four media resorted largely to the major photographic news agencies. While the iconographic dominance of destruction and human tragedy may be expected, the non-publication of photographs of Gazan authorities at any level –political, social, civil – contributes to portraying a society incapable of self-management and where chaos is the norm.

The partiality and imbalance regarding photographic representation also spills over into professional journalistic praxis regarding sourcing techniques. Chinese, Russian and French reporters systematically resort to hegemonic news agencies such as Reuters and AFP (TeleSUR is the exception here), mainstream press and vaguely referenced 'official' sources. This situation implies that the media presence of the Palestinian version of events undergoes a double exclusion: firstly because airstrike victims and the homeless in Gaza are left with no sounding board as they are denied access to these elite self-citing source circles and secondly the Palestinian authorities –and those leaders allied with them – are ousted from the narrative in stark comparison to the omnipresence of Biden, Macron and Netanyahu.

Conclusion

By cross-referencing the coverage of events in Gaza and Israel in May 2021 on the four television channels presented here, it is possible to identify certain common traits which cut across these platforms to form a divergent journalistic narrative vis-à-vis the conflict. In this sense, discourse markers, sourcing practices, semantic techniques and the analysis of graphic elements reveal an overarching triple narrative consisting in (i) generalized empathy towards the plight of the Palestinians and Gazan victims in particular; (ii) condemnation of what is seen as disproportionate action and disrespect for international law by the Israeli armed forces and (iii) an underlying critical tone towards the unconditional support to Israel of the Biden administration considered by these media as an obstacle to peace negotiations. This general news framework aside, additional aspects of their news coverage can also be detected such as the projection of their respective leaders – and financial backers – as peace-brokers in the midst of the conflict, the outcry caused by the air strike on the international media building in Gaza and the projection of Hamas as the dominant Palestinian voice and leading adversary to Israel. Media-specific findings – such as CGTN's use of the 'human rights' factor, RT's critical stance on neutrality or France 24's fear of 'civil war' – offer a third level of critical analysis.

While these emerging media platforms may offer an alternative perspective on the Israel–Palestine conflict, many of the newsgathering techniques employed by these channels (with the exception of France 24) feature production patterns typical of 'hegemonic' Western newsrooms such as an overdependence on official sources, the invisibilization of both Palestinian and Israeli civilian voices or the photographic projection of Palestine as a 'lost cause'. Along with the outsourcing of dissident opinion to columnists of limited credibility these practices need reconsidering not only to address the historical imbalances with regard to the media projection of the Israel–Palestine story but also to strengthen their presence and legitimacy on the world news stage.

Before concluding, one final point. Three of the media platforms analysed here – CGTN, RT and France 24 – are financed by permanent members of the UNSC. The former two – China and Russia along with Venezuela and Cuba – founding members of TeleSUR – voted in favour of a Human Rights Council resolution dated 27 May 2021 to carry out an investigation into the violations of International Humanitarian Law that may have been committed during the eleven-day conflict between Israel and Gaza following the Sheikh Jarrah protests. France abstained, a position which coincides with the cautious nature of its state-funded channel. How the image of the state of Israel is to be affected by the alternative narratives generated and distributed by these counter-hegemonic media and how the articulation of the 'Palestinian cause' on these very same platforms may be subordinate to the geostrategic interests of these global players is worthy of close attention over the coming years.

References

Alkalliny, S. (2017), 'Framing of Media Coverage of the Palestinian-Israeli Conflict in CNN and Fox News', *International Journal of English Literature and Social Sciences* (IJELS), 2(4): 161–5.

Bandurski, D. (2017), 'The Baffling Makeover of CCTV's Global Push', *Medium*, 5 January 2017.

Chalaby. J. (2003), 'Television for a New Global Order: Transnational Television Networks and the Formation of Global Systems', *Gazette: The International Journal for Communication Studies*, 65(6): 457–72.

Cull, N. (2008), 'Public Diplomacy: Taxonomies and Histories', *Annals of the American Academy of Political and Social Science*, 61: 31–54.

Elswah, M., and P. Howard (2020), ' "Anything that Causes Chaos": The Organizational Behaviour of Russia Today (RT)', *Journal of Communication*, 70(5): 623–45.

Freedman, Des. (2020), 'The State of Political Communications'. In A. Davis, N. Fenton, D. Freedman and G. Khlabany (eds), *Media, Democracy, Change: Reimagining Political Communications*, London: Sage.

Macbride, S. (1980), *Many Voices One World. Towards a New, More Just and More Efficient World Information and Communication Order*, New York: UNESCO.

Maihold, G. (2014), 'TeleSUR: la creacion televisiva de "lo latinoamericano" ', *Iberoamericana*, 8(29): 183–8.

Nicolás Gavilán, M. T. (2014), *El enfoque del conflicto israelí-palestino. Análisis de los factores culturales que influyen en los corresponsales de guerra*, Madrid: Fragua.

Nye, J. S. (2008), 'Public Diplomacy and Soft Power', *The Annals of the American Academy of Political and Social Science*, 616(81): 94–109.

Painter, J. (2007), 'The Boom in Counter-Hegemonic News Channels: A Case Study of Tele Sur', *Reuters Institute for the Study of Journalism: Oxford University*, 8 July: 1–56.

Pappé, I. (2008a), 'Zionism as Colonialism: A Comparative View of Diluted Colonialism in Asia and Africa', *South Atlantic Quarterly*, 107(4): 611–33.

Pappé, I. (2008b), *The Ethnic Cleansing of Palestine*, Oxford: Oneworld Publications. Citation from the Spanish translation: *La limpieza étnica de Palestina*, Barcelona: Crítica.

Pappé, I. (2020), 'From Balfour to the Nakba: The Settler Colonialism Experience of Palestine', 4 November, *Middle East Eye*, https://www.middleeasteye.net/opinion/balf our-nakba-settler-colonial-experience-palestine (accessed 2 October 2021).

Rai, Mugdha, and S. Cottle (2007), 'Global Mediations: On the Changing Ecology of Satellite Television News', *Global Media and Communications*, 31(1): 51–78.

Rawnsley, G. (2015), 'To Know Us Is to Love Us: Public Diplomacy and International Broadcasting in Contemporary Russia and China', *Politics*, 35(3–4): 273–86.

Ruigrok, N., W. Atteveldt and J. Takens (2013), 'Shifting Frames in a Deadlocked Conflict'. In J. Seethaler (ed.), *Selling War. The Role of the Mass Media in Hostile Conflicts*, Bristol: Intellect, 259–89.

Sand, S. (2013), *La invención de la Tierra de Israel (The Invention of the Land of Israel)*, Madrid: Akal.

Seib, P. (2010), 'Transnational Journalism, Public Diplomacy and Virtual States', *Journalism Studies*, 11(5): 734–44.

Thussu, D. (ed.) (2006), *Media on the Move: Global Flow and Contra-flow*, London: Routledge.

Tulloch, C. (2004), *Corresponsales en el extranjero: Mito y realidad*, Pamplona: Eunsa.

Tunstall, J. (2008), *The Media Were American*, New York: Oxford University Press.

Voltmer, I. (2003), 'The Global Networked Society and the Global Public Sphere', *Development*, 46(1): 9–16.

Wright, K., M. Scott and M. Bunce (2020), 'Soft Power, Hard News: How Journalists at State-Funded Transnational Media Legitimize Their Work', *The International Journal of Press/Politics*, 25(4): 607–31.

Yablokov, I. (2015), 'Conspiracy Theories as a Russian Public Diplomacy Tool: The Case of Russia Today (RT)', *Politics*, 35(3): 301–15.

News articles consulted

The complete list of news reports consulted during this study ran to 169 articles. For reasons of space only those specifically referenced in this chapter are listed below.
CGTN

13 May 2021	The Newest IP Conflict Explained
14 May 2021	China Accuses U.S. of Obstructing UN Operation on Israeli-Palestinian Conflict
15 May 2021	U.S. Blocks Friday UN Security Council Meeting on Gaza, Israel
15 May 2021	Building Used by International Media in Gaza Destroyed by Airstrike
16 May 2021	Xinjiang vs Palestine: The United States Distortion of Human Rights
17 May 2021	China Says Ceasefire, End to Violence the Top Priority in Palestine–Israel Conflict
18 May 2021	Palestinian Lives Matter
18 May 2021	China Condemns U.S. for Fueling Tension in Gaza after Failed UNSC Statement
19 May 2021	UN Official Calls for Humanitarian Pause in Violence in Israel, Gaza
20 May 2021	China Offers to Host Israel–Palestine Direct Negotiations

Russia Today (RT)

10 May 2021	Gaza Health Ministry Says 20 Palestinians Killed in Israeli Air Strikes, Including 9 Kids, Multiple Injured
12 May 2021	UN Middle East Envoy Warns of 'Full-Scale War' in Gaza as Diplomats Claim US Is Holding Up Security Council Statement
12 May 2021	'Our Intel Was Better': IDF Brags about Killing Top Hamas Spies
12 May 2021	War Crimes Court Monitoring Developments in West Bank: ICC Prosecutor Registers 'Great Concern'
13 May 2021	Russia Calls on Israel to 'Immediately' End Settlement of Palestinian Territories & Maintain Peace at Jerusalem's Sacred Sites
16 May 2021	UN Chief 'Deeply Disturbed' by Civilian Casualties & IDF Bombing of Gaza Media Building
17 May 2021	'Unacceptable Neutrality' Iran Calls Upon International Community to Stop Israeli 'Aggression' against Palestine

17 May 2021	Russian Foreign Minister Condemns Attacks in Israel & Palestine, Pledging Moscow Will Help Begin Peace Negotiations
17 May 2021	Israel Strikes on Gaza Hit Red Crescent Building Killing, 2 Aid Group Says
18 May 2021	Israeli Airstrikes on Gaza Resume as Tel Aviv Thanks Biden Administration for Blocking UN Statement Calling for Ceasefire

France 24

12 May 2021	Dozen Dead as Israel and Hamas Hurtle Towards 'Full Scale War'
13 May 2021	The Political Calculation behind Hamas' Escalating Conflict with Israel
13 May 2021	Pro-Palestinian Rally in Paris Banned amid Rising Israel–Gaza Tensions
14 May 2021	Paris Organisers Vow to Go Ahead with Pro-Palestinian Rally despite Court Ban
15 May 2021	Paris Clash with Pro-Palestinian Protesters at Banned Rally
15 May 2021	Israel Air Strike Flattens Gaza Building Housing AP, Al-Jazeera as Violence Spirals
19 May 2021	Tensions Emerge between US, France at the United Nations over Gaza Conflict

TeleSUR

11 May 2021	Israel Uses Disproportionate Force Against Palestinians
12 May 2021	Netanyahu Pledges More Violence over Palestine
13 May 2021	ICC Prosecutor Warns against Crimes in Recent Gaza Conflict
15 May 2021	Israel Bombs Attempt to Silence International Media in Gaza
16 May 2021	The US Does Not Urge Immediate Halt to Israel Attacks in Gaza
16 May 2021	US Supports Israel's Massacre of Palestinians in Gaza Strip
17 May 2021	China Push for United Nations Action to Defuse Tension in Gaza
17 May 2021	US Approves $735m Sale of Precision-Guided Munitions to Israel
19 May 2021	Israel Does Not Plan to End Its Military Assaults on Gaza
19 May 2021	Israel Shells Southern Lebanon and Blames Palestinians for It
20 May 2021	Israel Security Cabinet Approves Ceasefire with Hamas

Media coverage of the Palestinian-Israeli conflict, comparing Al Jazeera English and i24News

Noureddine Miladi, Rania El-Malky and Karima Miladi

Introduction

This chapter discusses the discrepancies between the news coverage of Al Jazeera English TV (AJE) and Israeli TV channel i24News of the Sheikh Jarrah events and the violent conflict between the Palestinians and the Israelis in May 2021. It analyses the news agenda and editorial lines of both satellite TV channels by studying the language used, news sources, framing of the events and the historical narrative advanced by each network. Based on video recordings from two weeks of turbulent events, we attempt to compare news values of each network, especially issues related to objectivity and impartiality. We will analyse this against internationally accepted standards of news reporting especially in conflict zones.

Discrepancies in the global news reporting of the Palestinian-Israeli conflict

International media reporting of the Palestinian-Israeli conflict is one of the most complex and controversial stories dealt with by international media. Over the years, journalists have spoken about the pressure they face when reporting the Palestinian viewpoint. A few also find it difficult to talk about academic studies that criticize the media coverage of the conflict (Philo and Berry 2004). Western global media outlets have been criticized for their biased reporting of the region. Oftentimes global networks like CNN, BBC, Sky and others tend to portray a perspective more in line with the Israeli narrative at the expense of the Palestinian. Most studies done on the Western media's coverage come to almost the same conclusion, that there is a systematic bias in favour of the Israeli narrative (Abdelmoula and Miladi, 2016; Aouragh, 2008; Artz, 2014; Barkho, 2007, 2011; Downey et al., 2019; Marzano, 2011; Miladi, 2006; Philo and Berry, 2011;; Martin (2011); Rinnawi, 2012; Sanz Sabido, 2015; Said, 1984; El Damanhoury and Saleh (2017); Sanz Sabido (2019). Reporting the conflict, as scores of extensive studies show, is usually 'slanted heavily in favor of Israeli perspectives' (Elmasry et al., 2013: 2).

The Sheikh Jarrah events of May 2021 garnered unprecedented international attention. Both regional and international media outlets dedicated their prime coverage to the dramatic conflict in Jerusalem and other parts of the occupied Palestinian territories. The Israeli state media exhausted every possible platform to promote the Israeli narrative in reporting the events. In this chapter we focus on analysing the coverage of Israeli i24 News and the Qatari Al Jazeera English satellite TV channels. Launched in July 2013, i24News broadcasts from Tel Aviv in English, Arabic and French. It is available via satellite in the Middle East and various other countries. According to its proprietors, the channel sets itself up against Al Jazeera to penetrate public opinion in the region and other parts of the world (Margalit, 2013). i24News also claims to be independent of the Israeli government, but one of its stated goals is to 'change the point of view about Israel' (Margalit, 2013).

Recently, a few researchers looked at news reporting of the same events by the Arabic service of i24News. Based on the analysis of twenty-two episodes of TV programme 'This Evening', Harb (2021) for instance, argues that i24News focused mainly on Israeli human casualties and marginalized all other casualties from the Palestinian side. The channel also put the blame for the escalation of the war on Palestinians. Gaza and Palestinian groups like Hamas and Islamic Jihad were presented as the main culprits. The channel also blamed the international community, and to a much lesser extent, the Israeli side. According to the study, their biased media coverage is evident in the frames through which the events were reported and through the selective inclusions and omissions in the i24News narrative.

As noted earlier, AJE is the news outlet that this study will compare with i24News. Much has been written about Al Jazeera satellite channel since its inception in 1996. The network has been hailed as revolutionizing Arab broadcasting, bringing a new angle to reporting the region. Coverage of the Palestinian-Israeli conflict is one of the key areas where Al Jazeera introduced a new perspective absent in other global networks (Abdelmoula and Miladi, 2016). The advent of AJE in 2007 made Al Jazeera's broadcasting service even more accessible to viewers beyond the Arabic-speaking world. The network further succeeded in capturing the mood of the Arab street. News from the occupied territories have always been high on the agenda of Arab public opinion, and AJE connected with that. The original Arabic channel, Al Jazeera, brought live coverage of the conflict to people's homes in a daring and unusual manner. For instance, it was the first Arab channel to give voice to both sides of the conflict. Adversarial debates about the day-to-day tension in Jerusalem and other occupied territories, between Israeli settlers and Palestinians, were brought to light by Al Jazeera through a new zoom lens. In fact, members of the Israeli cabinet did not have the opportunity to speak directly to an Arab audience before 1996. Al Jazeera was the first channel to provide that platform. AJE continued in the same path when it was launched in 2007. Covering Palestine remains one of the key areas, which differentiates AJE from other international broadcasters, as it provides an informed narrative, rich in historical context about the long Palestinian struggle for survival under Israeli occupation.

The reconstruction of a pan-Arab narrative

Al Jazeera's coverage of the Palestinian Intifada in 2000 was a turning point for Arab viewers. Images of the twelve-year-old Palestinian boy Mohammed al-Durra shot dead live on air by Israeli forces as his father tried to protect him captured the world's attention. The narrative repeatedly broadcast by Al Jazeera at the time triggered a new way of looking at the conflict. It reported the Israeli army as an occupying force brutally executing Palestinian civilians. In her study on the 'Al Jazeera's coverage of the "6th Arab-Israeli War" in Lebanon', Saber (2016) argues that the channel compared the Israeli army's unexpected withdrawal from Southern Lebanon on 24 May 2000 to the 1975 American troops withdrawal from Vietnam. The 'invincible Israeli army' like the US 'invincible army', was defeated and forced to end its occupation. The result of this pan-Arab trend, as suggested by Saber (2016: 83–4), is that

> Palestine is at the heart of Al Jazeera's narrative, thus participating in the reconstruction of Palestinian memory in the Arab space. The representation of the Israeli-Arab conflict is no longer limited to mere accounts of Israeli raids, pictures of funerals in Gaza, and children throwing stones in the West Bank. Al Jazeera's talk shows and documentaries have, since the early 2000s, framed the Palestine War of 1948, and more broadly the Palestinian cause, within its historic, social, economic, cultural and political contexts.

Moreover, the Palestinian perspective was no longer merely represented by the Palestinian Authority. New players got introduced through Al Jazeera's news and current affairs programmes. Fatah, the dominant political party in the Palestinian government in Ramallah, no longer holds a monopoly on the narrative. Leaders of groups like Hamas, Islamic Jihad, Alkassam Brigades, academics and civil society organizations, all contributed during the last few years to the articulation of the Palestinian narrative. Through this reconstruction of the Arab-Israeli conflict, the channel has helped re-appropriate Palestinian history and memory. Al Jazeera's online presence has also become one of its strongest tools of global influence. In 2021, Forbes Middle East ranked Al Jazeera as second for online TV streaming in the Arab world with 277.88 million visits and 21 million followers on its breaking news Twitter Accounts @AJABreaking (Forbes Middle East, 2021).

Sheikh Jarrah conflict in context

In May 2021, a renewed violent conflict broke out between the Israeli Occupation Forces and the Palestinians. This was the deadliest violence since the 2014 seven-weeks war on Gaza, when the Israeli Army launched what it called 'Operation Protective Edge'. The United Nations Office for the Coordination of Humanitarian Affairs (OCHA), accounted for more than 2,251 Gazans killed and more than 11,000 wounded, while 67 Israeli soldiers and 6 Israeli civilians were killed and 1,600 injured (OCHA, 2021).

The 2021 renewed conflict was sparked by a confluence of events which reached crisis point on 6 May, but the events are historically rooted in Israel's settler colonialist project to Judaize Jerusalem since the occupation of Palestine in 1948. As far back as 1950, according to the Washington DC-based Arab Center for Research and Policy Studies (2021) (ACRPS), Israel had promulgated a set of laws with the aim of displacing and dispossessing Palestinian neighbourhoods . In the aftermath of the 1967 war, Israel annexed East Jerusalem and continued to consolidate its control over Palestinian properties with impunity, even though the annexation was considered illegal under international law. UN Security Council Resolution 446, referring to the Fourth Geneva Convention, called upon Israel to desist from building settlements in territories under illegal occupation with the aim of changing their demographics. Yet despite international condemnation, Israel has continued to surround the eastern part of the city with Jewish settlements, effectively separating East Jerusalem from the West bank.

By mid-2017, according to ACRPS, the settlements covered about 35 per cent of East Jerusalem, accounting for about half of the total number of settlers in the West Bank, where it also built an Apartheid Wall separating tens of thousands of Jerusalemites from their city. Furthermore, the Israeli occupying forces employed a mechanism called the Absentee Property Law to revoke the 'permanent residency' status of Jerusalemites who do not live in the city for more than three years Arab Center for Research and Policy Studies (2021).

The systematic Israeli provocations reached a boiling point on 13 April 2021, the eve of the start of the holy month of Ramadan. According to a report by the *New York Times*, on that day, a squad of Israeli police raided the al-Aqsa Mosque and cut the cables to the loudspeakers attached to its minarets. The day coincided with Memorial Day in Israel, and Israeli officials did not want the prayers to drown out a speech to be delivered by the Israeli president at the Western Wall, which is below the mosque. Shortly after the loudspeaker incident, which was seen as an insult and a desecration of the holy mosque, Israeli police closed off a popular plaza outside one of the main entrances to the old city where Palestinian youth usually gather on Ramadan nights. The decision led to nightly clashes between the police and Palestinian youth, unbending about reclaiming their space.

Concurrently, another storm was brewing in the Sheikh Jarrah area on the back of an Israeli law that allows Jews to claim ownership of land that belonged to Palestine before 1948. On 1 May 2021, a Jerusalem District Court ruled that at least six families must vacate their homes in Sheikh Jarrah within a week, and seven other families to leave by 1 August 2021, making way for Jewish settlers to invade the Palestinian properties. Violence erupted between Palestinians and Israeli police at Al-Aqsa Mosque, escalating on the holy night of *Laylatul Qadr* on 8 May, which coincided with Jerusalem Day, an Israeli national holiday.

With hundreds of Palestinians injured in Al-Aqsa Mosque, leaders of the Palestinian group Hamas gave Israel an ultimatum on 10 May to withdraw from both the mosque area and Sheikh Jarrah quarter. Israel ignored the warning and as inter-communal violence continued, Hamas and the Islamic Jihad movements launched retaliatory rocket attacks towards Tel Aviv and various Israeli settlements. In a dramatic turn, the Israeli army launched a military offensive on Gaza, destroying Al-Jalaa high-rise, which housed the offices of Al Jazeera and the Associated Press, in addition to scores of other media organizations, claiming that the building harboured Hamas members. Israeli authorities failed to produce evidence to support this claim.

The conflict destroyed Gaza's infrastructure and left a heavy civilian death toll. According to a report by OCHA, '256 Palestinians, including 66 children and 40 women, were killed in Gaza and almost 2,000 others were injured in the course of two weeks. In Israel, 13 people were killed, including two children and six women. In the West Bank, 26 Palestinians were killed and about 6,900 were injured' (OCHA, 2021). Approximately 250 housing and commercial buildings were destroyed in the Gaza Strip, which has been under siege since 2007, with a land, air and sea blockade imposed by Israel.

Even though the war on Gaza had ended with both sides claiming victory, on May 24, Israeli police launched a new offensive called 'Operation Law and Order' to carry out mass arrests of suspected rioters. According to the *New York Times*, more than 70 per cent of the 1,550 people arrested were Arabs, including twins Muna and Mohammed Al-Kurd, who had been at the forefront of the campaign to stop the expulsion of Palestinians from their homes and to save their own home from that fate.

Research methodology

In order to gather relevant stories as a sample for this study, the research team did broad searches on YouTube, specifically on the Sheikh Jarrah events in Jerusalem, pertaining to both AJE and i24 News satellite TV channels. The period is limited to the duration of the conflict and its aftermath (between 8 and 28 May 2021). The actual data set derived consisted of a total of ninety videos. We first identified 115 news stories from Al Jazeera English and 95 news stories from i24News. All news clips were downloaded from AJE and i24News YouTube channels, then classified in chronological order along with a description of key events that took place. The next step was to scale down the sample by randomly choosing fifteen news stories per week for the duration of three weeks (i.e. between 8 May and 28 May 2021) for each channel. As a result, a total of forty-five video stories were logged for Al Jazeera English and forty-five video stories logged for i24News.

The qualitative analysis of the news stories draws on various media scholarship (Altheide and Schneider, 2013; Cohen and de Peuter, 2018; Entman, 1993; Kuehn, 2018). The research team devised an improvised four-point grid to unearth the deeper picture of news reporting for each media outlet. The proposed analytical techniques took advantage of various procedures and methods followed in the above-mentioned studies. This provided us with a broader framework to enhance our approach to the data set.

The analysis focused on the following levels, which were deemed significant enough to bring about a thorough discussion vis-à-vis the research aims set in this study:

(i) **Stories:** Here we looked at the basic narrative structure of the news stories in each channel. For instance, we were interested in finding out the competing narratives that existed. What stories came from i24News as compared to stories coming from AJE? We also scrutinized the frames through which the conflict was reported by both channels.

(ii) **Subjects:** Here we focused on the agents or central actors of the news reporting. We specifically looked at what constitutes a major subject of interest to each channel. Where does the emphasis of each channel stand with regard to human agency and human values?

(iii) **Sources:** Taking as our point of departure Kuehn's (2018: 405) proposition that 'Sources are messengers used to support frames', in this level of analysis we ask what voices a story selects and affirms as authoritative on its topic. Assuming that media outlets are often consciously selective about the sources of news they refer to, through this technique of analysis we attempt to find out who are the present and absent voices in the news stories. More importantly, to what extent do the voices that are given a platform help shape the intended narrative for each channel. Also, to what extent does this intended selection of sources significantly affect the credibility of news stories and news values?

(iv) **Signs:** Here we consider the characteristic metaphors, historical references, keywords, stock phrases and jargon that condense the narratives and subject positions discussed earlier. It is worth noting here that both AJE and i24News reflect specific world views and broadcast their news to intended audiences locally and internationally. Their points of reference vis-à-vis this conflict can be significantly different. Both cultural and religious symbols referred to, in addition to historical references drawn upon in the course of their news reporting, are loaded with signs and meanings, which also shape the way the conflict is understood. By deciphering the sign system relating to the news stories of each channel, we attempt to offer an understanding of the world view pertaining to each broadcaster and the extent to which such intended symbolism is crucial in affecting the reception of news among the intended audiences.

Research findings

As stated earlier, analysis of the news stories from each channel was performed following the four-point grid: (i) news stories and narrative structure, (ii) sources of the news, (iii) subjects and central actors in the news and (iv) signs and metaphors in the news narratives. The qualitative analysis approach to these levels of enquiry is presented separately for each channel. This was intentional to keep findings from each data set distinct to understand and decipher. In the discussion section, we attempt to compare and contrast the emergent themes and highlight discrepancies in the news coverage between AJE and i24News.

AJE

What follows is an analysis of AJE news reporting. Examination of the news stories retrieved as part of the selected sample, referred to as Video 1, 2, 3 and so on, will be discussed depending on their relevance to each of the four categories detailed earlier.

(i)   News stories and narrative structure

The May 2021 conflict was mainly reported through a victimization frame by AJE. For example, the 'Inside Story' report on 8 May 2021, about legal details of evictions in Sheikh Jarrah, positions Palestinians as victims, being evicted from their homes so that settlers can move in and 'steal' them (AJE, Video 3, 00:01, 8 May).[1] Following on from the news story cited earlier, on 9 May 2021, Al Jazeera reported live on Israeli forces violently forcing protestors and worshippers at Al-Aqsa out of the mosque compound. The narrative structure of the report firstly details the sixty injured Palestinian protestors and the nature of the 'clashes' (Israeli violence, Palestinians only throwing water bottles), why people are protesting (people gathering for Ramadan, stun grenades inside the mosque and the Sheikh Jarrah evictions) and then tensions that may cause future clashes. Overall, it frames Palestinians as the victims, peacefully protesting (AJE, Video 4: 01.11, 9 May)[2] while going to Al-Aqsa for Ramadan and being violently forced out of the area by Israeli forces.

The live report on 10 May details the same narrative while covering further Al Aqsa clashes and the mosque being stormed again – Israelis are in a position of power, while Palestinians face police brutality while peacefully protesting or just worshipping. The narrative structure emphasizes cause and effect: after first detailing the violent protests, the hundreds injured and weapons involved (Israeli stun grenades and rubber-coated steel bullets versus Palestinians throwing 'stones' and objects (AJE, Video 5, 00:20, 10 May),[3] the report *instantly* explains what sparked the day's violence, which was a peaceful 'sit-in protest' inside the mosque being stormed by Israeli police (Video 5, 00:40). This then caused Palestinians to protest aggressively. In comparison is AJE's report on 11 May 2021, which details the rockets fired towards Tel Aviv by Hamas's military wing, and the residential building in Gaza destroyed by Israel (AJE, Video 11, 11 May).[4] This is not as stark a victimization frame – it reports violence inflicted by both sides, and injuries and deaths caused in both Gaza and Israel. However, by explaining the timeline of cause and effect of the conflict, it demonstrates how Israeli forces sparked the tension. The timeline starts from most recent events to last; Hamas fires rockets on Israel, in retaliation to Israeli strikes destroying a Gaza residential tower. This in return was a reply to Hamas rockets heading for Jerusalem, which occurred because Israeli forces were attacking Al-Aqsa and worshippers, and so on (Video 11).

The report also contextualizes the violence in a history of oppression, 'ethnic cleansing' and the 'apartheid state' (Video 11) that Palestinians live in and emphasizes the discrepancy between the military power of Israel versus Hamas. This last point especially demonstrates the victimization frame, portraying an oppressed people trying to defend and stand up for themselves, against a colonizer with lethal military power.

The following four news stories have narratives that structurally break down causes and effects, and competing narratives, in a methodical way. This narrative structure follows events to their root causes and counteracts Israeli views with Palestinian and other sources, which leads to the general underpinning argument of Palestinians as victims.

Firstly, the live report on 10 May 2021 has a narrative structure that fastidiously explains the cause and effect of events, following them to the root causes that position Palestinians as the victims. It begins with reporting on nine Palestinians killed by Israeli air raids on Gaza (AJE, Video 6, 10 May).[5] It then explains how this was in reply to Hamas sending rockets, which in turn was because of Israel's violent attack inside Al-Aqsa Mosque on 'worshippers' (Video 6, 00:40). Thus, this root cause that flared up violence demonstrates the victimization frame, as Israel caused this beginning.

Only then was the Israeli perspective provided in what could be called a 'devil's advocate' frame, with footage of Israeli prime minister Netanyahu. This competing narrative is that of the criminality of the protests – Palestinians as disrupting the secure, stable, 'tolerant' society of Israeli rule by being violent and unlawful. Netanyahu states that he is 'upholding law and order' – that this is about Palestinian law-breaking and violence, 'tolerance and intolerance' (Video 6, 01:15).

Nevertheless, the narrative continues explaining cause and effect, such as the warning Hamas gave Israel to retreat from Al-Aqsa, as well as catalysts of tensions caused by Israel – the Jerusalem Day march and Sheikh Jarrah court hearing. It then reports on Palestinian political officials condemning Israel, thus counteracting the footage cited earlier of Netanyahu.

Similarly, the news story on 11 May could be considered to follow a 'devil's advocate' frame in its narrative structure. It reports on international reactions to Israeli forces wounding hundreds in an Al-Aqsa raid. First of all, it begins with the 'Western' perspective, the competing narrative of a 'conflict' between Israel and Palestine, implying an equal power dynamic. The Jordanian and US representatives urge de-escalation on both sides, with the US spokesman affirming Israel's right to 'defend itself' (AJE, Video 8, 11 May).[6]

However, immediately after this, the opposite narrative is introduced. The news story covers the international support for Palestinians, not Israelis, by worldwide protests and US democrats. After this, the victimization frame is much more distinct – the Palestinian point of view is brought on with a Palestinian political analyst. The presenter posits the Israeli perspective on having to 'impose a law and order situation' because of stone-throwing, and this is swiftly refuted (Video 8, 04:00). Therefore, Israel is positioned as the aggressor, while the narrative structure manages to create some balance through multiple perspectives.

Meanwhile, the report on 13 May does not so starkly display a victimization frame for Palestinians. It details armed Israeli civilians attacking Palestinians, shops and mosques in Israel, while Palestinian civilians give similar treatment to them. It states that the Israeli police are allowing these attacks on Palestinians (AJE, Video 19, 13 May).[7]

This report makes a point of listening to and portraying the Palestinian point of view, but also gives weight to the Israeli perspective on mobs, and questions the attacks on synagogues for example (Video 19). It provides a competing narrative of an Israeli police official. This is still by no means a terrorist frame, but does not frame Palestinian mobs as entirely guiltless or justified in attacking civilians, especially in places of worship. Nevertheless, the segment gives significant screen time to a Palestinian activist, who explains the oppression and colonization of Palestinians, demonstrating the reasoning behind all the anger.

The live report on 14 May 2021 details the four Palestinian protestors killed in the occupied West Bank, and explains that they are protesting against attacks on Gaza, as well as the occupation generally. Its narrative structure follows four different locations of protests, one by one, assessing damage and how peaceful they are. As usual, it explains causes (here it is the deaths in Gaza), and then gives time to the competing narrative, that protestors who were killed were trying to 'conduct an attack' (AJE, Video 28, 02:35, 14 May),[8] when this was not the case. This is methodically refuted through live reporting of some Palestinians attacking soldiers using rocks, Molotov cocktails and fireworks, but with 'minimal' effect (Video 28, 03:00). In this way, the news segment goes back and forth. It also explains more root causes by the end of the report – the catalyst of the Nakba anniversary and the civilian deaths in Gaza (Video 28).

(ii)   Subjects: Agents or central actors of the news reporting.

In terms of central actors, AJE's report on 8 May 2021 (on Sheikh Jarrah evictions and the protests this triggered) emphasizes the human agency of Palestinians, in particular Sheikh Jarrah residents. It focuses on specific residents and their livelihoods. They are also the agents of action in the report, protesting about the evictions. Furthermore, the report emphasizes how more than two hundred people were injured in protests the day before (Video 3). Similarly, on 9 May, residents threatened with eviction are the focal point and are interviewed (Video 4, 01:10). The major subject of interest is the reason for the protests around Al-Aqsa and the injuries Palestinians received from Israeli forces.

Meanwhile, in the report on 11 May 2021 (about Palestinian rockets fired on Tel Aviv and Israeli strikes on Gaza) the agents of action are the forces on both sides. However, AJE markedly specifies that the Palestinians firing the rockets are 'Palestinian armed groups' (Video 11, 00:05). It also specifies them as Hamas's 'military wing' (Al-Qassam Brigades) (Video 11, 00:30), as opposed to the Hamas political group generally, or indeed simply Palestinians. This emphasizes that Palestinian civilians are not responsible for inflicting this violence, and so removes their accountability, in contrast with the Israeli news coverage.

AJE's focus here, in terms of human agency and value, is on civilian casualties on both sides. It also emphasizes the significant differences, for example in the number of people injured, deaths, destroyed buildings and the extent to which civilians can protect themselves. For example, it explains how the majority of Israelis have bomb shelters to go to after the siren warning is issued, while civilians in Gaza do not, with no option but to stay in their homes (Video 11, 21:37). This AJE report also emphasizes how most rockets from Hamas are being deflected by Israel's 'iron dome' defence, while

Gaza has no such thing. Nevertheless, the report explains that some rockets are getting through to Tel Aviv and nearby areas and causing some injuries/casualties.

For example, the text in the report states: 'at least 28 Palestinians killed by Israeli air strikes' (Video 11, 02:16). This clearly displays the victim and perpetrator, putting Palestinians at the focal point of the sentence. Meanwhile, concerning Israeli casualties, the text reads: 'Rockets land in Southern Israel city of Ashkelon, killing two people' (Video 11, 02:27). While this does not specify who sent the rockets, it *is* very obvious contextually, as the entire news report is about Palestinian rockets targeting Israel.

(iii)   News sources:

Overall, the sources that AJE selects and affirms as authoritative tend not to be Israeli. They mainly select international sources or Palestinian ones. If there are Israeli sources, they are not people being interviewed, but instead raw footage from, for example, Israeli news channels, or indirect quotes from Israeli officials. The people that AJE interviews on the ground, or calls into the studio as analysts, are international or Palestinian. These are people given a platform and so help set the intended narrative.

The report on Sheikh Jarrah evictions aired on 8 May 2021 gives a platform to a range of voices, from actual Palestinian residents evicted to more neutral voices, like the British consul general and two Professors at both UK and US universities. There are also more authoritatively positioned Palestinians, such as a political activist and the defence lawyer for Sheikh Jarrah residents. Furthermore, AJE's journalists on the ground are key sources reporting the development of events (Video 3).

Meanwhile, the absent voices are those of Israeli police and army. An Israeli settler gets a voice, but for a very short time, during found footage where he speaks organically. A Sheikh Jarrah resident tells him 'You are stealing my house', and he replies: 'And if I don't steal it, someone else is going to steal it' (Video 3, 00:02).

Similarly, the story on 9 May concerning Al-Aqsa clashes sourced its information from journalists on the ground, Palestinians' raw mobile footage, Palestinian residents threatened with eviction, a political journalist and the secretary general of the Palestinian National Initiative Political Party (Video 4). The report gives a voice to Palestinians, positioning them as victims. It values their raw footage as authoritative and truthful.

In slight contrast is the report on 10 May 2021, documenting protests at Al-Aqsa where Israeli forces used stun grenades and rubber-coated steel bullets, leaving more than two hundred injured (Video 5, 00:20; 02:50). This report gives a limited voice to Israeli sources while explaining what the upcoming Jerusalem day march is, and why it is likely to cause increased tensions. It quotes common Israelis on the meaning of Jerusalem Day, as commemorating the 'unification' of Jerusalem in 1967, versus what Palestinians view as the 'occupation' (Video 5, 05:16). It also reports on the Israeli police commissioner stating that the future Jerusalem day parade would still go ahead.

However, it does not give voice to any Israeli views of the Al-Aqsa protests or actively interview any Israelis. That is given to Palestinians, thus being able to control their own narrative. In addition to raw mobile footage and AJE's journalists on the ground, the sources were a Palestinian political activist (advocacy director) and Palestinian medics (the Palestinian Red Crescent), who reported 215 wounded (Video 5).

The report on 11 May is a 36-minute special segment, so naturally has a larger array of sources than those discussed earlier, including Israeli. It concerned Hamas firing rockets into the Tel Aviv area, after Israeli air strikes destroyed a residential tower in Gaza. Generally, there is raw footage in both Israel and Gaza of the destruction. The story gave considerable screen time to Israeli news footage of the damage in Tel Aviv, including fires burning in streets and an empty burning bus. Furthermore, the Israeli ambulance service is sourced on numbers injured by the rockets, and an Israeli army spokesperson is an indirect source (Video 11). Similarly, the Gaza Health Ministry is sourced for the Palestinian death toll after the Israeli air strikes.

Some of the international sources are quoted indirectly too: the UN Secretary General, the President of the General Assembly, the US State Department, Reuters News Agency and Human Rights Watch. The latter is quoted by an academic, calling Israel an 'apartheid state' in how it treats Palestinians (Video 11, 36:00). The only literal 'voices' we hear are that of AJE journalists, their senior political analyst and William Schabas, a professor of international law at Middlesex University in London. He discusses the roots of the conflict, both from the 1940s and recently: tensions escalating about Israeli settlers trying to move into occupied territory, when they are not meant to (East Jerusalem and the West Bank) and so kicking residents out (Video 11, 33:20 onwards).

Within the following four AJE reports, a range of sources are selected:

Firstly, AJE has its own sources: studio journalists, correspondents on the ground and live and recorded footage (Video 6; 8; 19; 28). It also looks to international sources for credibility and thorough reporting – commentators like a former White House official (Video 8) and an intelligence analyst (Video 19) as well as political representatives. For example, a spokesperson for the United States (Video 6) and a press conference with Jordan and the United States (Video 8, 00:05). Other international sources include footage and voices of protesters around the world in solidarity with Palestinians (Video 8) and the important quotation of a UN school/shelter spokesperson in Palestine (Video 28).

Examples of Palestinian sources include, firstly, those summarized indirectly by AJE either in text or by the correspondents. Hamas commonly self-reports on its own actions, such as rocket attacks (Video 6; Video 8). Official statements are also summarized, including those by the Palestinian presidency spokesperson, Foreign Minister and others (Video 6). Statements made by protestors in Gaza are summarized by correspondents, on their grievances and so on (Video 6). Lastly, medical services sourced for death and injury statistics: the Gaza Health Ministry (Video 6; Video 19), Palestinian Red Crescent (Video 6) and the Minister of Health and other ambulance services (Video 28).

Other Palestinian sources include voices very literally heard. In terms of people interviewed, these include political analysts (Video 8) and activists (Video 19). There are also press conferences and related footage, such as an excerpt of a government meeting, where the Palestinian prime minister calls Israel fully responsible for escalations, and asks the international community to condemn Israel for 'ethnic cleansing' (Video 6).

Lastly, AJE uses raw footage by Palestinian civilians as authoritative sources, for example, footage from inside Al-Aqsa when it was attacked (Video 6).

Meanwhile, Israeli sources tend to mostly be summaries by correspondents or in text form on screen and statements of facts rather than subjective judgements. Usually, these are announcements of the military's future plans, attacks and general updates. Text examples include an Israeli military spokesperson announcing the coming 'several days' of fighting against Hamas (Video 8, 07:05; Video 6), and the Israeli prime minister Netanyahu stating that Hamas has 'crossed a red line' with rocket attacks targeting Israel (Video 8, 07:13). Summaries by correspondents include Israeli military tweets about their future plans (Video 28).

However, one summary of an official police statement gives voice to an Israeli judgement about Palestinian protests. He is quoted by a journalist, saying that police are trying to 'put a lid on violence' after Palestinians attacked synagogues and enacted 'mob violence' too (Video 19, 02:30). In this case, it is in the context of mosques being burnt down and Israeli mobs attacking Palestinians, which he says occurred only *after* Palestinians attacked synagogues. Giving an Israeli voice in this context may demonstrate AJE's value of human life and religious freedoms, emphasizing safety for all civilians, and that mob justice on both sides is problematic. The remaining Israeli sources are, firstly, video footage of Hamas rockets and an Israeli police video of protests (Video 19), as well as one example of a 'literal' voice being given to Israel – Prime Minister Netanyahu's press conference is televised, where he praises security forces for their 'just struggle' and 'upholding law and order' (Video 6).

(iv)   Signs and metaphors in the news narratives:

This final part of analysing AJE's news reports looks at the role played by cultural and historical signs as well as metaphorical language to support the intended narrative. The report on 8 May 2021, on the legality of the Sheikh Jarrah evictions, contains many repeated keywords and phrases that summarize the AJE narrative on Sheikh Jarrah and Palestine in general. Palestinians as subjects are positioned as the victims and labelled as 'residents' or 'protestors'. The Israelis are repeatedly labelled as 'settlers', emphasizing how they are new to the area, in contrast to the original Palestinian 'residents'. Israeli officials attacking protestors are labelled with the neutral 'Israeli forces/police' (Video 3). Stock phrases for the situation in Sheikh Jarrah frame the Israeli settlement as oppressive, using words such as 'occupation', 'evictions', 'ethnic cleansing' and perhaps in its strongest form, 'apartheid', used by both AJE and its interviewed guests (Video 3, 15:49). Overall, this positions Israelis as the wrongful settlers.

Importantly, this news segment also makes historical references, which contextualize the story within a history of racial oppression and occupation in Palestine. Moreover, using the word 'apartheid', referencing the previous racist system in South Africa, the video frames Palestinian-Israeli history: the Nakba of 1947/48 (and framing Sheikh Jarrah as a second Nakba) (Video 3, 09:00), the Balfour Declaration of 1917 where the UK gave their support' for a 'National Home for the Jewish people' (Video 3, 14:00), and key words and phrases like 'Zionist' and the 'two-state solution'. This shows how the conflict is expected to be understood, as an asymmetrical power dynamic and a history of Palestinians being unlawfully, violently evicted from their own homes and land, which continues to the present day.

Overall, the intended audience appears to be international, but perhaps more aware of Middle Eastern issues than the average Western viewer. Nevertheless, journalists and analysts interviewed explain the historical references, the Nakba and Balfour Declaration, making this news accessible to viewers with little background about the conflict.

Meanwhile, the report on 9 May, on Al-Aqsa compound protests, references a historically loaded allegory for the asymmetrical power dynamic between Palestinian civilians and Israeli forces. The journalist states that in the clashes at Al-Aqsa, 'Palestinian protestors threw water bottles. Israeli security forces used stun grenades, foul-smelling chemically laced water jets, and close-up physical force' (Video 4: 00.07). This is a well-known symbol of the power dynamic, similar to the image of Palestinians throwing stones at gun-toting Israeli soldiers. Such imagery provides the historical undercurrent of the channel's narrative and demonstrates AJE's positioning of Palestinians as powerless victims. While this reference to historical events may not be caught by viewers uneducated on the conflict, the contrast in power will not be lost on them.

Other keywords historically and religiously contextualize the news story. The importance of Al-Aqsa is explained, and the anger of Palestinians at it being attacked, especially on the holiest nights of Ramadan. This references the repeated historical issue of Palestinians trying to protect the holy mosque as off limits to Israeli forces. Like the report on 8 May, it frames the conflict as illegal colonization, referencing the 1967 'seizure of Jerusalem' by Israeli forces (Video 4, 02:30), and using the stock phrases 'ethnic cleansing', 'forcibly evict' (Video 4, 00:54), 'racism', 'occupied' and 'apartheid' (Video 4, 02:50; 03:15).

Extending this frame, the report on 10 May includes phrases like 'Occupier and occupied, coloniser and colonised'. These binaries exemplify how the conflict, in particular the attack on Al-Aqsa in this report, is not a 'both sides issue' (Video 5, 10:50). The phrases clearly set out the subject positions and power dynamic according to AJE's sources. It signifies a narrative that is *not* grey – Palestinians are a colonized people trying to stand up for themselves and their right to live and worship peacefully. The report also emphasizes this by calling those attacked in the mosque 'unarmed worshippers' (Video 5). Similar to the report on 9 May, the historical symbol of Palestinians only having stones (and in this case also empty bottles) to fight is raised, as a signifier of their lack of power against Israeli forces, who have tear gas and rubber-coated bullets (Video 5, 10:33). The historical reference to the seizure of Jerusalem is again made, stating that 'Right-wing Israeli nationalists will be celebrating it as a "Jerusalem day" parade that will march through the city' (Video 5, 00:22).

The apartheid framing of the occupation again repeated in the long news segment on 11 May 2021, which is a live report on Hamas firing rockets to the Tel Aviv area, following Israeli strikes on Gaza (Video 11, 36:00). AJE's political analyst Marwan Bishara emphasizes the 'asymmetrical nature of this conflict' in terms of civilian bomb shelters, quality of weapons, military power and infrastructure (Video 11, 24:35). Therefore, he communicates that 'there are no two sides' – this is not how the conflict should be understood (Video 11, 24:48). He even calls Gaza a 'big concentration camp of refugees' (Video 11, 23:53), a historically loaded reference that effectively communicates the oppression and discrimination facing Palestinians.

Lastly, this report portrays a narrative that does not generalize or villainize Palestinian civilians. Keywords used to describe those launching the rockets on Israel are called Palestinian 'fighting groups' (Video 11: 21.10), the 'military wing' of Hamas (Video 11, 00:30), and 'Palestinian armed groups' (Video 11, 00:05). This specifies that civilians are not responsible for military violence and that these neutral keywords do not give a moral judgement, unlike, for example 'terrorists'.

Analysis of four other AJE reports finds historical references that summarize the narrative of illegal occupation and colonization. The reports again reference the Nakba of 1948 (Video 8, 03:40), particularly the discrepancy in its meaning: the 'creation' of the Israeli state, according to Israel, versus the 'forceful displacement' (called *Al-Nakba*) of hundreds of thousands of Palestinians to make way for the state of Israel (Video 28, 04:19). A Palestinian activist, in a report dated 13 May 2021, calls Palestinians a 'colonised people', and Israel 'Palestine 48', a common term that refers to the year of the *Nakba* (1948) and the 'colonisation' of Palestine (Video 19: 00:35).

Generally, the stock phrases used to describe Palestinian land are around 'occupation' (Video 6; Video 8: 03:00; Video 19; Video 28). Israeli citizens are called 'settlers' (Video 8, 03:30) and their settlements 'illegal' (Video 28, 03:00). The 1967 Jerusalem Day celebration is described as the beginning of the 'military occupation' and 'capture' of Jerusalem (Video 6, 06:30), emphasizing the forcefulness and colonial takeover, rather than a unification of the country. Another key phrase used is 'ethnic cleansing', as stated by the Palestinian prime minister in relation to evictions/displacement (Video 6, 10:50).

A key symbol, found again in these four videos, is Al-Aqsa Mosque. Its importance religiously and culturally to Palestinians is emphasized, particularly when explaining why protests were held in its compound. It is described as 'Islam's third holiest site' (Video 6, 00:30), the 'holiest shrine' (Video 8, 04:35), and therefore protestors and 'worshippers' want to protect it from being 'desecrated' by Israeli forces and civilians, even standing guard (Video 8, 04:35; Video 6, 01:00). Al-Aqsa is a vital historical symbol of Palestinians holding on defiantly to their history and culture – not letting Israel erase it, even if they decide to take everything else.

Once again, these reports feature the symbol of stone-throwing as representing the asymmetrical power structure between Israel and Palestine. Palestinians are 'defending themselves with stones' versus the guns and military strength of Israeli forces (Video 8, 07:25). In the report from 14 May, rocks, fireworks and Molotov cocktails are used by Palestinian protestors against soldiers in Ramallah, at a checkpoint near an 'illegal' Jewish settlement (Video 28, 03:00). At this point, tensions are extremely high, with violence between civilians in Israel, and air strikes pounding Gaza. However, the emphasis is on the minimal damage caused by these rocks – the aggression is more a point of showing that they are not afraid and will not stand down (Video 28, 03:50).

One important key phrase, which summarizes AJE's view of Palestinian sovereignty and independence, is describing Hamas as the elected 'Palestinian Authority' in the Gaza Strip (Video 6, 09:00). By describing them as a governmental political authority in charge of Gaza, rather than as a 'terrorist' group, they are presented as a people of their own who have a right to protect their land and indeed defend themselves, like any country with a military.

i24News

What follows is an analysis of i24News reporting of the same events during the same period. In doing so, we followed similar steps employed to analyse AJE's news stories cited earlier. Examination of the news stories, referred to as Video 1, 2, 3 and so on, will be discussed depending on their relevance to each of the four analytical categories (1 – News stories, 2 – Subjects, 3 – News sources and 4 – Signs).

(i) News stories and narrative structure

In the lead up to the Israeli military offensive on Palestinians in Gaza, the coverage of i24News English set the stage for the network's editorial agenda over the next three weeks. In a three-minute news analysis segment (i24News, Video 1, 3 May),[9] a security analyst answers a question regarding the heightened threats to Israel's security in light of a drive-by shooting that targeted Israeli students in the West bank. The analyst frames the single event as a sinister conspiracy 'with an organization and preparation behind it'. The assailants, later referred to as 'terrorists', are described as 'well-trained' and supported.

The guest repeatedly states that this is 'no longer lone-wolf' terrorism, but something else that is a huge cause for concern for the Israeli establishment. He does not mention the IDF's provocations at Al Aqsa Mosque during Ramadan and the controversy over the Sheikh Jarrah evictions. The Palestinian 'enemy' is represented as ferocious and immoral to justify Israel's constant need for self-defence. The subjects of the news are Israeli citizens and victims of terror, and the sources are mostly Israeli or 'international' experts partial to the Jewish state.

On the day following the violent clashes which broke out between Palestinians and Israeli police at Al Aqsa, culminating in provocations on the Muslim holy night of *Laylatul Qadr*, a news analysis segment (i24News, Video 2, 9 May)[10] reveals another frame for the conflict: The guest attributes the escalation of violence in Jerusalem to the domestic power struggle between Fatah and Hamas. Hamas is presented as responsible for the clashes through incitement, which is viewed as a new 'strategy' to move the core of the conflict into Jerusalem, and hence prove that their strategy of violent confrontation is more effective than the Palestinian Authority's (PA) negotiations.

In a news bulletin posted on the same day (i24News, Video 3, 9 May)[11] a field reporter in Sheikh Jarrah frames the scene of Palestinian and Israeli youth protesters as a triumph of self-control by the Israeli border police, who are shown in full riot gear containing only the Palestinians. This framing is typical of i24News's coverage of Israeli forces whose violence is rarely aired.

With hundreds of Palestinians injured at Al Aqsa Mosque, the site of Israeli aggression, Hamas leaders gave Israel an ultimatum on 10 May to withdraw from both the mosque and Sheikh Jarrah quarter. Israel ignored the warning and as inter-communal violence continued in Sheikh Jarrah, Hamas and the Islamic Jihad movement launched rockets into Israel, unleashing retaliatory attacks that indiscriminately destroyed schools and hospitals via 1,500 air, land and sea strikes.

In a news analysis segment covering these developments (i24News, Video 4, 10 May)[12] the guest uses typical rhetoric in his comments on the escalating violence. Here, Israel is framed as the 'victim'. The source mentions Iran's support for Islamic Jihad, in effect conflating both 'enemies' in a bid to trigger the audience. He also frames the Sheikh Jarrah evictions as a cover-up for the real motive of the Palestinians, which is to take control of Jerusalem and wipe Israel off the map. Palestinian infighting is presented as the root cause of the violence.

Another framing of the conflict is introduced in the coverage of Israeli police chasing and attacking Muslim worshippers (i24News, Video 5, 10 May).[13] The interviewed guest depicts Hamas and the PA as 'two sides of the same coin', both equally guilty of deliberately inciting riots and conspiring against Israel in an extension of the 'victim' framing. This is a departure from the network's former distinction between the two political parties, who are now accused of collaborating to undermine Israeli authority in Jerusalem, hence justifying police violence.

Yet another framing of the conflict is introduced here: the notion that the majority of Palestinians in East Jerusalem are in favour of the status quo, and want to continue living under Israeli authority. The implication is that the conflict is contrived and does not reflect what Palestinians actually want.

In Video 11, with talk of a looming ceasefire, a military source expands on the idea that the PA believes that Hamas is an 'existential threat' to them (Video 11, 04:30) and so it is essential for Israel to collaborate with the PA to maintain some calm in the West Bank. The implication here is, once more, that the Palestinians are happy living under Israeli occupation.

(ii)   Subjects: agents or central actors of the news reporting.

The central protagonists prevailing in i24News coverage are unequivocally the Israeli citizens, the Israeli military or police and the State of Israel (both an entity and an idea), who are pitted against Hamas, the PA and Arabs holding Israeli citizenship. The two sides are portrayed through a good/evil, victim/aggressor lens. In both Videos 4 and 5 for instance, Israeli forces and the 'restraint' they show against the rioting Palestinians are the focal points of the reporting and analysis. The emphasis is on justifying police violence and framing it as a necessary evil to protect innocent Israeli citizens and the Jewish state at large, against the threat of 'terrorist' Palestinians who pose an existential threat to their country.

In a 5:36-minute report (i24News, Video 6, 11 May),[14] a reporter walks viewers through a home destroyed by a rocket fired by Hamas in Ashkelon, where one woman was killed. A scene of destruction and panic is displayed for almost two minutes as sirens sound in the background. Throughout, there is an emphasis on the IDF's military capability and in turn the power and steadfastness of the Jewish State, which looms large as one of the central actors in the conflict.

Typically, coverage of the escalation is presented through the network's defence correspondent (i24News, Video 7, 12 May)[15] over scenes of chaos and destruction in Ashkelon, a city close to Gaza. The focus is on the dozens of innocent Israelis hospitalized and killed and how residents under attack have no access to shelters (Video 7, 03:30). This piece of information is juxtaposed with a description of how the IDF 'warns' Gaza residents before bombing them. The implication, which permeates the coverage, is that Israeli raids are ethical and justified acts of self-defence, while indiscriminate rockets fired by Hamas are unethical acts of terrorism. No mention is made of the casualties in Gaza.

Furthermore, i24News's coverage intentionally and systematically dehumanizes and demonizes Palestinians. In a 13 May news segment (i24News, Video 8, 13 May),[16] the anchor interviews the Israeli police spokesperson who portrays violence perpetrated by 'Arab citizens of Israel' as violent rioters being confronted by police who exercise self-control by using only stun grenades (Video 8, 00:35). Responding to the anchor, who says he is angry by the fact that Israel cannot stop the 'lynching' of Israeli citizens, the spokesperson says that the problem lies in the 'Israeli Arab' communities who are attacking 'innocent victims' and 'burning vehicles'.

The power of the IDF as a central agent in the conflict is exemplified in a news analysis segment that ran on 18 May (i24News, Video 9, 18 May).[17] Amid official talk of a pending ceasefire as global media turned the spotlight on the indiscriminate destruction of civilian property, including the bombing of *Al-Jalaa* Tower, which housed the offices of Al Jazeera and the Associated Press three days earlier, the network interviewed a military source and member of a group called Commanders for Israel's security. In the interview, the source applauds the IDF's capacity to 'minimize uninvolved fatalities' (Video 9, 01:20). He explains that Operation Guardian of the Walls will require more days to fight Hamas, emphasizing that this fight will take place in all areas where Palestinians reside, even Arab-Israeli neighbourhoods inside Israel.

(iii)   News sources:

An analysis of the sources used by i24News in the coverage of the events reveals a consistent pattern. The vast majority of sources given a platform are Israeli. They are either the network's correspondents reporting live from the field where they exclusively interview Israeli sources or they are sources identified as experts. Only six news stories out of the whole sample analysed included Palestinians. However, their statements were framed to support the Israeli narrative. International 'experts', although presented as impartial observers, are always unequivocally partial to the Israeli viewpoint.

Video 1, for instance, features i24News security analyst, Jonathan Regev, who is the only outside source interviewed in this segment. He blatantly states that Palestinians are 'terrorists' (Video 1, 01:00) and avoids mentioning the Sheikh Jarrah evictions as the context for the escalation. In Video 2, Yaron Schneider, identified as an Arab Affairs Reporter for another Israeli Channel 12, is interviewed. He introduces the notion that Israel is 'trapped' (Video 2, 00:15) in the conflict between Fatah and Hamas, who are both guilty of deliberately transporting the Palestinian-Israeli conflict to Jerusalem. Again, no context is provided here.

As the fighting intensified on 10 May, sources featured in i24News coverage and analysis become increasingly radical. Right-wing, avowed religious Zionist and scholar Mordechai Kedar heightens the threat of Hamas by conflating it with Iran's support for Islamic Jihad and describes the Sheikh Jarrah evictions as a 'fig leaf' to conceal the ulterior motive of destroying Israel (Video 4, 00:10). Similarly, Efrain Inbar, a university professor and president of the Jerusalem Institute for Strategic Studies (JISS) is interviewed in Video 5, where he justifies the brutal attacks of Israeli forces against Muslim worshippers at Al Aqsa Mosque. He concludes his contribution by stating that the 'majority of Palestinians continue a normal life under Israeli authority' (Video 5, 03:00) and that only a minority of Islamists and nationalists in East Jerusalem stand behind this contrived confrontation.

In the first of only three instances in the sample period, where a Palestinian source is interviewed, i24News speaks to a Ramallah-based journalist Mohamed Najib (i24News, Video 10, 10 May).[18] Najib states that Hamas has 30,000 fighters and a massive weapons cache including long- and short-range missiles on which they were trained by Iran and Hezbollah (Video 10, 02:28). He conveniently plays up the level of coordination between the armed Palestinian factions, in effect raising the prospect of more violence against Israel. His statements are in sync with i24News's editorial line, dramatically exaggerating Hamas's military capability and in turn justifying Israel's disproportionate retaliation.

A second Palestinian source is interviewed on 11 May, Ghaith Al-Omari, a former Palestinian negotiator based in Washington, DC (i24News, Video 11, 11 May).[19] Despite pushing back on the Israeli narrative that the Sheikh Jarrah evictions are a mere real-estate dispute, Al-Omari is unequivocal in his sweeping condemnation of Hamas's strategy of violence, which he describes as ineffective and politically motivated to assert the group as the stronger voice of the Palestinian people (Video 11, 02:00). This, once more, plays into the network's broader narrative.

In a unique case, Palestinian activist Samer Sinijlawi is present in the i24News studios, where he comments on the devastation that has befallen Gaza and the dramatic death toll (i24News Video 12, 19 May).[20] Atypically, Sinijlawi is given a platform to present the Gazan point of view. But, even though he mentions the devastating impact of the fourteen-year-old siege, his tone is overwhelmingly conciliatory. He praises values that Judaism has brought to the world, naming 'human dignity' as one of them and the importance of coexistence (Video 12, 02:00). In the same segment, a member of the Knesset for the religious Zionist party Simcha Rothman is also interviewed (Video 12, 03:52) and given equal time to refute claims that Arabs are denied equal rights under Israeli law, blames the Palestinians for the failure of the two-state solution and accuses them of wanting to eliminate Israel altogether.

As global public opinion turned against Israel, i24News turned to their new allies in the region, diversifying their sources by interviewing Emirati social media influencer and self-proclaimed peace activist Loay Shareef live from Abu Dhabi (i24News, Video 13, 16 May).[21] Commenting on the 'current cycle of violence', Shareef reiterates the official statement of the UAE government, which called for an immediate ceasefire. i24News succeeded in using Shareef as a mouthpiece for a tamed Gulf region as he voiced his support for the newly minted Abraham Accords, which normalized relations between the UAE, Bahrain and Israel. He symbolizes the 'good' Arab, depoliticized Muslim, who is peace loving and condemns 'terrorism'. His comments bestow a false legitimacy to the recent accords, which were summarily denounced by the PA for failing to guarantee a contiguous Palestinian state according to the 1967 borders.

Interestingly, Shareef is interviewed again the next day (i24News, Video 14, 17 May)[22] in a bid to present the 'view from the Gulf'. In a more vocal and emotional appeal to normalization, Shareef refers to Jews as 'our cousins' and condemns attempts to try to destroy the relationship between the Jewish people and Muslims, in an oblique reference to Hamas (Video 14, 00:40). He further emphasizes that 'we are seeking stability ... the Jewish people belong to this region and we have to live with our Jewish neighbors' (Video 14, 04:00), ironically as the split screen shows images of destruction caused by Israeli tanks.

(iv) Signs and metaphors in the news narratives:

The analysis of i24News coverage of the May 2021 conflict reveals certain patterns in the use of metaphors and cultural references to support the network's editorial agenda. These signs revolve around the historical and present-day dispute over the status of Jerusalem as both a spiritual hub for Muslims, Christians and Jews and, politically, as the self-declared capital of Israel, unrecognized as such by the United Nations.

In an 11 May interview, as the Sheikh Jarrah confrontations escalated and the Israeli army began its counter attacks on Gaza (i24News, Video 15, 11 May),[23] Hebrew University professor Robbie Sabel, former legal advisor to Israel's Ministry of Foreign Affairs, justifies the Israeli police's decision to storm Al Aqsa, but adds that it incites 'Arab hatred' (Video 15, 00:30). He refers to stones thrown at the worshipping Jews in the context of unjustified aggression. Asked about the legal dispute over the properties in Sheikh Jarrah, Sabel says there is no doubt over the Jewish ownership of the land but that current residents should be granted 'tenancy' and allowed to stay there, relegating the issue to the courts as a real-estate dispute and embodying i24News's framing of the issue.

As part of the intentional framing of the Palestinian-Israeli conflict as a religious, rather than a political and territorial, dispute and a case of settler colonialism, i24News gives Israel's right-wing leaders an open platform to express this view. In a joint press conference by former Israeli prime minister Benjamin Netanyahu, Defense Minister Benny Gantz and then head of Shin Bet Nadav Argaman (i24News, Video 16, 11 May),[24] the IDF's precision capabilities and Iron Dome interceptors are glorified and portrayed as equally protective of 'all Israeli citizens', Jews and Arabs (Video 16, 02:45). The disproportionate attacks on Gaza are thus sanitized and justified as the IDF perpetuates the myth of targeting Hamas weapons caches and senior operatives and going out of its way to protect and warn civilians.

In a live report from Jerusalem a day later (i24News, Video 17, 12 May),[25] the correspondent describes scenes of chaos using the symbolism of bottles of water thrown at Israeli police who respond with stun grenades. The description is reminiscent of Palestinian stone-throwing during the *Intifida*. The reporter subliminally underscores the religious nature of the conflict by noting that the end of Ramadan's night prayers, the *Tarawih*, is 'a kind of signal for the youth to start clashing against Israeli forces' (Video 17, 01:00). Damascus Gate (Bab Al Amud) is presented as the main flashpoint in the area, a reference that carries symbolic weight as it epitomizes the historical feud between Muslims and Jews regarding claims of rightful sovereignty over the Holy City.

The notion of the violent Arab 'mob' is another ongoing image evident in i24News coverage. In a news package voice over (i24News, Video 18, 12 May 12)[26] reported from the city of Lod, the reporter describes 'Arab mobs' who 'torched Jewish-owned businesses and synagogues' as we see scenes of chaos and destruction. It also shows images of Gaza on fire as the IDF launches targeted operations, again glorifying Israel's military capability.

A significant interview with a Likud party hawk and former mayor of Jerusalem, MP Nir Barkat, at the height of Israel's offensive on Gaza, exemplifies the prevailing narrative of i24News on the conflict (i24News, Video 19, 16 May).[27] He underlines the notion that Israel's 'innocent civilians' are being attacked by a 'terrorist organization'. The language of vengeance and threat is used to justify the disproportionate Israeli offensive ('they have to pay a heavy price', 'we will take them back 30 years in their infrastructure' (Video 19, 00:45). Palestinian civilian casualties are, according to him, unintentional 'collateral damage'. For him Hamas targets Israeli civilians and hides behind its own civilians and the international media. A 'good-guys/bad-guys' dichotomy is repeated and so is the false implication that this is a symmetrical conflict between Israel and Hamas, which does not represent the Palestinian people. This plays into the Israeli narrative that a majority of Palestinians are happy living under Israeli occupation.

A speech by Israeli envoy to the United States and United Nations Gilad Erdan at the UN captures it best (i24News, Video 20, 20 May).[28] Erdan repeats typical Israeli tropes about Hamas's hatred of Israel and Jews (framing the conflict as religious). Like the Nazis, he insinuates, Hamas hates the Jews. Typical of Israeli political messaging, Erdan creates false binaries, for example, Israel's 'moral courage' versus Hamas's 'moral depravity' (Video 20, 02:50). Hyperbole and outrage pepper his speech, reflecting the editorial line of i24News, despite attempts to appear balanced and professional.

Discussion

The findings given earlier from news reports of i24News and AJE reveal substantial discrepancies. Evidently, the differences in the narrative based on analysing the various levels addressed reflect a well-established news culture and unique editorial policy for each channel. AJE recognizes the rights of the Palestinian people over their homeland, and its news narrative is critical of the occupation. The editorial policy regarding the coverage of the Palestinian Israeli conflict is part of the world view that constitutes Al Jazeera Network's approach to the conflict as a whole, which is generally in support of the Palestinian cause. On the other hand, i24News supports the Zionist views that Israel has the historical right to occupy the land of Palestine and that Jewish people are victims of Palestinian violence and hence have the right to defend themselves by all possible means.

A significant theme, which emerges from the earlier discussion, is how the narrative about the conflict is presented. In AJE's coverage, the Palestinian story is told by various actors, not only the official figures of the PA in Ramallah. Palestinians' daily struggle is not anymore exclusively narrated by the Fatah leadership. In fact, representatives of the PA come second after activists, ordinary people and leaders of resistance movements like Hamas and Islamic Jihad.

However, i24News clearly reflects the official Israeli viewpoint of the conflict. In spite of its claim to be objective, the channel is in line with the professed narrative of the state of Israel. For instance, i24News still regards Palestinian activists as troublemakers and even 'terrorists', whereas AJE views them as 'freedom fighters' and 'activists' defending their homes and properties. The discourse reinforces an image of them as part of a 'resistance movement' and not mere victims of occupation. As suggested by Kaposi (2014) in another study, both the Palestinian side as well as the Israeli side have their own narratives on the conflict. International organizations and governments around the world also have their own established perspectives. Each camp brings in its own 'truths' to the table. But one may argue that those truths on the history of the conflict are partly constructed by the media narrative itself. Media outlets routinely reflect specific world views in their news reporting, and they cannot be considered simply neutral or impartial.

One recurrent imagery reiterated by i24News during the Sheikh Jarrah events and the war on Gaza was highlighting the moral superiority of the Israeli Army. The discourse goes along the presentation of sophisticated Israeli machinery that is particularly doing its best to minimize civilian casualties while attacking Gaza. The air bombardment of a selected number of buildings in a surgical way is presented as a must-do tactic to target Hamas members. On the contrary, AJE's reporting highlights the scale of material damage and the disproportionate destruction of Palestinian infrastructure and buildings, hence characterizing the whole operation as pure aggression.

Sources of news reports drawn upon by each channel are also key in understanding the duelling narratives of the conflict. The two channels differ exponentially in this regard. AJE's reporting capitalizes on its widespread network of reporters on the ground. The presence of its journalists in almost every hotspot related to the tensions between Palestinians and the Israeli army or Israeli settlers is a key advantage. The vivid accounts of victims draw more sympathy and make its reporting genuine. The viewer follows the intense experiences of Palestinian women, children and the elderly at Al Aqsa Mosque as reported by the AJE cameras without the need for commentary by reporters. Examples of eyewitness accounts regarding Sheikh Jarrah's violent evictions, for instance, are numerous. Also, accounts of Palestinian activists who report events as they happen add further support to this claim. Israeli channel i24News in contrast does not interview Palestinian victims of Israeli police aggression or settlers' assaults. Eyewitnesses from the Palestinian side would be brought in purely to support the Israeli narrative. Although the channel may refer to Palestinian sufferings in reports of aggression by Israeli police against protesters or worshippers, this is always followed by a whitewash or a justification. The Israeli side is never blamed, but is presented as exercising self-restraint to protect the greater good of Israel against troublemaking Palestinians bent on eliminating the Jewish state.

One distinguishing feature of the AJE reporting was the constant employment of graphical illustrations about facts on the conflict. When Hamas started its rocket launch campaign, AJE would produce facts and figures about these rockets, their power and range and possible damage. The channel also furnishes its viewers with ample contextual information about various problematic issues in relation to this conflict such as statistical data on the increase of Israeli settlements built on Palestinian land during the last few decades, reports from local and international organizations about Palestinian prisoners in Israeli jails, inhumane treatment of Palestinians in Israeli checkpoints and the suffocation of the Palestinian economy. As suggested by Carpenter (2017: 68) in his study, 'AJE, as a source of contraflow in English, constituted a direct response and challenge to the dominance of Western news media in the global news sphere by introducing perspectives from the Global South into the English-speaking global news sphere.' The power of presenting solid facts about the history of the occupation and changes on the ground regarding the confiscation of Palestinian land, backed up with statistical data, is what makes AJE's reporting impactful and challenging to the Israeli narrative.

Newsmedia and newsworthiness

As argued earlier, analysing a sample of the coverage offered by AJE and i24News shows that both channels have diverse approaches to covering the conflict. AJE is clearly pro-Palestinian in its framing of Israel as a colonizing power, whereas i24News is pro-Israeli and therefore regards Israel as the only authority over historical Palestine. Another aspect of reporting the conflict as seen through the analysis given earlier is the weight each channel places on selective events. What makes a news story worthy is predicated on each channel's editorial line. A top story, according to AJE, will not necessarily make its way to the newsroom of i24News. A useful reference would be to French philosopher Paul Ricoeur in *Time and Narrative* where he argues that the correlation, or what he calls 'healthy circle' between time, in this case the telling of a story in a certain modality, and chronological order and the narrative, is not accidental. The understanding and perception of time is a selective set of modes and a 'transcultural form of necessity'. In Ricoeur's view

> between the activity of narrating a story and the temporal character of human experience there exists a correlation that is not merely accidental but that presents a transcultural form of necessity. To put it in another way, time becomes human to the extent that it is articulated through a narrative mode, and narrative attains its full meaning when it becomes a condition of temporal existence. (Ricoeur, 1984: 52)

Another theme which emerges from the comparison of news reporting between two channels is the focus of i24 Network on a normalization narrative towards the end of the conflict. By comparison, AJE pursues a singular stance/narrative against the 'Zionist state' and settler colonialism before, during and after the war and sees the

Israeli left-wing as an ally of the right-wing extremism. It is no surprise that Al Jazeera network faced various criticisms from the Israeli side regarding its stance in reporting the conflict. Attacks on its journalists have been amply recorded over the years.

Significance of context in understanding the news

A final point reflecting on the news reporting of AJE and i24News is the advantage of providing ample historical and social context for any news story. Detailed information backed by statistical data can be crucial in the way a narrative is received by viewers around the world, especially those not familiar with the complex developments of the Palestinian-Israeli conflict over the last few decades. The power of background information about any conflict is crucial in understanding its history as articulated by Ricoeur (1984: 58): 'A symbolic system thus furnishes a descriptive context for particular actions.' A historical narrative is loaded with symbols that help understand the present. 'The term "symbol" immediately accentuates the public character of any meaningful articulation … [and] symbolism is not in the mind, not a psychological operation destined to guide action, but a meaning incorporated into action and decipherable from it by other actors in the social interplay' (Ricoeur, 1984: 57). And according to him, 'if, in fact, human action can be narrated, it is because it is always already articulated by signs, rules, and norms. It is always already symbolically mediated' (Ricoeur, 1984: 57).

The analysis given earlier reveals that the Israeli channel's narrative focuses on the construction of Israel in the international public opinion as a peaceful country not as a colonizing power. More importantly, the picture that it promotes focuses on the obliteration of historical Palestine that existed before the 1948 *Nakba* (Palestinian catastrophe). Israel was promoted by Western powers since then as a nation attempting to live in peace with its Arab neighbours, and that Palestinians are a 'troublesome' minority living within Israel.

Zeina Khodr, AJE correspondent, reports on how important it is for journalists to gather background information from various voices to tell an informative and complete story. She argues: 'You will really have to spend your time listening, talking to people, understanding. It is not only what politicians say … A lot of the conflicts today have a past and you need to understand the past in order to understand the present' (Joumaa and Ramadan, 2018: 51).

Notes

1. AJE (2021), 'What Can Stop Palestinians Being Evicted from Sheikh Jarrah?', 8 May, https://www.youtube.com/watch?v=Ac3YqXsc9Kw&list=PLyMzSMPZdJtcgt-Z4y pBO5x1_g5eYsyhC&index=2 (accessed 13 June 2021).
2. AJE (2021), 'More than 60 Palestinians Injured in New Jerusalem Clashes', https:// www.youtube.com/watch?v=Ac3YqXsc9Kw&list=PLyMzSMPZdJtcgt-Z4ypBO5x1_g 5eYsyhC&index=2 (accessed 14 June 2021).

3. AJE (2021), 'Dozens Wounded as Israeli Forces Raid Al-Aqsa Compound', 10 May, https://www.youtube.com/watch?v=COLYY4Y0iJY&list=PLyMzSMPZdJtcgt-Z4y pBO5x1_g5eYsyhC&index=3 (accessed 14 June 2021).

4. AJE (2021), 'Hamas Retaliates after Israel Attack Destroys Gaza Residential Tower', 11 May, https://www.youtube.com/watch?v=_sWyski92ME&list=PLyMzSMPZdJtcgt-Z4ypBO5x1_g5eYsyhC&index=9 (accessed 15 June 2021).

5. AJE (2021), 'Palestinians Report Several Killed in Israeli Air Raids on Gaza', 10 May, https://www.youtube.com/watch?v=ZxKjF6eAxqw&list=PLyMzSMPZdJtcgt-Z4y pBO5x1_g5eYsyhC&index=4 (accessed 14 June 2021).

6. AJE (2021), 'World Reacts after Israeli Forces Wound Hundreds in Al-Aqsa Raid', 11 May, https://www.youtube.com/watch?v=tlTsHJgeVyE&list=PLyMzSMPZdJtcgt-Z4y pBO5x1_g5eYsyhC&index=6 (accessed 15 June 2021).

7. AJE (2021), 'Israeli Police "Allowing Attacks" on Palestinians: Activist', 13 May, https://www.youtube.com/watch?v=tPX7BskyGLc&list=PLyMzSMPZdJtcgt-Z4ypBO5x1_g 5eYsyhC&index=17 (accessed 16 June 2021).

8. AJE (2021), '4 Palestinians Killed in West Bank', 14 May, https://www.youtube.com/watch?v=zywsJcsghAc&list=PLyMzSMPZdJtcgt-Z4ypBO5x1_g5eYsyhC&index=26 (accessed 16 June 2021).

9. i24NEWS (2021), 'Jonathan Regev Discusses Israeli Security Concerns after West Bank Shooting', 3 May, https://www.youtube.com/watch?v=liNjpnw1fP4&list=PLyMzSM PZdJtdfcye9WMxM0RqeNqB_Mp3T&index=7 (accessed 24 May 2021).

10. i24NEWS (2021), 'High Alert after 2 Days of Violent Jerusalem Clashes', 9 May, https://www.youtube.com/watch?v=ali7nH-JfFk&list=PLyMzSMPZdJtdfcye9W MxM0RqeNqB_Mp3T&index=10 (accessed 24 May 2021).

11. i24NEWS (2021), 'On the Ground in #SheikhJarrah Neighborhood in East Jerusalem', 9 May, https://www.youtube.com/watch?v=mKLDatLhdis&list=PLyMzSMPZdJtdfc ye9WMxM0RqeNqB_Mp3T&index=13 (accessed 24 May 2021).

12. i24NEWS (2021), 'Middle East Scholar on Jerusalem Tensions, Gaza Flare-Up', 10 May, https://www.youtube.com/watch?v=UgWS8zuh5HA&list=PLyMzSMPZdJtdfc ye9WMxM0RqeNqB_Mp3T&index=14 (accessed 24 May 2021).

13. i24NEWS (2021), 'Tensions Boil Over ahead of Jerusalem Day Celebrations', 10 May, https://www.youtube.com/watch?v=4s7ouY-QPas&list=PLyMzSMPZdJtdfcye9W MxM0RqeNqB_Mp3T&index=16 (accessed 24 May 2021).

14. I24NEWS (2021), 'More Than 150 Gazan Rockets Target Israel amid Clashes between IDF, Palestinians at Temple Mount', 11 May, https://www.youtube.com/watch?v=PPBtn-MSvkg&list=PLyMzSMPZdJtdfcye9WMxM0RqeNqB_Mp3T&index=24 (accessed 24 May 2021).

15. I24NEWS (2021), 'Dozens of Israelis Hospitalized, Several Killed as Rocket Attacks Target Tel Aviv', 12 May, https://www.youtube.com/watch?v=l6MlnO8k _B8&list=PLyMzSMPZdJtdfcye9WMxM0RqeNqB_Mp3T&index=27 (accessed 24 May 2021).

16. I24NEWS (2021), 'Israel Police Spox on Lynching of Jews, Arabs in Riots throughout Country', 13 May, https://www.youtube.com/watch?v=tknOXF4Xxlk&list=PLyMzSM PZdJtdfcye9WMxM0RqeNqB_Mp3T&index=31 (accessed 24 May 2021).

17. I24NEWS (2021), 'IDF "Operation Guardian of the Walls" to Last Until Deterrence Is Re-Established', 18 May, https://www.youtube.com/watch?v=JaU-VKcA M8k&list=PLyMzSMPZdJtdfcye9WMxM0RqeNqB_Mp3T&index=45 (accessed 24 May 2021).

18. i24NEWS (2021), 'Palestinian Journalist: Unprecedented Escalation, Hamas Has Not Attacked Jerusalem Since 2014', 10 May, https://www.youtube.com/watch?v=MFV7 Ml2Qar0&list=PLyMzSMPZdJtdfcye9WMxM0RqeNqB_Mp3T&index=19 (accessed: 24 May 2021).

19. i24NEWS (2021), 'More Than 150 Gazan Rockets Target Israel Amid Clashes Between IDF, Palestinians at Temple Mount', 11 May, https://www.youtube.com/watch?v=34FB ZoejPaQ&list=PLyMzSMPZdJtdfcye9WMxM0RqeNqB_Mp3T&index=22 (accessed 24 May 2021).

20. i24NEWS (2021), 'Religious Zionist and Palestinian Activists Debate Israel–Gaza Conflict', 19 May, https://www.youtube.com/watch?v=lYsq0LsZGdc&list=PLyMzSM PZdJtdfcye9WMxM0RqeNqB_Mp3T&index=51 (accessed 25 May 2021).

21. i24NEWS (2021), 'Speaking from Abu Dhabi, Social Media Influencer and Activist Loay Shareef', 16 May, https://www.youtube.com/watch?v=TEyTlx0U CcI&list=PLyMzSMPZdJtdfcye9WMxM0RqeNqB_Mp3T&index=40 (accessed 25 May 2021).

22. i24NEWS (2021), 'Social Media Activist Loay Shareef Still Hopeful for Jewish-Muslim Relations', 17 May, https://www.youtube.com/watch?v=FkDmvNPm D_Y&list=PLyMzSMPZdJtdfcye9WMxM0RqeNqB_Mp3T&index=43 (accessed 25 May 2021).

23. i24NEWS (2021), 'Legal Expert on Israeli Conduct in Jerusalem as Escalation Continues', 11 May, https://www.youtube.com/watch?v=ykzyDeYbR_g&list= PLyMzSMPZdJtdfcye9WMxM0RqeNqB_Mp3T&index=21 (accessed 25 May 2021).

24. i24NEWS (2021), 'Netanyahu and Gantz Address Public on Israel/Gaza Escalation', 11 May, https://www.youtube.com/watch?v=6KrcWSp4t8k&list=PLyMzSMPZdJtdfc ye9WMxM0RqeNqB_Mp3T&index=25 (accessed 25 May 2021).

25. i24NEWS (2021), 'Jerusalem Protests Continue as Gaza Militants Rain Rockets Over Israel', 12 May, https://www.youtube.com/watch?v=eSGQ_zz3b4w&list=PLyMzSM PZdJtdfcye9WMxM0RqeNqB_Mp3T&index=26 (accessed 24 May 2021).

26. i24NEWS (2021), 'Hamas Fires Endless Rocket Barrage into Israel', 12 May, https:// www.youtube.com/watch?v=8wftpRI7m_Y&list=PLyMzSMPZdJtdfcye9WMxM0 RqeNqB_Mp3T&index=29 (accessed 24 May 2021).

27. i24NEWS (2021), 'Likud MP Nir Barkat Speaks to i24NEWS about Israel's Ongoing Battle against Hamas', 16 May, https://www.youtube.com/watch?v=qQ31GOYD 2Mo&list=PLyMzSMPZdJtdfcye9WMxM0RqeNqB_Mp3T&index=42 (accessed 25 May 2021).

28. i24NEWS (2021), 'Israeli Envoy to US and UN Gilad Erdan: "United Nations Gives Hamas a Free Pass" ', 20 May, https://www.youtube.com/watch?v=wRiz R85-75w&list=PLyMzSMPZdJtdfcye9WMxM0RqeNqB_Mp3T&index=62 (accessed 25 May 2021).

References

Abdelmoula, E., and N. Miladi (eds) (2016), *Mapping the Al Jazeera Phenomenon 20 Years On*, Doha: Al Jazeera Centre for Studies.

Al Jazeera (2011), 'Al Jazeera Vindicated over Palestine Papers', *Al Jazeera English*, https://www.aljazeera.com/features/2011/10/10/al-jazeeraAl Jazeera-vindicated-over-palestine-papers (accessed 31 July 2021).

Aouragh, M. (2008), 'Everyday Resistance on the Internet: The Palestinian Context', *Journal of Arab and Muslim Media Research*, 1(2): 109–30, doi: 10.1386/jammr.1.2.109_1.

Arab Center for Research and Policy Studies (2021), 'The Palestinian Popular Revolt: Background, Causes, and Characteristic', 21 May, https://arabcenterdc.org/resource/the-palestinian-popular-revolt-background-causes-and-characteristics/ (accessed 24 November 2021).

Artz, L. (2014), 'Banal Balance, Selective Identification and Factual Omissions: The *New York Times* Coverage of the 2014 War in Gaza', *Journal of Arab & Muslim Media Research*, 7(2+3): 97–112, doi: 10.1386/jammr.7.2-3.97_1.

Barkho, L. (2007), 'Unpacking the Discursive and Social Links in BBC, CNN and Al-Jazeera's Middle East Reporting', *Journal of Arab and Muslim Media Research*, 1(1): 11–29, doi: 10.1386/jammr.1.1.11/1.

Barkho, L. (2011), 'The Discursive and Social Paradigm of Al-Jazeera English in Comparison and Parallel with the BBC', *Communication Studies*, 62(1): 23–40, doi: 10.1080/10510974.2011.535408.

Carpenter, J. (2017), 'Creating English as a Language of Global News Contraflow: Al Jazeera at the Intersection of Language, Globalization and Journalism', *Journal of Arab & Muslim Media Research*, 10(1): 65–83, doi: 10.1386/jammr.10.1.65_1.

Cohen, N., and G. de Peuter (2018), 'Interns Talk Back: Disrupting Media Narratives about Unpaid Work', *The Political Economy of Communication*, 6(2): 3–24, https://www.polecom.org/index.php/polecom/article/view/96.

Downey, J., D. Deacon, P. Golding, B. Oldfield and D. Wring (2019), 'The BBC's Reporting of the Israeli-Palestinian Conflict', Loughborough University: Communications Research Centre, https://hdl.handle.net/2134/3158 (accessed 29 October 2021).

El Damanhoury, K., and F. Saleh (2017), 'Is It the Same Fight? Comparative Analysis of CNN and Al Jazeera America's Online Coverage of the 2014 Gaza War', *Journal of Arab & Muslim Media Research*, 10(1): 3–23, doi: 10.1386/jammr.10.1.3_1.

Emasry, M., A. Elshamy, P. Manning, A. Millas and P. Auter (2013), 'Al-Jazeera and Al-Arabiya Framing of the Israel–Palestine Conflict during War and Calm Periods', *The International Communication Gazette*, 75(8): 750–68, doi: 10.1177/1748048513482545.

Entman R. M. (1993), 'Framing: Toward Clarification of a Fractured Paradigm', *Journal of Communication*, 43(4): 51–8.

Forbes Middle East (2021), 'Top TV Channels Online in the Arab World', https://www.forbesmiddleeast.com/list/top-tv-channels-online-in-the-arab-world/ (accessed 30 July 2022).

Harb, G. (2021), 'News Framing of the Israeli Aggression on Gaza in 2021 on i24 Israeli Channel' (in Arabic), *Al-Bahith Al-A'alami*, 13(53): 7–30.

Joumaa, A., and K. Ramadan (eds) (2018), *Journalism in Times of War*. Al Jazeera Media Institute, https://institute.aljazeera.net/sites/default/files/2018/JOURNALISM%20IN%20TIMES%20OF%20WAR.pdf (accessed 31 July 2022).

Kaposi, D. (2014), *Violence and Understanding in Gaza. The British Broadsheets' Coverage of the War*, London: Palgrave Macmillan.

Kuehn, K. M. (2018), 'Framing Mass Surveillance: Analyzing New Zealand's Media Coverage of the Early Snowden Files', *Journalism*, 19(3): 402–19, https://doi.org/10.1177/1464884917699238.

Margalit, R. (2013), 'The Israeli Answer to Al Jazeera', *The New Yorker*, 29 July, https://www.newyorker.com/news/news-desk/the-israeli-answer-to-al-jazeera (accessed 29 July 2022).

Martin, J. D. (2011), 'Palestinian Women, the Western Press and the First Intifada', *Journal of Arab & Muslim Media Research*, 4(1): 95–107, doi: 10.1386/jammr.4.1.95_1.

Marzano, A. (2011), 'Reading the Israeli–Palestinian Conflict through an Islamophobic Prism: The Italian Press and the Gaza War', *Journal of Arab & Muslim Media Research*, 4(1): 63–78, doi: 10.1386/jammr.4.1.63_1.

Miladi, N. (2006), 'Satellite TV News and the Arab Diaspora in Britain: Comparing Al-Jazeera, the BBC and CNN', *Journal of Ethnic and Migration Studies (JEMS)*, 32(6): 947–60, doi: 10.1080/13691830600761552.

OCHA (2021a), 'West Bank: Escalation of Violence 13 April–21 May 2021', United Nations Office for the Coordination of Humanitarian Affairs, 6 June, https://www.ocha opt.org/ (accessed 24 November 2021).

OCHA (2021b), 'Protection of Civilians Report, 24–31 May 2021', United Nations Office for the Coordination of Humanitarian Affairs, 4 June, https://www.ochaopt.org/poc/24-31-may-2021 (accessed 24 November 2021).

Philo, G., and M. Berry (2004), *Bad News from Israel*, Glasgow: Pluto Press.

Philo, G., and M. Berry (2011), *More Bad News from Israel*, London: Pluto.

Ricoeur, P. (1984), *Time and Narrative*, Chicago: University of Chicago Press.

Rinnawi, K. (2012), 'Al Jazeera Invades Israel: Is Satellite TV Challenging the Sovereignty of the Nation State?', *Journal of Arab & Muslim Media Research*, 5(3): 245–57, doi: 10.1386/jammr.5.3.245_1.

Saber, D. (2016), 'From Pan-Arab Nationalism to Political Islam: A Ricoeurian Reading of Al Jazeera's Coverage of the "6th Arab-Israeli War" in Lebanon', *Journal of Arab & Muslim Media Research*, 9(1): 81–98, doi: 10.1386/ jammr.9.1.81_1.

Said, E. (1984), 'Permission to Narrate', *Journal of Palestine Studies*, 13(3): 27– 48.

Sanz Sabido, R. (2015), 'Palestine in the British Press: A Postcolonial Critical Discourse Analysis', *Journal of Arab & Muslim Media Research*, 8(3): 199–216, doi: 10.1386/jammr.8.3.199_1.

Sanz Sabido, R. (2019), *The Israeli-Palestinian Conflict in the British Press*, Basingstoke: Palgrave Macmillan.

5

SDG16 in the news: Digital news coverage of Sheikh Jarrah in Nigerian newspapers

Muhammad Jameel Yusha'u

Introduction: SDG16 – 2030 agenda and sustainable peace

The year 2015 was a watershed moment in international development. A total of 193 member states of the United Nations came together to agree on the Sustainable Development Goals (SDGs), also called the global goals or the 2030 Agenda for Development. All the SDGs are important, yet without peace, justice and stability it is difficult for any of the SDGs to be achieved. As discussed by Olayide, Mauerhofer and Cerin (2017), there was renewed hope for peace and stability at the end of the Cold War.

This renewed hope was partly informed by the desire to end conflicts, war and military confrontations which have become a major hallmark in the twentieth and twenty-first centuries. From the 1940s when the Palestinian conflict erupted, there have been major wars and conflicts between and within nations. Among these conflicts, the Palestinian conflict has been the most endless and, based on current developments, there is no end in sight for the crisis. For this alone, adding SDG16 on peace, justice and strong institution to the global goals is justified.

SDG16 is the sixteenth goal among the SDGs that aims to promote security, justice and strong institutions and ensure an equitable society. According to the United Nations, the estimated number of people suffering from conflict or fleeing war have exceeded 70 million as of 2018 (UN 2021). SDG16 includes twelve targets, which if achieved, could help in ending war, conflict and ensure peace and justice across the globe (UN SDGs 2021: para 5)

Due to the criticality of SDG16 in ensuring peace and justice and ending conflicts, scholars and researchers are paying attention and providing a critique on SDG16 from a variety of perspectives. Such studies include Berbeito (2020) and Franco and Derbyshire (2020). Takien and Rajaeieh (2020) conducted a study on the relationship between health, peace and sustainable development in the middle east. The conclusion of their study was that 'lack of peace has direct and indirect impact on health, as well as health workers, the civil society, and the whole community who have in turn a critical role in creating peace. Strong and resilient health systems are essential in reaching out to citizens during war, while achieving SDGs would be impossible if SDG 16 is compromised. Health and peace are interchangeable and achieving either is impossible without the other' (23). Mickler and Wachira (2020) focused their research on the role of African Union's African Governance Architecture in peace-keeping operations to help achieve SDG16 on sustainable peace.

There are a variety of approaches in trying to understand the role of SDG16 in achieving sustainable peace, reduce conflicts and utilize digital media and technologies for peaceful coexistence. Such studies include fake news (Mensah, Awini and Mensah 2021), artificial intelligence driven technologies (Pigola et al., 2021), data ecosystem mapping in Bangladesh (Bhattacharya and Khan, 2016), public administration (Walsh et al., 2020), information poverty (Vargas and Lee, 2018) and digital government (Janowski (2016). With specific reference to the Palestinian crisis, which is the core subject of this chapter, researchers have explored the role of SDG16 in this ongoing conflict. These studies include Ballasiotes et al. (2019); Elyan and Al-Doulat (2021); Marian (2022) and Sabboubeh, Farrell and Osman (2019).

Media and conflict reporting of Africa

The African continent has been a major victim of conflict for ages. These conflicts were either self-inflicted or caused by foreign interference. Discussing conflicts in Africa and their causes has been explored by scholars both within the continent and outside. Such studies see constant conflicts in the continent as products of weak governance, poverty, inept leadership, ethnicity and creation of colonial boarders (Aremu, 2010), boarder issues, civil wars, change of government and cessation conflicts left by the colonialists (Bujra, 2002;Deng, 1996), civil strife (Annan, 2014), impact on refugees (Atim, 2013) and ethnic and identity politics (Ottoh, 2018).

As discussed by Yusha'u (2018) African countries are nations within nations. Several researchers have documented the role of the media in reporting conflict in the continent. Maweu and Mare (2021) have distinguished the role of the media in Africa in reporting conflict between good and bad journalism. Good journalism according to them is represented by peace journalism, while bad journalism is exemplified by war journalism. Wahutu (2018) conducted a study on the coverage of the Darfur crises in Kenyan, South African, Rwandan and Egyptian newspapers. The study found the dominance of ethnic frames in the reporting of the newspapers, of course with variations. The utilization of radio as a tool for propaganda to set Rwandans against each other was noteworthy.

Such studies about the role of the radio in Rwandan conflict include Barnett (2002) and Berry and Berry (1999). Gulseth (2004), who conducted an in-depth study on the role of RTLM, one of the leading radio stations that employed propaganda tactics in the Rwandan genocide, concluded that 'some of the techniques are clearly pure propaganda techniques, such as the use of negative name-calling of the other part in a conflict and the use of euphemisms when describing the activities of one's own group. In addition, this thesis has drawn upon a lot of literature that stresses the role of RTLM in promoting the Hutu Power ideology and inciting violence against the Tutsi.' (119).

Shaw (2007) studied the African media coverage of humanitarian interventions in Somalia, Ethiopia and Rwanda. What he found in the study is the domination of elite dominated frames.

In the last decade, the *Boko Haram* crisis is one of the major conflicts that received significant local, regional and international media attention. Several scholars have explored the nature of the reporting of this conflict by various media platforms in Nigeria and beyond. Osisanwo (2016) studied the linguistic discourse of the *Boko Haram* crisis in four Nigerian newspapers. Demarest, Godefroidt and Langer (2020) conducted a study on the news coverage of the *Boko Haram* crisis in Nigerian newspapers. However, their study focused on interviews with journalists where they tried to identify whether the northern and southern based news organizations link the *Boko Haram* crisis with religion, that is Islam, in when compared to the Western media. The study found similarity in the coverage in that the newspapers do not link the coverage with religion. They pointed out that

> By unravelling a predominantly war-oriented coverage of the *Boko Haram* insurgency in Nigerian newspapers, our findings corroborate the general patterns in conflict journalism outlined by the peace journalism framework. But, by highlighting important differences between Nigerian and Western media in the outgroup categorization of Muslims, we also drew attention to the dynamics of group categorization and its determinants. We suggested that a country's political-religious demography is an important explanatory factor for media outgroup categorization. Our findings on the representation of radical Islamist violence may hold for other countries where Muslims form a sizeable group in the population, including those on West-Africa's coastal line. (Demarest, Godefroidt and Langer 2020: 568)

An interesting theme that emerged from the literature reviewed in this section is the discussion on peace journalism in the media reporting of conflict in Africa. It shows that media scholars are paying attention to the role of the media in peace building or promoting peace through the power of journalism. This is important because the central theme of this chapter is identifying whether the reporting of Sheikh Jarrah conflict takes into consideration the tenets contained in SDG16, which in essence is about peace, justice and strong institutions.

Digital media coverage of conflict in Africa

Since the explosion of information and communication technologies, there has been transformation in the way news is reported by the news media. The emergence of the internet into the public domain in the 1990s has brought a major transformation in the way news is consumed. It created an avenue for newspapers and other forms of media to have an online presence. This presence has created a digital community that consumes news mainly through the internet. As such, news reporting of conflict in Africa receives more global prominence after the proliferation of the internet in both international media organizations and those within the continent.

According to Robert and Marchais (2018: 9–42):

> The use of social media and digital technologies has radically changed the way that information about violence is captured, reported, analysed and acted upon. People's use of social media played a significant role in the Egyptian revolution, post-election violence in Kenya, and drug-cartel violence in Mexico.

Ottosen and Mudhai (2009) have looked at the challenges of reporting conflict by the news media in Africa in the digital age. From their perspective digital tools such as blogs, websites and other digital platforms present an opportunity and a challenge. The challenges are the potential of the news media to be used as a tool for propaganda. It can easily be exploited to promote, ethnic, religious and sectional interests. In contrast to that is the potential to use the digital tools in promoting peace and societal coexistence.

The points made by Roberts and Marchais (2018) and Ottosen and Mudhai (2009) are pertinent in the recent reporting and interest in conflict in Africa. The Kenyan elections as discussed by Yusha'u (2018) and social media inspired violence such as End Sars in Nigeria have shown how the digital and social media could be utilized by the both citizens and governments to try and outdo each other in the scramble to influence public opinion.

As such several studies have researched how the news media in Africa reported violence in the African continent. Such studies include the impact of social media in post-election violence in Kenya (Mutarhi and Kimari, 2017), hate speech and citizen journalism in Kenya (Kimotho and Nyaga, 2016), digital media and conflict in the horn of Africa (Gagliardone and Stremlau, 2011), patterns of destruction in the reporting of the crises in Darfur and complexity in the digital reporting of terror advertisements in the *Boko Haram* crisis (Chukwu, Ani and Thobejane, 2021).

Digital media reporting of Sheikh Jarrah in African newspapers

The conflict in Sheikh Jarrah has attracted attention in different regions of the world. Before delving into an analysis of the Nigerian newspapers, this section of the chapter will provide a general survey of the reporting of the conflict in the digital version of newspapers in different African countries. This provides a window to the dominant themes/frames in reporting the conflict, looking specifically at the Nigerian newspapers. Do African newspapers take sides in the reporting of a conflict? Does the reporting embody the tenets of SDG16 on peace and justice?

The *Nation* newspaper in Kenya is one of the prominent English newspapers in the African continent. In its reporting on 18 May 2021, the online version of the paper published a story with the headline 'Kenya Labels Israel–Palestine Conflict "Dark

Moment", Calls for Truce' (*The Nation*, 2021). In the introduction of the story, the newspaper stated that 'Kenya has joined the United Nations Security Council (UNSC) in calling for diplomatic negotiations to achieve a solution to the escalating violence in Israel and Palestine.' It quoted Kenya's Permanent Representative to the United Nations calling for truce to avoid the possibility of making a two-state solution impossible. The dominant frames in the story were 'two state solution', 'illegal settlements', 'condemning violent rioting', 'deescalate the violence', 'return to peace mediation', 'Palestinian militant group', 'support a more peaceful future' and 'demilitarization of Gaza Strip', among others.

Although the report appears to be balanced on the surface, it also imports common assumption found in the Western news organizations by featuring Palestinians as the aggressors and Israel as a victim that responds to Palestinian militancy. For instance, the report stated that 'two Palestinian militant groups – Hamas and Palestinian Islamic Jihad – on May 10 fired rockets into Israel from the Gaza Strip, hitting multiple residences and a school', and then concluded that 'Israel retaliated with air strikes against Gaza, targeting multiple apartment buildings and a news office building'.

The *Mail & Guardian* of South Africa equally provided coverage of the story on Sheikh Jarrah. The digital version of the newspaper dedicated space to both sides of the conflict. One of the prominent pieces that emerged upon searching for the *Mail & Guardian* is the letter written by President Cyril Ramaphosa to fellow South Africans on the conflict. A few quotes from the letter provide a perspective on how the South African government, which until 1994 was suffering from apartheid through white minority rule, views the conflict. President Ramaphosa stated in the letter:

> Our experience with the democratic transition is a lesson about the power of empathy, negotiation and compromise. The escalating situation in Israel and Palestine affirms once more what we South Africans know too well, that intractable conflicts can only be solved through peaceful negotiation. It also demonstrates that unless the root causes of a conflict are addressed, in this case the illegal occupation by Israel of Palestinian land and the denial of the Palestinian people's right to self-determination, there will never be peace. (*Mail & Guardian*, 2021a: para 1–6)

After looking at the background on the escalation of the violence in Sheikh Jarrah, the then president Ramaphosa's letter focused on the need for peace.

> Far too many lives have been lost to this intractable conflict. The continued occupation of Palestinian land and the suffering of the Palestinian people is a blight on the conscience of humanity. As South Africa we are committed to being part of international efforts aimed at reviving a political process that will lead to the establishment of a viable Palestinian state existing side-by-side in peace with Israel, and within internationally recognised borders. The two-state solution remains the most viable option for the peoples of Israel and Palestine, and must continue to be supported. (*Mail & Guardian*, 2021a: para 1–6)

While the letter from President Ramophosa sounds more pro-Palestinian in content, with clear themes seeking peace and the implementation of a two-state solution, the newspaper also published an opinion piece with a contrasting perspective. An opinion article by a journalist called Paula Slier on 21 May 2021 with the title 'Media Coverage Fails to Provide the Facts' (*Mail & Guardian*, 2021b) suggested that 'the global loathing for Israel doesn't reflect the facts on the ground'. The opinion piece added: 'Recent events in the small East Jerusalem neighbourhood of Sheikh Jarrah that some claim sparked the latest round of violence, centre on a complicated property rights battle. In 1875, Jews bought land in the area but in 1948 they were expelled. A Palestinian population moved in. Surely this is a matter better left to the courts than world opinion to rule on?'

The two pieces published by the *Mail & Guardian* differ significantly from the story by the *Nation* in Kenya. This suggests the diversity of the coverage in the African continent. In the *Nation* newspaper there was no reference to Sheikh Jarrah as it is called in Arabic, while the *Mail & Guardian* made clear reference to Sheikh Jarrah. The two pieces by the *Mail & Guardian* depicted the two contrasting perspectives in the conflict, while the *Nation* seems to take the 'sitting on the fence' or the neutrality approach. Though these examples are inadequate to generalize the nature of the coverage, they highlight the diversity in the way the conflict was covered in the digital version of the newspapers. The two newspapers though converge in using frames that seek peace and a two-state solution.

The African continent is quite diverse in terms of regions, ethnic nationalities and media diversity. English newspapers with a strong interest in reporting the Palestinian conflict are not restricted to the Anglophone countries in Africa such as Nigeria, Kenya and even South Africa. *Al Ahram* newspaper is one of the English language newspapers that provides uninterrupted coverage of the conflict in Sheikh Jarrah. In the English website of the newspaper, english.ahram.org.eg, there were several news stories and opinion pieces dedicated to the coverage of the conflict in Sheikh Jarrah. So far, among the newspapers searched, *Al Ahram* has the highest number of stories among English online newspapers in Africa. This is understandable due to the role of Egypt in the Palestinian crisis and the sentiment among the readers of the English version of the newspaper globally. Yet its coverage also has some similarities with other African newspapers in the call for peace. From a story published on 20 May 2021, 'Biden's Call for Netanyahu to De-escalate Israel's Gaza Campaign Raises Questions' (*Al Ahram* 2021), the key themes that emerged include Biden calling for immediate 'significant de-escalation', 'Israel aggression on Gaza', the readiness of the United States to 'push for ending Israel's brutal use of force on Gaza', 'UN's resolution on ceasefire', 'France submitting a draft resolution', 'US turning a blind eye to Sheikh Jarrah evictions', 'Egypt and Western Governments taking diplomatic steps' and 'reviving peace process'.

What is clear from a snapshot of reports from the digital versions of the newspapers from Kenya, South Africa and Egypt is that themes about peace and resolution of the conflict in Sheikh Jarrah have featured in the stories. It is also clear that there is an absence of veiled reference to SDG16 on peace, justice and strong institutions, which the UN aims to achieve by 2030.

Methodology

This chapter employs a qualitative approach to studying the coverage of Sheikh Jarrah in the digital version of newspapers in the African continent with specific focus on newspapers from Nigeria. Nigeria was selected for this study for a number of reasons. The Nigerian media landscape is perhaps the most vibrant in the African continent. Nigeria has a population estimated to be around 200 million. The population of the country is complex and diverse which, as discussed by Yusha'u (2018), is reflected in the character of the Nigerian media. Conflicts in the Middle East generate a lot of interest in Nigeria partly because of the size of the Muslim population and because of the interest of Nigerian Christians in Jerusalem. Public discourse on the Middle East can generate hot debates in the media. The diversity of the Nigerian media would be crucial in understanding how the conflict is reported. It is noteworthy that in the last two decades Nigeria has witnessed the escalation of ethnic and religious crises in which the media has come under serious scrutiny for alleged bias or amplifying the conflict. These conflicts include the farmer/herder's conflict in which Nigerian media was accused of bias and amplifying the conflict. The *New African* published a piece on this in which it states

> Sadly, in virtue of the identity of the two groups, the debate has the propensity to escalate by exposing certain fault lines within Nigerian society. Herders are traditionally Muslim and of the Fulani ethnic group; who, in the circumstances of competing interests, may be seen as intrinsically opposed to middle-belt farmers who are Christian and not associated with the extreme north … indeed, it is worth considering that many of Nigeria's large media houses are based in the south, an area traditionally associated with Christianity. As such, Tayo argues that the herders are overwhelmingly portrayed as the engine of aggression in the conflict. (*New African*, 2018: para 12–14)

The Boko Haram conflict and periodic ethno-religious conflicts in various parts of Nigeria have attracted media scrutiny within and outside the country. But how does the Nigerian media report international conflicts, especially one from the Middle East where there is a religious fault line involved?

To address this, a search was conducted on Lexis-Nexis for Nigerian newspapers. The initial focus was on four newspapers to examine how they reported the Sheikh Jarrah conflict. The newspapers are *Daily Trust* located in Abuja with predominant Northern ownership, *Punch* from Southwestern Nigeria, *Guardian* located in Southwestern Nigeria but with ownership from the Niger-Delta or what is referred to as the South-South in the Nigeria media and *Premium Times*, located in Abuja with mixed editorial and structural ownership from northern and southern Nigeria and staffing that reflects the religious diversity of Nigeria to some extent. Despite the influence of their location, all the newspapers are national in terms of acceptance and reach. *Premium Times* is different though because it is purely digital, while the other three newspapers have both print and digital versions.

The timeline for the study is from 10– to 21 May 2021, when the story about Sheikh Jarrah broke to the time a ceasefire was negotiated. The entire content of the newspapers was retrieved from Lexis-Nexis by using the following search terms: Sheikh Jarrah, East Jerusalem, Jerusalem, Israeli-Palestinian Conflict and Israel-Gaza. This search yielded very little result, and therefore the search was modified to cover all Nigerian newspapers available via Lexis-Nexis – this produced slightly better results. The search for Jerusalem produced only thirty-one stories, which was the highest compared to other search terms. This necessitated a modification of the approach to focus mainly on the newspapers that reported the conflict online. Despite the global interest in the Sheikh Jarrah conflict, it seems it didn't generate as much coverage in the digital versions of Nigerian newspapers as the researcher envisaged.

The analysis therefore focused on the newspapers that appeared using the stated search terms on Lexis-Nexis. The newspapers are: *Premium Times, ionigeria, News Chronicle, Nigerian Tribune, the Nation* and *PM News*. The analysis will focus on the headlines with few extracts from the text. The analysis will be conducted using framing analysis.

Framing refers to exclusion or inclusion of words and phrases in the news. Through the selection of words certain aspects are made more prominent than others. The way stories are framed can give a clue on the editorial direction and the ideology of the news media. According to Vreese et al. (2001: 108) 'the central dimension of a frame seems to be the selection, organisation, and emphasis of certain aspects of reality, to the exclusion of others'"

> Bateson introduced the notion of frame in 1955 to explain how individuals exchange signals that allow them to agree upon the level of abstraction at which any message is intended. The term frame is associated most often with the anthropological/sociological orientation of Hymes, Goffman, and Frake, and with the artificial intelligence research of Minsky. Their use of the term stems from Bateson. (Tannen, 1993: 15)

Framing analysis is also a way of selecting and ignoring some aspects of a report. The selected aspect is given enough prominence and is well promoted while the ignored one is left to gradually wither away. The frames are used to justify a given political approach or ideology via the news medium. This can be achieved by choosing specific words to describe issues and events so that a given world view can be established in the mind of the audience.

One of the advantages of framing analysis is that it provides a theoretical platform for scrutinizing media messages (Dimitrova and Lee, 2009).

Reporting Sheikh Jarrah in Nigerian newspapers

Based on the results from the search on Lexis-Nexis, three major frames emerged from the headlines of online newspapers in Nigeria on the Sheikh Jarrah conflict in 2021. The frames are violence frame, peace frame and humanitarian frame. The violence frame refers to stories that focus on the clashes or similar actions demonstrating power in the conflict. The peace frame refers to the frames that seek resolution of the conflict or point towards ceasefire. The humanitarian frame refers to the casualties or victims of the clashes. There could be some similarities or overlap in some of the frames, but the one that is closest to the theme of the frame is selected for discussion.

Violence frame

The *Nigerian Tribune* is one of the oldest surviving traditional newspapers in Nigeria with both print and online versions. In its headline of 10 May 2021, the newspaper reported a story with the headline 'Hundreds Injured in Renewed Fighting at Jerusalem's Al-Aqsa Mosque'. The newspaper stated in the story that 'some Palestinian families in Sheikh Jarrah facing eviction from their homes by Israeli authorities further heighten tensions'. The text of the story tried to show some balance by providing perspectives from both sides of the conflict. The story adds that 'In an effort to minimize violence, Israeli authorities have banned parades by Jewish groups through the Old City and to the Temple Mount'. And then it quoted a Palestinian official for a perspective on Sheikh Jarrah. 'Hussein al-Sheikh, the advisor to Palestinian president Mahmoud Abbas, criticized the "storming" of the Temple Mount by Israeli police officers and said the Palestinian leadership was keeping all options open for its response.'

Another newspaper from Nigeria that paid attention to the reporting of the Sheikh Jarrah conflict is *PM News*, an online newspaper. In its headline of May 13 2021, it captioned a story: 'Hamas Hammers Jerusalem, Tel Aviv with 1,500 Rockets'.

Other headlines that focused on violence in the reporting of the conflict in Sheikh Jarrah were:

'Israel Intensifies Attacks in Gaza as Conflict Enters Fifth Day' *ionigeria*, 14 May 2021;
'Israel-Gaza Violence: Senior Hamas Commander Killed in Airstrike' *ionigeria* 12 May 2021;
'World Reacts as Violence Escalates in Israel-Gaza Conflict' *Premium Times*, 12 May 2021;
'Israeli Air Strikes Kill Over 200 People in Gaza, US Newspaper Reports' *News Chronicle* (Nigeria), 19 May 2021;
'31 Dead as Israel, Hamas Fight Again' *PM News*, 11 May 2021;
'Updated: Israel Kills 16 Hamas Leaders, Gaza Death Toll Hits 56' *PM News*, 12 May 2021.

An important point to note in the headlines is that stories on violence in the online newspapers were reported between 10 May 2021 and 14 May 2021. In this case it suggests that the pattern of reporting was influenced by the clashes between the Israeli military and the Palestinians in Sheikh Jarrah. Although it doesn't mean that there were no other frames in those days, there were more stories about the conflict at the beginning when the clashes were in top gear compared to the days that followed when ceasefire was being considered.

Paying attention to stories about violence in newspapers is common because it attracts the attention of the reader. Studies on newsworthiness such as Harcup & O'Neill (2001, 2017) have thoroughly discussed the criteria for news selection.

Peace frame

The peace frame is very important for this chapter in that it fits perfectly with the themes of SDG16 on peace and strong institutions. The headlines under the peace frame combined news stories and some opinion pieces. For instance, the first headline in this section, 'Why Peace Loving Nations Must Join Hands To Liberate Palestine', was a by columnist, Murtadha Gusau, in the *Premium Times* Newspaper of 14 May 2021.

The opinion piece by Mr Gusau went on to provide some context to the Palestinian conflict by stating that 'until 1948, Palestine typically referred to the geographic region located between the Mediterranean Sea and the Jordan River. Arab people who call this territory home have been known as Palestinians since the early 20th century. Much of this land is now considered present-day Israel. Today, Palestine theoretically includes the West Bank (a territory that sits between modern-day Israel and Jordan) and the Gaza Strip (which borders modern-day Israel and Egypt). However, control over this region is a complex and evolving situation. There is no international consensus concerning the borders, and many areas claimed by Palestinians have been forcefully occupied by Israelis for years.' Other headlines focused more on the effort for ceasefire by fellow Arab countries. For instance, on 12 May 2021, *PM News* reported that 'Iraq Sues for Peace between Israel–Palestine'. The *Nation* newspaper also focused on the de-escalation of the conflict in its headline of 13 May 2021. The newspaper reported that 'De-escalation "An Absolute Must" in Israel–Palestine Conflict – UN Chief'. The *News Chronicle* reported on the diplomatic effort for ceasefire with a headline 'Israel–Gaza Conflict: US President, Joe Biden Calls for Ceasefire' (18 May 2021).

For quite some time communication scholars such as Galtung (2003) have strongly advocated for the use of peace frames in reporting. Although the stories with peace frames were less than those with violence frame, at least there was an attempt to capture the Sheikh Jarrah story from a peace perspective.

Humanitarian frame

Every conflict that involves clashes, especially a delicate one like the Israeli-Palestinian conflict, is likely to create a humanitarian situation. This is exactly the case with the conflict in Sheikh Jarrah. The digital versions of Nigerian newspapers have reflected that in their reporting. This can be seen from the following headlines.

'UN Chief Says Mounting Death Toll Unacceptable as Scores of Women, Children Killed in Palestine–Israel Conflict' *News Chronicle*, 14 May 2021;
'UN Agencies Scale-Up Activities to Avert Humanitarian Nightmare in Gaza' *News Chronicle*, 21 May 2021;

'Quibbling Over Cruelties: Human Rights Watch, Israel and Apartheid' *News Chronicle*, 10 May 2021;
'Ten Family Members Killed in Israeli Airstrike on Gaza' *ionigeria*, 15 May 2021.

It was quite interesting that the stories on the humanitarian frame were captured from the international angle focusing on UN and human rights organizations. This could be due to the heavy reliance on foreign news agencies because Nigerian newspapers do not have reporters on ground to report the conflict. It could also mean the absence of an effort to report the humanitarian angle using local sources. Nigeria has participated in several peacekeeping missions in Africa, Europe and the Middle East. Getting sources to provide perspective on the situation in Gaza from local perspective could have brought the story closer to the comprehension of Nigerian readers.

Conclusion

This chapter has shown the complexity in the reporting of international conflicts by local newspapers. The Sheikh Jarrah conflict has certainly attracted attention in different parts of the world, but based on this research, it shows that the story deserves more coverage from the media in the African continent at least in the digital version of the newspapers.

The African continent has undergone and continues to face challenges about insecurity and ethnic and religious crises. Perhaps these crises, for instance, the persistence of Boko Haram and the bandits' challenges, have occupied the attention of the Nigerian media; as a result conflicts from other regions do not receive the attention they deserve.

In addition, countries like South Africa have experienced apartheid similar to what Palestinians are facing in the hands of Israel. When South Africa was facing apartheid, there was strong solidarity from every part of the world. The media in the South–South or developing countries gave strong prominence to stories about the challenges faced by South Africans. The letter from President Ramophosa quoted earlier in this chapter is a testimony to that. Has the interest in the Israeli-Palestinian conflict waned overtime, or are the challenges that African countries are facing becoming more severe to the extent that there is less coverage of the conflict in individual news platforms than expected?

In the coverage of the conflict studied in this chapter, there is clear evidence that the reporting on peace, resolution and ceasefire are themes that resonate with SDG16 on peace and justice. There is no single story that made reference to SDG16 in the reporting of the Sheikh Jarrah conflict. Why is this important? It is important because, 2030 is very much around the corner, will the international community claim to be making progress in achieving global peace if the Israeli-Palestinian conflict is not resolved? White (2016) might be right in asking the question whether achieving SDG16 is asking for achieving the impossible.

References

Al Ahram (2021), 'Biden's Call for Netanyahu to De-escalate Israel's Gaza Campaign Raises Questions', https://english.ahram.org.eg/NewsContent/2/8/411499/World/Region/Biden's-call-for-Netanyahu-to-deescalate-Israel's-.aspx (accessed 19 February 2022).

Annan, N. (2014), 'Violent Conflicts and Civil Strife in West Africa: Causes, Challenges and Prospects', *Stability: International Journal of Security and Development*, 3(1): 1–16.

Aremu, J. Johnson Olaosebikan (2010), 'Conflicts in Africa: Meaning, Causes, Impact and Solution', *African Research Review*, 4 (4): 549–60.

Atim, G. (2013), 'The Impact of Refugees on Conflicts in Africa', *IOSR Journal of Humanities and Social Science*, 14(2): 4–9.

Ballasiotes, A. D.,J. Van Den Hoek, H. Friedrich, P. Murillo-Sandoval and B. Roberts-Pierel (2019), 'Earth Observations to Assess SDG 16: Monitoring Terrestrial and Coastal Signals of Conflict in Gaza via Satellite Imagery'. In *AGU Fall Meeting Abstracts* (Vol. 2019), IN51C-09).

Barnett, Michael (2002), *Eyewitness to a Genocide: The United Nations and Rwanda*, Ithaca, NY: Cornell University Press.

Berbeito, Cecile (2020), 'Conflict Matters. Peace and Conflict Education Practices towards SDG16', *Revista Internacional de Educación para la Justicia Social (RIEJS)*, 8(1): 181–200.

Berry, J. and C. Berry (eds) (1999), *Genocide in Rwanda: A Collective Memory*, Washington DC: Howard University Press.

Bhattacharya, Debapriya, and Towfiqul Islam Khan (2016), 'Data Ecosystem Mapping in the Context of SDG 16 in Bangladesh', Centre for Policy Dialogue Bangladesh, file:///C:/Users/320170/Downloads/Bangladesh%20-%20Data%20Ecosystem%20Mapping%20Country%20Report.pdf (accessed 15 February 2022).

Bujra, Abdalla (2002), *African Conflicts: Their Causes and Their Political and Social Environment*, Addis Ababa: Development Policy Management Forum, https://repository.uneca.org/handle/10855/10432 (accessed 15 February 2022).

Chukwu, J. N., K. J. Ani and T. D. Thobejane (2021), 'Digital Media Reportage and the Boko Haram Insurgency in Nigeria', *African Journal of Development Studies (formerly AFFRIKA Journal of Politics, Economics and Society)*, 2021(si2): 197–208.

Demarest, L., A. Godefroidt and A. Langer (2020), 'Understanding News Coverage of Religious-Based Violence: Empirical and Theoretical Insights from Media Representations of Boko Haram in Nigeria', *Journal of Communication*, 70 (4): 548–73.

Deng F. M. (1996), 'Anatomy of Conflicts in Africa'. In L. van de Goor, K. Rupesinghe and P. Sciarone (eds), *Between Development and Destruction,* London: Palgrave Macmillan, https://doi.org/10.1007/978-1-349-24794-3_11.

Dimitrova, D. V., and K. S. Lee (2009), 'Framing Saddam's Execution in the US Press', *Journalism Studies*, 10(4): 536–50.

Elyan, Rabiha, and Adnan Al-Doulat (2021), 'Evaluating the Content of Palestinian Curricula in Light of the Sustainable Development Goals 2030', *Journal of Multi Disciplinary Evaluation*, 17(41): 1–22.

Franco I. B., and E. Derbyshire (2020), 'SDG 16 Peace, Justice and Strong Institutions'. In I. Franco, T. Chatterji, E. Derbyshire and J. Tracey (eds), *Actioning the Global Goals for Local Impact. Science for Sustainable Societies*, Singapore: Springer, https://doi.org/10.1007/978-981-32-9927-6_17.

Gagliardone, I., and N. Stremlau (2011), *Digital Media, Conflict and Diasporas in the Horn of Africa*, New York: Open Society Foundations.

Gulseth, H. L. (2004), 'The Use of Propaganda in the Rwandan Genocide: A Study of Radio-Télévision Libre des Mille Collines (RTLM)', Master's Thesis, University of Oslo.

Harcup, T., and D. O'neill (2001), 'What Is News? Galtung and Ruge Revisited', *Journalism Studies*, 2(2): 261–80.

Harcup, T., and D. O'neill (2017), 'What Is News? News Values Revisited (Again)', *Journalism Studies*, 18(12): 1470–88.

Kimotho, S. G., and R. N. Nyaga (2016), 'Digitized Ethnic Hate Speech: Understanding Effects of Digital Media Hate Speech on Citizen Journalism in Kenya', *Advances in Language and Literary Studies*, 7(3): 189–200.

Liebmann, Marian (2022), 'Faith in the United Nations and Arts Approaches to Conflict Prevention and Resolution'. In Slawomir Redo (ed.), *The Rule of Law in Retreat: Challenges to Justice in the United Nations World* (2022), 323, London: Lexington Books.

Mail & Guardian (2021), 'Ramaphosa's Letter on the Israel–Palestine Conflict', https://mg.co.za/news/2021-05-17-ramaphosas-letter-on-the-palestine-israel-conflict/ (accessed 19 February 2022).

Mail & Guardian (2021b), 'Media Coverage Fails to Provide the Facts', https://mg.co.za/opinion/2021-05-21-media-coverage-fails-to-provide-the-facts/ (accessed 19 February 2022).

Maweu, J., and A. Mare (eds) (2021), *Media, Conflict and Peacebuilding in Africa: Conceptual and Empirical Considerations*, London: Routledge.

Mensah K., G. Awini and G. K. Mensah (2021), 'Fake News and SDG16: The Situation in Ghana'. In M. J. Yusha'u and J. Servaes (eds), *The Palgrave Handbook of International Communication and Sustainable Development*, Cham: Palgrave Macmillan, https://doi.org/10.1007/978-3-030-69770-9_15.

Mickler, D., and G. M. Wachira (2020), 'The AU's African Governance Architecture and SDG 16: Examining Intersections'. In M. Ramutsindela and D. Mickler (eds), *Africa and the Sustainable Development Goals*. Sustainable Development Goals Series, Cham: Springer, https://doi.org/10.1007/978-3-030-14857-7_5.

Mutahi, P., and B. Kimari (2017), *The Impact of Social Media and Digital Technology on Electoral Violence in Kenya*, United Kingdom: IDS.

New African (2018), 'Is the Media Fueling Herder vs Farmer Clashes?', https://newafricanmagazine.com/17208/ (accessed 20 February 2022).

Olayide, Olawale, Volker Mauerhofer and Pontus Cerin (2017), 'Sustainable Development Goals and Sustainable Peace', *ISDRS Newsletter*, Issue 3, https://www.researchgate.net/publication/336265903_Sustainable_Development_Goals_and_Sustainable_Peace (accessed 10 February 2022).

Osisanwo, A. (2016), 'Discursive Representation of Boko Haram Terrorism in Selected Nigerian Newspapers', *Discourse & Communication*, 10 (4): 341–62.

Ottoh F. O. (2018), 'Ethnic Identity and Conflicts in Africa'. In S. Oloruntoba and T. Falola (eds), *The Palgrave Handbook of African Politics, Governance and Development*, New York: Palgrave Macmillan, https://doi.org/10.1057/978-1-349-95232-8_20.

Ottosen, R., and O. F. Mudhai (2009), 'Conflict Coverage in a Digital Age: Challenges for African Media'. In O. F. Mudhai, J. T. Wisdom and F. Banda (eds), *African Media and the Digital Public Sphere*, New York: Palgrave Macmillan, 239–53.

Pigola A., P. R. da Costa, L. C. Carvalho, L. Fd. Silva, C. T. Kniess and E. A. Maccari (2021), 'Artificial Intelligence-Driven Digital Technologies to the Implementation of the Sustainable Development Goals: A Perspective from Brazil and Portugal', *Sustainability*, 13(24): 1–28, https://doi.org/10.3390/su132413669.

Roberts, T., and G. Marchais (2018), 'Assessing the Role of Social Media and Digital Technology in Violence Reporting', *Contemporary Readings in Law & Social Justice*, 10(2): 9–42.

Sabboubeh, Heba, Peter Farrell and Osman Yassin (2019), 'Establishing Sustainable Construction in War Zones; Palestine as a Case Study', 14th International Postgraduate Research Conference 2019: Contemporary and Future Directions in the Built Environment, University of Salford. 16–17 December 2019.

Shaw, I. S. (2007), 'Historical Frames and the Politics of Humanitarian Intervention: From Ethiopia, Somalia to Rwanda', *Globalisation, Societies and Education*, 5(3): 351–71.

Takian, A., and G. Rajaeieh (2020), 'Peace, Health, and Sustainable Development in the Middle East', *Archives of Iranian Medicine*, 23(4Suppl1): S23–S26, https://doi.org/10.34172/aim.2020.s5.

Tannen, D. (1993), 'What's in a Frame? Surface Evidence for Underlying Expectations'. In D. Tannen (ed.), *Framing in Discourse*, Oxford: Oxford University Press.

The Nation (2021), 'Kenya Labels Israel–Palestine Conflict "Dark Moment", Calls for Truce', https://allafrica.com/stories/202105170160.html (accessed 19 February 2022).

UN (2021), 'Goal 16: Promote Justice, Peace and Inclusive Societies', https://www.inf oplease.com/history/us/major-military-operations-since-world-war-ii (accessed 13 February 2022).

UN SDGs (2021), 'The Global Goals for Sustainable Development', https://www.globalgo als.org/16-peace-justice-and-strong-institutions (accessed 13 February 2022).

Vargas, Lorezo, and Philip Lee (2018), 'Addressing Communication and Information Poverty in the Context of the Sustainable Development Goals (SDGS)', *Journal of Latin American Communication Research*, 6 (1–2).

Vreese De, C., J. Peter and A. Holli Semetko (2001), 'Framing Politics at the Launch of Euro: A Cross-National Comparative Study of Frames in the News', *Political Communication*, 18 (2): 107–22.

Wahutu, J. S. (2018), 'Representations of Africa in African Media: The Case of the Darfur Violence', *African Affairs*, 117(466): 44–61.

Walsh, Grace Sheila, Adegboyega Ojo, Fatemeh Ahmadi Zeleti, and Emer Mulligan (2020), 'Generating SDG-Related Public Value – A Systematic Review on the Use of Emerging Digital Technologies in Public Administration', https://ssrn.com/abstr act=3927083 (accessed 20 February 2022).

White, A. (2016), 'SDG16: Achieving the Impossible. Govnet Background Paper No. 22', https://www.seedsrenewables.com/wp-content/uploads/attachments/Achieving%20 the%20Impossible%20can%20we%20be%20SDG16%20believers.pdf (accessed 20 February 2022).

Yusha'u, M. J. (2018), *Regional Parallelism and Corruption Scandals in Nigeria: Intranational Approaches to African Media Systems*, Cham: Springer.

6

Reporting the Sheikh Jarrah evictions on TRT World's Twitter account

Yusuf Devran

Introduction

This study analyses the content of TRT World's Twitter account between 14 and 20 May 2021 regarding the coverage of Israeli invasion of Sheikh Jarrah area (in Jerusalem) and the military offensive on Gaza. TRT World is a Turkish based satellite television channel. This study will only focus on the analysis of the Twitter account of the channel during the coverage of the Israeli onslaught. The foundation of TRT World, which broadcasts in English, is a reflection of the development that Turkey has made in global broadcasting. The channel reflects the approach and perspective of the Turkish state. Since its launch in October 2015, TRT World has been covering events in the region from an impartial perspective based on the philosophy of collective responsibility to attract the attention of a global audience.

In this chapter, TRT World's Twitter content was analysed following a Critical Discourse Analysis framework as suggested by Teun van Dijk (van Dijk, 1998: 21–45), namely, at the micro level, within the framework of basic criteria such as words, sentence structures, cause and effect relations, news sources, expert opinions, background information and rhetorical dimensions. Discourse is defined as the use of language to convey meanings, where language is central in the formation of power and maintaining hegemony (Matheson, 2005: 6). Discourse also explains the purpose, intention, ideology and power of the person who utters and reveals how he or she positions the 'other'. Every discourse is a construction of reality and therefore there are realities corresponding to discourses (Sözen, 1999: 12). One may argue that the realities built with discourses can be destroyed by reversing the existing discourses and thus a new discursive reality can be built. Since discourse constructs the meaning of the external world, the meaning cannot remain fixed and unchangeable due to the radical changes in language. Therefore, the 'discursive struggle' is extremely important as suggested by Jorgensen and Phillips (2002: 1–6).

In light of this, the main issue this chapter addresses is that despite Israel's step-by-step occupation of Palestine since 1948, it maintains its policies with discursive superiority and ensures that the worldwide public opinion remains silent about what is taking place. The main claim of this study therefore is that due to the broadcasts and messages shared by TRT World and similar media organizations on the events of May 2021, the discursive supremacy of the Israeli government was challenged on a global scale. As a result, many anti-Israel protests broke out in different countries. The US administration itself, which has always protected Israel, faced effective public pressure for the first time.

TRT World as a voice for Palestine

Between 14 and 20 May 2021, TRT World allocated its television channel and social media platforms' content primarily to reporting on the events that took place in Sheikh Jarrah. While conveying the dramatic events in Palestine to the global public in detail, it also covered the statements, meetings and reactions from around the world on the subject. Furthermore, it was observed that a common broadcasting policy and coordination were followed by different TRT TV channels and platforms. For example, news that was broadcast on television was also uploaded on internet news portals, and this content was also shared on Twitter in the form of short sentences with embedded links. Although the Israeli government attempted to silence journalists by bombing the media buildings in Gaza, media houses such as TRT World conveyed their updates in all possible formats: written, verbal and visual news. The channel also managed to draw the attention of the world to the attacks, massacre and occupation in Palestine by providing live broadcasting from the region.

The Palestinian administration managed to have their voices heard through TRT World while being denied access by many other global media outlets. This includes Palestinian officials such as President Abbas, the Minister of Foreign Affairs Riyad Malik, the minister of health and Khaled Mashal from Hamas. In particular, the 'death toll' list announced daily by the Ministry of Health was constantly shared in the news.

The call by the Palestinian foreign minister to the UN Security Council was shared with the following summary sentence: 'Israel is committing "war crimes" with its indiscriminate bombing of civilian areas in blocked Gaza, says Palestinian FM Riyad al Maliki and calls on UNSC to impose sanctions and arms embargo on Tel Aviv' (TRT World, 2021c). President Mahmoud Abbas also emphasized in his statements that Israel systematically commits state terrorism and that the international community should hold Israel accountable.

Between 14 and 20 May 2021, a total of 366 posts regarding Sheikh Jarrah and the events in Gaza were posted on TRT World's Twitter account. This number corresponds to an average of 52 posts per day. This shows the importance TRT World gave to the subject. The subjects mentioned in these posts were as follows: Israel's attacks, the political reasons for these attacks, the pressures on media, the historical background of the issue, the massacres and the women, children and other civilians who lost their lives and the various reactions of the leaders of different countries, international organizations, foreign artists, academics and politicians.

Israel perceived as 'aggressive' and 'occupying' state

Most of the posts published on TRT World's Twitter account were related to Israel's attacks. In these posts, Israel was described as a 'brutal aggressor', 'occupier', 'torturer' as well as a 'rogue state' that kills Palestinians without discrimination between civilians, women, men, children or the elderly. In various instances, Israeli Army was also described as destroying houses with air bombardments, killing journalists without hesitation to hide their aggression from the world (TRT World, 2021d,e,f).

In addition, Israel, which was reported to carry out an 'ethnic cleansing' and 'massacre' of Palestinians in the region, was also labelled as a state that evicted the Palestinians from their homes and settled the Zionist migrants instead. For this purpose, words such as 'ethnic, religious and cultural cleansing', 'massacre' and 'genocide' were frequently used in the news. These adjectives and descriptions are expressions used by the president of the Republic of Turkey, the Pakistani administration and other global leaders, as well as the Palestinians. In his speeches, Erdoğan describes Israel as a country that carries out religious, cultural and ethnic cleansing. He states that Israel has always been an aggressive occupier state, not only today but throughout history. For instance, 'Turkey's Erdoğan calls on Pope Francis to keep denouncing Israeli violence in Gaza, saying Tel Aviv is carrying out "ethnic, religious and cultural cleansing" of blockaded Palestinians' (TRT World, 2021g). Pakistani officials, meanwhile, objected to the description of the events as a conflict, and emphasized that what happened was a massacre perpetrated by Israel: 'Pakistan is averse to calling Israeli aggression on Palestine a "conflict", says it's a "massacre" committed by Israeli occupation forces' (TRT World, 2021h). During the march in support of Palestine in Buenos Aires, the demonstrators chanted 'no to the Palestine genocide' (TRT World, 2021i).

Palestine, on the other hand, was defined by TRT World as a country that is occupied, oppressed, continually bombarded, turned into an open-air prison and trying to respond to the attacks against it with the scarce means at its disposal (TRT World, 2021j). Thus, the Palestinian response to Israel is represented as perfectly legitimate. In TRT World's discourses, the subject has been definitively emphasized, whether the sentence structures are active or passive. For example, 'Israeli warplanes destroy Mushtaha Tower in besieged Gaza hours after destroying a 12-storey building housing several media outlets' (TRT World, 2021k). This is an active sentence in which the subject is at the beginning. In passive sentences on the same issue, the subject was aimed to be disclosed by using the phrase 'by Israel'. For example, 'More than 5,700 Palestinians have been killed by Israelis since 2008, including more than 110 in Gaza since Monday' (TRT World, 2021l). When TRT World's posts were examined, it was found that active sentences about Israel's attacks were generally preferred.

Suffering of Palestinian victims emphasized

In TRT World posts, the Palestinians who were rescued hours later from the wreckage of buildings, or destroyed by bombings, were especially featured, and the dimensions of the brutality, massacre and destruction by Israel were emphasized: 'In pictures: Gaza girl survives Israeli attack that shattered her family and home. Suzy Eshkuntana, 6, was pulled from the rubble of a building in Gaza City after remaining trapped for seven hours under the debris' (TRT World, 2021m).

In its social media posts, TRT World pointed out the brutality of Israel especially by emphasizing the victims – innocent and defenceless people including pregnant women, children and the elderly. Thus, by raising the emotions of its social media followers, TRT World tried to make them pay more attention to the issue and act accordingly. For example, 'Six-year-old Suzy Eshkuntana wakes up alone in Gaza's largest hospital after surviving an Israeli air strike that destroyed her home and killed her mother and all four of her siblings' (TRT World, 2021n).

Photographs and video footage documenting the loss of lives among Palestinians highlight the brutality of the bombardments. With these images, the extent of the ruthlessness of the war is presented to the reader in detail. Due to these photographs, the possibility of denying the massacre committed by the Israeli side was made impossible. Riyadh, a Palestinian whose house was destroyed, expressed his desperation by saying, 'My children were trapped under the rubble, crying for me to help them, but I was also buried … They were crying: Dad, Dad. But I couldn't do anything to help them, I was stuck. Four of my children and my wife have been killed' (TRT World, 2021o). These images not only shocked Muslims but any individual with conscience and compassion living anywhere in the world. It paved the way for huge demonstrations even in Western capitals.

It was pointed out that in addition to killing children, the war also badly affected the surviving Palestinian children psychologically. Five-months-old Omar Hadid survived the destruction of buildings in the attacks and became the clearest evidence of Israeli brutality. In another video, a child said, 'I'm scared that we are all going to die' (TRT World, 2021p), while another girl in tears expressed her fear by saying that their house would be destroyed and they would die. Furthermore, on TRT World's Twitter account, stories about how some children rescued their toys from the ruins of their homes were also published.

The use of violence by Israeli soldiers against Palestinian women in Sheikh Jarrah also attracted the attention of the public. In its posts, TRT World has always shown and emphasized that the morale and self-confidence of the Palestinians is very high despite all the destruction. Videos of women and children who emerged from the ruins of bombed houses and made a victory sign were frequently shared. Those who read and see these posts can easily comprehend that under no circumstances will the Palestinians bow and submit to Israel, especially the youngsters. In addition, the smile of a young girl who was handcuffed while looking at her friends infuriated the Israeli soldiers. The young Palestinian girl said later that she was not afraid of Israeli soldiers because she was doing the right thing. These images had reached world media and received much more appreciation. Due to international pressure, Israel had to release the Palestinian girl shortly after (TRT World, 2021r).

On the other hand, TRT World also reported on angry Israeli citizens who were disturbed by the heartbreaking events and aggression of Israeli soldiers. For example: 'Few Israeli citizens are resisting the mandatory military draft due to Israel's abuses against Palestinians and its current bombardment of besieged Gaza' (TRT World, 2021s). Through these posts, it was pointed out that the Israeli public was not behind its government as a whole.

Exposure of Israeli propaganda and media bias

During May 2021, Israeli prime minister Benjamin Netanyahu consistently spoke about Israel's right to protect itself, claiming that they would continue their operations in Palestine. Producing arguments in his own way to expel the Palestinians from their homes, Netanyahu tried to spread this narrative by producing videos with the title 'Share the truth'. TRT World released these videos, stating that 'Israel's PM Netanyahu released a propaganda video asking people to "share the truth". Here's the Israeli-inflicted truth from Palestine' (TRT World, 2021t). This drew attention to how Israel distorted the facts. In the posts, it was stated that these video messages were just propaganda, and it was also pointed out that Netanyahu constantly lied; Netanyahu was promising to protect civilians in Gaza, while at the same time massacring women, children and the elderly with bombardments.

In TRT World's tweets, it was also stated that the main reason for Netanyahu's attack on Gaza was to make the Israeli public believe that the Palestinians continue to act as a threat to their national security, and that only Netanyahu can fight them. Thus, it has been widely indicated with the following post that he assumes he will gain the support of the voters in the upcoming elections: 'Is Netanyahu trying to gain political capital by bombing Palestinians in Gaza?'(TRT World, 2021v). In other words, TRT World reveals how the problem is orchestrated for the benefit of Israel's internal politics.

The Israeli government has also heavily used social media and internet facilities for their political propaganda. For instance, on an official account, the government shared some verses of the Qur'an with an image of Gaza, in order to justify the bombing of Gaza. TRT World, on the other hand, reflected the public's anger towards this misuse of the Qur'an by tweeting: 'People reacted angrily to a post by Israel's official Arabic language Twitter account that used verses from the Qur'an to justify its bombing of Gaza' (TRT World, 2021y). Also, in order to justify its attacks, the Israeli administration claimed that the Palestinians fired missiles at them and attacked the citizens of Israel. TRT World shared the incident, in which a Palestinian person stabbed an Israeli in the back, with the following sentences: 'Israeli forces have shot dead a young Palestinian man, Mohammed Rawhy Hammad, in north Ramallah, alleging he attempted to stab a soldier. Hammad is the fourth Palestinian killed by Israelis in occupied West Bank since Monday' (TRT World, 2021z). In the posts, the phrase 'Israel claimed' was used to indicate that this information was doubtful. Furthermore, TRT World has constantly tried to refute Israel's unrealistic claims through its content. It was also stated that the Israeli side had launched the attacks first, and that the Palestinians tried to respond to them from time to time, legitimizing the Palestinians' struggle to protect their land.

The Israeli army bombed the media tower in Gaza, which hosted Al-Jazeera studios and the Associated Press news agency, and tried to arrest journalists and confiscate their equipment by force in order to prevent news about the attacks and massacres.

TRT World shared these events in detail on its social media platforms. Additionally, it reported the statements made by journalists whose office buildings were destroyed and made their voices heard throughout the world.

Netanyahu said that the building in Gaza, in which Al-Jazeera and the AP offices were located, was a legitimate target. By sharing these video messages, TRT World clearly revealed Netanyahu's aggression, denial of rights and law and unlawful attitude towards media freedom. In the posts about Israel's bombing of media buildings, the word 'flatten' is used to indicate that the buildings were completely destroyed. For example, 'Israeli air strike flattens high-rise building housing AP offices and other media organizations in Gaza' (TRT World, 2021a1). The expression 'other' in the sentence also refers to all other media outlets. Therefore, it is stated that Israel is targeting and trying to destroy all media institutions operating in Gaza.

The following statement by an Al-Jazeera official to TRT World was also shared on Twitter to highlight Israel's desperation: 'Israel gave journalists just a few minutes as they abandoned their "memories and equipment" before Israeli army reduced the entire building into mangled heap of concrete, glass and iron' (TRT World, 2021a2). It similarly reported on the statement of the chairman of the AP: 'The world will know less about what is happening in Gaza because of what happened today' (TRT World, 2021a3), and TRT General Manager İbrahim Eren's statement: 'We are ready to support our colleagues in Gaza in any way possible' (TRT World, 2021a4).

Israeli soldiers also continuously attacked journalists in order to prevent news about the massacres and subsequent events from being covered in the media. TRT World has shared many written and visual posts in this regard. For instance, 'This is how Israeli forces attacked photojournalist Latifa Abd al Latif while she was covering protests at Damascus Gate' (TRT World, 2021a5). In addition, TRT World has included the statements of the employees of different media institutions about how Israel is committing atrocities. For example, 'Talk show hosts are calling out Israel's brutal attacks against Palestinians. Here is what John Oliver and Trevor Noah said' (TRT World, 2021a6).

Israeli forces did not hesitate to silence journalists with armed and bomb attacks. For example, this post regarding Muhammad Dahlan was shared: 'Anadolu Agency photojournalist Mohammad Dahlan sustained shrapnel injuries to his leg from an Israeli missile attack on Gaza' (TRT World, 2021a7). Additionally, the following message shows how Israeli soldiers mistreated journalists: 'Israeli police were filmed pushing CNN correspondent Ben Wedeman and his crew. Sky News correspondent Mark Stone shared this video on Twitter, saying it "happened to us all this week"' (TRT World, 2021a8).

Erdoğan's political manoeuvres and their global impact

Since the beginning of the Sheikh Jarrah events, the president of the Republic of Turkey, Recep Tayyip Erdoğan, took the initiative and discussed the Israel–Palestine issue with world leaders, seeking to join forces in isolating Israel and pressuring it to stop its attacks immediately. In TRT World's Twitter posts, it was stated that

Erdoğan urges world leaders to take action. This discourse reveals how determined he is, and also points to Erdoğan's position and power at the international level. Erdoğan attempted to put pressure on Israel by acting as the shield and advocate of Palestinians. The harsh expressions used by Erdoğan were especially echoed in TRT's tweets. Erdoğan made a very strong statement to stimulate global public opinion on the issue, and those messages were conveyed by TRT World in detail. In his speeches, Erdoğan also criticized the international community that was not condemning Israel's attacks on Palestinian cities and emphasized that supporting innocent Palestinians is a matter of honour for humanity (TRT World, 2021a9). After Erdoğan's harsh stance against Israel and his emphasis on Israel being the aggressor, the US administration made a statement criticizing his speech. Turkey's official response to this statement was announced on the TRT World account: 'Turkey strongly rejects the USA State Department's statement accusing President Erdoğan of being anti-Semitic, after he called Israel a "terrorist state" for bombing civilians in Gaza'(TRT World, 2021a11).

Global public takes action

Initially, TRT World criticized the international community who lacked interest in the Palestinian crisis, but in the following days, voices of support for Palestine began to resound from all over the world. Israel's efforts to hide its 'atrocities' from the mainstream media and worldwide public opinion remained insufficient. People who followed the events in all their detail on both traditional and new media platforms began to react. Individuals in a number of countries and cities of the world, from America to Australia, organized demonstrations to condemn Israel and support Palestine.

It is evident that TRT World made a significant contribution to unveiling the day-to-day harsh conditions of the Palestinian people. It also acted as a voice not only for the Palestinians, but also for the citizens of other countries and the organizations who supported Palestine. These countries include Bangladesh, Pakistan, Jordan, the United States, Canada, Australia, France, England, Germany, Chile, Spain, and so on. The purpose of TRT World's inclusion of statements from these countries was to create a strong global voice and ensure that Israel put an end to its attacks and occupation. Videos of the protests were widely featured on the TRT World account, showing the support of different nations for Palestine's cause. TRT World's headlines, such as 'Large Pro-Palestinian Protests across the US and Europe Show a Shifting Dynamic against Israel in the Western World' (TRT World, 2021a12), emphasized the increasing condemnation in the West. In fact, the discourse of 'People around the world' was used to underline how the global public, from Chile to Buenos Aires, supported Palestine.

Many people who empathized with the Palestinians attended these demonstrations. For the first time the world observed impactful reactions against Israel while supporting Palestine. For instance, a person in San Francisco made a Palestinian flag by combining different pieces of his clothes in the colours of the flag and hung it on the balcony of his house. During a march against Israel in England, a policeman chanted 'Free Palestine' and additionally, British Member of Parliament Richard

Burgon demanded an embargo against Israel for continuing the violence and asked the UK government 'How many more Palestinian children have to be killed?' (TRT World, 2021a13).

TRT World also broadcast messages of support for Palestine from celebrities such as artists, musicians and athletes from different countries. Players of Manchester United football team Paul Pogba and Amad Diallo supported Palestine by waving the Palestinian flag after the match they played with Fulham. Their manager reacted on the subject by saying that acts of the players should be respected (TRT World, 2021a14). A special tweet in support of the Palestinian cause made by Elneny, a football player for Arsenal, is also a prominent example. On the TRT World Twitter account, Elneny's football fans also supported the voice of Elneny with their comments (TRT World, 2021a15). Singer Zayn Malik's support for Palestine was given voice on TRT World's Twitter account with the following message: 'British singer Zayn Malik has reacted to the deadly Israeli attack on besieged Gaza on his Instagram account, joining other celebrities who have expressed their solidarity with Palestinians. The singer's post garnered over 3.5 million likes' (TRT World, 2021a16).

It has been argued that as a result of these intense reactions by the global public, the myth that the Israel lobby cannot be challenged in the United States has begun to change. For instance, political analyst Omar Baddar commented by saying: 'The claim that the Israel lobby in the US cannot be challenged is a myth and it's beginning to break' (TRT World, 2021a17). In fact, during this period, the US supply of weapons to Israel was also frequently criticized. Moreover, when voices were loud enough in the form of demonstrations and various statements that Israel was committing and continues to commit war crimes were made, Amnesty International also had to state that 'Israel's attacks on Palestinian civilians may amount to war crimes or crimes against humanity' (TRT World, 2021a18). Few demonstrators also called for the International Criminal Court to decide whether Israel's bombing and demolition of the building where the media offices were located in Gaza was a war crime.

Global public opinion pressure became effective in the UN

UN Secretary General Antonio Guterres did not show much interest in the issue during the first days of the events. For this reason, he was criticized by TRT World with the following message: 'UN Secretary General Antonio Guterres enjoyed a "fantastic performance" by Bolshoi Theater during Israel's intensified bombardments on Gaza last night. Following backlash on Twitter, he later called for an "immediate cessation of hostilities in Gaza and Israel"' (TRT World, 2021a19).

However, because of the global criticism of Israeli aggression, in his second statement, Guterres warned about the incalculable crises in Palestine and called for the fighting in the region to stop immediately (TRT World, 2021a20). Although Guterres did not refer to the Israeli occupation and massacres in his statement, his words on Palestinian children's lives in Gaza as 'hell on earth' were notable. It is noteworthy that in the emergency meeting of the UN, Guterres did not condemn Israel as an aggressor state while calling for the parties to stop the massacre and destruction, urging them to return to peace talks. In his speech, Guterres described the event as a fight, stating that 'Fighting must stop immediately' (TRT World, 2021a21).

Like Guterres, the UN Security Council was silent in the beginning of the conflict. In response, TRT World harshly criticized this silence on its Twitter account and shared the below statement of the Malaysian prime minister Yassin, who criticized the fact that the resolutions taken in the UN Security Council on Israel's attacks could not be implemented due to the US veto: 'The United Nations Security Council's inability to stop Israeli atrocities was "disappointing"' (TRT World, 2021a22). The Chinese foreign minister also expressed regret over the behaviour of the United States. TRT World, by including the statements of the leaders of different countries, foreign ministers or officials at the UN, tried to highlight the fact that the whole world finds Israel aggressor. These statements not only increased public pressure on Israel on a global scale, but also weakened the support that Netanyahu used to receive from the outside world, including the United States.

The US policy in the face of these events drew a reaction from various quarters. In TRT World's posts, it was emphasized that the attitude of the United States towards the crisis was hypocritical. Joe Biden, the president of the United States, signed an arms sale agreement with Israel at the time of the outbreak of the events and openly expressed his support for Israel in his phone call with Netanyahu. TRT World's posts on the subject were exactly as follows: 'US President Biden on a phone call with Israeli PM Netanyahu: – Expresses "grave concern" over fresh violence – Reaffirms "strong support for Israel's right to defend itself" – Raises concerns about "safety and security" of journalists' (TRT World, 2021a23). Biden described what happened in the region as 'violence' and spoke of Israel's right to self-defence. This discourse implies that the Palestinians launched the war and attacked the Israeli side.

Moreover, the United States failed to condemn Israel's bombing of the tower building in Gaza hosting various media organizations. Only the minister of foreign affairs made a statement to refute Israel's claims regarding the demolition of the media building and said, 'I have not seen any Israeli evidence of Hamas operating in the Gaza media office building hit by air strike' (TRT World, 2021a24). Since Israel killed many people using the weapons supplied by the United States, and because of the increasing pressure of the global public opinion, the United States had to put pressure on Israel to reduce tensions.

Conclusion

In its reporting of the Shaikh Jarrah events and war on Gaza in May 2021, TRT World Twitter account echoed much detail of the dramatic developments that took place. It has provided a voice for the Palestinians and has contributed to the formation of a global agenda by bringing the events in the region to the attention of the mainstream media. In almost all posts, it was emphasized that Israel was an aggressive and occupying state. For this reason, TRT World points out that Palestine's self-defence is legitimate. While emphasizing the aggressive practices of the Israeli side, active sentences were generally preferred in the posts, whereas in passive sentences, the expression 'by Israeli officials' was used.

The 'death toll' list, announced daily by the Palestinian ministry, was consecutively published. When reporting on the number of people who died and were injured, it was stated that the sources were reliable, and the figures were accurate by claiming, 'in the statements made by the authorities'. The posts appealed to the conscience of the global public by including the emotional statements of Palestinians whose homes were destroyed and children were lost. For this reason, many people from different countries, regardless of their faith and affiliations, reacted to the matter. Even some empathetic Israeli citizens did not hesitate to criticize Prime Minister Netanyahu for his actions.

A pro-Palestinian discourse was carefully constructed by giving references in the posts, such that the name and title of the person who made the statement was included in the posts. Again, the comments of experts on the subject were included from time to time to provide satisfactory information about the issue. Among the outspoken critics of the Israeli hostility was Turkish president Erdoğan. TRT World gave ample space to his critical statements. Erdoğan's accusation of Israel committing cultural, religious and ethnic genocide against the Palestinians had great impact globally, and it led both the Israeli and American administrations to react accordingly. It was the first time that the United States and EU countries were at odds with their own public opinion.

The United Nations secretary general did not show enough interest in the issue at the beginning; however, after observing the reaction of the public on a global scale, he was pressured to react and invite the parties to peace. In addition, the veto of the United States on the raised resolutions taken against Israel in the UN Security Council was also criticized by many member states. Despite the fact that Israel destroyed the media buildings and put pressure on the media, it could not prevent the events from influencing the global public opinion. It can be said that TRT World's broadcasting policy in this sense was very effective. The United States and Western countries, which are sensitive about press freedom, unfortunately did not uphold their standards on Israel's destruction of the media building in Gaza.

References

Jorgenson, M., and L. J. Phillips (2002), *Discourse Analysis as Theory and Method*, London: Sage.

Matheson, D. (2005), *Media Discourse: Analysing Media Text*, Berkshire: Open University Press.

Sözen, E. (1999), *Söylem, Belirsizlik, Mücadele, Bilgi/Güç ve Refleksivite*, İstanbul: Paradigma Yayınları.

TRT World (2021a, 20 May), https://twitter.com/trtworld/status/1395408687095767050 (accessed 27 May 2021).

TRT World (2021b, 19 May), https://twitter.com/TRTWorldNow/status/139504067193 8097155 (accessed 27 May 2021).

TRT World (2021c, 16 May), https://twitter.com/trtworld/status/1393948715484844035 (accessed 27 May 2021).

TRT World (2021d, 14 May), https://twitter.com/trtworld/status/1393172613418061824 (accessed 27 May 2021).

TRT World (2021e, 15 May), https://twitter.com/trtworld/status/1393554588918296578 (accessed 27 May 2021).

TRT World (2021f, 14 May), https://twitter.com/trtworld/status/1393306204655529988 (accessed 27 May 2021).

TRT World (2021g, 17 May), https://twitter.com/trtworld/status/1394299306815918080 (accessed 27 May 2021).

TRT World (2021h, 15 May), https://twitter.com/trtworld/status/1393547964774223873 (accessed 27 May 2021).

TRT World (2021i, 18 May), https://twitter.com/TRTWorldNow/status/139446148385 4086148 (accessed 27 May 2021).

TRT World (2021j, 16 May), https://twitter.com/trtworld/status/1394008954263441409 (accessed 27 May 2021).

TRT World (2021k, 15 May), https://twitter.com/TRTWorldNow/status/139360658968 9602048 (accessed 27 May 2021).

TRT World (2021l, 14 May), https://twitter.com/trtworld/status/1393149877320880130 (accessed 27 May 2021).

TRT World (2021m, 16 May), https://twitter.com/TRTWorldNow/status/139401183348 5438989 (accessed 27 May 2021).

TRT World (2021n, 17 May), https://twitter.com/trtworld/status/1394046248026521600 (accessed 27 May 2021).

TRT World (2021o, 17 May), https://twitter.com/TRTWorldNow/status/139438598661 7024513 (accessed 27 May 2021).

TRT World (2021p 18 May), https://twitter.com/trtworld/status/1394423483296362497 (accessed 27 May 2021).

TRT World (2021r, 16 May), https://twitter.com/trtworld/status/1394023282056343553 (accessed 27 May 2021).

TRT World (2021s, 20 May), https://twitter.com/trtworld/status/1395426440418627584 (accessed 27 May 2021).

TRT World (2021t, 14 May), https://twitter.com/trtworld/status/1393142525876125696 (accessed 27 May 2021).

TRT World (2021v, 14 May), https://twitter.com/trtworld/status/1393274160290439171 (accessed 27 May 2021).

TRT World (2021y, 19 May), https://twitter.com/trtworld/status/1394962638992457729 (accessed 27 May 2021).

TRT World (2021z, 14 May), https://twitter.com/TRTWorldNow/status/139317765518 9643268 (accessed 27 May 2021).

TRT World (2021, a1, 15 May), https://twitter.com/TRTWorldNow/status/139354270872 8303620 (accessed 27 May 2021).

TRT World (2021, a2, 15 May), https://twitter.com/TRTWorldNow/status/139359251178 4960005 (accessed 27 May 2021).

TRT World (2021, a3, 15 May), https://twitter.com/TRTWorldNow/status/139357678163 9307268 (accessed 27 May 2021).

TRT World (2021, a4, 15 May), https://twitter.com/trtworld/status/1393604370110074888 (accessed 27 May 2021).

TRT World (2021, a5, 18 May), https://twitter.com/trtworld/status/1394650705261207558 (accessed 27 May 2021).

TRT World (2021, a6, 18 May), https://twitter.com/trtworld/status/1394701817435598856 (accessed 27 May 2021).

TRT World (2021, a7, 19 May), https://twitter.com/trtworld/status/1395007372419117060 (accessed 27 May 2021).

TRT World (2021, a8, 19 May), https://twitter.com/trtworld/status/1394917109046599681 (accessed 27 May 2021).

TRT World (2021, a9, 14 May), https://twitter.com/trtworld/status/1393133161299783682 (accessed 27 May 2021).

TRT World (2021, a10, 17 May), https://twitter.com/trtworld/status/1394299306815918 080 (accessed 27 May 2021).

TRT World (2021, a11, 19 May), https://twitter.com/trtworld/status/1395020165784408 068 (accessed 27 May 2021).

TRT World (2021, a12, 17 May), https://twitter.com/trtworld/status/1394323582520541 191 (accessed 27 May 2021).

TRT World (2021, a13, 20 May), https://twitter.com/trtworld/status/1395332546427301 888 (accessed 27 May 2021).

TRT World (2021, a14, 19 May), https://twitter.com/trtworld/status/1394771739918405 632 (accessed 27 May 2021).

TRT World (2021, a15, 17 May), https://twitter.com/trtworld/status/1394110423683633 153 (accessed 27 May 2021).

TRT World (2021, a16, 14 May), https://twitter.com/trtworld/status/1393228861966405 634 (accessed 27 May 2021).

TRT World (2021, a17, 20 May), https://twitter.com/The_Newsmakers/status/13953427 24577079296 (accessed 27 May 2021).

TRT World (2021, a18, 18 May), https://twitter.com/trtworld/status/1394662845036515 332 (accessed 27 May 2021).

TRT World (2021, a19, 14 May), https://twitter.com/trtworld/status/1393228931667566 592 (accessed 27 May 2021).

TRT World (2021, a20, 16May), https://twitter.com/TRTWorldNow/status/139393505597 9008007 (accessed 27 May 2021).

TRT World (2021, a21, 16May), https://twitter.com/TRTWorldNow/status/139393505597 9008007 (accessed 27 May 2021).

TRT World (2021, a22, 15 May), https://twitter.com/trtworld/status/1393521546287849 475 (accessed 27 May 2021).

TRT World (2021, a23, 15 May), https://twitter.com/TRTWorldNow/status/139364318940 8522243 (accessed 27 May 2021).

TRT World (2021, a24, 17 May), https://twitter.com/TRTWorldNow/status/139425881792 4452352 (accessed 27 May 2021).

Van Dijk, T. (1988), *News as Discourse. Hillsdale*, NJ: Lawrance Erlbaum Associates.

Van Dijk, T. (1998), *Approaches to Media Discourse*, UK: Blackwell Publishers.

Part Two

Digital Media and the Competing Media Narratives

7

Digital activism and the politics of protest: Palestine and the struggle for global popular representation

Mazhar Al-Zo'by

The tragic limit of reporting the Palestinian plight in global media persists in its denial of the Palestinian self-narration and the writing of its own collective communal identity into history. The rare impulse in traditional media to focus on witness images to document Israeli state violence and transgressions against the Palestinians during military conflict as well as during everyday occupation has seldomly incited the global moral outrage or human indignation to warrant serious collective reaction. However, the dramatic evolution of the global public sphere has ushered in alternative and shifting forms and features in social advocacy and political mobilization in many cotemporary societies. The shift from the conventional 'mediated broadcasting' to the reciprocal 'unmediated narrowcasting' along with the evolution of the global media landscape from 'vertical to horizontal communication' capture the essence of the crucial transformation in the function and character of both political activism and political communication alike. In this regard, the evolving media ecology represents a critical analytical vision from which to understand contemporary and shifting forms of sociopolitical protest and mobilization in collective action.

During the Israeli military assault on Gaza and East Jerusalem in the summer of 2021, it was amply clear that alternative social media as well as global mass-mediated digital discourse played a vital and transformative role in the coverage and representation of the Palestinian struggle, experiences and realities under occupation and assault. However, it would be misleading to intimate that social media simply enables global activism under the simple premise of its own communicative structure. Despite its decentralized and somewhat egalitarian character, social media still requires organization, leadership and dissemination strategies. Furthermore, beyond digital-networked optimism as an instrument in the promotion of social and political activism, social media has been equally mobilized as a catalyst in the service of hegemonic powers and mass surveillance. Digital orientalism, like traditional orientalism, persists and manifests, for example, in the Draconian restrictions on Palestinian rights to represent themselves and express their struggle on major social media platforms such as Facebook, Twitter, YouTube and Google (see Mashkoor, 2021). Nonetheless, examining the character and function of Palestinian mass-mediated digital activism during the Israeli military attacks of 2021 on Gaza and East Jerusalem illustrates the dynamic capacity of these media platforms in articulating various political and communal narratives in local, regional and global discourse. Within this political environment, this chapter argues that celebrities as public figures can and have assumed a critical role in advocacy communication strategies as well as the mobilization of discursive tactics in mass media politics. Therefore, the rise of political celebrity activism should not be conceived as 'the trivialization of the public sphere', or as a sign of the diminishing spirit of revolutionary narratives, but rather as a marker of a sweeping change in modern social movements and their function in political life in general. The reciprocal and strategic alliance between discourse production, distribution and consumption in the mobilization of collective action enables us to capture the significant function of some celebrity tweeting and retweeting in a networked political and social infrastructure.

In order to analyse the critical features of this form of celebrity-powered activism related to Palestine, this chapter will revisit the Gramscian notion of the 'organic intellectual' as *dirigenti,* where the public figure assumes a 'directive' role to guide frame public and popular discourse for transformative collective action and political change. This notion will prove crucial to understanding counter-hegemonic ideological formation in political and social mobilization because of the vital significance it accords to popular culture (including social media) as the vital site and domain of popular struggle. By analysing celebrity social media discourse and narratives, this chapter contends that celebrity social media platforms critically challenged the hegemonic capacity of conventional media narratives to manage and regulate the production, framing and dissemination of mass communications and information related to the war.

To this end, this chapter will comprise four sections. The first section will examine the representational politics of the Palestinian national struggle and argue that the denial of a Palestinian homeland has tragically formed a corollary to the denial of a Palestinian communal and historical narrative under the Israeli colonial eraser. In order to overcome this narrative of the annihilation inflicted on Palestine and its struggle, it is essential to confront the silence of narration as an indispensable stage in the politics of resistance. The second section seeks to illustrate how news as forms of hegemonic representations embodies the essence of the denial of Palestinian communal and historical narratives, especially as mainstream media ideological conventions merge in the construction of the very ideas and attitudes which shape mass, popular knowledge about Palestine and Palestinians. Alternatively, digital communication platforms, it will be argued, have facilitated new modes of political activism for many hitherto marginalized communities like the Palestinians, thereby enabling new forms of protest movement and political activism. However, a radical political engagement with social media must not be confined to the simple function of such platforms. As the third section of this chapter will explain, a political and revolutionary struggle aimed against oppression demands multiple modes of resistance strategies. In this regard, and as Gramsci explains in his concept of the 'organic intellectual' as *dirigenti,* the ultimate revolutionary vison in the deconstruction of oppressive sociopolitical conditions is to be located in, and crucially directed at, civil and popular consciousness and not simply confined to conventional military and physical power. To specify and examine the character and function of the popular agency and popular consciousness advanced by Gramsci, the fourth section will focus on how some prominent celebrities as public figures assumed a critical role in the advocacy communication strategies as well as the mobilization of discursive tactics during the Israeli military assaults on Gaza and the West Bank.

Palestine and the (un)permission to narrate

In Jean-Luc Godard's profound ruminations on loss, memory and collective trauma in his 2004 narrative-documentary film *Notre Musique*, the Palestinian poet Mahmoud Darwish appears in one of the most compelling scenes to reflect on what he considers to be the monumental burden of Palestinian metaphorical and real survival. In a war of symbolic as well as real annihilation, Darwish (2006:126) reveals that narrating the self is an existential and ethical imperative. Strongly believing that 'whoever writes his story will inherit the earth of the story', Darwish decrees that 'if they defeat us in poetry [collective self-narration], then it's the end' (quoted in Williams, 2016: 171). Elaborating further on the material as well symbolic domination of Palestinian communal narration, Darwish explains that even in defeat, the tragedy lies not in the 'loss' but in the silence and silencing of the vanquished. 'I wanted to speak in the name of the absentee' (ibid.), as 'there is more poetic inspiration and humanity in defeat than in victory' (ibid.). For Darwish as for Palestine, the 'permission to narrate' is sometimes more crucial than victory itself. Paradoxically, however, Darwish explains how the Palestinian voice (both as the dispossessed and the excluded victim of Israeli colonial domination) is only visible through Israel's global discursive hegemony: 'Palestinians', he laments,

> have the misfortune of having as their enemy Israel, a state that enjoys unlimited international support, yet they also enjoy the great fortune of having the world's media focused on their plight precisely because the Jews are the center of attention: 'You [the Jews] have brought us defeat and renown … they [the world's media] only take an interest in me [Arab] because of you [Jew]. (ibid.)

Like Darwish, Edward Said despairingly mourns that the denial of a Palestinian homeland has tragically formed a corollary to the denial of a Palestinian communal and historical narrative. As he once famously remarked, 'unlike other colonial experiences – we weren't exploited, we were excluded. And that is the essence of the Palestinian struggle' (Middle East Revised, 2014). Nowhere has this anguish of silence been more evident than in the fragmentation of the Palestinian national voice. 'Since our history is forbidden', Said (1985) writes of the Palestinian people,

> narratives are rare; the story of origins, of home, of a nation is underground. When it appears it is broken, often wayward and meandering in the extreme,

always coded, usually in outrageous forms … that make little sense to an outsider. Thus the Palestinian life is scattered, discontinuous, marked by the artificial and imposed arrangements of interrupted or confined space, by the dislocations and unsynchronized rhythms of disturbed time … . We linger in nondescript places, neither here nor there. (20–1)

Although Said is keen to speak on behalf of a Palestinian community built on loss, dispersion and exile, he unequivocally insists that the search for a Palestinian identity, community and history remains the inner experience that resists the Zionist colonial erasure. Thus through the unconventional, hybrid and fragmentary forms of expression, Palestinians must 'write back' and narrate their own presence in history and in struggle.

For Said the Zionist project in Palestine, like other settler-colonial movements, has little to do with Jewish liberation or 'Messianic' fulfilment. It is rather a conquering colonial movement which has expropriated Palestinian land and dispossessed and displaced the Palestinian people. The success of the Zionist occupation of Palestine, however, is primarily attributed to its effective embrace of European Orientalist narrative, in which Zionism and Israel were associated with freedom, enlightenment, democracy and civilization, and by contrast, 'Zionism's enemies' were simply a twentieth-century version of the alien spirit of Oriental despotism, ignorance and similar forms of barbarity and backwardness. In effect, the European Zionists saw and still see the 'Oriental' Palestinians as lesser beings and unworthy of human dignity, a narrative that has been manufactured and propagated rather effectively on global media circuits among both conservatives and liberals alike.[1] It is in this context that the question of the Palestinian struggle must be invoked: the obligation to condemn and to bear witness to the crimes, abuse and destruction against Palestinians must be accompanied by the will and permission to self-narrate.

Reporting the Palestinian plight in global media both historically and during the Israeli military attack in May 2021, however, goes beyond the denial of self-narrative and writing the Palestinian collective communal identity into existence. In most cases, mainstream media platforms render the witness-spectator powerless and helpless, as they present news narratives to a viewer who consumes the news passively. As Edward Said (1984) perceptively explained almost four decades ago, 'facts do not at all speak for themselves, but require a socially acceptable narrative to absorb, sustain and circulate them. Such a narrative has to have a beginning and end: in the Palestinian case, a homeland for the resolution of its exile since 1948' (34).

However, during the events in the occupied East Jerusalem neighbourhood of Sheikh Jarrah and the ensuing massive air strikes on Gaza, and relying on alternative social media networks,

the witness's narrative proliferated as a new mode of aesthetic expression linked to experimentations with modes of archiving, alternative forms of writing [and presenting the war] … . In this form of ethical-aesthetic expression, images and their origin are unquestionably 'true' to each other: the space between face

[Palestine/occupation] and voice [Palestinians/humans] is also obliterated. (Emmelhainz, 2019:180)

More significantly perhaps, during these events, social media platforms challenged the hegemonic capacity of conventional media narratives to manage and regulate the production, framing and dissemination of mass communications and information related to the war, a process that allowed the emergence of new strategies for political activism and mobilization both locally and globally. In prior military assaults, the Israeli state was able to exploit its traditionally effective and sweeping networks of both social media as well traditional media channels to shape and fashion a favourable global narrative for its colonial occupation of Palestine, 'portraying itself as a nation unjustly under attack with the sole goal of defending itself' (Ward, 2021). However, during the military assault on East Jerusalem and Gaza Strip, the Palestinian self-narratives 'have had far more success in telling their side of the story on social media – eroding Israel's edge in the battle of perspectives and gaining a rapt audience in the US [and around the globe]' (ibid.). As the advocacy director for the Palestine Institute for Public Diplomacy Ines Razek confirms, 'We're the weak ones. Social media – our cameras and our videos – is one of the only means that we have. They have the weapons and the laws and the infrastructure' (quoted in Ward, 2021).

From ideological broadcasting to popular narrowcasting

The rise and institutionalization of the global news industry regarding the Arab world and particularly the question of Palestine has always been intertwined with ideological practices and attitudes. News as a form of representation, as Said (1981) explains, embodies the essence of this process as media narrative conventions and ideological values merge in the construction of 'reality', as he concludes that

> despite the variety and the differences, and however much we proclaim the contrary, what the media produce is neither spontaneous nor completely 'free': 'news' does not just happen, pictures and ideas do not merely spring from reality into our eyes and minds, truth is not directly available, we do not have unrestrained variety at our disposal. For like all modes of communication, television, radio, and newspapers observe certain rules and conventions to get things across intelligibly, and it is these, often more than the reality being conveyed, that shape the material delivered by the media. (47)

The news coverage of Palestine in traditional media outlets is further complicated by the convergence of the tropes of orientalist discourse and how they 'have largely become a form of mass-discourse disseminated in public forums and mass media platforms and function as a masquerade that provide a moral legitimacy for [Israeli] American/western neo-imperial designs' (Al-Zo'by, 2015: 218) in the region. Even though Edward Said recognizes that 'we do not … live at the mercy of a centralized propaganda apparatus', he upholds that for most Americans (the same is generally true for Europeans) the branch of the cultural apparatus that has been delivering Islam to them for the most part includes the television and radio networks, the daily newspapers, and the mass-circulation news magazines; films play a role, of course, if only because to the extent that a visual sense of history and distant lands informs our own, it often comes by way of the cinema. Together, this powerful concentration of mass media can be said to constitute a communal core of interpretations providing a certain picture of Islam and, of course, reflecting powerful interests in the society served by the media. (1981: 47)

In this context, the conception of media as an ideological mediation enables us to recognize how such media narratives constitute the very ideas, values and ideals that shape popular representations of cultural and political difference, especially on the question of Palestine. Following the analytical tools and critical approach of the 'Hegemonic Model' of media analysis (Hall, 1997:76), it is clear that the dominant representational strategies employed in this context demonstrate 'the process of making, maintaining and reproducing … authoritative sets of meanings and practices' related to Palestine and its struggle. (Barker 2008: 262). Accordingly, and as Al-Zo'by (2015) observes,

> The articulation of such hegemonic practices in media conventions, codes and attitudes, in turn, creates hegemonic discourses, authoritative views and common-sense assumptions and idioms. Understood accordingly, hegemonic media discourses do not describe the linguistic expressions of media discourse strictly speaking, but rather illuminate the wider scope of ideological formations that determine and regulate (include or exclude) possible public knowledge production – that is, they assemble ideological attitudes and world views and provide us with the framework to understand, naturalize and justify those views. (219)

Subsequently, as Hall (1979) maintains, hegemonic discourses are not consciously chosen by encoders to reconstruct news events within the domain 'of the dominant ideology', but constitute the field of meanings within which they must choose. Precisely because they have become 'universalized and naturalized', they appear to be the only forms of intelligibility available; they have become sedimented as the 'only rational, universally valid ones' (343). However, and because hegemonic discursive attitudes and practices demand perpetual and constant preservation and validation, they, following Foucault (1977), 'regulate not only what can be articulated and declared, but most importantly who can speak and under what conditions' (Al-Zo'by 2015: 221). Thus, dominant media attitudes and analysis fabricated by news and media 'elites/ experts' in this case 'do not only sanction those interpretations as "truth-claims", but in fact function also as a source of power that re-authorizes their perspectives as objective knowledge' (ibid.). Therefore, and notwithstanding its potential divergent views, the cycle of ideological news reproduction is linked directly to the authority and authorization of power through media elites and experts, who will always strive to secure and sustain discourse into conventional ideology. As Hall (2018) further elaborates,

> How the broadcasting professionals are able both to operate with 'relatively autonomous' codes of their own and to act in such a way as to reproduce the hegemonic signification of events is a complex matter .... It must suffice to say that the professionals are linked with the defining elites not only by the institutional position of broadcasting itself as an 'ideological apparatus', but also by the structure of access (that is, the systematic 'over-accessing' of selective elite personnel and their 'definition of the situation' in television). (196)

Similarly, and as Mouffe (2013: 2) strongly confirms, 'Hegemonic practices are the practices of articulation through which a given order is created and the meaning of social institutions is fixed.'

The trouble with reporting the Palestinian plight in general and the Palestinian struggle during the Israeli military attacks in May 2021 is that most of the traditional media coverage was rendered within this symbiotic duality between dominant ideology and conventional media consensus. However, for some observers, digital communication platforms have facilitated new modes of political activism for many hitherto marginalized communities like the Palestinians, thereby enabling new forms of protest movement and political activism. More importantly, therefore, 'social and digital media networks for many defied the hegemonic capacity of central powers to control the dissemination of mass communications and information, which gave rise to new strategies for social and political mobilization around the world' (Al-Zo'by 2019: 193). The focus on the capacity and agency of individual expressive narratives in everyday political life in digital networked platforms 'signals the emergence of an alternative virtual public sphere within networked societies' (ibid.). In her analysis of the 'digital formations of the powerful and the powerless', Sassen (2013) further defines the globally networked public sphere as fashioned by three critical features of digital communication – 'decentralized access/distributed outcomes, simultaneity, and interconnectivity'. Sassen insists that these digital networks are the ideal mediums for popular forces to advance a more democratic civil society and transnational global activism. Through these platforms, local struggles can emerge as part of a network of trans-border global connections 'while still remaining specific to local concerns. She notes that cyberspace is often a more concrete space for the articulation of social struggles than many orthodox national political systems. This is because it accommodates a broader range of issues and persons than more traditional discourses and institutions'. (Barker, 2008: 452).

During the Israeli military assault on Gaza and East Jerusalem in the summer of 2022, it was manifestly clear that alternative social media as well as global mass-mediated digital discourse had played a vital role in the representation of the indigenous Palestinian struggles, experiences and realities under occupation. Examining the character and function of social media during those assaults illustrates the dynamic capacity of such media platforms in articulating various political and communal narratives in local, regional and global discourse. In this regard, 'the distinct and central feature of social and digital media, therefore, is not simply that it facilitates and mediates mass communication among political and social activists [inside Palestine and beyond], but rather that social and digital media constitute a mode of production of radically transformative, empowering' and defying political narratives about Palestine and its struggles (Al-Zo'by 2019: 193). In this case, alternative digital media networks and social media platforms represent a constructive as well as inventive new form of political activism, solidarity and resistance. As Castells explains in a different context,

> Enthusiastic networked individuals … are transformed into a conscious, collective actor. Thus [political and] social change results from communicative action that involves connection between networks … from a communicative environment through communications networks. The technology and morphology of these communications networks shapes the process of mobilization, and thus social [and political] change, both as a process and an outcome. (2012: 219–20)

It is, thus, abundantly clear that collective protest action has been transformed by digital networked activism in Palestine as well as among protest movements around the globe. The utilization of social media activism has likewise enabled social and protest movements to shift from conventional and vertical-ranked forms of decision-making commonly associated with the more traditional forms of orthodox collective action. As Shirky (2008) proclaims, the advent of the 'power of organizing without organizations' is upon us as exemplified by leaderless collective movements. Therefore, and as Hardt and Negri (2017) contend, 'the rejection of leadership is a symptom of a profound historical transformation: hierarchical structures have been overturned and dismantled within the movements as a function of both the crisis of representation and a deep aspiration to democracy' (8).

However, it is very important that a distinction is made between connective activism (as a logic of individual expressions) and collective activism (as a logic of collective and communal struggle). Therefore, it would be misleading to intimate that social media enables global activism simply under the premise of its distinctive communicative structural attributes. Despite its decentralized and informal character, social media still requires an organization, leadership and dissemination strategies. In this case, vital voices in the production of Palestinian narratives are well documented in digital media-facilitated protest activism (including, Muna Al Kurd, Suhad Abdel Latif, Mohammed Almadhoun, Khalid Safi, Khalid Omar to name just a few). Furthermore, and notwithstanding the digital-networked optimism associated with its utility in the promotion of political and protest activism, social media has been equally mobilized in the service of hegemonic powers and mass surveillance (for detailed account of this critique, see Al-Zo'by, 2019). One only has to document the way oppositional right-wing settlers along with major social media companies attempted to silence Palestinian voices during the conflict and beyond. Facebook alone closed more than three hundred and fifty Palestinian accounts which documented the Israeli state and settler violence in Gaza and the West bank. Accordingly, a radical political engagement with social media must not be confined to the simple function of such platforms. For this, and as Gramsci insists, a political and revolutionary struggle aimed against oppression demands multiple modes of resistance strategies. This is precisely because 'hegemony, understood as a fluid and temporary series of alliances, needs to be constantly rewon and renegotiated. The creation and dissolution of cultural hegemony is an ongoing process and culture a terrain of continuous struggle over meanings' (Barker, 2008: 564). I would like to turn to Gramsci's argument here in order to better illustrate his counter-hegemonic approach and how it would apply to Palestinian counter narratives during the conflict of 2021.

Media, hegemony and popular protest

In his classical model of revolutionary struggle, Gramsci (1971) distinguishes between two types of strategic protest operations (wars): 'war of maneuver' and a 'war of position'. In the former, the revolutionary struggle against oppression is conducted through armed insurrection and military force campaigns. However, for Gramsci a more effective political and revolutionary struggle aimed against oppression demands multiple modes of resistance strategies. Whereas one is pursued as a war of manoeuvre, another is directed at the cultural and hegemonic production of global power and should involve a 'war of position' (a war of narratives and counter narratives). In this regard, for Gramsci the cultural counter-hegemonic struggle against oppression is sometimes more significant than an actual armed struggle. This is because the deconstruction of a dominant ideology should assume a priority over a military one, especially if oppressive forces maintain the monopoly over structural means of ideological discursive production. As Gramsci (1971: 232) explains, 'to fix one's mind on the military model is the mark of a fool: politics, here too, must have priority over its military aspect and only politics creates the possibility for maneuver and movement'. Critical of the singular strategy of military struggle, for Gramsci the art of politics (war of position) is conceived as a more sophisticated and multifaceted strategy of political-cultural resistance. As he further elaborates,

> The massive structures of the modern [power], both as State organizations, and as complexes of associations of civil society, constitute for the art of politics as it were the 'trenches' and the permanent fortifications of the front in the war of position: they render merely 'partial' the element of movement which before used to be 'the whole' of war, etc. (242–3)

For Gramsci, then, political violence (oppression and control) is a condition where the political, social and economic elite exercise domination over the subordinate and powerless classes through a combination of force, coercion and more crucially, consent. As he further emphasizes,

> The normal exercise of hegemony … is characterized by the combination of force and consent, which balance each other reciprocally without force predominating excessively over consent. Indeed, the attempt is always to ensure that force would appear to be based on the consent of the majority expressed by the so-called organs of public opinion – newspapers and associations. (Gramsci, 1971: 80)

It is, therefore, a central feature of Gramscian political analysis that counter-hegemonic practices should focus on education and the reclamation of popular consciousness rather than the utilization of force, military struggle and correction, something that Edward Said himself has advocated in the context of Palestine.

Accordingly, the ultimate revolutionary strategy in the deconstruction of oppressive sociopolitical conditions is to be located in, and crucially directed at, civil and popular consciousness and not simply confined to conventional military and physical power. Correspondingly, this will require the mobilization of local and global narratives of popular and mass-mediated platforms in order to express and disseminate counter-hegemonic ideological and secure persuasion and support for collective popular struggles. Thus, Gramsci is interested in the character of mass-mediated ideology (common sense) as well as popular culture because these are the crucial sites where hegemonic ideology is both secured and contested. As Gramsci (1971: 362) explains,

> Common sense is not rigid and immobile but is continually transforming itself, enriching itself with scientific ideas and with philosophical opinions which have entered ordinary life. Common sense creates the folklore of the future, that is as a relatively rigid phase of popular knowledge at a given place and time.

While for Gramsci these counter-hegemonic narratives (war of position) are designed by the oppressed and marginalized, at 'the vanguard of this proposed war of position, he identifies the 'organic intellectuals', ... who have taken up the mantle of cultural leadership' (Lydon, 2020: 35) and who reflect the feelings, struggles and experiences of the masses. In this context, 'organic intellectuals' seek to assume the capacity of what Gramsci calls '*dirigenti*' (Williams, 1960), a 'directive' role to guide and frame public and popular discourse for transformative collective action and political change.

The use of the Gramscian notion of organic intellectual as *dirigenti* has proved crucial to understanding counter-hegemonic ideological formation in political and social mobilization because of the vital significance accorded to popular culture (including social media) as the site and domain of popular struggle. Moreover, and as Fiske (1987) argues, popular social sovereignty is shaped by a terrain of sociopolitical semiotics generated by people and activists alike. In fact, Fiske sees 'popular culture as a site of semiotic warfare and of popular tactics deployed to evade or resist the meanings produced and inscribed' by hegemonic powers through collective action (quoted in Barker, 2008: 443). The Gramscian concept of counter-hegemonic organic intellectual was deployed in its original inception in relation to class struggle. However, political action and activism in contemporary societies require a broader conception of both popular mobilization and collective action. Therefore, we must 'dislodge the concept from its strictly class-centered semantic field and to apply it to the composition of more diverse and fluid disaffected, or otherwise subaltern, groups' (Bakardjieva, Felt and Dumitrica, 2018: 95).

Furthermore, the articulation of counter-hegemonic collective action cannot situate the organic activist strictly within the confines of discourse production; it must rather approach the process as a symbolic and connective flow between production, diffusion and consumption. The reciprocal and strategic alliance between discourse production, distribution and consumption in the mobilization of collective action enables us to capture the significant function of some celebrity tweeting and retweeting in a networked political and social infrastructure. As Thrall et al. (2008) acknowledge,

> The problem with web sites and other online communication efforts, of course, is that they are hidden in a vast cyberspace full of voices competing for attention. No one except those who are already aware of the group and supportive of the mission is likely to visit the web site. To overcome this problem groups have begun to use celebrities to help target specific groups of people and draw them to their web sites. (375)

Accordingly, and as this chapter will argue, the notion of the 'organic intellectual' must be revisited and deployed as a function and labour of activism as participation in social struggles regardless of profession, affiliation and locale. Moreover, its domain of intervention transcends the limitations of class struggle to other forms of political and social protest movements (anti-colonial, racial, gender, etc.). In this case, the Gramscian notion emerges as an expansive view of the organic intellectual, whose role is performed by popular figures, social media personalities, writers, musicians, actors, teachers, community organizers alike.

In social media, therefore, the mantle of the public intellectual activism and digital mass-mediated popular mobilization for collective action have acquired a unique and different status. For example, 'social media now allows celebrities the possibility to instantly secure mobilization and direct action from an audience without the filters of news media' (Bennett, 2014: 139). In this articulation of digital activism, the revisited Gramscian 'organic intellectual' assumes a pivotal function in the deconstruction of hegemonic and dominant ideology. As Lydon further explains,

> These new organic intellectuals … are not professional politicians or members of the mainstream media; they are simply social progressives determined to challenge the dominance of [hegemonic] ideology and savvy enough to recognize the amazing potential of [social media] to assist in accomplishing this goal … . [They] successfully connect with millennial audiences in their formative years and influence their social perspectives and political affiliations more deeply than members of the mainstream media could ever hope to do. (2020: 36)

In the context of the Palestinian struggle, and especially during the Israeli military assault on Gaza and East Jerusalem in the summer of 2021, celebrity-powered activism was crucial for the diffusion of public protest discourse, to which I would like to turn at this point.

Palestine, digital activism and celebrities

As indicated earlier, during the military campaign in the occupied East Jerusalem neighbourhood of Sheikh Jarrah and the ensuing overwhelming military assault on

Gaza, social media was utilized to challenge the hegemonic capacity of conventional media narratives to regulate the production, framing and dissemination of mass communications related to the events. While Israel undeniably had the military dominance, in its effort to manage the 'public narrative of the conflict, Israel's edge seems to be slipping' (Ward, 2021). In prior military conflicts, the Israeli official communication strategy exploited its traditionally effective and sweeping networks of both social media as well as mainstream media channels to shape and fashion a favourable global narrative for its own side, 'portraying itself as a nation unjustly under attack with the sole goal of defending itself' (ibid.). However, during the military attacks, the Palestinian voice and self-narratives 'have had far more success in telling their side of the story on social media – eroding Israel's edge in the battle of perspectives and gaining a rapt audience in the US [and around the globe]' (ibid.). In previous military conflicts, digital networked activism was also mobilized to report and document Israeli transgressions in real time. However, the 'emergence of new platforms like Telegram and TikTok have allowed more – and younger – people to engage with this flare-up online ... and in real time, muddying the usual easy storylines (ibid.). As Ward (2021) further explains,

> From making solidarity videos on TikTok to using Twitter to organize international protests to posting videos to Instagram showing Israeli airstrikes on Gaza, Palestinians and those around the world sympathetic to their plight have made social media a central weapon in the narrative fight against Israel. Those weapons are deployed on many fronts: using different platforms to target multiple audiences – in the region and around the world – while also using apps to coordinate actions among themselves.

It is unquestionably clear that alternative social media as well as global mass-mediated digital discourse played a vital role in the coverage of the self-representation of the indigenous Palestinian struggles. Nonetheless, studying the character of such narratives during those assaults also illustrates how many prominent celebrities as public figures assumed a critical role in the advocacy communication strategies and the global mobilization of discursive tactics in mass media politics. Relying on unmediated direct engagement and interaction with the public followers regarding Palestine, 'emerging celebrity advocacy efforts [in this regard] are better understood as part of a strategy to circumvent the mainstream mass media news than as a strategy to leverage its power' (Thrall et al., 2008: 364). That is, celebrity-powered activism in the case of this military assault was crucial for facilitating the digital communication infrastructure for the diffusion of the protest narratives produced inside Palestine and beyond in a media landscape residing outside the formal policy process.

The massive air strikes and overwhelming bombardment of the Palestinians gripped global media platforms – both mainstream as well as social media – and attracted unprecedented attention from many prominent celebrities, media personalities and socialites from around the world. They included actors, musicians and popular media personalities like Susan Sarandon, Mark Buffalo, Rihanna, Roger Waters, Lena Headey, Kendall Jenner, Paris Hilton, race-car driver Lewis Hamilton,

Models and sisters Gigi and Bella Hadid and Dua Lipa to name just a few. Among the many celebrities who had expressed solidarity with the Palestinians during the bombardment, no one had been as actively vocal as the American actress, Susan Sarandon. With almost 770,000 followers on Twitter, Sarandon vigorously retweeted a 'Slow Factory Foundation' multimedia text image with pictures of utter human and residential destruction in Palestinian neighbourhoods. The captivating text caption was divided into two segments. The first, entitled 'Myth: Palestine and Israel are in "conflict"' was followed by a second caption entitled, 'Fact: What is happening in Palestine is settler colonialism, military occupation, land theft, and ethnic cleansing. A conflict means there is equal footing, which is not the case … . This is not a conflict'. (@SusanSarandon,12 May 2021: 1:55 pm). On 6 May, the day this tweet appeared on Sarandon's Twitter account, it was retweeted 14,400 times and it was 'liked' almost 36,900 times. The ensuing discussion on the thread of this tweet was very illuminating as many of her followers debated the ideological as well as the real pushback against Palestinian supporters in the West. One follower commented that: 'Vanessa Redgrave learned the hard way what standing up for Palestinians caused', in reference to the British actress who had encountered an intense repercussion after her Oscar acceptance speech in 1978, in 'which she congratulated the Academy for standing up to "a small bunch of Zionist hoodlums" who had attacked her for producing and appearing in a documentary about Palestine' (Roxborough, 2018). Responding to the cautionary post cited earlier, another follower replied: 'She's not alone this time .@ violadavis & @MarkRuffalo are on the right side of justice too' (@emykat03, 13 May 2021: 6:47am). This was in reference to other celebrities who had expressed solidarity with the Palestinians.

Like Sarandon, the veteran and legendary British rock musician Roger Waters expressed very strong solidarity with the people of the occupied West Bank and Gaza and their struggle for justice and freedom. Waters' widely circulated video, entitled 'It's Official Israel Is an Apartheid State. Check Out Sheikh Jarrah Genocidal House Clearings', called into attention Western hypocrisy on the plight of the Palestinians . In this video, frustrated with President Biden's silence on Israel's 'atrocities', Waters addresses Biden directly, stating, 'How would you like it, Joe Biden? You're sitting at home … and [someone] comes along and goes, that's ours. I'm a settler I'm going to take your house from you. I don't care what you do. Die … that would be the very best' (@rogerwaters, 7 May 2021: 6:38 am). The video received more than 27,000 likes and was retweeted close to 12,000 times on the day of its release, but has been viewed close to 700,000 times as of the date the video was accessed.

Likewise, the supermodel sisters Gigi and Bella Hadid, whose followers on Instagram reached 66.4 million and 42.3 million respectively, posted often during the first days of the military attacks under the hashtag '#FreePalestine' and '#SaveSheikhJarrah'. In one post, Bella wrote,

> I have a lot to say about this but for now, please read and educate yourself. This is not about religion. This is not about spewing hate on one or the other. This is about Israeli colonization, ethnic cleansing, military occupation and apartheid over the Palestinian people that has been going on for YEARS! (Quoted in Lampen, 2021)

In addition to their own posts, the Hadid sisters shared numerous clips chronicling Palestinian suffering under Israeli military occupation since 1967. In a striking 30-second video clip from 'This Is Palestine' podcast, the shocking facts about Israel's '73 year ethnic cleansing' of Palestinians (since 1948) and the '54 year brutal occupation' of Palestinians (since 1967) are flashed on the screen. The video as of 12 May 2021 received 3,748,072 views, like many of their other posts on this issue (@bellahadid, 12 May 2021).

So effective and widespread was the Hadid sisters' social media outreach that the Israeli government responded with numerus posts on its own official Twitter account, with 834,400 followers. Admonishing the sisters, the Israeli government accused the two celebrities of 'advocating for the elimination of the Jewish State'. However, many on social media saw this as a desperate reaction to the popular sisters influence on youth perceptions of the conflict around the world. As one follower commented on the Israeli thread,

> THIS is why celebrity influence is SO important. When Bella Hadid got involved, they felt threatened. Now imagine if internationally recognized celebs like Beyonce, Taylor Swift etc. say something. This is why statements from public figures are important right now. (@dezgostang, 17 May 2021: 1:17 am)

Deploying other strategies to confront such influence on social media, some Israelis implored other Israeli celebrities to get involved in the digital mass-mediated wars for public opinion. Lamenting the Hadid sisters' sweeping influence, Netanyahu's outspoken son of the then prime minister tweeted:

> The models of Palestinian descent Gigi and Bella Hadid, with millions of followers, have been conducting antisemitic propaganda against Israel 24/7 since the beginning of the mess [military attacks]. The only Israeli figure, with the same number of followers, and with the power of an international celeb, who can give them a fight in publicity is Gal Gadot. She chose to write a neutral post as if she was from Switzerland. (Quoted in Dutton 2021)

Other expressions of support for the Palestinian plight came from unlikely sources. Using the hashtags #SavePalestine #GazaUnderAttack #stopthegenocide, the popular American socialite, Paris Hilton, tweeted on 16 May 2021: 'This is so heartbreaking. This needs to stop' (quoted in Uddin, 2021). In a sequel post, Hilton shared a video clip of one of the most haunting and most viral accounts of the military attack in which a young Palestinian girl breaks down weeping after one of the air strikes demolished and devastated her neighbour's homes, killing eight young children. 'This hurts my heart', Hilton shared with her 17 million followers, 'No one should have to live in fear. My heart goes out to the little girl and the other children around her' (ibid.). Like Hilton, the usually apolitical race-car driver Lewis Hamilton tweeted a 'Statista' gripping infographic data-flow illustrating the dramatic difference between Palestinian deaths and injuries compared to the Israeli ones during the recent military conflicts. This was followed by another dramatic image depicting the shrinking of Palestinian land since the inception of the state of Israel today, highlighting the annihilation of Palestinian spatial sovereignty and thus its existence (Cancian, 2021). However, and under the ire of the pro-Israel lobby in the United States, both Hamilton and Hilton, like many others before them, including Kendal Jenner, had to delete these pro-Palestinian posts. Nonetheless, the original posts and their subsequent deletion incited wide debate on the plight of Palestinians both during the military attacks and in general under occupation.

Employing a different medium, and challenging one of the great Western liberal attitudes about the occupation, John Oliver, host of the HBO's *Last Week Tonight* (with 1 million viewers) condemned the 'false equivalencies and euphemisms that prevent us from talking honestly about the situation' (Dessem, 2021). As Oliver declared in a blazing monologue on his show,

> Look, there is a real tendency, particularly in America, to both-sides this situation. And I am not saying that there aren't some areas where that's warranted, but it's important to recognize there are also areas where it's simply not. Both sides are firing rockets, but one side has one of the most advanced militaries in the world. Both sides are suffering heartbreaking casualties, but one side is suffering them exponentially. And it's not like the U.S. is operating from the moral high ground here. It's obviously no stranger to drone striking weddings and saying, 'We were just trying to target enemy combatants.' This country has blood on its hands too. And look, if you believe Israel's actions are warranted and proportionate this week, you're welcome to try and make that argument. (Ibid.)

The episode, in which the segment on Palestine was aired, was later viewed 5.5 million times, sparking hundreds of thousands of tweets and retweets in addition to a number of YouTube videos both in support and against Oliver's monologue.

Like John Oliver, tens of high-profile and prominent celebrities waded in on the side of the Palestinians, offering solidarity with Palestinians and condemnation of Israeli oppression and violence. Many others contributed to a collective broader discourse which shaped the debate on Palestine. These include Trevor Noah (11.6 million followers) to Mark Ruffalo (7.9 million followers), and from actress Lena Headey (1.1 million followers) to Academy-Award-winning actress Viola Davis (8.9 million followers) to Gael García Bernal (2.4 million followers) to Emma Watson (65.7 million followers). Commenting on the glimmer of hope for narrating a Palestinian voice on a global stage, Roger Waters stated,

> The huge backlash if you mentioned the word apartheid ... ten years ago you couldn't mention the word ever. Completely forbidden. We have made huge progress and the BDS has made huge strides, and there are huge strides being made on the campuses in the United States of America ... and we are going to reach a tipping point. (Quoted in Moini 2021)

Conclusion

As the Palestinian social activist Muhammad el-Kurd so eloquently put it, 'I didn't believe that a post or a picture could change anything in reality ... But I discovered that our first and last battle is one of words, the battle of narratives and the battle of public opinion' (France 24, 2021). Therefore, given its communication media landscape resides outside the formal and official policy process, celebrity-powered activism is more crucial for protest 'mobilization and building social movement infrastructure than it is for mass agenda setting' (Thrall et al., 2008: 364). Thus, celebrity tweeting and retweeting of Palestinian voices has enabled a penetration of mainstream public discourse, diminishing the familiar monopoly, which the Israeli state has, on global narratives of the conflict. In fact, Israel's extreme pressure on social media platforms to restrict Palestinian digital media protests has only made them more intense. This happened precisely 'when the hashtag [#SaveSheikhJarrah] reached public figures, celebrities, diplomats, and politicians', said Khaled Safi, a social media consultant (quoted in Abu Jahal 2021). 'They all interacted positively', Safi said, 'and shared posts and videos they came across, thus reaching more people and raising awareness about the issue of Jerusalem and Sheikh Jarrah' (ibid). Additionally, the widespread dissemination of Palestinian voices via celebrity social media platforms enabled a cross social movement alliance. Here the Palestinian plight was linked with the other global movements like Black Lives Matter and other progressive groups around the world. For instance, the Black Lives Matter (BLM) Twitter account (with over 1 million followers) tweeted a solidarity message in support of hashtag #freepalestine:

> Black Lives Matter stands in solidarity with Palestinians. We are a movement committed to ending settler colonialism in all forms and will continue to advocate for Palestinian liberation. (always have. And always will be). #freepalestine (@Blklivesmatter, 17 May 2021: 4:52pm)

While social and progressive movements like BLM may not have direct impact on policy outcomes, building a discursive alliance with such movements through the mediation of celebrity social media support serves to maintain public attention to the cause, and more importantly reconfirms the Palestinian right to self-narrate through successful cross-movement solidarity building alliance.

Note

1. Part of the passage on Said's ideas included here was part of a speech delivered at his memorial reading held at Macslester College (St. Paul, MN) in April 2004.

References

Abu Jahal, E. (2021), 'Sheikh Jarrah Activists Say Israel Pressuring Twitter to Block Them', *Al Monitor*, May 12, https://www.al-monitor.com/originals/2021/05/sheikh-jarrah-activists-say-israel-pressuring-twitter-block-them (accessed 1 January 2022).

Al-Zo'by, M. (2015), 'Representing Islam in the Age of Neo-orientalism: Media, Politics and Identity', *Journal of Arab & Muslim Media Research*, 8(3): 217–38.

Al-Zo'by, M. (2019), 'Social Media and Power in the Arab World: From Dominant Ideology to Popular Agency', *Journal of Arab & Muslim Media Research*, 12(2): 191–211.

Barker, C. (2008), *Cultural Studies: Theory and Practice*, London: Sage.

Bakardjieva, M., M. Felt and D. Dumitrica (2018), 'The Mediatization of Leadership: Grassroots Digital Facilitators as Organic Intellectuals, Sociometric Stars and Caretakers', *Information, Communication & Society*, 21(6): 899–914.

Bennett, L. (2014), 'If We Stick Together We Can Do Anything: Lady Gaga Fandom, Philanthropy and Activism through Social Media', *Celebrity Studies*, 5(1–2): 138–52.

Cancian, D. (2021), 'Kendall Jenner, Lewis Hamilton and Other Celebs Delete Pro-Palestine Social Media Posts', *Newsweek*, 18 May, https://www.newsweek.com/kend all-jenner-lewis-hamilton-paris-hilton-delete-pro-palestine-posts-1592475 (accessed 1 February 2022).

Castells, M. (2012), *Networks of Outrage and Hope: Social Movements in the Internet Age*, Cambridge: Polity.

Darwish, M. (2006), *Why Did You Leave the Horse Alone?*, trans. Jeffrey Sacks, New York: Archipelago Books.

Dessem, M. (2021), 'John Oliver Accuses Israel of Committing War Crimes, Practicing Apartheid', *Slate*, 17 May, https://slate.com/culture/2021/05/last-week-tonight-john-oliver-israel-palestine-apartheid-war-crimes-stand-your-ground.html (accessed 9 November 2021).

Dutton, J. (2021), 'Gal Gadot Acting More Swiss Than Israeli Over Conflict, Says Son of PM Benjamin Netanyahu', *Newsweek*, 18 May, https://www.newsweek.com/gal-gadot-acting-more-swiss-israeli-conflict-netanyahu-son-1592420 (accessed 1 December 2021).

Emmelhainz, I. (2019), *Jean-Luc Godard's Political Filmmaking*, London: Palgrave Macmillan.

Fiske, J. (1987) *Television Culture*, London: Methuen.

Foucault, M. (1977), *Discipline and Punish*, London: Allen Lane.

France 24 (2021), '#SheikhJarrah: From Jerusalem Neighbourhood to Global Hashtag', 6 June, https://www.france24.com/en/live-news/20210606-sheikhjarrah-from-jerusa lem-neighbourhood-to-global-hashtag (accessed 10 December 2021).

Gramsci, A. (1971), *Selections from the Prison Notebooks*. New York: International Publishers.

Hall, S. (1979), 'Culture, the Media and the Ideological Effect'. In J. Curran, M. Gurevitch and J. Woollacott (eds), *Mass Communication and Society*, London: Edward Arnold, 315–48.

Hall, S. (1997), 'Introduction'. In S. Hall (ed.), *Representation: Cultural Representations and Signifying Practices*, London: Sage Publications.

Hall, S. (2018), 'Encoding/Decoding'. In J. Bardzell, S. Bardzel and M. Blythe, *Critical Theory and Interaction Design*, Cambridge, MA: MIT Press, 187–97.

Hardt, M., and A. Negri (2017), *Assembly*, New York: Oxford University Press.

Lampen, C. (2021), 'Bella Hadid Protests for Palestinian Rights in Brooklyn', *Vulture*, 17 May, https://www.vulture.com/2021/05/bella-hadid-joined-a-pro-palestine-protest-in-brooklyn.html (accessed 11 January 2022).

Lydon, K. (2020), 'Gramsci in the Digital Age: YouTubers as New Organic Intellectuals', *The Graduate Review*, 5: 34–45.

Mashkoor, L. (2021), 'Sheikh Jarrah Content Takedowns Reveal Pattern of Online Restrictions in Palestine', *The National News*, 10 May, https://www.thenationalnews.com/mena/sheikh-jarrah-content-takedowns-reveal-pattern-of-online-restrictions-in-palestine-1.1220037 (accessed 7 January 2022).

Middle East Revised (2014), 'Edward Said and Salman Rushdie Ta(l)king the Box Away', https://middleeastrevised.com/2014/03/22/edward-said-and-salman-rushdie-talking-the-box-away/ (accessed 11 December 2021).

Moini, R. (2021), 'Roger Waters' Pro-Palestine Activism Is a Lesson for the West', *The Express Tribune*, 20 May, https://tribune.com.pk/story/2300850/roger-waters-pro-palestine-activism-is-a-lesson-for-the-west (accessed 5 December 2021).

Mouffe, C. (2013), *Agonistics: Thinking the World Politically*, London: Verso Books.

Roxborough, S. (2018), 'Vanessa Redgrave Recalls Unapologetic Political Speech at 1978 Oscars: "I Had to Do My Bit"', *The Hollywood Reporter*, 28 August, https://www.hollywoodreporter.com/movies/movie-news/vanessa-redgrave-recalls-unapologetic-political-speech-at-1978-oscars-1136251/ (accessed 4 January 2022).

Said, E. (1981), *Covering Islam: How the Media and the Experts Determine How We See the Rest of the World*, New York: Pantheon Books.

Said, E. (1984), 'Permission to Narrate', *Journal of Palestine Studies*, Spring, 13 (3): 27–48.

Said, E. (1985) *After the Last Sky*, New York: Pantheon Books.

Sassen, S. (2013), 'Interactions of the Technical and the Social: Digital Formations of the Powerful and the Powerless', *Eurozine*, 13 November, https://www.eurozine.com/interactions-of-the-technical-and-the-social/ (accessed 25 December 2021).

Shirky, C. (2008), *Here Comes Everybody: The Power of Organizing without Organizations*, New York: Penguin Press.

Thrall, A., J. Lollio-Fakhreddine, J. Berent, L. Donnelly, W. Herrin, Z. Paquette, R. Wenglinski and A. Wyatt (2008), 'Star Power: Celebrity Advocacy and the Evolution of the Public Sphere', *The International Journal of Press/Politics*, 13(4): 362–85.

Uddin, R. (2021), 'Paris Hilton Deletes Palestine Tweets, Bella Hadid Attacked by Israel', *Middle East Eye*, 17 May, https://www.middleeasteye.net/news/israel-palestine-paris-hilton-bella-hadid-celebrities-delete-attacked (accessed 12 January 2022).

Ward, A. (2021), 'The "TikTok Intifada"', *Vox*, 22 May, https://www.vox.com/22436208/palestinians-gaza-israel-tiktok-social-media (accessed 10 January 2022).

Williams, G. (1960), 'The Concept of "Egemonia" in the Thought of Antonio Gramsci: Some Notes on Interpretation', *Journal of the History of Ideas*, 21 (4) (October–December): 586–99.

Williams, J. (2016), *Encounters with Godard: Ethics, Aesthetics, Politics*, Albany, NY: SUNY Press.

8

The orchestration of activist events: Making protests heard (and seen)

Konstantin Aal, Sarah Rüller, Peter Tolmie and Volker Wulf

Introduction

Digitization and the internet have changed the media landscape enormously. An important part of this is the circulation of media content via the world wide web (www). Social media has played an increasingly important role in this. The behaviour of users has changed: they are now active participants in the generation of content, be it via posts, comments, annotations, wikis, blogs or microblogs (Thurman, 2008). These activities have evolved into a commonplace feature of conflicts around the world. Activists, just like everyone else, use social media and other online tools to share their perspectives along with videos and pictures that support their views. While social media use is ' first and foremost … social' and 'mostly revolve[s] around fun, self-expression and social gain' (Lim, 2013: 19), it also allows individuals and groups to debate political developments and concerns and, where relevant, transform these debates into active resistance (Lim, 2018).

Social networking sites (SNSs) have had a major impact in a number of countries, especially in the Middle East. Social media played a pivotal role in the organization of the political protests that led to the so-called Arab Spring (the generic term for the protests and uprisings that began in the Arab world in December 2010) (Howard et al., 2011; Wilson and Dunn, 2011), which led to the overthrow of political regimes in Tunisia, Egypt and Libya and the ongoing conflict in Syria. Although conventional mass media played a major role later in the democratization process, social media was particularly important for the mobilization of protesters during the early days of the uprisings. However, as pointed out by Rodriguez, Ferron and Shamas, most extant studies 'focus on the "newness" of ICTs [and] reduce the richly contextual human relations that surround media use into a flat and unrevealing technological determinism' (2014: 3). Thus, there remains a need to understand the relationship between the use of social media and users' everyday political activities 'on the ground'. Arriving at this understanding involves taking a closer look at people's actual practices, the extent to which they are premised on the use of ICT, and how they are exercised over longer periods of time. We know little about the influence of the shifting platform characteristics and platform policies on their use by activists. This study shows how activists react to such changes by following a hybrid social media approach, with different IT platforms and tools being used at different times. It looks at how activists, together with friends and family members, have used social media and other technologies over the past eight years as they sought to organize demonstrations against the Israeli construction of a wall in their village. In particular, it reveals how these activities were embedded in other everyday chores and the ordinary business of their lives.

Protests in the MENA

Over the last few decades, a number of major protests and conflicts have occurred around the world, especially in the MENA (Middle East and Northern Africa) region, beginning with Tunisia in 2010 (Lotan et al., 2011; Wulf et al., 2013b). Social media, such as Facebook and Twitter, and satellite television, for example, Al-Jazeera, proved to be instrumental tools during the Arab Spring (Kavanaugh et al., 2011a, b; Lotan et al., 2011), especially during the Tunisian revolution (Kavanaugh et al., 2013; Warnick and Heineman, 2012). Social media helped citizens to quickly spread self-generated news and information, and activists, in particular, used social media to spread news and organize protests. This made it clear that social media can play a role in promoting democratic processes (Wulf et al., 2013b). In follow-up work in Tunisia two years after the uprising, it was found that Facebook had evolved and was now mainly being used to consume other user-generated content (UGC), across a range of topics, rather than purely political information. SNSs were still playing an important role, but to support a new and evolved form of 'normality' (Aal et al., 2018). A later study by Rohde et al. (2016) described the practices of Syrian activists, where users had developed sophisticated practices to increase their credibility and to verify information. Here, Facebook was largely only being used to find out more about the current political situation, though some users had created multiple accounts to protect them when using it more actively. Importantly, different forms of use were visible before, during and after the uprising (Rohde et al., 2016).

Protests in the Palestinian context

In Palestine, most people in the West Bank and Gaza Strip rely solely on telecommunications. Most of the infrastructure and resources in the West Bank, including the air-waves, are controlled and allocated by the Israeli authorities. This affects both the TV and radio stations and the mobile operators. Access to the global network is also provided by Israeli companies. Nonetheless, websites and SNSs like Google, YouTube, Twitter and Facebook have become increasingly popular. In mid-2011 Facebook counted 600,000 Palestinian users. In 2019, this had risen to 1,600,000 users (Internetworldstats, 2019). As the use of digital media has grown, the Israeli-Palestinian conflict has become more than just a political, partially armed conflict. Now it is also a media war. Aouragh's analysis of the use of new ICTs in Palestine and their social and political impact shows that the internet is now one of the most important tools for achieving cross-border self-determination (Aouragh, 2011).

However, the role played by the internet and digital media has also changed in recent years. During the Second Intifada, their use for political mobilization and activism was limited. The main focus was on supporting mutual assistance by keeping people inside Palestine connected and keeping Palestinians outside of Palestine informed about current developments (Aouragh, 2008, 2011; Bishara, 2009). Over time, there has been a shift towards using the internet for civil journalism projects, media projects, blogs and the creation of other websites, so it has now become an important platform for free speech (Iazzolino, 2010).

The most important difference between the Occupied Palestinian Territories and other countries in the Arab world has always been control and censorship. The weakness of the Palestinian Authority (PA) has resulted in there being few formalized media restrictions in comparison to other Arab countries (Zayyan and Carter, 2009). However, Palestinian society remains subject to two types of surveillance: one by the Israeli Occupation; the other by their own local PA. Furthermore, Palestinian activists and their international supporters are faced with a new type of censorship from the SNSs and other platforms themselves.

Research methodology

The study reported here adopted an ethnographic approach. All the authors of this essay visited a Palestinian activist, Hasan, over a period of ten years and spent time with him and his family. Semi-structured interviews were also conducted and he was followed to demonstrations. We present this process in more detail later in the text.

Study phases

Qualitative, 'on the ground' studies of the kind we conducted stand in strong contrast to quantitative ones, where the focus is on enumeration and statistical analyses. Many studies focusing on social media are quantitative and use downloadable, online data in their investigations. However, as our goal was to acquire a rich understanding of actual practices, an ethnographic approach was essential. The insights are revealing when compared to online data – social media use and political participation was situated in people's everyday lives, the organizational and mobilizing processes they were involved in, their motives and reasoning and their broader patterns of communication (Wulf et al., 2013b).

Over the eight-year period we studied activism in Palestine, we used a variety of ethnographic techniques, including observations, interviews and online interactions. This helped us to fully understand the daily routines and practices of the activists and other inhabitants living in the village. Our intent, here, is not to link specific local practices to more general cultural issues, but rather a working analysis of a particular series of events and how the practices they reveal changed and evolved over time. As we were working under challenging conditions, talking to

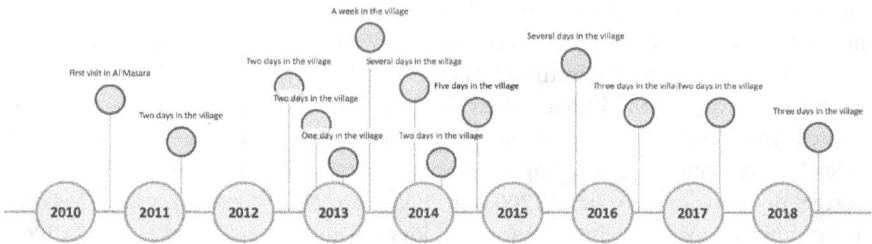

Figure 8.1 Visits to the village

people and observing their behaviour had to be done carefully and infrequently. This made a long-term engagement crucial to building trust and getting to see the things we needed to see. We spent time with activists not only during demonstrations, but also in our free time. This added insight into their activities and further helped with building trust.

From 2010 onwards, we paid recurrent visits to the village to conduct interviews, observe the weekly demonstrations and spend time with the main activists to understand how they structured their activities and routine (Figure 8.1). We focused on: the organization of the demonstrations; the use of ICT, the internet and social media; their consumption of mass media such as radio and TV; and how whole families got involved both before and after the demonstrations.

Our first visit to the village happened during the establishment of a computer club project in the West Bank (Aal et al., 2014, 2015; Yerousis et al., 2015). During the visit, Hasan explained the geopolitical environment and how the Al'Masara demonstrations were organized.

The following year, we contacted Hasan again and spent two days with him. This time, we conducted interviews with other activists who were living there, most of them members of Hasan's family. The following day, we observed the weekly demonstration and conducted informal interviews with participants from the village, Israel and various European countries.

In May 2012 we visited the village again and conducted informal interviews with different political activists while visiting the newly established computer club, where Hasan's children could now access the internet. In September 2012, all four of the authors spent another two days in the village, interviewing and recording conversations with various local and international activists and village residents. This time, we actually took part in the weekly demonstrations as observers and watched the subsequent use of (social) media.

In 2013, two researchers spent a week in the village, bunking down in Hasan's living room and spending most of their time with him. Every day, Hasan added insights into how he was fighting the construction of the wall at different locations and voicing his opposition to the Israeli occupation. In this way, we became not only a part of Hasan's political life, but also his social life: we visited his friends together, his workplace and even attended a wedding as guests.

In 2014, another two researchers undertook a six-week research trip to the West Bank to conduct 3D-printing workshops in the newly established computer clubs (Stickel et al., 2015) and took the opportunity to visit Hasan again. This time, they saw how he organized 'virtual' Friday demonstrations in a different location and how he talked to media representatives and newspapers about the demonstrations and their success.

During a further three-week trip in 2015, we found that Hasan had changed his strategy regarding the demonstrations: they were no longer conducted in Al'Masara, because a favourable court ruling meant that the construction of the wall had stopped.

In 2016, Hasan showed us his new Palestinian 'settlement' project. The settlement belonged to a rich Palestinian citizen living in the United States, who had donated the land. A house was built, and a small family lived there in close proximity to three different Israeli settlements.

In 2017, we spent another half a day in the growing Palestinian settlement. The house had now been rebuilt in brick and extended. More members of the family were living there and they had started to grow vegetables in greenhouses. We conducted unstructured interviews with the settlers and obtained some insight into their lifestyle and how they were using technology in this remote place.

Our last visit happened in 2018. This time, we spent three days with Hasan and discussed how things had changed over the years, and projects old and new developed, how the demonstrations had evolved and how both he and other activists had changed their use of ICT (and how it had changed them).

Analytic approach

Over the eight years we were visiting the village, we wrote more than 160 pages of field notes, captured videos and pictures, recorded interviews and amassed digital data, including e-mails and WhatsApp messages, Facebook posts and tweets. We also followed the activists on Facebook, Instagram, Twitter and YouTube and were part of various Facebook groups that disseminated information about the village and the current activities. Apart from this, we monitored news media, SNS and blogs to stay on top of the overall situation in Palestine and the village. We have retained contact with the activists, and this has helped us find answers to questions that arose during the analysis.

In a shared analysis of the materials, the field notes and interviews were open-coded into themes, which have informed the narrative of this essay. All the authors discussed and compared the codes and themes in detail across a number of meetings, until a consensus of understanding was reached.

We should emphasize, here, that the focus of this essay is on the activities of one specific actor and the people around him. For an activist, these activities are nothing special and there are only so many ways to solve the organizational problems that activists confront in their everyday lives. Throughout, he was striving to develop a clear mechanism to orchestrate his own activities and the activities of others, so as to give voice to their grievances and concerns. Unsurprisingly, the methods he used are in no way unique to him, even if certain features were distinct. Nonetheless, we are aware that this is a one-sided account.

Palestinian organized protests: Background

The overall conflict

The conflict between Israel and Palestine has a long history. To understand the current study, an elementary understanding of the conflict is required. The following will provide a brief overview of how the resistance in several villages (including Al'Masara) arose. We will also look at the history of the family responsible for the demonstrations in Al'Masara. After the First World War destroyed the Ottoman Empire, Britain took on administration of Palestine, while the French Mandates ruled in Syria and Lebanon. The goal was to prepare the local population for self-government. However, in Palestine, the Balfour Declaration guaranteed a national home for Jewish People. This resulted in tensions in the Middle East and Northern Africa. The 1948 war that led to the founding of the State of Israel effectively destroyed Palestinian society and the Israel that was established was called 'Nakba' in Arabic, meaning 'catastrophe' (Sa'di and Abu-Lughod, 2007). To this day, the Palestinian population is divided. One part lives in the West Bank and Gaza, the other in the diaspora in neighbouring countries such as Jordan, Syria and Lebanon, where the majority fled after 1948.

After the 1967 Six-Day War, the West Bank was occupied by Israel. Shortly afterwards, the first Israeli settlers began to build settlements in the occupied territories. Between 1977 and 1984, an average of ten to nineteen new settlements were established each year. These developments, a growing sense of political inertia and loss of direction, and economic depression in the Palestinian Occupied Territories (POT) led to the first Intifada ('uprising' in Arabic) in 1987 (Khawaja, 1993). This continued until the 1991 Madrid Conference, where Palestine and Israel met to revive the peace process with the support of the United States and the Soviet Union (Hiltermann, 1993; Sayigh, 1997). The signing of the Oslo Accords in 1993 put an official end to the uprising (Nasrallah, 2013).

After the Oslo Accords, parts of the West Bank fell under the control of the PA. This created a quasi-state that was run mainly by the Fatah party, but with clashes over time with the Hamas party. The occupied West Bank was divided into three administrative units: Areas A, B and C. Area A covers about 3 per cent of the West Bank and is controlled completely by the PA, excluding East Jerusalem. Area B (another 22 per cent of the West Bank) is under Palestinian civil control, but joint Israeli-Palestinian security control. Area C (the remaining 75 per cent) is completely under the control of Israel and nearly all of the settlements are located in this area (B'Tselem, n.d.). In 2003, during the second Intifada, the Israeli government began to build a 'Separation' wall around and within the West Bank. Though argued to facilitate self-defence against Palestinian terrorists, the wall was mainly built on Palestinian land, separating the Palestinian population and further undermining the coherence of their country (Barak-Erez, 2006).

As a response, Palestinian villages began regular demonstrations, starting with Bi'lin, where demonstrations have taken place every Friday since 2003 and are still ongoing. Several other villages followed suit, with Al'Masara demonstrating every Friday from 2006 until a 2014 court ruling stopped the building of the wall around their village. Most instances of popular resistance emerged as a response to perceived threats to the local community. Many local people found that the wall blocked them from gaining access to their own land and imposed hurdles when leaving or returning to their village (Darweish and Rigby, 2015).

Al'Masara and its protests

Analysis of Al'Masara's political activities necessitates understanding the background of the families living in the village and the main actor discussed in this chapter, 'Hasan'. The village dates back to 1930. Its residents originate from the Az Zawahra and At Ta'amra tribes and are composed of several families, mainly: 'Alaa'ed Deen, Brijieh, Abu Al'Adas and Salah. Al'Masara is at the south-west of Bethlehem, and most of the land is in Areas B and, primarily, C. This prohibits the residents from constructing anything on the land or from using it for other purposes (such as agriculture).

Hasan and his family are all politically active (see Figure 8.2). They have paid a heavy price for this. While they were organizing demonstrations against the building of the wall, Hasan was arrested by the Israeli army five times. Each time, an Israeli lawyer managed to secure his release after a few weeks. The Israeli army has searched the family house many times, typically the night before the Friday demonstrations. One of Hasan's younger brothers was imprisoned in Israel for fifteen years. He was released in 2018 and now supports the rest in their political activities. During his stay in prison,

Figure 8.2 Demonstrations in Al'Masara

he maintained his demonstration by refusing to eat (Maan News, 2017). Although the village has suffered for its political activities, it has also received political support and investment in its infrastructure. Supporting the villages opposing the expropriation of land and construction of the wall has been an apparent priority for the PA.

Fieldwork findings: Galvanizing the protests

The following shows how Hasan used ICT daily in his struggle against Israel and how we helped to expand his knowledge, enabling him to reach more people outside of his immediate activist 'bubble'. Over time, he realized that the Israeli secret service was following his Facebook account and actively used this information to confuse the soldiers designated to attend the demonstrations.

Learning how to use social media effectively

Over time, Hasan's use of IT and SNS evolved from posting basic messages to mailing lists and Facebook (Wulf et al., 2013a) to a more sophisticated use of Twitter, YouTube, Instagram and WhatsApp, which gave access to more supporters and activists. This diversity was important because, if there were problems with one account, he could easily switch to another. He learnt how to use Twitter (*less space to describe situations and developments, but opportunities to add pictures*) after he heard that Facebook was blocking other activists' accounts: *You do not put all your eggs into one basket* (Hasan, 28 April 2018).

Facebook is an important tool in a country where all mass media are censored. After a UN vote on Palestine, Mahmood (a close friend of Hasan and an activist) gave an interview to a French television crew that later featured in the French news. Very few of their supporters in France recorded it and, when he saw it, he found they had only used the least political part of what he said. Hasan therefore said, 'FB offers him the opportunity to express what he really wants to say' (Hasan, 28 April 2018).

The activists in the village learnt over time how to use the different functionality offered by each SNS to their advantage (e.g. by creating groups to stay in touch with international activists and creating pages about the village itself to share news and invite greater engagement). Not only Hasan's ICT use, but also his behaviour towards the mass media in Palestine evolved. He said he wanted to 'reach the people on the ground' (Hasan, 28 April 2018) and added new channels to reach a wider variety of people, but remained in constant contact with a variety of journalists, who called him regularly to ask about things like the latest demonstration or what the theme of the next demonstration would be.

The orchestration and performance of protests

Over the course of our engagement, we observed several demonstrations and witnessed a difference between the more recent demonstrations and earlier ones, where social media had not played any role. The demonstrations were actively transformed to exploit the new opportunities offered by social media, as illustrated by the following examples.

During one particular visit, Hasan described how he was using social media to confuse the soldiers who attended the weekly demonstrations. He showed us a Facebook post from him saying a demonstration would be beginning shortly, with many international activists, and that it would start from his home and try to reach the centre of the village. However, he had actually organized several cars to drive about twenty-five people to the gate of a nearby settlement. Here, he took photos in front of the security cameras while the activists began to celebrate and play football. Hasan was aware that the Israeli forces were following his Facebook account and would pick up on the declared demonstration. After a while the Israel Defense Forces (IDF) soldiers arrived and the usual demonstrations began instead, with the activists trying to walk through the streets and the soldiers stopping them. On another occasion, two researchers spent a demonstration day with Hasan. While touring Bethlehem, he received a call from a reporter to ask about the weekly demonstrations. He replied that the demonstrations were 'quite peaceful today', with some thirty participants and a 'German delegation' taking part. When we asked another activist, we found that no demonstrations occurred that day.

Hasan also increasingly turned to using staged pictures. This showed an awareness of his Facebook audience and how images would be 'liked' and shared. Once, he even positioned and photographed his daughter in front of soldiers to create a particular effect (see Figure 8.3), even though his daughter was terrified. He shared the photos on his Facebook page and they later appeared on several 'News' pages. His daughter was in no real danger, but, for Hasan, the picture served to 'capture the fight of the Palestinians against the powerful soldiers'.

Figure 8.3 Hasan's daughter in front of soldiers during a demonstration

Discussion

The role of ICTs in the orchestration of protests

As he took on new projects, Hasan developed his media strategy to reach a wider range of target groups. He increasingly drew upon a hybrid network consisting of social media (Facebook and Instagram), mass media (e.g. news agencies such as Maan News) and small media (e.g. cameras, WhatsApp, etc.). The intermodality of these different tools, where social media is combined with other networks, is a crucial part of modern activism (Lim, 2018: 22). For instance, in Malaysia, the Bersih movement employed low-tech communication networks (flyers and SMS) to reach rural areas and gave lectures in mosques and community centres while starting a campaign to motivate Malaysians with online access to deliver Bersih messages to offline communities by printing hard copies or by copying them to CDs (Khoo, 2014). Hasan similarly expanded his palette by broadening the number of platforms and networks he used. He also gave weekly radio broadcasts to reach people who otherwise had little contact with activism or the movement in Al'Masara. Thus, there was a strong interrelationship between his evolving strategies and his use of ICT.

Preserving a visible protest routine

After Hasan won a court action in 2014 stopping construction of the wall around the village, he launched several new projects. However, he deliberately delayed the announcement of his success and continued to post about the demonstrations, as though they were still ongoing. He wanted to keep close control over the flow of information, so as to maximize its effect. Only after he had successfully publicized his new projects did announce his victory in court. This may seem duplicitous, but it needs to be remembered that, for social movements and activists, it is important to occupy public spaces and to make public performances of their resistance visible. For Hasan, the public manifestation of their resistance was the walk to the centre of Al'Masara, where 'bodies and their visibility to the public are central in the struggle for power' (Lim, 2015: 121), and he had to manage that visibility accordingly.

This attention to the performativity of protest was visible from the outset. From early on, the demonstrations were actively themed around mottos and events, such as the football world cup, the fall of the wall in Germany and a wedding of friends (Darweish and Rigby, 2015). Movements have to retain their presence beyond any original protest through public demonstration of their opposition, regardless of the potential risks (Al Saleh and Arefin, 2011).

Conclusion

As digital media becomes increasingly embedded in everyday life, political conversations and actions are increasingly tied to it. It is therefore unsurprising that the effective use of digital media has become an important aspect of political projects, including protests and social movements. Most of the current literature on media use focuses on Western democracies, setting aside other political contexts where different constraints and opportunities hold sway (though there are a few exceptions, e.g. Dawson, 2003). Our long-term engagement with local activists in Palestine enabled us to see how activism and political resistance has changed over a period where the very nature of the media landscape has also changed. We have seen how one activist, amongst many, has had to learn how to adapt his strategies for orchestrating protests and demonstrations and embrace new tools and outlets that can preserve the public visibility of his resistance. He has also had to learn how to use new media to preserve the creativity and performativity of protest that is an essential part of its power to engage and motivate. Hasan is fully aware of this power, but he is also aware how much trust and authenticity matter when it comes to making good use of such tools, hence the skilful way he interweaves activism with his private life (Wulf et al., 2013a).

More than anything, this study has brought to the fore the extent to which the orchestration of protests, rendering them visible and imbuing them with the right elements to capture the attention of the right people, involves a capacity to not only embrace a variety of digital and physical tools, but to be able to adapt and reconfigure practices to stay in line with the evolution of the tools themselves. Were Hasan still the same activist he was when we first met him, still using the same tools in the same kinds of ways, his effectiveness as an activist would, at the least, be much diminished and the visibility of his protests would have been washed away in a tide of new activism that has grown up with digital resources.

In May 2021, new tensions arose in Sheikh Jarrah and in Gaza. Palestinian families were detained in their homes and intense fighting broke out in the Gaza Strip (Bateman, 2021). As a result, young activists used online posts and media appearances to give the world a glimpse of the living conditions under the occupation in East Jerusalem. Like Hasan, they had to adapt their strategies and use social media to show the world the daily struggles they typically had to face. These materials were reposted and retweeted and became visible in the mainstream media (Yee and El-Naggar, 2021). Around the world, this helped to inspire the Palestinian diaspora and reinvigorate the protest movement. In the United States, more and more people are voicing their support for Palestinians and putting pressure on their government to adopt a more critical stance towards Israel (Yee and El-Naggar, 2021). This new generation of activists know how to navigate the digital realm, because they have grown up under not just a real, but also a virtual occupation (Human Rights Watch, 2021), so they know what they can post online and what to avoid (De Vries and Majlaton, 2021). This is central to understanding what the orchestration of protests outside of Western democracies looks like. While Hasan had to learn how to use various tools for different purposes (e.g. Twitter, Facebook, WhatsApp, radio), the new generation of activists are already familiar with how to proceed in a world dominated by digital media and powerful platforms (Yee and El-Naggar, 2021). Thus, they know just how to make sure that their contributions are not only noticed, but also added to by an array of global actors (e.g. fashion influencers on Instagram), institutions and NGOs (e.g. Human Rights Watch) (Yee and El-Naggar, 2021). This has changed the narrative of the Israel–Palestine conflict and, with the new scope for citizen journalism, this narrative can now be elaborated upon by ordinary

Palestinians, who have the ability to use their smartphones to broadcast their stories to the world (Murtaza, 2021).

References

Aal, K., M. Schorch, E. B. H. Elkilani and V. Wulf (2018), 'Facebook and the Mass Media in Tunisia', *Media in Action: Interdisciplinary Journal on Cooperative Media*, 2018 (1) (Socio-Informatics – ISSN 2567-9082, S.): 135–68.

Aal, K., T. von Rekowski, G. Yerousis, V. Wulf and A. Weibert (2015), ,Bridging (Gender-Related) Barriers: A Comparative Study of Intercultural Computer Clubs'.I In *Proceedings of the Third Conference on GenderIT, GenderIT '15*, New York: Association for Computing Machinery, 17–23, https://doi.org/10.1145/2807565.2807708.

Aal, K., G. Yerousis, K. Schubert, D. Hornung, O. Stickel and V. Wulf (2014), 'Come_in@palestine: Adapting a German Computer Club Concept to a Palestinian Refugee Camp'.I In *Proceedings of the 5th ACM International Conference on Collaboration across Boundaries: Culture, Distance & Technology*, New York: Association for Computing Machinery, 111–20.

Al Saleh, D., and M. R. Arefin (2011), 'Five Days of Anger in Cairo', https://www.thepolisblog.org/2011/01/five-days-of-anger-in-cairo.html (accessed 19 July 2021).

Aouragh, M. (2011), *Palestine Online: Transnationalism, the Internet and Construction of Identity*, London: IB Tauris.

Aouragh, M. (2008), 'Everyday Resistance on the Internet: The Palestinian Context', *Journal of Arab & Muslim Media Research*, 1: 109–30.

Barak-Erez, D. (2006), 'Israel: The Security Barrier—between International Law, Constitutional Law, and Domestic Judicial Review', *International Journal of Constitutional Law*, 4: 540–52.

Bateman, T. (2021), 'Jerusalem Violence: Deadly Air Strikes Hit Gaza after Rocket Attacks', BBC News, https://www.bbc.com/news/world-middle-east-57053074 (accessed 29 January 2022).

Bishara, A. (2009), 'New Media and Political Change: The Case of the Two Palestinian Intifadas', Working Paper, EUI RSCAS, 2009/21, Mediterranean Programme Series, http://hdl.handle.net/1814/11487 (accessed 25 March 2022).

B'Tselem (2019), 'Planning Policy in the West Bank', https://www.btselem.org/planning_and_building (accessed 18 July 2021).

Darweish, M., and A. Rigby (2015), *Popular Protest in Palestine: The Uncertain Future of Unarmed Resistance*, London: Pluto Press.

Dawson, A. (2003), 'Documenting Democratization: New Media Practices in Post-Apartheid South Africa', paper presented at the Media in Transition Conference at the Massachusetts Institute of Technology, October, web.mit.edu/m-I-t/articles/dawson.html.

De Vries, M., and M. Majlaton (2021), 'The Voice of Silence: Patterns of Digital Participation among Palestinian Women in East Jerusalem', *Media and Communication*, 9: 309–19, https://doi.org/10.17645/mac.v9i4.4391

Hiltermann, J. R. (1993), *Behind the Intifada: Labor and Women's Movements in the Occupied Territories*, Princeton, NJ: Princeton University Press.

Howard, P. N., A. Duffy, D. Freelon, M. M. Hussain, W. Mari and M. Mazaid (2011), 'Opening Closed Regimes: What Was the Role of Social Media During the Arab Spring?', *SSRN Electronic Journal*, https://doi.org/10.2139/ssrn.2595096.

Human Rights Watch (2021), 'Israel/Palestine: Facebook Censors Discussion of Rights Issues', https://www.hrw.org/news/2021/10/08/israel/palestine-facebook-censors-dis cussion-rights-issues (accessed 29 January 2022).

Iazzolino, G. (2010), 'Digital Shahid-Palestinians Covering Occupied Palestine: From Broadcast Media to Citizen Journalism', *Arab Media Society*, 10 (3): 1–14, https://www. arabmediasociety.com/digital-shahid-from-broadcast-media-to-citizen-journalism-in-palestine/ (accessed 5 February 2023).

Internetworldstats (2019), 'Middle East Internet Statistics, Population, Facebook and Telecommunications Reports', https://www.internetworldstats.com/stats5.htm (accessed 14 July 2021).

Kavanaugh, A., S. Yang, S. Sheetz, L. T. Li and E. A. Fox (2011a), 'Between a Rock and a Cell Phone: Social Media Use during Mass Protests in Iran, Tunisia and Egypt', ACM Transactions on Computer–Human Interaction.

Kavanaugh, A., S. Yang, S. Sheetz, L. Li and E. Fox (2011b), 'Microblogging in Crisis Situations: Mass Protests in Iran, Tunisia, Egypt'. In Proceedings of the Conference on Human Factors in Computing Systems (CHI), ACM, Association for Computing Machinery, New York, 1–7.

Kavanaugh, A., S. D. Sheetz, R. Hassan, S. Yang, H. G. Elmongui, E. A. Fox, M. Magdy and D. J. Shoemaker (2013), Between a Rock and a Cell Phone: Communication and Information Technology Use during the 2011 Uprisings in Tunisia and Egypt', *International Journal of Information Systems for Crisis Response and Management*, 5: 1–21.

Khawaja, M. (1993), 'Repression and Popular Collective Action: Evidence from the West Bank', *Sociol Forum*, 8: 47–71, https://doi.org/10.1007/BF01112330 (accessed 5 February 2023).

Khoo, Y. H. (2014), 'Mobilization Potential and Democratization Processes of the Coalition for Clean and Fair Elections (Bersih) in Malaysia: An Interview with Hishamuddin Rais', ASEAS-Österreichische Zeitschrift für Südostasienwissenschaften, 7: 111–20.

Lim, M. (2018), 'Sticks and Stones, Clicks and Phones: Contextualizing the Role of Digital Media in the Politics of Transformation'. In C. Richter, A. Antonakis and C. Harders (eds), *Digital Media and the Politics of Transformation in the Arab World and Asia*, Wiesbaden, Germany: Springer, 9–34.

Lim, M. (2013), 'Many Clicks but Little Sticks: Social Media Activism in Indonesia', *Journal of Contemporary Asia*, 43: 636–57, https://doi.org/10.1080/00472336.2013.769386.

Lim, M. (2015), 'A CyberUrban Space Odyssey. The Spatiality of Contemporary Social Movements', *New Geographies*, 7: 117–23.

Lotan, G., E. Graeff, M. Ananny, D. Gaffney, I. Pearce and D. Boyd (2011), 'The Arab Spring – The Revolutions Were Tweeted: Information Flows during the 2011 Tunisian and Egyptian Revolutions', *International Journal of Communication*, 5: 31.

Maan News (2017), 'Israeli Authorities Release Former Hunger Striker after 12 Years in Prison', http://www.maannews.com/Content.aspx?ID=777410 (accessed 17 July 2021).

Murtaza, H. (2021), 'States Can't Control the Narrative on Israel–Palestine Anymore', The Intercept, https://theintercept.com/2021/05/12/israel-palestine-jerusalem-soc ial-media/ (accessed 29 January 2022).

Nasrallah, R. (2013), 'The First and Second Palestinian Intifadas'. In J. Peters and D. Newman (eds), *Routledge Handbook on the Israeli-Palestinian Conflict*, Oxfordshire, UK: Routledge, 74–86.

Rodríguez, C., B. Ferron and K. Shamas (2014), 'Four Challenges in the Field of Alternative, Radical and Citizens' Media Research', *Media, Culture & Society* 36: 150–66, https://doi.org/10.1177/0163443714523877.

Rohde, M., K. Aal, K. Misaki, D. Randall, A. Weibert and V. Wulf (2016), 'Out of Syria: Mobile Media in Use at the Time of Civil War', *International Journal of Human-Computer Interaction*, 32: 515–31, https://doi.org/10.1080/10447318.2016.1177300.

Sa'di, A. H., and L. Abu-Lughod (2007), *Nakba: Palestine, 1948, and the Claims of Memory*, New York: Columbia University Press.

Sayigh, Y. (1997), *Armed Struggle and the Search for State: The Palestinian National Movement, 1949–1993*, Oxford, UK: Clarendon Press.

Stickel, O., D. Hornung, K. Aal, M. Rohde and V. Wulf (2015), '3D Printing with Marginalized Children—An Exploration in a Palestinian Refugee Camp'. In N. Boulus-Rødje, G. Ellingsen, T. Bratteteig, M. Aanestad and P. Bjørn (eds), *ECSCW 2015: Proceedings of the 14th European Conference on Computer Supported Cooperative Work, 19–23 September 2015, Oslo, Norway*, Cham: Springer International Publishing, 83–102.

Thurman, N. (2008), 'Forums for Citizen Journalists? Adoption of User Generated Content Initiatives by Online News Media', *New Media & Society*, 10: 139–57.

Warnick, B., and D. Heineman (2012). *Rhetoric Online: The Politics of New Media*, 2nd ed., Bern, Switzerland: Peter Lang Publishing.

Wilson, C., and A. Dunn (2011), 'Digital Media in the Egyptian Revolution: Descriptive Analysis from the Tahrir Data Sets', *International Journal of Communication*, 5: 25.

Wulf, V., K. Aal, I. Abu Kteish, M. Atam, K. Schubert, M. Rohde, G. P. Yerousis and D. Randall (2013a), 'Fighting against the Wall: Social Media Use by Political Activists in a Palestinian Village'. In *Proceedings of the SIGCHI Conference on Human Factors in Computing Systems*, New York: Association for Computing Machinery, 1979–88.

Wulf, V., K. Misaki, M. Atam, D. Randall and M. Rohde (2013b), ' "On the Ground" in Sidi Bouzid: Investigating Social Media Use during the Tunisian Revolution'. In *Proceedings of the 2013 Conference on Computer Supported Cooperative Work*, New York: Association for Computing Machinery, 1409–18.

Yee, V., and M. El-Naggar (2021), ' "Social Media Is the Mass Protest": Solidarity with Palestinians Grows Online', *The New York Times*, https://www.nytimes.com/2021/05/18/world/middleeast/palestinians-social-media.html (accessed 29 January 2022).

Yerousis, G., K. Aal, T. von Rekowski, D. W. Randall, M. Rohde and V. Wulf (2015), 'Computer-Enabled Project Spaces: Connecting with Palestinian Refugees across Camp Boundaries'. In *Proceedings of the 33rd Annual ACM Conference on Human Factors in Computing Systems, CHI '15*, New York: ACM, 3749–58, https://doi.org/10.1145/2702123.2702283.

Zayyan, H., and C. Carter (2009), 'Human Rights and Wrongs: Blogging News of Everyday Life in Palestine'. In S. Allan and E. Thorson (eds), *Citizen Journalism: Global Perspective*, Bern, Switzerland: Peter Lang, 85–94.

9

#PalDigiplomacy: Palestinian online public diplomacy during Israel's 2021 attacks

Loreley Hahn-Herrera

Introduction

On 10 May 2021, Israel began the bombardment of the Gaza Strip. The attack was the fourth large-scale military operation against the air, land and sea blockaded and densely populated Palestinian enclave in the last thirteen years. As Israel robbed Palestinians of their properties, denied them access to their religious sites and inflicted psychological and physical injuries on them, their plight became visible online. Social media allowed Palestinians and their international supporters to articulate and frame their stories within the historical and political contexts in which they develop. Consequently, they can challenge hegemonic media and political elites (Kuntsman and Stein, 2010; Tawil-Souri and Aouragh, 2014; Ward, 2009) and break away from the traditional coverage of mainstream media that misrepresents or ignores the Palestinian narrative and allows Israeli voices to speak unchallenged (Noakes and Wilkins, 2002; Philo and Berry, 2004, 2011).

Recent research has centred on the use of social media platforms by the Palestinian grassroots and the international solidarity network that supports them (Aouragh, 2012; Collins, 2011; Monshipouri and Prompichai, 2018; Siapera, 2013; Tawil-Souri and Aouragh, 2014). The present work is one of the first (Manor and Holmes, 2018; Yarchi, 2018) to look at the institutional efforts of the Palestinian leadership's use of social media platforms for public diplomacy. It analyses how the Palestinian Ministry of Foreign Affairs (PMoFA) used Twitter and Instagram to articulate and advance strategic narratives during the Israeli attacks on the oPt and the Gaza Strip between 6 and 21 May 2021.

Examining Palestinian digital diplomacy is crucial because it provides a window into how the State of Palestine self-represents and how it uses social media channels to bypass negative and contentious portrayals of its cause and people while attempting to establish direct links with foreign governments and publics. The exercise of public diplomacy is one essential facet where public opinion can change in favour of the Palestinian cause on a global level. It is also a way to refocus international attention on the Palestinian plight during a time when the peace process went stale after the Oslo

Accords' failure. Additionally, the complicit US–Israel relationship has furthered the occupation of Palestine with the establishment of more illegal settlements in the West Bank and the moving of the US embassy to Jerusalem. Moreover, it relocates Palestine as a central issue in the Middle East after Arab countries have abandoned their commitment to the Palestinian cause in exchange for economic gains by normalizing relations with Israel, more saliently with the Abraham Accords.

This chapter has four sections. First, it looks at the history of Palestinian diplomacy and the situation in which the PMoFA works, linking it to the current context of public diplomacy, particularly the emergence of digital diplomacy and its relation to soft power and strategic narratives. The second section explains the methodology used. The third section consists of the frame analysis of the PMoFA social media posts and how they function as strategic narratives aiming to advance the Palestinian cause. Finally, the conclusion highlights and reflects on the key findings.

From the PLO to the PMoFA: Palestinian public diplomacy and the use of soft power

Studies focusing on the history and structure of Palestinian diplomatic institutions and their work are scarce (Abusada, 2017; Hassan et al., 2021; Manor and Holmes, 2018; Rumley and Rasgon, 2016; Safieh, 2006; Segal, 1989; Yarchi, 2018) although there is a vast literature on the Palestinian-Israeli diplomatic peace process. In *Reviving a Palestinian Power. The Diaspora and the Diplomatic Corps*, Hassan and others (2021) outline the most recent and comprehensive report on the history of the Palestinian diplomatic structures.

The authors explain how Palestine's foreign diplomacy efforts emerged along the foundation of the Palestine Liberation Organization (PLO) in 1964 and its strategy to establish representative offices in different parts of the world to build international support for the Palestinian cause (Hassan et al., 2021). These efforts accelerated in 1974 when the PLO was granted observer status in the United Nations (UNGA, 1974).

After the signing of the Oslo Accords in 1993, the PLO could operate in the occupied Palestinian territories (oPt). The Oslo framework meant that as long as the leadership of the PLO was the same as that of the Palestinian National Authority (PNA), the organizations could be considered undistinguishable, which was the case with Yassir Arafat and his successor Mahmoud Abbas. As long as the PLO chairman is president of the PNA, the 'PLO primacy is ensured, and the redundant foreign relations structures existing between the PNA and the PLO are not in conflict' (Hassan et al., 2021:14). Nevertheless, there is a problem of representation because the PLO is the sole official representative of the Palestinian people, both the ones in the oPt and the diaspora. The PNA was supposed to be a transitional government that only represents Palestinians in the oPt but has effectively held power since 1994.

The PLO is responsible for the diplomatic capabilities of Palestine and is the only organization able to negotiate international agreements on behalf of the entire Palestinian people (Hassan et al., 2021). However, the gradual establishment of parallel structures from the PNA has led to a vacuum within the PLO. Regarding diplomacy, the PLO's political bureau has been sidelined, first by the PNA's Ministry of Planning and International Cooperation (MoPIC) and since 2005 by the establishment of the Ministry of Foreign Affairs (MoFA).

The transfer of responsibilities has voided the PLO's diplomatic role and altered its activities' focus. One of its main interests was towards advancing the rights of the diaspora and refugees, but it has shifted towards the internationalization of the Palestinian cause and prioritizing 'symbolic victories over pragmatic ones' (Rumley and Rasgon, 2016), such as gaining international recognition for the State of Palestine and obtaining funding and support towards sate-building (Hassan et al., 2021). Nevertheless, one of the main problems is that the transfer of power and responsibilities has not been complete. Thus, duplicating PLO/PNA structures make determining who is in charge confusing. There is also the infighting between Fatah and Hamas, which poses obstacles to the national liberation movement, undermines the grassroots Palestinian civil society advocacy, the international solidarity movement and the role of Palestinian diplomats.

Despite these problems, the PMoFA has become the organism in charge of Palestinian public diplomacy, which consists of creating a positive climate amongst foreign publics to facilitate the acceptance of another country's foreign policy (Kampf, Manor and Segev, 2015). It relies on activities such as information, education, tourism and cultural events that help improve the image of a country, position it vis-à-vis the rest of the world and advance its reputation and foreign policy goals (Bollier, 2003).

In the twenty-first century, the internet and social media platforms gave way to a new type of public diplomacy: digital diplomacy. This phenomenon refers to the use of social media networks to foster dialogue with online publics (Duncombe, 2019; Kampf, Manor and Segev, 2015; Olubukola, 2017). It is a practice that co-exists with traditional diplomatic channels and can implement public diplomacy's objectives – inform, educate and project a positive image – in a fast, low-cost and global way. Digital diplomacy also aids states and non-state actors in gathering and processing large amounts of information for traditional diplomatic activities and providing consular services and emergency assistance to its citizens abroad (Olubukola, 2017). It is a tool for public engagement (Kampf, Manor and Segev, 2015) that has transformed the role of public diplomacy to go beyond the mere transmission of information and towards the building and leveraging of relations with other state and non-state actors and with foreign publics (Hayden, 2012).

The internet allows countries, non-state actors, diasporic communities, non-governmental organizations (NGOs) and interested individuals to partake in foreign policy discussions and, for these discussions, to be a two-way communication system instead of a monologue. As Bollier (2003: 12) highlights, in this new media ecology, the marginalized and powerless are able 'to bypass traditional intermediaries whose power revolved around the control of information'. In the case of the PMoFA, engaging in digital diplomatic practice lets it bypass negative mainstream media coverage and framing and challenge the postures of hegemonic state powers and international organizations vis-à-vis Israel and the Palestinian question.

Another element of digital diplomacy is that it allows for knowledge construction (Bjola and Holmes, 2015). Using information communication technologies (ICTs) as public diplomacy tools means that countries, international organizations and NGOs can develop and share information to advance their objectives. Therefore, digital diplomatic practice creates and strategically controls the information output, making knowledge and cognition available to a global public. For Palestinians, a systematic and encompassing digital diplomacy allows them to tell their story and articulate their narrative, silenced for more than seventy years. It also provides them the possibility to engage foreign audiences who are interested or learning for the first time about the Palestinian plight. Thus, the digitalization of diplomacy permits the diffusion of power that facilitates bottom-up change for grassroots activism and the less powerful countries and non-state actors, as is the case of Palestine, while making soft power a sought-after commodity able to shape global outcomes (Bjola and Holmes, 2015).

Soft power is central to understanding public and digital diplomatic practice. The term developed in the 1990s refers to 'the ability to get preferred outcomes through the co-optive means of agenda-setting, persuasion and attraction' (Nye, 2011: 16). It is the ability to use ideology, values and culture as opposed to military and economic might (hard power). In what Nye (2009) has defined as 'smart power', international actors often use hard and soft power to achieve their means. Recently, not only states but also individuals and non-state actors have implemented hard power, that is, through terrorism. Consequently, soft power, often used by NGOs and civil society, has now become of utmost importance for governments (Bollier, 2003) because, as Nye (2013: 3) argues, in the information age, 'it is not just whose army wins it is also whose story wins'.

Roselle et al. (2014: 71) explain that strategic narratives are 'soft power in the 21st century'. Strategic narratives focus on how persuasion and influence work and in which contexts and conditions they would be successfully implemented. They are a way of developing, crafting and diffusing ideas in the international system. Soft power and strategic narratives attempt to build shared meanings by using culture, values, policies and affective components to persuade and attract foreign publics. In more complex media environments, strategic narratives are a relevant element of contestation used by international actors to sway target audiences into their camps (Roselle et al., 2014).

Duncombe (2019) furthers the idea of using affect and emotion in digital diplomacy. She highlights that this is key to understanding the power of using social media in public diplomacy. Ideology, culture and values are assets for persuasion and elements that help construct the state identity that governments want to use to represent and advance on the global stage. The way states portray themselves – the ideas they support and the emotions they mobilize – speak to the policies and interests they want to legitimize.

Consequently, emotion helps construct national identity frames that aim to make the country, its values and its culture attractive while also creating and spreading state identity knowledge that can further foreign interest. Additionally, using emotion in social media allows for building trust that can help solidify diplomatic relations and increase public opinion support. This is enhanced by what Duncombe (2019: 104) calls 'emotional contagion', which is the idea that emotions can spread from one person to another and that social media, particularly Twitter, facilitates this. Polleta's (2002) and Papacharissi's (2015) works further elaborate this by arguing that emotive frames appeal to people's passions and can help mobilize support.

While Polleta (2002) and Papacharissi (2015) look at emotion and affect within social movements, their work can help look at how public and digital diplomacy use soft power and strategic narratives to advance a state's policies and reputation in the international arena. For Polleta (2002), one of the main ways to increase support is through storytelling, which allows for the narration of a coherent event where emotions, even when not explicitly articulated, can be elicited by the severity of that event and lead to action. Additionally, stories are 'persuasive rhetorical devices' (Polleta and Chen, 2012: 487) because they can change people's opinions, particularly when they are not fully informed or cognizant of an issue. In her research on storytelling on digital media platforms, Papacharissi (2015) speaks of 'affective publics' as those publics that are mobilized through and mobilize affect. Saliently, Papacharissi found that hashtags on Twitter work as framing devices that allow publics to construct a collaborative narrative, thus providing a way to organize and have a long-term engagement.

Hashtags serve as an indexing system on social media (Xiong et al., 2019) through which users can search and identify topics and conversations that are relevant to them. They also allow users to contribute to discourse (Gunson, 2021) and become active participants in framing issues, which lets online users have the power to establish the salience of a topic and follow its development in real-time or 'trending'. Using hashtags means that user-generated content can bypass mainstream media routines that determine what is news and allow grassroots activism as well as politicians and people in power the capabilities of agenda-setting. In the case of Palestinian digital diplomacy, I argue that the PMoFA aims to frame Palestine and the Palestinian plight through a narrative that builds affective publics. Consequently, the discourse, frames and hashtags used aim to portray Palestinians as human beings with rights, hopes and desires continually crushed by the Israeli occupation.

Methodology

This research examines the frames the PMoFA used on Twitter and Instagram between 6 and 21 May 2021. The study began with the assumption that the PMoFA would use these digital platforms to depict an alternative narrative to the one presented in traditional mainstream media that was favourable for the Palestinian state and its people. A second assumption was that through strategic narratives, the PMoFA would attempt to build knowledge on the historical background of the Palestinian plight that could help foreign publics learn and understand the current status of the Palestinian-Israeli conflict, aid in the legitimization of the Palestinian cause and increase support in public opinion towards Palestine.

All of PMoFA's Twitter and Instagram posts were collected manually through screenshots. In total, the PMoFA published 297 social media posts, 252 on its official Twitter account @pmofa, 34 on its associated Twitter account @MofaPPD, and 11 on its Instagram account @palestine.mofa. This research analysed 297 posts. It is essential to clarify that because of the 280-character limit of Twitter, a post can be published individually or be part of a thread where two or more posts are related. Of the 286 tweets analysed, the PMoFA used 39 threads comprising between 2 and up to 25 tweets. In the case of Instagram, the platform allows for a maximum of 10 different photographs or videos to be part of a single post with one caption, and out of the 18 posts, 8 included more than 1 photograph.

Based on the textual nature of social media and digital diplomacy, a frame analysis methodology was used to identify the strategic narratives used in the 297 social media posts. Borrowing from the work of Benford and Snow (1992), frames are defined as selected ways to understand the world. Frames attempt to make a complex reality comprehensible by placing it within specific categories. In their words:

> It [Frame] refers to an interpretive schemata that simplifies and condenses the 'world out there' by selectively punctuating and encoding objects, situations, events, experiences, and sequences of actions within one's present or past environment. (Benford and Snow, 1992: 137)

Frame analysis helps to understand the strategic approach to the use of language and overall communicative activity in a specific context (Lindekilde, 2014). It is a technique for approaching a text and understanding how different ideas and cultural elements are linked together to construct meaning and be implemented in context-specific discursive practices (Creed, Langstraat and Scully, 2002). It revolves around the idea that social actors use strategic and deliberate language, where specific ideas, events, culture and ideology are actively put to work to ascribe meaning or challenge the existing meaning of a topic to focus it on a specific direction.

A codebook was developed by reading the posts and examining the accompanying photographs to determine how the language and imagery used fit themes that could comprise different frames. The posts were analysed again against the categories in the codebook to determine if there was a need to create new categories. In most cases, more than one frame appeared in a single post.

Framing Palestinian Digiplomacy

In a 2020 report, Burson, Cohn and Wolfe (2020) write that 189 countries have either personal or institutional accounts for their heads of state and/or Ministries of Foreign Affairs (MFAs). They add that 'foreign ministries continue to expand their digital diplomatic networks, encouraging their missions and ambassadors worldwide to become active on social media'. One of the attractive aspects of the platform is that heads of state and MFAs can quickly react to and comment on world affairs (Kampf, Manor and Segev, 2015) and broadcast relevant information to local and foreign publics.

Twitter's central purpose as a microblogging service is to share and transmit information without interaction being a prerequisite, as in other social networks. Thus, its high usage for digital diplomacy means that most world leaders and MFAs continuously publish information instead of interacting with their followers (Kamp, Manor and Segev, 2015).

On the other hand, the photo-sharing app Instagram has become the third most popular social network for diplomats, behind Twitter and Facebook, with 81 per cent of UN member states having an account to share videos and photographs. While it has been underutilized by governments, its importance has become apparent. Some of its appeal is that it helps draw a younger audience, a group not typically attuned to foreign diplomacy and public affairs issues (Clay, 2019), but that can be key for shaping the future of diplomacy since influencing young people at an early age could prove strategic for policymaking and increasing political support. Its strong reliance on user-generated, image-based content (Sprott, 2019) can make it a prominent channel for advancing marginalized voices and challenging hegemonic narratives. Its content can be organized by location data and hashtags, which, as Papacharissi (2015) argued, allow for narratives to be collectively framed and constructed by affective publics.

The PMoFA has two separate Twitter accounts: @pmofa, established in July 2012, has 8,060 followers and follows 132 accounts. The second one @MofaPPD has operated since November 2018. It currently has 707 followers and follows 116 accounts. Its Instagram account @palestine.mofa first posted on 11 March 2019. It has 3,520 followers, is following 0 accounts, and has 527 posts at the time of writing. Between 6 and 21 May 2021, the PMoFA published 297 social media posts on its Twitter and Instagram accounts, 252 tweets from the @pmofa account, 34 from the @mofaPPD account and 18 Instagram posts, respectively.

Among the general characteristics of the posts is that English was the primary language used on both platforms during the research period, with 184 posts written in English. The analysis shows that the Twitter account @mofaPPD tweets in English systematically. However, the @pmofa Twitter account and its Instagram account tweet mainly in Arabic. Therefore, the use of English signals a departure from most posts before and after those dates. Consequently, the PMoFA recognized the opportunity to reach an international audience during the escalation of the conflict by changing the language it uses to communicate on Instagram and Twitter.

Additionally, the PMoFA understood that sharing photographs and videos along with English text would increase the likelihood of the content being understood and shared by foreign publics. Consequently, posts shared on both platforms used photographs or videos to accompany the messages. While Instagram requires an image to be associated with the post and is the app's central feature, Twitter is a text-based platform. Still, out of the 286 tweets, 66 had image-based content, meaning that 23 per cent of Twitter posts had visual imagery. Tweets with photos and videos tend to perform better and receive higher engagement, thus helping drive the Palestinian narrative further. Moreover, Duncombe (2019) argues that adding images to text-based social media platforms provides an extra layer of emotional complexity to digital diplomacy. She writes:

Texts and images shared on social media are powerful not only because of the emotions they evoke but also because they frame representations of identity. (Duncombe, 2019: 112)

The analysis showed that the PMoFA relied on five frames: Affect and emotion, settler colonialism, violence, human rights and international solidarity. However, frames were not used in the same way on Twitter and Instagram; there was different content and language used on each platform, and the use of hashtags also differed. In most cases, several frames were articulated in one single post and used hashtags in combination with one another, which shows that frames are overlapping and interdependent because, in this form, they can articulate a more encompassing narrative and construct a comprehensive meaning.

Affect and emotion frame

This frame was the most prominent on Twitter and Instagram. It relied on different narrative devices that appealed to the conscience and emotions of the audience, such as injured children (Figure 9.1), cultural destruction (Figure 9.2), as well as discourse and images that speak of fear and suffering (Figure 9.3) and elicit an emotional response from the social media user.

Using an emotional frame, the PMoFA implements a strategic narrative that portrays Palestinians as the victims and Israel as the aggressor. This way, the Palestinian state bypasses mainstream media narratives and challenges adversarial reporting to gain the support of foreign publics. Using these storytelling mechanisms, the PMoFA is structuring a clear and cohesive story that can be easily shared online and can help

State of Palestine - MFA ✔ @pmofa · May 18, 2021   ···
7/10 Israel, the occupying Power, is also deliberately targeting children. Over 40 percent of those willfully killed have been children, and the number is rising;

♡ 1   ⟲ 1   ♡ 1   ↥

Show this thread

Figure 9.1 Tweet about Israel's targeting of Palestinian children

Palestinian Public Diplomacy   ···
@MofaPPD

In #Gaza, the Israeli occupation targets and destroys holy sights to demoralize Palestinians and attempt to erase their culture.

7:38 PM · May 21, 2021 · Twitter for iPhone

Figure 9.2 Tweet about Israel's destruction of Palestinian religious sites

> **State of Palestine - MFA** ✅ @pmofa · May 14, 2021   ...
> 3/3 **Families** in #GazaStrip are living in sheer terror for their lives,
> compounded by their knowledge of their absolute helplessness.
> #GazaUnderAttack #FreePalestine #EndOpression #SaveSheikhJarrah
>
> ♡   ⇄ 3   ♡ 3   ↑

Figure 9.3 Tweet narrating Palestinians' experiences during Israel's attacks

increase international solidarity with Palestine while constructing and representing its own state identity (Duncombe, 2019) as one of resistance in the face of adversity, of victimhood and of wanting their own story acknowledged and legitimized by the international community.

While the portrayal of Palestinian suffering is not new, the representation of victimhood by Palestinians themselves is a storytelling device that elicits an emotional reaction while constructing cognitive frames. It is an implementation of soft power that works on several levels, the ideological one showing Palestinian perseverance. The cultural and historical one portrays the history of the conflict and how Israel aims to ethnically cleanse the Palestinians and eradicate or appropriate their culture. Lastly, the emotional aspect, where all these facets work together to educate foreign publics and generate a response from them that can translate into long-term support while also aiming to delegitimize the Israeli narrative and undermine their hasbara, their diplomatic support and international standing.

Settler colonialism frame

Both platforms used this frame in the posts' text content, hashtags and images associated with each post. Some of the recurring hashtags on Twitter and Instagram were: #IsraeliOccupation, #EndOccupation, #Jerusalem, #SaveSheikhJarrah, #TheNakbaContinues, #Nakba, #Nakba73, #FreePalestine, #Palestine and #SavePalestine. The PMoFA also used three hashtags in Arabic: انقذوا_حي_الشيخ_جراح# مستمرة_النكبة# and #القصف_تحت_غزة# on Twitter but not on Instagram.

Using the settler-colonial frame is a strategic device for Palestinians that captures their historical experience as the country's indigenous people (Figure 9.4) while establishing that their cause is just and legitimate (Hijab and Jaradat, 2017). It is a tool that addresses the history of the conflict and its different elements and portrays them as part of a broader system of control and oppression (Figure 9.5), not as disjointed attacks or isolated events (Salamanca et al., 2012). This frame also advances the narratives of decolonization and self-determination and establishes links with other former colonized nations.

Violence frame

Violence is one of the most prevalent characteristics of the Palestine–Israel conflict, and it underlines its origins, development and current state. During Israel's attacks

State of Palestine - MFA ✔
@pmofa

...

(1/5) Today, 15 May 2021, is the 73th anniversary of Al-Nakba (catastrophe) that befell the Palestinian people in 1948, as Zionists militias forcibly uprooted and ethnically cleansed the 800,000 Palestinians from their homes in 400 villages and made them refugees; #Nakba73

11:12 AM · May 15, 2021 · Twitter for Android

8 Retweets   **7** Likes

Figure 9.4 Tweet commemorating the Nakba

State of Palestine - MFA ✔
@pmofa

...

(4/5) Regrettably, the Palestinian people continue to suffer an ongoing Nakba, as Israel, the occupying Power, persists with its cruel denial of the rights of the Palestinian people; #EndtheOccupation #SaveSheikhJarraj #GazaUnderAttack

11:12 AM · May 15, 2021 · Twitter for Android

2 Retweets   **5** Likes

Figure 9.5 Tweet on the ongoing Israeli occupation of Palestine

in May 2021, this was one of the main frames used by the PMoFA as the escalation in violence draws attention to the Palestine–Israel conflict and garners traditional news media coverage. Furthermore, the linkages between social media and traditional news media amplify public diplomacy messages as it is now common to have social media posts form the basis for news stories (Duncombe, 2019).

Using war, destruction, death and fear (Figures 9.6, 9.7 and 9.8) as online storytelling mechanisms is a way to make news headlines and obtain emotional reactions that establish affective connections with the audiences. Thus, the

State of Palestine - MFA ☑
@pmofa

        ⋯

4/22In the occupied #GazaStrip, Israel, the occupying
Power, has killed 122 Palestinians, including 31
children and 19 women, and wounded more than 830;
In there rest of the State of Palestine;

11:01 PM · May 14, 2021 · Twitter for Android

1 Like

Figure 9.6 Tweet highlighting Palestinian casualties' numbers

State of Palestine - MFA ☑
@pmofa

        ⋯

13/22Jewish supremacist settlers continue rampaging
in Palestinian neighborhoods
in #EastJerusalem, in Sheikh Jarrah, Silwan, Al-Tur
and other areas, terrorizing families, causing injuries
and damage to homes and properties,attacking
Palestinians in their own homes;

11:01 PM · May 14, 2021 · Twitter for Android

1 Quote Tweet   1 Like

Figure 9.7 Tweet about Israel's ongoing attacks on the oPt and Gaza

violence frame, along with hashtags such as #GazaUnderAttack, #Gaza, #SaveGaza, #IsraeliCrimes and #WarCrimes, serves the aims of traditional public diplomacy by informing foreign publics and constructing knowledge about the specific situation of Palestine while contributing to the construction of emotional frames and national identity.

Human rights frame

Framing Palestine as a human rights issue has been more common since the 1980s, coinciding with the events of the First Intifada. It is a frame that has shifted Palestine

State of Palestine - MFA ✓
@pmofa   ...

5/22Despite the callous narrative spread by Israel's
constant dehumanization and demonization of
thePalestinian people, these human lives are being
mourned, tears are flowing, the pain is searing, lives
have been forever ruined;

11:01 PM · May 14, 2021 · Twitter for Android

1 Like

Figure 9.8 Tweet humanizing Palestinians

State of Palestine - MFA ✓
@pmofa   ...

19/22Once again, we call upon the #SecurityCouncil
to act in respect of its Charter duty to maintain
international peace and security. The Palestinian
people cannot be left without protection at the mercy
of an occupying Power armed to the teeth;

11:01 PM · May 14, 2021 · Twitter for Android

1 Like

Figure 9.9 Tweet calling on the UN Security Council

away from the predominant frameworks of settler colonialism and national liberation
that were prevalent since the origins of the Palestinian question. The PMoFA used
this frame to call on international organizations (Figure 9.9), such as the UN Security
Council, and denounced Israel for committing war crimes and violating Palestinians'
human rights by militarily attacking civilians, destroying infrastructure and obstructing
the work of humanitarian agencies (Figure 9.10).

Allen (2018) highlights that the use of the human rights framework has become a
hegemonic discourse for Palestinians and their international supporters. Through this
narrative device, Palestinians could break away from the images of the armed struggle
that permeated media coverage of Palestinians in the 1960s and 1970s (Collins,

State of Palestine - MFA ✓
@pmofa
⋯

21/22There must be a clear demand for an end to all attacks, provocations and incitement and for full respect of #internationallaw, including #humanitarianlaw, and a demand for a halt of Israel's criminal aggression against Gaza and a cessation of all illegal Israeli actions;

11:01 PM · May 14, 2021 · Twitter for Android

1 Quote Tweet   **4** Likes

Figure 9.10 Tweet highlighting Israel's violation of international and humanitarian law

2011) and instead be seen and heard as human beings deserving of rights. The use of human rights as a framing strategy has been critiqued for de-contextualizing and de-politicizing the Palestinian cause (Tawil-Souri, 2015). Nevertheless, this framework prevails because the media portrayal of the violent reality of Palestine produces images that are themselves a vehicle for the articulation of the human rights discourse and a witnessing technique that allows Palestinians the right to claim-making and legitimacy based on their identity as a 'nation of sufferers' (Allen, 2009: 165). Moreover, it enables Palestinians to elicit sympathy and empathy from foreign publics based on having shared humanity.

While initially international NGOs relied on this frame, Palestinians have adopted it as a way to portray themselves, which coincides with Duncombe's (2019) notion of how framing aids states in identity construction. In Allen's words:

Human rights informs how Palestinians see themselves, how they create solidarities internationally and locally, and how they forge channels through which to mobilize forms of support, to empathize, and to provide national pedagogy. (Allen, 2009: 165)

International solidarity frame

The international solidarity framework helps portray Palestine as a prominent example of a global fight against injustice and oppression while allowing the Palestinian cause to establish links with other justice, anti-colonial and human rights movements worldwide. Because of the protracted nature of the Palestinian issue and the emergence of other international crises, internationalizing it is a mechanism to maintain Palestine in the political and media agenda and exercise pressure for its just and prompt

Palestinian Public Diplomacy
@MofaPPD
···

Countries around the world are rising up to stand in solidarity with the Palestinian people. Friends of #Palestine from all over are speaking out against the illegal occupation and the inhumane treatment Palestinians suffer at the hands of the #IsraeliOccupation.

9:07 AM · May 19, 2021 · Twitter for iPhone

1 Retweet   **3** Likes

Figure 9.11 Tweet showing international protests in support of Palestine

resolution. The PMoFA used the frame to highlight the international protests to call for an end to the Israeli military attack on Gaza and, more broadly, the occupation of Palestine (Figures 9.11, 9.12 and 9.13).

The solidarity frame contributes to the construction and maintenance of affective publics. It is a way to bond with foreign audiences and recognize how grassroots activism has the mobilizing capabilities to challenge the international status quo. By acknowledging transnational solidarity with Palestine, the PMoFA uses strategic narratives that advance a history of dispossession and oppression that international activists legitimize. As the protests took place offline, it also demonstrates how online framing can have a spillover into offline grassroots collective action.

Figure 9.12 Tweet thanking global solidarity with Palestine

Figure 9.13 Tweet thanking international solidarity with Palestine

Conclusions

This chapter examined the Twitter and Instagram output of the PMoFA during the Israeli military attack against the oPt and the Gaza Strip to understand which frames the PMoFA advanced online and how they can work as strategic narratives for online public diplomacy. The research found that the most prevalent frames were affect and emotion, settler colonialism, violence, human rights and international solidarity.

The analysis demonstrates that the use of these specific frames is an active exercise of narrative and storytelling that relies on the overlapping and interdependent use of frames and hashtags to provide context on the situation of Palestine and construct a resonant meaning that can be understood and shared by online publics.

The prevalence of the affect and emotion frame on both social media platforms aligns with the notions of Duncombe (2019), Nye (2011), Papacharissi (2015), Polleta (2002) and Roselle et al. (2014) about the importance of eliciting an emotional reaction and constructing affective publics as a way of exercising soft power and articulating strategic narratives. Using English as the primary language of the publications and including images and videos provided the social media postings with further emotional complexity than if they had been solely textual.

The frames operate on an individual level, but their joint usage contributes to constructing a coherent and cohesive narrative that articulates Palestine's history and its people's stories. It also helps the PMoFA construct and portray a national identity that aids in legitimizing the Palestinian narrative and the role of the PNA and its foreign ministry vis-à-vis local and foreign publics and the international community.

Understanding how the PMoFA exercises its public diplomacy online provides insight into how the Palestinian state positions itself in the broader international relations landscape and the ideological resources it uses to construct its identity vis-à-vis its population and the foreign publics it seeks to influence. It provides a window into Palestinian leadership's narrative tools to counteract Israel's hegemonic narrative on the conflict and its pervasiveness in global mainstream media. As such, this work seeks to contribute to the literature on the practice of digital diplomacy and strategic narratives (Bjola and Holmes, 2015; Bollier, 2003; Duncombe, 2019; Kampf, Manor and Segev, 2015; Olubukola, 2017, Roselle et al., 2014) and specifically, on the gap that exists on the field of Palestine's public diplomatic practice, which has only been studied by Manor and Holmes (2018) when they looked at the Facebook page of Palestine in Hebrew.

References

Abusada, M. (2017), 'Palestinian Diplomacy: Past and Present'. In G. Gürbey, S. Hoffmann and F. I. Seyder (eds.), *Between State and Non-State. Politics and Society in Kurdistan-Iraq and Palestine*, New York: Palgrave Macmillan, 197–212.

Allen, L. A. (2009), 'Martyr Bodies in the Media: Human Rights, Aesthetics, and the Politics of Immediation in the Palestinian Intifada', *American Ethnologist*, 36 (1): 161–80.

Allen, L. A. (2018), 'What's in a Link?', *South Atlantic Quarterly*, 117 (1): 111–33.

Aouragh, M. (2012), *Palestine Online: Transnationalism, the Internet and the Construction of Identity*, London: IB Tauris.

Benford, R., and D. Snow (1992), 'Master Frames and Cycles of Protest'. In A. D. Morris and C. M. Mueller (eds), *Frontiers in Social Movement Theory*, New Haven, CT: Yale University Press, 133–55.

Bjola, C., and M. Holmes (2015), *Digital Diplomacy: Theory and Practice*, New York: Routledge.

Bollier, D. (2003), 'The Rise of Netpolitik: How the Internet Is Changing International Politics and Diplomacy', A Report of the Annual Aspen Institute Roundtable on

Information Technology, The Aspen Institute, Communications and Society Program, USA, http://www.bollier.org/files/aspen_reports/NETPOLITIK.PDF (accessed 20 September 2021).

Burson, Cohn and Wolfe (2020), 'Twiplomacy Study 2020', https://www.twiplomacy.com/twiplomacy-study-2020 (accessed 10 October 2021).

Clay, J. (2019), 'How Twitter, Instagram and Other Social Media Are Transforming Diplomacy', School of Communication and Journalism, University of Southern California, 25 February, https://annenberg.usc.edu/news/research-and-impact/how-twitter-instagram-and-other-social-media-are-transforming-diplomacy (accessed 25 September 2021).

Collins, J. (2011), *Global Palestine*, London: Hurst.

Creed, D., J. Langstraat and M. Scully (2002) (2002), 'A Picture of the Frame: Frame Analysis as a Technique and as Politics', *Organizational Research Methods*, 5(1): 34–55.

Duncombe, C. (2019), 'Digital Diplomacy: Emotion and Identity in the Public Realm', *The Hague Journal of Diplomacy*, 14: 102–16.

Gunson, M. (2021), 'Web 2.0: Hashtag Activism', https://michaelwgunson.info/Hashtag-Activism (accessed 15 October 2021).

Hassan, Z., N. Hijab, I. Abdel Razek and M. Younis (2021), 'Reviving a Palestinian Power. The Diaspora and the Diplomatic Corps', *Al Shabaka*, May 2021, https://al-shabaka.org/reports/reviving-a-palestinian-power-the-diaspora-and-the-diplomatic-corps/ (accessed 1 October 2021).

Hayden, C. (2012), 'Social Media at State: Power, Practice, and Conceptual Limits for US Public Diplomacy', *Global Media Journal*, 11: 1–21.

Hijab, N., and I. Jaradat (2017), 'Talking Palestine: What Frame of Analysis? Which Goals and Messages?', *Al-Shabaka*, 12 April, https://al-shabaka.org/commentaries/talking-palestine-frame-analysis-goals-messages/ (accessed 13 October 2021).

Kampf, R., I. Manor and E. Segev (2015), 'Digital Diplomacy 2.0? A Cross-National Comparison of Public Engagement in Facebook and Twitter', *The Hague Journal of Diplomacy*, 10: 331–62.

Kuntsman, A., and R. Stein (2010), 'Another War Zone. Social Media in the Israeli-Palestinian Conflict', *Middle East Research and Information Project*, 20 September, https://merip.org/2010/09/another-war-zone/ (accessed 13 October 2021).

Lindekilde, L. (2014), 'Discourse and Frame Analysis'. In D. Della Porta (ed.), *Methodological Practices in Social Movement Research*, Oxford: Oxford University Press, 195–227.

Manor, I., and M. Holmes (2018), 'Palestine in Hebrew: Overcoming the Limitation of Traditional Diplomacy', *Revista Mexicana de Política Exterior*, 113: 1–17.

Monshipouri, M., and T. Prompichai (2018), 'Digital Activism in Perspective: Palestinian Resistance via Social Media', *International Studies Journal*, 14 (4): 37–58.

Noakes, J. A., and K. G. Wilkins (2002), 'Shifting Frames of the Palestinian Movement in US News', *Media, Culture & Society*, 24: 649–71.

Nye, J. (2009), 'Get Smart: Combining Hard and Soft Power', *Foreign Affairs*, 88 (4): 160–3.

Nye, J. (2011), *The Future of Power*, New York: Public Affairs.

Nye, J. (2013), 'Transcript of Witness Testimony to the House of Lords Select Committee on Soft Power and the UK's Influence', 15 October, https://www.parliament.uk/globalassets/documents/lords-committees/soft-power-uk-influence/uc151013Ev10.pdf (accessed 20 September 2021).

Olubukola, A. (2017), 'Foreign Policy in an Era of Digital Diplomacy', *Cogent Social Sciences*, 3 (1): 129–75.

Papacharissi, Z. (2015), 'Affective Publics and Structures of Storytelling: Sentiment, Events and Mediality', *Information, Communication & Society*, 19: 307–24.

Philo, G., and M. Berry (2004), *Bad News from Israel*, London: Pluto Press.

Philo, G., and M. Berry (2011), *More Bad News from Israel*, London: Pluto Press.

Polleta, F. (2002), 'Plotting Protest'. In J. E. Davis (ed.), *Stories of Change: Narrative and Social Movements*, Albany: State University of New York Press.

Polleta, F., and B. Chen (2012), 'Narrative and Social Movements'. In J. C. Alexander, R. N. Jacobs and P. Smith (eds), *The Oxford Handbook of Cultural Sociology*, Oxford: Oxford University Press.

Roselle, L., A. Miskimmon and B. O'Loughlin (2014), 'Strategic Narrative: A New Means to Understand Soft Power', *Media, War & Conflict*, 7 (1): 70–84.

Rumley, G., and A. Rasgon (2016), 'Assessing the Palestinian Authority's Foreign Policy', *Fathom*, https://fathomjournal.org/assessing-the-palestinian-authoritys-foreign-pol icy/ (accessed 1 October 2021).

Safieh, A. (2006), *On Palestinian Diplomacy*, Beltsville, Maryland: International Graphics.

Salamanca, O., M. Qato, K. Rabie and S. Samour (2012), 'Past Is Present: Settler Colonialism in Palestine', *Settler Colonial Studies*, 2 (1): 1–8.

Segal, J. (1989), 'A Foreign Policy for the State of Palestine', *Journal of Palestine Studies*, 18 (2): 16–28.

Siapera, E. (2013), 'Tweeting #Palestine: Twitter and the Mediation of Palestine', *International Journal of Cultural Studies*, 17 (6): 539–55.

Sprott, B. (2019), 'The Next Phase of PD: Instagram Diplomacy', Centre for Public Diplomacy Blog, University of Southern California, USA, https://uscpublicdiplomacy. org/blog/next-phase-pd-instagram-diplomacy (accessed 25 September 2021).

Tawil-Souri, H. (2015), 'Media, Globalization, and the (Un)Making of the Palestinian Cause', *Popular Communication*, 13 (2): 145–57.

Tawil-Souri, H., and M. Aouragh (2014), 'Intifada 3.0? Cyber Colonialism and Palestinian Resistance', *The Arab Studies Journal*, 22 (1): 102–33.

Yarchi, M. (2018), 'Two Stories for Two Nations: Public Diplomacy in the Israeli-Palestinian Conflict', *Studies in Conflict and Terrorism*, 41 (9): 677–95.

UNGA (1974), *Resolution 3237 (XXIX) Observer Status for the Palestine Liberation Organization*, United Nations General Assembly, 22 November, https://www.un.org/ ga/search/view_doc.asp?symbol=A/RES/3237(XXIX) (accessed 1 October 2021).

Ward, W. (2009), 'Social Media and the Gaza Conflict', *Arab Media & Society*, 7: 1–6.

Xion, Y., C. Moonhee and B. Boatwright (2019), 'Hashtag Activism and Message Frames among Social Movement Organizations: Semantic Network Analysis and Thematic Analysis of Twitter during the #MeToo Movement', *Public Relations Review*, 45: 10–23.

10

Social media, activism and mass protest: Framed narratives of the May 2021 Sheikh Jarrah events

Shadi Abu-Ayyash and Hussein AlAhmad

Introduction

One might claim that the contentious debate in academia, media and politics about the potentialities of communication technologies in providing possibilities for citizens to bring about social and political change will not cease to exist as long as new technologies are used and produced. Historically, advanced communication technologies have had their role in mediating conflicts and influencing the routes and outcomes of many struggles. Kellner (2003) emphasizes the media's influence, primarily how it represents a wide series of conflicts, in ever-changing shapes of interaction with its audience, in a way that is powerful enough to instigate new conflicts of varied nature. In a contemporary mediatized era, social media offers a refuge to social and political actors in their endeavour to exert influence on public opinion. Polarizing and mobilizing publics relies on several tools including the use of media. New media, according to Cottle (2006), plays a role in providing the powerless with tools to counter the imbalance in power. Social media contents that are generated in times of conflicts are mostly produced in forms of framed narratives, which seek to influence public opinion and impose agendas on public debate. Framing is a building process that consists of 'narrowing' or focusing of public attention towards certain aspects/stories in the conflict (Entman, 1993).

Our overall argument, in this chapter, is in line with the body of literature that advances the idea of media framing, primarily how internet users produce framed narratives on social media to mobilize domestic and regional publics to achieve their aims. These frames, when further analysed, may produce narratives that intersect with the thoughts and interests of other users with similar standpoints and contribute to the production of collective online framed narratives.

One method adopted in this chapter is through providing a case study that sheds light on how narratives – in the digital venues – are constructed through the lens of framing. While many studies have tried to capture mediatized conflicts via traditional media lenses, this chapter attempts to examine and conceptualize mediatized conflicts from the new media's unique perspective, that is, social media production and consumption.

Research on mediatized conflicts is influenced by the dynamics of the media's role in bringing attention to certain aspects of an event, the production of framed content and power relations among actors via communications practices (Eskjær, Hjarvard and Mortensen, 2015; Lundby, 2018) and narrating conflicts (Matar and Harb, 2013). This chapter, however, provides an opportunity to understand the relationship between communication and conflict – with regard to ordinary people's narratives. A recent case of conflict, with evident social media influence, took place during the recent round of confrontations erupting on 6 May 2021 in the Sheikh Jarrah neighbourhood of occupied Jerusalem. This was a result of an Israeli court order evicting at least seven Palestinian families from their homes for the benefit of Israeli settlers. A few days later, during the holy month of Ramadan, Israeli forces invaded Al-Aqsa Mosque, one of the holiest places for Muslims. The escalation attracted local, regional and international media and political attention. This was embodied in the popular hashtag #SaveSheikhJarrah, which both widely and constantly reported the on-ground confrontations and was disseminated over multiple social media platforms. In this geopolitical context, the Palestinians have relied on social media platforms to advance their narratives in their struggle for national liberation and ending the Israeli colonization of their land. These digital zones provided an alternate space to reach international viewers, especially that the Western mainstream media accused of being biased to the Israeli narrative (Jackson, 2021). Exploring this recent round of confrontations in Jerusalem, this chapter explores – from a mediatized conflict perspective – how and to what extent activists relied on framing in their narrative via social media platforms (precisely Facebook and Twitter).

In the context of framed narratives, understanding the dynamics of online users' narratives requires two steps of content deconstruction. First, deconstruction of the mediated narrative through analysing how main actors, events, venues and time were incorporated and structured in the content (Bontje and Slinger, 2017), followed by identifying frames and narrative relations (Aukes, Bontje and Slinger, 2020). In this text, the social media content produced by Palestinians and their global supporters pertaining to the recent confrontations, using the popular hashtag of #SaveSheikhJarrah, are analysed in terms of three related analytical tools that we propose combining in this chapter: narrative deconstruction, frames analysis and binary opposition.

Literature review

Mediatized conflicts and framing narratives

Although mediatization research gained attention from communication and media scholars, with many adopting it as a theoretical and methodological framework in their research inquiries, it is still being developed in terms of conceptualization and application to practical research. Mediatization research, argues Lundby (2018), is concerned with understanding relations between changes of media and changes in culture and society, saying that mass and social media are being digitized and merged into global networks of communication – and 'mediatization is driven by big companies and big data, as well as by individual media users and producers' (300). Mediatization research inquiries are not focused on a particular domain, but have been applied to many areas in which digital communication and media-related practices are evident, including fields of contemporary conflicts, online political participation and activism, leading to the birth of new terms such as mediatized conflict – the focus of this chapter.

Studying mediatized conflicts requires looking into actions of the process, which can be applied to news media and social media alike. The process of mediatized conflict consists of three dynamics: first, the media raising an event in the news, followed by a second dynamic where framing is a central act in content production while the third dynamic lies in the role the media play in structuring the communications practices of power relations among publics and institutions (Eskjær, Hjarvard and Mortensen, 2015; Lundby, 2018).

Cottle (2006) has proposed research questions that inquire into mediatized representations of conflicts. These include questions centred on reasons behind visualizing some conflicts in the media while others are salient, and what roles could alternative or new media play in the process. Although these questions of his 2006 work may look overstudied, it can be argued that they are still legitimate research questions that can contribute to contemporary debates on alternative media and social media contributions to narrating conflicts from the 'powerless' point of view.

The body of literature addressing relations between media and conflicts mostly addresses traditional media forms with little attention to 'alternative diverse spaces in which conflicts are imagined and narrated' (Matar and Harb, 2013: 3). These alternative spaces are apparent in interactive social media platforms that have their own logic of narration production. The seemingly unrelated relation between framing process and narrative production is discussed by Aukes, Bontje and Slinger (2020) who state that the main difference between the two lies in the 'respective scale level, [in which] frames are actors' perspectives, whereas narratives are the expressed products of those perspectives' (1).

The classical news production approach to framing is conceptualized by Entman (1993), who classifies four elements of the framing process that involves selecting 'some aspects of a perceived reality and making them more salient in a communicating text in such a way as to promote a particular problem definition, causal interpretation, moral evaluation and/or treatment recommendation for the item described' (52). Building on that, we argue here that social media contents generated by activists and ordinary users, as alternative narratives to mainstream media news content, may also be examined and analysed from a 'framing elements' perspective.

Narrative co-construction in social media, argue Dawson and Mäkelä (2020), is different from what it has been conceptualized as traditionally in narrative research explaining that the dialogical relations between actors on interactive platforms contribute to formulating shared conceptualizations of events. Twitter content for example, as Sadler (2018) explains, provides elements of narrative which nevertheless require a process of reading to make sense of the seemingly separated unrelated tweets. Hashtags, according to Papacharissi (2016), are devices of framing process in which publics engage in politics through engaging in a collaborative process of their own stories' production and reproduction.

A study of how frames are produced in a mediatized conflict is provided by Abdel-Fadil and Liebmann (2018), in which they explain how the main actors in mediatized conflicts about religion, in Scandinavian case studies, are engaging with frames that are dominantly reproduced. They found that mediatized conflicts about religion are centred around the divide between 'good vs. bad' religion. Such analysis may be seen as a notion that resonates with Lévi-Strauss's explanation of human narrative structure that is driven by a binary way of thinking in which polarized themes come to produce binary oppositions (Dixon, 2019). The structuralism-oriented concept of *binary opposition* has been applied in many narrative deconstruction areas of inquiry. Coined by Ferdinand de Saussure, the term refers to the definition of language units where each unit is defined against its opposite meaning (Fogarty, 2005).

Social media and activism for Palestine

Despite the ongoing discussion on the role social media plays in aiding protesters in their efforts to challenge mainstream media narratives, arguments have been made for the idea that social media protesters are not necessarily able to draw public attention to alternative stories (Poell, 2020).

Limitations of social media have been discussed by Van-Dijck and Poell (2013), who clarify that social media logic is constructed based on four main acting pillars: programmability, popularity, connectivity and datafication. Social media platforms, mainly Facebook, practise censorship on Palestinian content as manifested in the role played by programmers and content moderators of that company, which overtly represses digital affiliation with basic Palestinians rights. Facebook has been described as 'the most egregious violator, with far reaching systemic problems and impact on Arab and pro-Palestine content' (Alimardani and Elswah, 2021: 69; see also Lewis, 2021).

Although social media logic may play a role in controlling content diffusion and limiting a message's popularity online, interactive social media platforms possess many unique aspects. Among them is the space they provide for users and activists to overcome the controlled traditional modes of information flow, enabling them to enjoy a 'horizontal mode of communication' in their collective action endeavours (Castells, 2009). Contemporary activists' reliance on digital media for solidarity, networking, organizing and framing narratives and message production is a central aspect of mediatized activism, in which organized and formulized social movements enjoy utilizing.

In war contexts, the key focus of this chapter, online content created and shared by citizens experiencing the armed conflict is no less important than content produced by activists, news media and politicians.

'Internet resistance' is considered as a part of the larger Palestinian political activism against the Zionist dispossession of the Palestinian people and not a separate form of resistance from the historical national resistance movement (Tawil-Souri and Aouragh, 2014). Production of framed narratives around Palestine on social media, including Twitter, is done by users and activists who frame Palestine-related issues based on similar positions in a mediation process that is different from mainstream media 'hard' news (Siapera, 2014). Moreover, social media platforms are utilized by global solidarity activists, who, in the process of organizing and connecting via social media, provide alternative pro-Palestine narratives to issues pertaining to Palestine (Abu-Ayyash, 2015). Meanwhile, the connectivity the internet provides has proven to be an effective tool for Palestinians in Palestine and in the diaspora to collaborate and connect (Aouragh, 2008).

Method and data collection

Contents from a number of accounts on Facebook (*n*=10) and Twitter (*n*=15) were coded. These accounts represent the most followed local news media pages, activists and politicians, in addition to other US- and UK-based Palestinians and solidarity groups.

The selection of accounts took into consideration two elements: the high number of followers based on a 2020 social media report in Palestine (Ipoke, 2020), and the users' high level of digital engagement with the news coming from Palestine. The selected Facebook pages were news media pages that provided ongoing coverage of events in Jerusalem: Palestine TV; Maydan Al-Quds; Al-Qastal; Hadith al-Youm news page and Al-Quds daily newspaper. Palestinian siblings Muna and Muhammad el-Kurd, whose house was occupied by Jewish settlers in the neighbourhood of Sheikh Jarrah, were both very active on social media and on the ground protests. The Facebook account of the Palestinian celebrity singer Mohammad Assaf was also included in the selected pages. An active Ireland-based solidarity group, Ireland Palestine Solidarity Campaign (IPSC), and the outspoken US-based group Jewish Voice for Peace were also chosen for their active online and offline advocacy for Palestine.

The selected accounts on Twitter platform included the American Jewish advocacy group of IfNotNow, the major UK-based solidarity group Palestine Solidarity Campaign (PSC) and the main account of the global Boycott, Divestments and Sanctions Campaign (BDS). Among the selected accounts of Palestinian academics that were vocal on Twitter is Yara Hawari, a writer and senior policy analyst for Al-Shabaka Policy Network. Digital rights activist and the founder and executive director of 7amleh – The Arab Centre for the Advancement of social media, Nadim Nashif's account on Twitter was also included. Palestinian politicians, who were active on Twitter as well as outspoken in addressing English-speaking media, Hanan Ashrawi and the Palestinian Ambassador to the UK Husam Zomlot were included. Twitter accounts of Palestinians living in the diaspora were also chosen, including the Palestinian-American Congress member Rashida Tlaib, Palestinian American activist Huwaid Aarraf, Palestinian-American activist and academic Noura Erakat and Rafeef Ziadah, a UK-based activist, poet and academic at King's College of London. Journalists who were also selected based on their Twitter accounts' activity during the May confrontation included Dima Khatib, the managing director of AJ+ Channels, the Palestinian-American journalist Dena Takruri, a senior presenter and producer at Aljazeera plus (AJ+), and the Palestinian-American journalist Samar Jarrah. Adalah, the legal justice centre protecting the human rights of Palestinian citizens of Israel and Palestinians in the Occupied Territories account on Twitter was also added to the selected sample.

Data analysis

The entire period of analysis (6 to 21 May 2021) was divided into phases that represent four major developments in the confrontation: the Israeli invasion of Al-Aqsa Mosque, the confrontations between Palestinians in the West Bank and Israeli army, the militarized confrontation between Palestinian factions in Gaza and the Israeli Army and the uprising of the Palestinian milieu inside Israel.

For the sampled data content, the authors searched a single and most popular hashtag during the selected period of analysis: Any tweet or post that contained the hashtag #SaveSheikhJarrah, from the selected accounts, during the four mentioned developments, was analysed.

The extracted data were analysed in three sequential phases: narrative deconstruction through categorization of extracted texts into indexical and non-indexical segments, followed by frame elements identification and lastly, binary opposition terms identification. The first phase of coding was borrowed from the Bontje and Slinger (2017) method that recruited biographical research approaches, in which narrative structure is divided into segments and coded into two groups: 'indexical' and 'non-indexical' segments. Indexical segments refer to questions of 'who did what, when, where and why' in relation to events, while non-indexical segments are concerned with how actors are experiencing the events and how these events are reconstructed. The second phase consists of identifying frame elements within the categorized segments. This step is crucial for understanding frames inside the constructed narrative for which a comprehensive coherent interpretation of framed narratives is possible, as frames help us understand how narratives are conveyed: 'frames serve as the underlying foundations on which narratives are expressed' (Aukes, Bontje and Slinger, 2020: 11).

The content of each segment is extracted and classified into four frame elements (see Entman, 1993). Each corresponding content is systematically grouped into specified and relevant groups of topics within the frame variable, providing the authors with a clear way to thematically analyse the extracted data (see Matthes and Kohring, 2008: model of 'patterns frames'). Every frame element that contains variables/topics related to certain themes is added to a table across from its corresponding element, followed by a description of each variable/topic.

A third and final level of analysis involves trancing terms that, within the coded texts of identified frames of narratives, represent binary oppositions. Binary oppositions are salient in narratives surrounding conflicts.

Findings and discussion

Distribution of content

The result of analysing 155 tweets (*n*=100) and posts (*n*=55) from the 25 accounts on Twitter (*n*=15) and Facebook (*n*=10), between 6 and 21 May, shows that visual elements of images and short videos were heavily present in mediating the confrontations. While 43 per cent of the analysed contents contained short videos, 27 per cent contained

Table 10.1 Distribution of content generation over the different periods throughout May confrontations

Date	Number of posts and tweets
From 6 to 11 May	47
From 13 to 15 May	52
From 17 to 19 May	30
From 20 to 21 May	26

still images. This visual content showed images of on-ground confrontations between Israeli soldiers and settlers and Palestinian citizens in Jerusalem, in the West Bank cities, and inside Israeli land of 1948. These visuals also showed extensive images of the destruction of Gaza, as well as images of protests and solidarity activities around the globe. Content dissemination on the two platforms, Twitter and Facebook, was affected by the developing confrontations on the ground in Palestine. The results show that the more the confrontations spread geographically and took a violent turn, the more content on it was posted and shared (see Table 10.1).

The social media scene in this case intersects with the mediatized conflict dynamics that are based on three layers of the media's role: mainly in bringing attention to events, framing of related content and the dynamic of relations among actors through the media (Eskjær, Hjarvard and Mortensen, 2015; Lundby, 2018).

Although traditional media have brought attention to the confrontations, it is the genuine images coming from the Palestinian citizens on ground, mainly in Jerusalem, that have also contributed to an amplification of events. Furthermore, the amplification of events is rather related to the rise of dramatics on the ground developments. That is to say, the more dramatic the developments become, the more they lead to extensive use of posting on social media.

These case results point to another factor that is in play within the dynamics of mediatized conflict, that is, platform policies. The role of social media policies in the conflict in which the platform, Instagram for example, has engaged in the mediatized conflict through limiting Palestinian voices (see Tables 10.2 and 10.3) is evident in the analysed data.

Narrative segments

(i) Indexical segments

Results of segmenting tweets and posts into indexical and non-indexical segments show close similarities between the sampled online activists' perception of events, including agreement among them in identifying the main actors. Grouping similar interpretations of events in indexical segments that correspondents to 5W questions of *who, what, when, where* and *why* provide a better understanding of collective narrative construction, in which narrative construction patterns occur. Activists' narratives on social media were centred around five main themes: the Israeli military occupation

Table 10.2 Identified main actors

Who/Actor	Percentage of occurrence
Colonial settlers	23.08
Social media – Instagram	7.69
Israeli soldiers	28.21
Israel state	12.82
Palestinian youth	5.13
The United States	5.13
Palestinian families	2.56
Palestinian women	7.69
Palestinian activists/protestors	5.13
Global solidarity protestors	2.56

and displacement policies; the Palestinian resistance of Apartheid policies; the global solidarity with Palestinians; the US administration's support for Israel and the social media companies' complicity in censoring Palestinian voices.

Who:
As shown in Table 10.2, data indicate that the Israeli military (28 per cent) followed by Jewish settlers (23 per cent) are the main actors responsible for the development of events. Each event may be interpreted in a different context, yet these two actors are seen as responsible for the violence on the ground. Meanwhile, different Palestinian groups, be they women (8 per cent), activists (5 per cent), youth or children (5 per cent) are subjected to settlers and Israeli soldiers' violence. Meanwhile, social media platforms including Instagram (8 per cent) received a negative perception as actors who are contributing to censorship on Palestinian content.

At the same time, the reactions of external players including the US government (5 per cent) and global solidarity activists (3 per cent) to the developments were present in the content.

What:
Descriptions of how users referred to the daily events of the confrontations is shown in Table 10.3, in which two explanations were evident: the violence against Palestinians (28 per cent) and the Palestinian resistance (25 per cent). Interpretations of *what* happened in these events were communicated by referring to terms such as: 'ethnic cleansing', 'displacement' and an 'ongoing Nakba', as these terms were present in the content of around 11 per cent. Added to this, the reference to Israeli policies was described as 'Apartheid state policies' (8 per cent).

'Palestinian suffering' (13 per cent) refers to tweets and posts about events that included death, injury, arrest and grief of Palestinians during the confrontations. Deleting Palestinian activists' accounts by social media platforms, mainly Instagram, was also present in the interpretation of events (4 per cent). In that, Instagram is seen as a force practising censorship of Palestinian voices.

Table 10.3 Topics identified as events interpretation

What	Percentage of occurrence
Displacement/ethnic cleansing/ongoing Nakba	11.32
Social media censorship	3.77
Violence against Palestinians	28.30
Violation of international law	1.89
International community 'both sides' discourse	1.89
Apartheid state policies	7.55
Global solidarity	3.77
US military support	3.77
Palestinian resistance	24.53
Palestinian suffering	13.21

Table 10.4 Places at the centre of activists' posts and tweets

Where	Percentage of occurrence
Jerusalem	51.79
West Bank cities	8.93
Gaza	19.64
Israel/the lands of 1948	8.93
The United States	3.57
Western cities	3.57
Social media platforms	3.57

When:

Most analysed content refers to the events in the present tense, as activists were commenting, tweeting and posting about daily on-ground developments. Thus, the 'when' in the narratives addressed contemporary events, with very limited reference to old developments. Results show that activists' references to Israeli actions of displacement and ethnic cleansing as forms of an ongoing Nakba is a way of describing continued policies of Israel that not only took place in 1948 but are still taking place in contemporary times.

Where:

The fourth indexical segment addresses how social media users' narratives refer to the locations of events. The question of 'Where' in the narrative is concerned with the venues in which events have taken place. As Table 10.4 shows, understandably, Jerusalem, where the confrontations initially erupted in Sheikh Jarrah and Al-Aqsa Mosque, received major proportion of places as the centre of social media attention, with more than half (51 per cent) of the content addressing events taking place in the city. After the start of the Israeli military attack on Gaza, a great deal of attention was moved to the Gaza Strip, as a place at the centre of Israeli airstrikes, receiving 20 per

Table 10.5 Themes showing the reasons why events took place

Why	Percentage of occurrence
US support	12.5
Social media companies' anti-resistance	6.25
Form of solidarity action	6.25
Military occupation and displacement policies	31.25
Resisting apartheid policies	43.75

cent of content, followed by 9 per cent for clashes in the West Bank cities and 9 per cent for the Palestinian populated cities inside 1948 Palestinian land.

Why:
Grouping the reasons and motives behind the occurrence of these events, according to activist social media contents, led to the rise of five themes (see Table 10.5). Themes that represent *why* these events took place are: Palestinians resisting Apartheid policies (44 per cent); Israeli military occupation and displacement policies (31 per cent); US support for Israel (13 per cent); actions of global solidarity (6 per cent); and social media companies anti-resistance policies (6 per cent).

Grouping the stories of social media users, and segmenting them, can provide a better understanding of their collective narratives. Furthermore, the similarities between activists' identification of the events' main actors, explanations, times, places and reasons behind the occurrence of these events also reaffirms our conclusion that Palestinian activists do capitalize on social media networks to express their views and share stories, with mainly those with similar points of view (Siapera 2014).

(ii) Non-indexical segments

The second level of analysing Palestinian contents on social media during the May confrontations relies on categorizing content into non-indexical segments, for which three categories are established: how activists experienced the events; what these events represent and what actions are called for in response to these events.

Experiencing the events:
As shown in Table 10.6, social media users, while tweeting and posting content, expressed feelings towards the events on the ground in Palestine. These feelings were categorized into five themes, each theme accompanied by a particular feeling they experienced. The results show that the most experienced feelings were fear and anger towards Israeli aggression and violence (34 per cent), followed by feelings of enthusiasm towards the Palestinian resistance and bravery (25 per cent). A third aspect that represents how the events were experienced was sadness for the Palestinian pain, loss of lives and properties (23 per cent). The fourth and fifth aspects were encouragement for the global popular solidarity activism (14 per cent), and anger over the world governments' silence (5 per cent).

Table 10.6 Feelings that represent how confrontations are experienced

How events are experienced	Percentage
(Anger) World silence	4.55
(Fear and Anger) Aggression and violence	34.09
(Enthusiasm) Resistance and bravery	25.00
(Sadness) Pain and loss	22.73
(Encouragement) Encouraged solidarity	13.64

Table 10.7 What events represent for the activists

Events representation	Percentage of occurrence
Colonial project action	38.71
Anti-freedom of speech	1.61
National struggle for liberation	35.48
US government complicity	4.84
Palestine cause gaining global support	19.35

Events representations:

Activists' perceptions of events are categorized into five themes as shown in Table 10.7, where each theme occupied a different percentage. Results show that 39 per cent of the content considered the events as part of the Israeli colonial project in Palestine, while 35 per cent of the tweets and posts have seen the Palestinian actions as part of the national struggle for liberation. Meanwhile, global activities that showed support for the Palestinians during the confrontations are seen as a sign of rising global support for the Palestinian cause (19 per cent). The US official position, mainly the support for Israel, is perceived as a form of complicity with the Israeli colonial project (5 per cent), while social media censorship of Palestinian activists' accounts is perceived as an act of suppressing freedom of speech (2 per cent). A further reflection on these themes is found in a later section, framing narratives. The *event's representations* are much closely related to the constructed frames that represent how activists see the event.

Call for Action:

The non-indexical segmentation lies in categorizing actions that activists called for in response to events (see Table 10.8). Results from this part show that actions which were most advocated for were joining solidarity activities (35 per cent) including calls for joining global protests for Palestine, followed by advocating the boycott, divestment and sanctions (BDS) of Israel (26 per cent). A third action advocated on social media centred on calls for writing to Western governments and Members of Parliaments around the globe to intervene to stop Israeli aggression (22 per cent). Meanwhile, 17 per cent of the actions called for were dedicated to taking legal action

Table 10.8 Actions called for by Palestinian social media activists during May confrontations

Actions Called for	Percentage of occurrence
Writing to world governments	21.74
Boycott, divestment, sanctions (BDS)	26.09
Join solidarity activities	34.78
Take legal action against Israel	17.39

against Israel, including calls to hold Israel accountable through the International Criminal Court (ICC).

Framed narratives

Examining how activists framed the events through analysing what these events represented to them led to the discovery of salient frames. As previously shown in Table 10.7, five themes in events representation existed, in which two of them were dominant. These two representative themes, analysed in this chapter as equivalent to narratives' dominant frames, are: 'conflict with colonial Israel' as well as 'resistance' frames. Examining these opposing frames by applying framing analysis to the text of event representation was conducted by the deconstruction of texts into four frame elements (Entman, 1993): problem definition, causal attribution, moral evaluation and treatment or recommendation (see Table 10.9).

Binary opposition

This last phase of analysis lies in categorizing the terms mostly used in the content that represents binary opposites. These terms are identified within the events representations (see Table 10.7) in which the narratives were framed. Table 10.10 shows how terms and opposite terms in the process of narratives' framing (those identified in the social media content of Palestinian voices) framed the Israeli actions and actors through a 'colonial frame'. In this, actors like 'settlers', 'soldiers', 'occupiers' versus Palestinian actors like 'citizens', 'protestors' and 'landowners' are shown in an opposing resistance frame.

The two identified frames of 'colonialism' and 'resistance' are opposite not only in their nature, but also in how the main actors identified within these frames are carrying meanings of binary opposition. Opposite terms found in this research do play a role in setting the stage for understanding the conflict between parties in the communicated stories. The opposing positions and roles of actors are established within the content of the frame.

Binary oppositions play an evident role in constructing narratives on social media content through characterizing the main players and events. Their characteristics are

Table 10.9 Frame elements, variables and description

Frame element	Variable	Descriptive sentences
Problem definition	Topic 1: Conflict with colonialism	An ongoing Nakba Policies of ethnic cleansing Apartheid policies Military occupation Colonial settlers
	Topic 2: Resistance	Struggle for independence Earning for liberation Little victories
Causal attribution	Topic 1: Benefit attribution	Liberation is within our reach
	Topic 1: Risk attribution	Facing state violence Ethno-national superiority
	Topic 2: Benefit attribution	Defiance and steadfastness Freedom is simple
	Topic 2: Risk attribution	Grief; loss of lives; property destruction
Moral evaluation	Topic 1	Inhumane treatment of Palestinians
	Topic 2	Landowners Sacrifices
Treatment/ recommendation	Topic 1: Judgement	Sanctions; BDS Legal countability in the international courts
	Topic 2: Judgement	Global solidarity

Table 10.10 Binary opposites in forms of terms and opposite terms

Terms	Opposite terms
Settlers	Residents
Soldiers	Activists
Aggressors	Protesters
Troops	Families
Occupiers	Citizens
Colonial powers	Landowners

framed either negatively or positively based on their actions and position towards the Palestinians – with a limited attribution to players who hold neutral positions towards the conflict.

In this context, Israeli occupation army and Jewish settlers, the US government and social media companies are framed as contributors to the inflaming of the conflict, while they are in alliance against the Palestinian people. Their roles are associated with aggression, colonization, complicity and censorship. Meanwhile, Palestinians and their supporters are presented as victims and resisters.

Framing of actions and positions of key players in the narratives is evident throughout the analysed text. Every segment of the narrative and identified frame carries opponents who hold opposing positions in the discussed event.

Conclusion

This chapter examined the dynamics of mediatized activism within the May 2021 events in Jerusalem, as a mediatized conflict, within which Palestinian content on social media witnessed a notable shift in its presentation as well as scope and level of influence.

Results show that activists' narratives on social media centred around five main themes: the Israeli military occupation and displacement policies; the Palestinian resistance of apartheid policies; the global solidarity with Palestinians; the US administration support for Israel and the social media companies' complicity in censoring Palestinian voices. Furthermore, the grouping and segmenting of bloggers and activists' stories on social media provided a better understanding of their collective narratives. Another conclusion is that social media platforms, mainly Facebook and Instagram, were silencing Palestinian voices through censorship and deleting proactive accounts. Nevertheless, a major conclusion is that Palestinian social media activists played a significant role in recruiting social media platforms, setting a unitary public agenda, which generated massive media attention and sympathy among Palestinians as well as Arab and other publics at global level, bringing high pressure on their rival.

Furthermore, utilization of the main hashtag, #savesheikhjarrah in most of tweets and posts contributed to providing collective narratives where the main actors, times, places and reasons behind events were similarly identified. The two identified dominant frames in the narratives – colonial policies frame and resistance frame – can be traced throughout the data. From the segmentation process of narratives to understanding what events represent for activists, to identifying binary opposition terms, these two frames were evident and salient in the text.

To sum up, combining an analysis of elements of narrative segments, frames and binary oppositions on conflicts would contribute to providing a rather comprehensive understanding of narrative structure and key drivers within it.

One significant aspect of the chapter case results is that despite the different and varied social media accounts that have been analysed, a similar presentation of events in Palestine has been found among users whose analysis of events, actions and actors' positions was nearly identical. This indicates that the Palestinian national narrative is not only collective, but it also strongly resonated on social media platforms in times of rise in on-ground conflict and confrontations.

This work contributes to the scholarly discussion on how narrative production – and reproduction – via social media platforms can play a major role, from below, within mediatized conflict cycles. The text examined the mediatized conflict and mediatized activism approaches in a Palestinian context which is a line of research that is slowly growing in the Arab world. The limited period considered in this analysis (two weeks of confrontations) played a role in selecting limited samples for analysis. Thus, further research should take into consideration expanding the period of analysis and the sample in trying to replicate the study with the same or different case studies.

References

Abdel-Fadil, M., and L. Liebmann (2018), 'Gender, Diversity and Mediatized Conflicts of Religion: Lessons from Scandinavian Case Studies'. In K. Lundby (ed.), *Contesting Religion: The Media Dynamics of Cultural Conflicts in Scandinavia*, Berlin: De Gruyter, 281–98.

Abu-Ayyash, S. (2015), 'The Palestine Solidarity Movement, Human Rights and Twitter', *Networking Knowledge: Journal of the MeCCSA Postgraduate Network*, 8 (2): 1–18.

Alimardani, M., and M. Elswah (2021), 'Digital Orientalism: #SaveSheikhJarrah and Arabic Content Moderation'. In POMEPS Studies 43, Elliott School of International Affairs, The George Washington University, USA, https://pomeps.org/digital-oriental ism-savesheikhjarrah-and-arabic-content-moderation (accessed 24 October 2021).

Aouragh, M. (2008), 'Palestine Online: Cyber Intifada and the Construction of a Virtual Community 2001–2005', PhD Dissertation, University of Amsterdam, https://dare. uva.nl/search?identifier=3e06c97c-9124-4d39-a651-97c3aa1ac46f (accessed 21 October 2021).

Aukes, E. J., L. E. Bontje and J. H. Slinger (2020), 'Narrative and Frame Analysis: Disentangling and Refining Two Close Relatives by Means of a Large Infrastructural Technology Case', *Forum Qualitative Sozialforschung/Forum: Qualitative Social Research*, 21 (2): 1–18.

Bontje, L. E., and J. H. Slinger (2017), 'A Narrative Method for Learning from Innovative Coastal Projects – Biographies of the Sand Engine', *Ocean & Coastal Management*, 142: 186–97.

Castells, M. (2009), *Communication Power*, Oxford: Oxford University Press.

Cottle, S. (2006), *Mediatized Conflicts: Developments in Media and Conflict Studies*, Berkshire: Open University Press.

Dawson, P., and M. Mäkelä (2020), 'The Story Logic of Social Media: Co-construction and Emergent Narrative Authority', *Style*, 54(1): 21–35.

Dixon, M. (2019), *Media Theory for A Level: The Essential Revision Guide*, New York: Routledge.

Entman, R. M. (1993), 'Framing: Toward Clarification of a Fractured Paradigm', *Journal of Communication*, 43 (4): 51–8.

Eskjær, M. F., S. Hjarvard and M. Mortensen (2015), *The Dynamics of Mediatized Conflicts*, New York: Peter Lang.

Fogarty, S. (2005), 'Binary Oppositions', *The Literary Encyclopaedia*, 15 February, https:// www.litencyc.com/php/stopics.php?rec=true&UID=122 (accessed 13 October 2021).

Ipoke (2020), 'Social Media Report in Palestine', https://bit.ly/3DHquO8 (accessed 24 September 2021).

Jackson, Holly M. (2021), 'The *New York Times* Distorts the Palestinian Struggle a Case Study of Anti-Palestinian Bias in American News Coverage of the First and Second Palestinian Intifadas', Preprint, http://web.mit.edu/hjackson/www/The_NYT_Distor ts_the_Palestinian_Struggle.pdf (accessed 24 January 2022).

Kellner, D. (2003), *Media Spectacle*, London: Routledge.

Lewis, K. (2021), 'Social Media Platforms Are Complicit in Censoring Palestinian Voices', *The Conversation*, 25 May, https://theconversation.com/social-media-platforms-are-complicit-in-censoring-palestinian-voices-161094 (accessed 12 October 2021).

Lundby, K. (2018), 'Interaction Dynamics in the Mediatization of Religion Thesis'. In K. Lundby (ed.), *Contesting Religion: The Media Dynamics of Cultural Conflicts in Scandinavia*, Berlin: De Gruyter, 299–314.

Matar, D., and Z. Harb (2013). *Narrating Conflict in the Middle East: Discourse, Image and Communications Practices in Lebanon and Palestine*, London: I.B. Tauris.

Matthes, J. and Kohring, M. (2008), The Content Analysis of Media Frames: Toward Improving Reliability and Validity. Journal of Communication, 58: 258-279. https://doi.org/10.1111/j.1460-2466.2008.00384.x

Papacharissi, Z. (2016), 'Affective Publics and Structures of Storytelling: Sentiment, Events and Mediality', *Information, Communication & Society*, 19 (3): 307–24.

Poell, T. (2020), 'Social Media, Temporality, and the Legitimacy of Protest', *Social Movement Studies*, 19 (5–6): 609–24.

Sadler, N. (2018), 'Narrative and Interpretation on Twitter: Reading Tweets by Telling Stories', *New Media & Society*, 20 (9): 3266–82.

Siapera, E. (2014), 'Tweeting #Palestine: Twitter and the Mediation of Palestine', *International Journal of Cultural Studies*, 17 (6): 539–55.

Tawil-Souri, H., and M. Aouragh (2014), 'Intifada 3.0? Cyber Colonialism and Palestinian Resistance', *The Arab Studies Journal*, 22 (1): 102–33.

Van Dijck, J., and T. Poell (2013), 'Understanding Social Media Logic', *Media and Communication*, 1 (1): 2–14.

11

Palestinian war narrative and social media: Ethnographic account of the victims of Israel–Palestine war during May 2021

Tawseef Majeed and Ali M. Abushbak

Introduction

As social media usage increases with advancing information and communication technologies (ICTs), the world becomes more reliant on digital archiving and memory storage. It is no different in conflict zones. Major sociopolitical conflicts around the world witness amassing literature regarding the consequences of war in the form of human rights violations, press (un)freedom, mis/disinformation and so on. Contextually, the Israel–Palestine conflict is one of the significant disputes that pose an immense threat to civilians and sociopolitical peace in Palestine and Israel. The recent war during May 2021 is one such aspect of the conflict that devastated the lives of the Palestinians and Israelis. The war was documented and disseminated by various media agencies and outlets. However, it is imperative to observe that people document what they experience during the skirmish using their mobile phones, sustaining the 'convergence culture' (Jenkins, 2006). The information is saved as memory, which not only reflects the victim-user perspective (space) but also presents an emotional and motivational attachment to the (documented) incident/s.

This chapter explores emotions, spaces and the perspective of the victim-users in the context of the war. Several different practices and patterns of usage have appeared on social media, which play a major role in mobilizing and advocating the Israel–Palestine conflict. For instance, digital archiving (Vlassenroot et al., 2021) is the process of converting non-digital content into a digital format that can be easily archived and retrieved at any time. However, it may face several challenges. The process has its own set of problems such as hacking, data leaks and ransomware attacks that can destroy the stored information (Jaillant and Caputo, 2022). Consequently, the (digital) memory always seems to be at odds with our culture's growing reliance on digital archiving. As we can store more data in the form of bytes, it becomes difficult for people to maintain their memories of certain events, which have no other means of access. Relying on the insights from mass communication theory (McQuail, 2005), network society theory (Castells, 1996) and cultural production theory (Manovich, 2001), the chapter employs a comprehensive theoretical framework and empirical lens to study digital documentation, archiving and dissemination of memories, emotions and so on in context to social media usage during the eleven days of the Israel–Palestine war of May 2021.

Theoretical considerations

This chapter comprehends diverse social practices digitally. Castells (1996, 2009) argues that new media could shape society in earnest. Nevertheless, the network society conception is related to the consequences and interpretations of globalization (Khondker, 2011) or even the 'global village' (McLuhan, 1964). Moreover, Castells defines the network society as 'a society whose social structure is made up of networks powered by micro-electronics-based information and communications technologies' (Castells, 2005: 3). However, for Castells, social networks are not new – through the stages of history, they were already present. The main factor is that the incorporation of digital technology in the modern network society creates new kind of social relationships, which could even facilitate memories, collective and individual. The author's insights would be helpful to understand how the Palestinian victims use social media platforms to document, archive and disseminate the war narratives to create diverse layers of memories including loss, war, solidarity with the sufferings of the people who die or are injured. The diverse aspects facilitate narratological nuances of the conflict. However, it is crucial to understand why do people document war, especially the losses and repercussions.

Bruns's (2007) produsage and Fishbein and Ajzen's (2010) theory of reasoned action are quite relevant to addressing embedded motivations of the users (victims) leading to content production. The prospects of the victim-user role in documenting and archiving the crucial information are often contextualized with the contemporary sociopolitical aspects of the Israel–Palestine conflict (Majeed and Abushbak, 2020). It is quite evident that such user-led content production is a kind of memory itself or at least preserves personal memories of the victim users. Besides, the political connotations of the conflict decentralize the users or civilians but the sociocultural characteristics reaffirm their place and role in shaping the conflict itself using ICTs – precisely, social media. The patterns of use of media to produce and shape the innate culture of Palestinian resistance against Israel's occupation is relevant to Manovich's (2001) screen and cultural production, which is the digital participation of the users and victims in addressing the war and its impact.

Technological determinism (Hauer, 2017) supports that technology available to a community or society determines its cultural values, social structure and history. Sociocultural advancement trails certain course (Diamond, 2010) that is facilitated by technological innovations (Hauer, 2017). It also affects several domains of society including politics, economics and even community-specific social norms. The social media landscape affects the intimate sociocultural patterns of Palestine and even Israel. It reinforces the physical prospects of the public who are directly or indirectly affected by the conflict. Social media, and new media, impacts the image of the conflict in front of the global audience; therefore, it stretches the physical limitations of the conflict and its consequences.

Several scholars confirm that social media and the internet are crucial instruments for sustaining democracy and liberation technology (Diamond, 2010; Khondker, 2011). In addition, they play a major role in shaping politics, opening a new public sphere, especially in societies where a real public sphere is absent (Khondker, 2011). In an asymmetric conflict like the Israeli-Palestinian one, victims turn to alternative tools to document and disseminate their stories. In– particular, the Israeli military operations in Gaza are usually accompanied by media blackout as well as Israel's surveillance and censorship of the information coming from the region (Ben-David, 2014). Furthermore, social media management put a new kind of censorship on the Palestinian narrative, to fight against the Israeli content, which poses newer challenges to the users. Such authoritarian tactics are quite visible across global conflicts. For instance, compared to the Israel–Palestine conflict, authoritarian censorship is significantly harsher in Indian-administered Kashmir (Majeed, 2021, 2022), a Himalayan region disputed between India and Pakistan. Kashmir is sometimes referred to as Asian Palestine.

Consequently, non-political platforms were used as an instrument for advocacy and sharing the experiences during the tension between Israel and Palestine (Majeed and Abushbak, 2020). It seemed to build, however, an effective image of the conflict internationally. The Palestinian victim-users shared their suffering on social media during the eleven days of the war, which influenced international users, who also took to the streets in solidarity with Palestine (Couzens, 2020). Although the narratives were personal, these also contributed to the collective war memory.

What is the 'personal' in the war narrative?

Fishbein (1967) and Fishbein and Ajzen (2010) suggest how attitude and subjective norms determine the intention and how the viewpoint towards behavioural outcome and public opinion determine individual behaviour (change). The theory stresses that intention shapes a particular behaviour which results in a specific attitude. The current context is of Palestinian victim-users' behavioural projections using social media as the sites of discussion and deliberation in documenting and portraying war memories.

On 29 July 2021 at 9:00 am, Palestinian Standard Time (PST), we met Anas Rehan, a Palestinian freelance photojournalist. Rehan recorded his personal experience of the eleven days of the war on his mobile phone. On the way, we noticed that the city still bore the scars of the war between Hamas and Israel; that was also quite visible in his mobile phone gallery and Instagram account. Destruction blotched the cityscape on Al-Jalaa Street, one of the main streets in Gaza city. We witnessed the rubble of three towers, bombed by Israeli air strikes which was shot by Rehan using his mobile phone. The buildings hosted the offices and headquarters of some prominent media organizations including Al Jazeera, Associated Press (AP) and other outlets. Rehan's office was destroyed too. Only debris remained of the *Al-Jawhara* building. We met him there. He could walk us through the pre-bombed building and the ruins, which he had captured on his smartphone. Middle-aged Rehan wore a striped t-shirt with jeans and a black cap. His untrimmed beard denoted his deteriorating economic situation. He lost his job after the Israeli aircraft bombed his office. We asked him how he knew the war started on 11 May 2021? He sighed and was quiet for a moment. He mentioned he was covering the situation during the Israeli raids against the al-Aqsa compound. 'At that time the violence escalated between the Palestinians and Israeli forces, and the situation was unstable. I predicted there would be some sort of severe violence within a day or two on a larger scale' (Rehan, 2021). The participatory approach of documentation by the users is possible because of the digital empowerment of the public, which is transformed into public 2.0 (see Papacharissi, 2008).

On 11 May in the afternoon Rehan documented his family's evacuation following Israel's bombing threat in Gaza. However, his response to the threat came through self-recording. He disseminated his personal experience to others on social media. Such action fits quite well with Bruns's (2007) idea of produsage, which considers the production and usage of the content that interests a user often governed by Fishbein and Ajzen's (2010) reasoned action. Produsage and reasoned action embed ICT usage including social media.

The projections of war memories have diverse perspectives (Barnes and Newton, 2018; Nevarez et al., 2017; Tripp, 2020). The significant one is the audience's viewpoint and participation. Also, personal memory contributes to and shapes collective memories (Capella, Jadhav and Moncrieff, 2020). Bruns (2007) produsage is a portmanteau of production and usage. The term constitutes producer behaviour and motivations that intend to document and disseminate content, which matters to society. In other words, it results in citizen journalism and activism. On the other hand, the reasoned action approach considers producer intentions that shape their behaviour to participate in content production and dissemination (Fishbein and Ajzen, 2010).

Social media offers a constructive space for political communication and democratic participation in political discussion in virtual public spheres (Bennett and Segerberg, 2012; Lev-On, 2012, 2018; Loader and Mercea, 2011). Besides, Papacharissi (2008) perceives digital spaces as virtual spaces 2.0, adding sociocultural dimensions to the online political discussion. With the advent of technological advancements and wired audience participation in the political processes, the citizens and even media professionals not only could influence the political processes but are empowered to challenge and destabilize the mainstream narratives. Rehan continued to speak about his experience and what he had forecasted became a reality. He not only documented the incidents but also shared the content on social media. 'Most of the time we, as journalists, follow the news, and if it is local, we cover it. At the same time, I would update the information on my social media account including Instagram, Facebook, Twitter etc. My colleagues call me a social media addict. But it is ironic, they do the same' (Rehan, 2021).

Citizens' mobile phone usage to record war is significant. The use of ICTs, socio-technological empowerment and intention to record personal narratives facilitates war memories (Castells, 1999; Wessels, 2017) especially their record and archiving. The personal account reflects and contributes a broader narrative in situations when the personal becomes political. The Israel–Palestine conflict has shaped diverse memories that are associated with the war. People, who also act like the mainstream audience, identify, narrate and portray such memories using diverse podia that even, at times, counter the mainstream narrative. The conventional narrative is usually reflected by mainstream media, which mostly functions from a specific vantage point and ideology (Majeed, 2022). It becomes significant to identify and understand the observations and reactions that take the shape of memories.

Given that we as common people physically observe and document the incidents/ events that surround us, we also archive and create memories digitally. Rehan was one among hundreds who tried to save their families during the war that started suddenly. On 11 May 2021, I met a forty-year-old man, Hashem al-Jarosha, a barber in Gaza. His eyes are hazel-coloured and he has a tanned skin. That day a nearby building was blown up and his shop was destroyed. Jarosha captured his demolished shop using his mobile phone and shared it on social media. He ran his shop over the debris and updated his account with the pictures.

The man stood on the rubble of what was once his home and recalls the memories associated with the building. The house no more stood tall but his memories did. The physical and psychological construction of the memories was structured according to the sociopolitical perception of war. Jarosha, in a sad tone, mentioned that he received the information about the war on Facebook. He read 'Israel Will Attack Gaza' in the news. 'As soon as I read the news, I rushed to my home in a hurry to make sure that my family is safe' (Jarosha, 2021). If victims own their testimonies (Azumah et al., 2020; Fohring, 2018), so do the perpetrators. The complexity of the memories is difficult to address. 'I was semi-conscious until now I can't imagine how my store got destroyed, you tell me! here is barber stuff, where is the military material, there is nothing, so why did Israel bomb my store. I recorded the Israeli violations against the human and unarmed people, and I disseminated it through social media to let everyone know the real face of Israel' (Jarosha, 2021).

War memories are complex. The comprehensive notions of the perpetrators and victims are weaved into composite perspectives. We as an audience perceive such diverse perceptions through media across varied podia, and as victims (Chang, Mukherjee and Coppel, 2021), we shape and archive our memories by our present (Walden, 2016). The contemporary, technologically driven environment legitimizes diverse public interpretations. Such meanings are essential for sustaining democracy. The content production patterns of the victims are reinforced by technological convergence (Madden and Alt, 2021). The empowered audience documents evidence, which tranforms into memory.

Mainstream news media, which broadly includes newspapers, radio and television along with their extended online representations, is the chief source of information and acts as the sites of memories. However, the term mainstream has become difficult to define due to the multimodal projections of the news content, affected by creed, ideology and philosophy in the world. On the other hand, alternate media platforms including social media, citizens and participatory journalism metamorphose the information/ news content generation and form broader memory narratives. Immediacy is one of the significant perspectives of social media. Jarosha says he 'received a lot of support messages and sympathy. My picture travelled to the entire world and thousands of people saw it; there are people and supporters from different countries, particularly from Europe, who contacted me and asked me about what happened with me. Due to social media everyone got to know about me, and how Israel bombed my only source of livelihood.'

Jenkins's (2006: 208) notion of 'monitorial' citizens offers a comprehensive understanding of the role of the audience in news content production. The conflict-related content is also produced on similar patterns where the citizens document, 'discuss, debate, and deliberate on the news complement and sometimes supplement the output of the mainstream journalism industry' (Bruns, 2009: 109). The recent escalation of war violence in Gaza is interpreted, disseminated and archived by the citizens who shape their response and opinions.

Israel–Palestine war of May 2021 and virtual sphere 2.0

The Israel-Palestine conflict, which commenced on 10 May and went on till 21 May 2021, can be seen to have reinforced the idea of virtual sphere 2.0. The practical connotation of the term embeds the virtual space, which offers sites of public discussion, facilitated by the internet. The use of ICTs by the public, who could be categorized as collective victims of Israel's intentional domination (Human Rights Watch, 2021), contributes to a broader narrative portrayal of the war memories. Social media finds a significant relevance with the victimization of the civilian population by a relatively powerful state.

The calculated execution of punitive populism (Bonner, 2019) reflects Israel's intentions towards the Palestinian Muslim community (BBC, 2021), which is interpreted as a war threat by Palestinians. The violence affected the civilian population predominantly, which is corroborated by the magnitude of digital/online content production by the victims. 'There is no doubt that the war affected me gravely. When the war started, I was on the field and I was far away from my family. I was worried for my children' (Rehan, 2021). The call for al-Zuhr prayer stopped us for a minute, and then Rehan continued, the idea of recording his daily experience during the eleven days of the war on his mobile phone. 'One of my basic intentions to use social media is to mobilize the people, locally and internationally, to have their opinion on what is happening with us, Palestinians. Even how journalists also suffer while working under Israeli occupation' (Rehan, 2021).

User-generated content constitutes the direct observation and reflection of a user. The observer–reflection phenomena are embedded performances that shape the users' intentions and subsequently experiences and memories. In the context of the May 2021 war, the Palestinian users responded to the repercussions by portraying diverse layers of violence, which reflected the personalized version of the embedded experience. It seems interesting to consider the identity of the war-torn public who intentionally documented themselves as the victims along with their response as social media users. For example, Rehan, along with his family, feels like a victim. However, 'as a person, I respond to Israel's hostility destroying my home. The images of my home are for memory, every moment I have lived with my family at my home is kind of saved on my mobile phone. Also, it is a memory for the future. But my elders do not do it. They feel emotional when they see the debris but it is a reality, it is gone' (Rehan, 2021).

The content recorded and disseminated on social media also proposes an opinion or a response constructed as memory and protest site. Rehan mentions, 'our elders do not encourage us to record what happens with us. During the Nakba, our elders stopped us from recording protests, which were organized to fight for our rights. The right to live with dignity. We could disseminate it to the entire world. Also, I think patriotism and civilian sacrifices include a few crucial motivations that make me personally responsible for sharing my opinion with others on social media' (Rehan, 2021). The individual presence on social media collaborates with developing war memory narratives.

Spaces and sites of war memories

According to Mayo (1988: 62), 'when physical settings, forms of sentiment, and social purpose are combined in memorials, war memory socially becomes either a part of everyday life or a celebration of the past'; it also preserves the embedded narrative. Addressing historical/war memory (Olick, 2018) empirically could be impartial because of its disconnection or deviation from the present, objective and factual reality. It is quite evident that the internet and social media have shifted the prospects of the 'physical settings' to 'virtual settings' while preserving the perspectives of war memories and memorials. The endless evolution of technology empowers individuals who either witness or personally experience war to respond and share their thoughts, circumstances and opinions with the world.

Malik Skaik, a fifteen-year-old Palestinian teenager, lost his home. Israeli aircraft bombed his home in Gaza city. On 12 May 2021 around 04:00 pm, his father received a call from an Israeli intelligence officer asking him to evacuate the building immediately. It was bombed after five minutes. Skaik was monitoring how the Israeli missile destroyed his home. 'When my father received the call, I held my phone. I started collecting my education and property documents. I, along with the family, left the building immediately and took shelter on a street corner. We were scared to death. I recorded those moments on my phone.'

'Whenever I pass by my home, I feel shattered. I loved my home, which is just history now. Sometimes I may look at my room and the ambience and even the last glimpse of the building that I recorded; it makes me feel sad. All the memories come back when I look at the photos and the video' (Skaik, 2021). Skaik, who now lives in a rented house, is very close to his lost home. In this case, the war memories are created with embedded despair and desolation. However, it is interesting to observe that physical memories shape virtual memories.

Common citizens are empowered by ICTs and they can contribute to decision-making democratically, and therefore, affect the 'individuals as they interact with each other in public life' (Papacharissi, 2008). The penetration of existing technology into the deeper layers of diverse societies reshapes and redesigns the conception of the information society (Castells, 1996, 1999) or the public. Online/digital ethnography is one of the methodologies that we employ to understand intimate phenomena of societies. The use of the internet, social media practice and cultural and technological convergence and divergence create a comprehensive operative medium, an asset or a detriment based on its usage. Such medium, in context, 'serves as a tool, and does not contain the agency to effect social change'. Individuals 'possess differing levels of agency, based on which they can employ the internet to varying ends, effects, and gratification' (Papacharissi, 2008).

War narratives are individualized to a certain extent depending on the effect and influence they have on the people (Callahan, Dubnick and Olshfski, 2006; Graef, da Silva and Lemay-Hebert, 2020; Kurtz and Upton, 2017). The use of social media for information dissemination and reaction is quite prominent within the war memory discourses. Such patterns of participation evoke a richer picture of the civilian population, reshaping its representation and portrayal. For instance, Skaik mentions that he 'disseminated the videos to reach to the international audience about my loss. Even though social media companies suppressed Palestinian digital content during the war, I did not give up. Facebook even removed my account; however, I constantly disseminated the Israeli's human rights violations and war crimes in Gaza. Israel kills us without any reason, my home got destroyed without any reason too.' Skaik clicks more photos of his demolished home from different angles and shares these on his newly created Facebook account.

Skaik uses social media to archive memories of war and shows resistance to Israel's occupation of Palestine. 'Any activity that makes Israel angry is seen as resistance. When we document the Israeli violations against us and disseminate them on social media it is a kind of resistance. I never imagined that I will have to witness and document my own home being demolished by Israel. I lost my childhood. I have to be a man to help my family to rebuild our home. Also, I'll share all the stories and disseminate the information until the occupation ends' (Skaik, 2021).

Intimate war memories: Patterns of participation

Civilians participate in information production, which is often referred to as user-led content. However, when a user is also a victim, it authenticates the participation and restructures a precise perspective of the victim-user. Their (produced) content is more provocative, often unbiased and just an impartial view of the situation the person is in. It strengthens the related narrative often disseminated and circulated on social media. It develops networking and strengthens the public engagement with the ongoing sociopolitical notions and, therefore, shapes memories. User-victims from diverse perspectives of the Israel–Palestine war of May 2021 evoke not only the war plans of Israel and Hamas group, human rights violations and the present status of the conflict but how the victims see, perceive, document, archive and disseminate it. It is quite significant to understand the role and space of the war victims who use ICTs and social media to share their first-hand experiences with the global audience.

War memories are structured around diverse memories of sociopolitical significance. Palestinian user-victims cast their representation from diverse standpoints, which cater to the wider prospects of memories (Nevarez et al., 2017; Tripp, 2020) and protest

(Fisher et al., 2019) and challenge the mainstream media. The layered roles of the public are contextualized with the virtual sphere, which is grounded within the public sphere systematics (Fraser, 1992). User-victim intentions and motivations construct the spaces that are associated with the chief narratives on social media. For instance, the Palestinians played many roles including social media users, victims, protesters and media content producers besides being the mainstream audience, looking for their representation.

This study uses the ethnographic intervention into the victim-user memories that were shaped during the war. Most of the respondents affirm that they document and disseminate their tragedies to make the world audience aware of Israel's violence towards Palestinians. It is quite evident that most users own smartphones, which empowers them. It helps them to amplify their voices against Israel's human rights violation in Gaza and West Bank regions. The ethnographic enquiries were carried out at the exact locations where the incidents took place to have a comprehensive understanding of the emotions attached. Even the reasons for their direct user-victim participation are justified and defensible. The information runs parallel to the mainstream media, which is often influenced by respective social, political and religious ideologies. However, social media plays a significant role in structuring the contrasting news narrative that may be sabotaged or even ignored by the mainstream.

Digital networking drives the narrative. It does not have any physical boundaries and even censorship is not able to completely screen and sabotage the information. It is quite evident in authoritarian environments including India, China, Russia and so on. There are 'spaces' (Chomsky, 2020) and strategic media practices (Majeed, 2021) that facilitate calculated information dissemination, thereby challenging authoritarianism and dictatorship. The social media networks contribute to broader narratives, especially on incidents of loss of humans, property and close family members and survival. Most of the time, the user-victims document, archive and even disseminate as an emotional burst with the online public/audience.

The user-victims use the technology to document information that challenges the mainstream and dominant narratives. Bruns's (2007) produsage reflects on the user engagement with what he or she witnesses or experiences and documents, archives and disseminates to the audience. Skaik, for instance, reflects on the (documented) memories of the war happening on the ground that he chooses to offer a precise perspective of to the civilians. The prospects are relevant to the user's behaviour to become a producer rather than just a consumer. The reasoned action by the users fashions the contextual information about their personal experiences. Jarosha's, or even Rehan's, testimonies about his experience of the war recount the horrors and consequences of Israel's bombing of Gaza.

Conclusion

Wars shape memories. Memories metamorphose into dissent. The first-hand experience of the Israel–Palestine war violence of May 2021 of the user-victims' constructs collective memories, which include consistent portrayal and diffusion of the recorded content. The embedded motivations, behavioural changes and spaces of war memories in the context of social media usage during the recent war advance the narratological portrayal of the war memories facilitated by social media. The patterns of inclusive behaviour of the public represent war narratives, including sociopolitico-technological ones, as their individual experiences and perceptions shape and contribute to virtual sphere 2.0. The virtual world provides a favourable space and site for portraying personal accounts of the public 2.0. The Palestinian user-victims use diverse platforms for digital activism, which contributes to their overall digital performance and production. Most of the respondents understand the power of social media, its penetration and its significance in the global village. Their personal stories exist as a part of a broader phenomenon, which is shaped and sustained by the long-standing conflict.

The user-victims' testimonies shape war narratives and memories, which is quite evident from the stories of Anas Rehan, Hashem al-Jarosha and others. The recollections of war, violence, loss and hope do construct a collective narrative that represents a broader perception of dissent. It seems imperative that ICTs and social media offer a lot to the common public, who can comprehend what happens within their vicinity and how it affects them. The ethnographic account of the user-victims evokes certain reminiscences of the Israel–Palestine war accounts to large-scale human rights violations, loss of property and even the deterioration of the long-standing conflict. The direct intervention of the users led to information production, which destabilizes the mainstream claims of normalcy in Gaza and the West Bank. Digital networking (Castells, 1996) forms an effective community that shapes the specific behaviour of the users who use ICTs and social media to convey their narratives to the public.

The strategic use of social media platforms affects the overall representation of the Israel–Palestine war. The user participation in documenting, archiving and disseminating personal narratives contributes to the collective representation of the repercussions of the war. It also supports the collective memories that not only shape the projection of diverse prospects of the conflict but also help comprehend what would otherwise go undocumented.

References

Abushbak, A. M., & Majeed, T. (2020). 'The Role of Social Media in Mobilizing Crowd Protest – A Case Study of Palestinian Anger Against Israel's Military Measures at Al-Aqsa Compound on Instagram', *Studies in Indian Place Names*, 40 (10): 1–15.

Azumah, F. D., J. O. Nachinaab, S. Krampah and P. N. Ayim (2020), 'Determinants of Target Victim Selection: A Case Study of Criminals from Gambaga Prisons', *Journal of Victimology and Victim Justice*, 3 (1): 93–112.

Barnes, V., and L. Newton (2018), 'War and Peace in Organizational Memory', *Management & Organizational History*, 13 (4): 303–8.

BBC (2021), 'Israel–Gaza Violence: The Conflict Explained', BBC News, 16 June, https://www.bbc.com/news/newsbeat-44124396 (accessed 30 October 2021).

Ben-David, A. (2014), 'Israeli-Palestinian Conflict'. In K. Harvey (ed.), *Encyclopedia of Social Media and Politics*, London: Sage Publications, 740–3.

Bennett, W. L., and A. Segerberg (2012), 'The Logic of Connective Action: Digital Media and the Personalization of Contentious Politics', *Information, Communication & Society*, 15: 739–68.

Bonner, M. D. (2019), *Tough on Crime: The Rise of Punitive Populism in Latin America*, Pittsburgh: University of Pittsburgh Press.

Bruns, A. (2007), 'Produsage: Towards a Broader Framework for User-Led Content Creation', *Proceedings of 6th ACM SIGCHI Conference on Creativity and Cognition 2007*, presented at the 6th ACM SIGCHI Conference on Creativity and Cognition 2007, Association for Computing Machinery, New York, 13–15 June 2007, 99–105.

Bruns, A. (2009), 'News Blogs, Online Media Forum and Citizen Journalism'. In K. Prasad (ed.), *e-Journalism: New Media and News Media*, New Delhi: B. R. Publishing Corporation, 101–26.

Callahan, K., M. J. Dubnick and D. Olshfski (2006), 'War Narratives: Framing Our Understanding of the War on Terror', *Public Administration Review* [American Society for Public Administration], 66 (4): 554–68.

Capella, M., S. Jadhav and J. Moncrieff, J. (2020), 'History, Violence and Collective Memory: Implications for Mental Health in Ecuador', *Transcultural Psychiatry*, 57 (1): 32–43.

Castells, M. (1996), *The Information Age: Economy, Society and Culture. The Rise of the Network Society*, Oxford: Blackwell.

Castells, M. (1999), *The Information Age, Volumes 1–3: Economy, Society and Culture*, West Sussex, UK: Wiley-Blackwell.

Castells, M. (ed.) (2005), *The Network Society: A Cross-Cultural Perspective*, Northampton, MA: Edward Elgar Pub.

Castells, M. (2009), *Communication Power*, 2nd edition (9 September 2009), New York: Oxford University Press.

Chang, L. Y. C., S. Mukherjee and N. Coppel (2021), 'We Are All Victims: Questionable Content and Collective Victimisation in the Digital Age', *Asian Journal of Criminology*, 16 (1): 37–50.

Chomsky, N. (2020), 'Internationalism or Extinction', *Progressive International*, 18 September, https://progressive.international/wire/2020-09-18-noam-chomsky-internationalism-or-extinction/en (accessed 21 May 2021).

Couzens, J. (2020), 'Thousands Protest in London over Israel-Gaza Violence', BBC News, 15 May, https://www.bbc.com/news/uk-57127628 (accessed 20 June 2021).

Diamond, L. (2010), 'Liberation Technology', *Journal of Democracy*, 21 (3): 69–83.

Fishbein, M. (1967), 'Attitude and the Prediction of Behavior'. In M. Fishbein (ed.), *Readings in Attitude Theory and Measurement*, New York: Wiley, 477–92.

Fishbein, M., and I. Ajzen (2010), *Predicting and Changing Behavior: The Reasoned Action Approach*, New York: Psychology Press.

Fisher, D. R., K. T. Andrews, N. Caren, E. Chenoweth, M. T. Heaney, T. Leung, L. N. Perkins and J. Pressman (2019), 'The Science of Contemporary Street Protest: New Efforts in the United States', *Science Advances*, American Association for the Advancement of Science, 5 (10): 1–15.

Fohring, S. (2018), 'What's in a Word? Victims on "Victim"', *International Review of Victimology*, 24 (2): 151–64.

Fraser, N. (1992), 'Rethinking the Public Sphere: A Contribution to the Critique of Actually Existing Democracy'. In Calhoun Craig (ed.), *Habermas and the Public Sphere*, London: MIT Press.

Gerbaudo, P. (2012), *Tweets and the Streets Social Media and Contemporary Activism*, London: Pluto Press.

Graef, J., R. da Silva and N. Lemay-Hebert (2020), 'Narrative, Political Violence, and Social Change', *Studies in Conflict & Terrorism*, 43 (6): 431–43.

Hauer, T. (2017), 'Technological Determinism and New Media', *International Journal of English, Literature and Social Science (IJELSS)*, 2 (2): 1–4.

Human Rights Watch (2021), *A Threshold Crossed: Israeli Authorities and the Crimes of Apartheid and Persecution*, Human Rights Watch, https://www.hrw.org/rep ort/2021/04/27/threshold-crossed/israeli-authorities-and-crimes-apartheid-and-pers ecution (accessed 30 October 2021).

Jaillant, L., and Caputo, A. (2022), 'Unlocking Digital Archives: Cross-Disciplinary Perspectives on AI and Born-Digital Data', *AI & SOCIETY*, https://doi.org/10.1007/s00 146-021-01367-x.

Jarosha, H. A. (2021), Palestinian freelance journalist, personal interview.

Jenkins, H. (2006), *Convergence Culture: Where Old and New Media Collide*, New York: New York University Press.

Khondker, H. H. (2011), 'Role of the New Media in the Arab Spring', *Globalizations*, 8 (5): 675–79.

Kurtz, D. L., and L. Upton (2017), 'War Stories and Occupying Soldiers: A Narrative Approach to Understanding Police Culture and Community Conflict', *Critical Criminology*, 25 (4): 539–58.

Lev-On, A. (2012), 'Communication, Community, Crisis: Mapping Uses and Gratifications in the Contemporary Media Environment', *New Media & Society*, 14: 98–116.

Lev-On, A. (2018), 'The Anti-Social Network? Framing Social Media in Wartime', *Social Media + Society*, 4 (3): 1–12.

Loader, B. D., and D. Mercea (2011), 'Networking Democracy?', *Information, Communication & Society*, 14 (6): 757–69.

Madden, S., and R. A. Alt (2021), 'Know Her Name: Open Dialogue on Social Media as a Form of Innovative Justice', *Social Media + Society*, 7 (1): 1–10.

Majeed, T. (2021), 'Strategic Journalism amid Media Repression in Kashmir', *Media Asia*, 48 (3): 207–9.

Majeed, T. (2022), 'Embedded Authoritarianism: The Politics of Poor Press Freedom in Indian Kashmir', *Media, Culture & Society*, 44 (3): 613–24.

Manovich, L. (2001), *The Language of New Media*, London: MIT Press.

Mayo, J. M. (1988), 'War Memorials as Political Memory', *Geographical Review*, American Geographical Society, 78 (1): 62–75.

McLuhan, M. (1964), *Understanding Media: The Extensions of Man*, London: McGraw-Hill.

McQuail, D. (2005), *Mass Communication Theory*, 5th edition, Thousand Oaks, CA: Sage Publications.

Nevarez, M. D., J. C. Malone, D. M. Rentz and R. J. Waldinger (2017), 'War and Remembrance: Combat Exposure in Young Adulthood and Memory Function Sixty Years Later', *Comprehensive Psychiatry*, 72: 97–105.

Olick, J. K. (2018), 'From the Memory of Violence to the Violence of Memory', *ENRS*, 18 February, https://enrs.eu/article/from-the-memory-of-violence-to-the-violence-of-memory (accessed 30 October 2021).

Papacharissi, Z. (2008), 'The Virtual Sphere 2.0. The Internet, the Public Sphere, and Beyond'. In Andrew Chadwick and Philip N. Howard (eds), *Routledge Handbook of Internet Politics*, London: Routledge.

Rehan, A. (2021), Palestinian freelance journalist, personal interview.

Skaik, M. (2021), Palestinian freelance journalist, personal interview.

Tripp, C. (2020), 'Memories of Violence: Introduction', *Journal of the British Academy*, 8 (3): 1–6.

Tufekci, Z. (2017), *Twitter and Tear Gas – The Power and Fragility of Networked Protest*, New Haven, CT: Yale University Press.

Vlassenroot, E., S. Chambers, S. Lieber, A. Michel, F. Geeraert, J. Pranger, J. Birkholz and P. Mechant (2021), 'Web-Archiving and Social Media: An Exploratory Analysis', *International Journal of Digital Humanities*, 2 (1): 107–28.

Walden, V. G. (2016), 'Animation and Memory'. In N. Dobson, A. H. Roe, A. Ratelle and C. Ruddell (eds.), *The Animation Studies Reader*, 69–80, London: Bloomsbury Publishing.

Wessels, J. I. (2017), 'Introduction: The Digital Age Opens Up New Terrains for Peace and Conflict Research', *Conflict and Society*, Berghahn Journals, 3 (1): 125–9.

Part Three

Social Media Management and Public Opinion Control

12

Comparative analysis of Israeli and PLO diplomacy practices during the May 2021 Israeli attacks against Gaza

Sherouk Maher and Dina Matar

Introduction

On 7 May 2021, a fresh round of military clashes broke out between Israel and the Palestinian group Hamas in Gaza after weeks of rising tensions in East Jerusalem, which started with an Israeli court ruling sanctioning the forceful eviction of several Palestinian families from their homes in the Sheikh Jarrah area of the city. The neighbourhood had become the symbol of a protracted struggle against what Palestinians call new practices of 'ethnic cleansing' since Israel's annexation of East Jerusalem in 1980 (Al-Sharif, 2021). During the eleven days of Israeli military strikes against Gaza, 240 Palestinians, mostly women and children, were killed and 12 Israelis were killed by rockets launched by the Palestinian group Hamas, which controls Gaza, before an Egyptian-brokered ceasefire on 21 May 2021 stopped the hostilities.

During the period of military actions, Israel used Twitter and other social media platforms to legitimize its military action in Gaza and win international support, as part of its persistent public diplomacy campaign to construct and manage its self-constructed image as a state defending its right to exist. In contrast, the Palestine Liberation Organization (PLO), which nominally represents all Palestinians, used its official Twitter feed to communicate an alternative narrative of the conflict, focusing more on the violence and the suffering the military attacks subjected Palestinians in Gaza to as well as on persistent Israeli settler-colonial practices in the occupied Palestinian territories. What was particularly remarkable, however, was the exponential rise in digital activism by ordinary Palestinians and activists on the ground, who used digital platforms to disseminate largely unmediated images of collapsed homes, casualties and displaced families in Gaza and tell alternative narratives of lived experiences during the hostilities, thus challenging the Israeli self-constructed narrative of its right to defend itself against what it calls terrorist actions by Hamas and the PLO's lukewarm approach to public diplomacy.

This chapter discusses the Israeli and PLO's digital practices as part of their diverse strategic public diplomacy campaigns that have become more sophisticated since the 11 September 2001 attacks in New York and since the monumental expansion of digital platforms that have enhanced the opportunities for new players to be involved in the battle over publics. Broadly speaking, public diplomacy is often discussed as a necessary taken-for-granted political practice that states instrumentalize to communicate their aims and ideologies to foreign audiences. Scholarly work on public diplomacy across a variety of disciplines – politics, political communication, war studies and international relations – often uses the term in instrumentalist and functional sense, such as its effect on public opinion and whether or how it could lead to an intended political outcome. As an ill-defined term and practice, public diplomacy is sometimes confused or used interchangeably with the concept of soft power, which has been used to refer to any established state's efforts to influence international publics through the communication of compelling narratives, or with the concept of propaganda defined as the dissemination of biased ideas or as a form of misinformation and deception. In addition, public diplomacy has been conflated with the concept of strategic communications, defined by Holtzhausen and Zerfass as 'the practice of deliberate and purposive communication that a communication agent enacts in the public sphere on behalf of a communicative entity to reach set goals' (2013: 74) or, more precisely, strategic political communication which incorporates the use of sophisticated knowledge of attributes of human behaviour, such as attitude, cultural tendencies and media-use patterns.

Within the field of international relations and political communication studies, Alister Miskimmon, Ben O'Loughlin and Laura Roselle (2013) suggest public diplomacy can be better understood by paying attention to what they call 'strategic narratives' – or the storytelling aspects of public diplomacy, soft power or strategic communication. For them, strategic narratives are the means for 'political actors to shape the behavior of domestic and international actors … . [They] are a tool for political actors to extend their influence, manage expectations and change the discursive environment in which they operate. They are narratives about both states and the system itself … the point of strategic narratives is to influence the behavior of others' (2013: 2). In their argument, the authors make three central claims concerning the importance of narratives in global politics. First, they argue that 'narratives are central to human relations' (ibid: 1) as they constrain and enable behaviour. Second, that people and political actors use narratives in strategic ways, and third, that the communication environment affects how narratives are communicated and what effects they have (ibid).

In the digital age, what is increasingly evident is the fact that public diplomacy, understood broadly as comprising official (state or non-state) discursive and visual communicative practices disseminated in diverse platforms and spaces, is increasingly being challenged by diverse local/national, regional and transnational actors seeking to tell their own narratives and gain public recognition of their claims. Such challenges have only served to underline the fault lines in public diplomacy's ability to construct 'monological views', particularly of contemporary conflicts, (Kaempf, 2013: 601) and exposed the 'continual risk of stray images emerging from the battlefield, which may shape public opinion both at home and among the population in the war zone' (Hoskins and O'Loughlin, 2010: 12). Furthermore, as Philip Seib (2012) has argued, the challenges posed by the digital era require a shift in diplomatic practice that matches the pace of real-time events and, as such, contemporary digital diplomatic practices must speak to the ordinary public, not only to elite government leaders, since 'power *can* emanate from the public, and so developing and maintaining ties with publics around the world is an essential element of foreign policy' (Seib, 2012: 8).

While debates continue around the digital divide and who can say to whom, there is a consensus that an ultra-saturated media and communication environment and the easy access to social media platforms provide ample opportunities for activists to resist, to exert their agency, to self-represent themselves and to defy structural constraints. Focusing more closely on the structural characteristics of Twitter to overcome such constraints, Zizi Papacharissi and Maria de Fatima Oliveira (2012) detail how the platform had changed the ways information is circulated because of its ability to enable what they call a 'collaborative construction of events' that brings together media outlets and online users during real-time events (ibid: 2), resulting in some dependence on members of the public for updates on events (Hoskins and O'Loughlin, 2010). Arguably, as more publics become producers and consumers of news, it becomes difficult for established states to control or influence public opinion through using discursive and visual communication or strategic narratives aimed at constructing a particular image of these states and securing them support. However, the debates on whether these narratives change public opinion and secure support remain unresolved, particularly in the contexts of prolonged and unequal conflicts as well as the changing sociopolitical conditions which would also determine what is said and who says it.

With this brief conceptual background, this chapter now offers a brief overview of public diplomacy practices by Israel and the PLO before turning to a comparative analysis of their official Twitter feed in the May 2021 armed conflict in which Israel repeatedly attacked Gaza and its people. It acknowledges from the outset that any comparative analysis of public diplomacy practices must take into account the broader aspects of the asymmetrical conflict between Israel and the Palestinian people and must acknowledge the fact that the entities under study here are different – Israel is an internationally recognized state and the PLO is a non-state actor still seeking to establish an independent state. This asymmetry has implications for the location of these actors in global power structures and their ability to act and reach out to a global audience, an asymmetry magnified by Israel's superior material, economic and symbolic power and its continuous occupation of Palestinian territory. As the superior power and as an established state, Israel not only holds, and has access, to significant military and institutional resources as well as foreign support, but also controls and limits the PLO resources as well as the Palestinian subjects under its settler-colonial regime.

Israeli, Palestinian public diplomacy in an asymmetrical conflict

Since its creation, Israel has used strategic and intentional public diplomacy as part of its constant campaign to dominate local and global politics and secure international legitimacy for its actions. This campaign is popularly known as *Hasbara* (literally meaning to explain), a practice through which strategic information and communication has been tied to the strategic objectives of the Israeli state – namely, to cultivate a positive image and achieve legitimacy for its actions in its permanent war against the Palestinians (Khalidi, 2019). Following its 2006 war in Lebanon and Operation Cast Lead in Gaza in 2008, both of which seriously damaged Israel's reputation, Israel shifted to what Miriyam Aouragh calls Hasbara 2.0 (2016), which can be described as an assertive digital diplomacy campaign in social media platforms and involving several state entities, including the Israeli Defense Forces (IDF) and the Israeli Ministry of Strategic Affairs established in 2008 to reach regional and international audiences.

The term *Hasbara* has been discussed as soft propaganda, public relations, government advocacy and public diplomacy (Aouragh, 2016; Shenhav, Sheafer and Gabay, 2010) or as persuasive strategic communication that the Jewish state has used to manage and control its image since even before its creation in 1948. Indeed, as historian Ilan Pappe has argued in his book *The Idea of Israel* (2016), Israel has been instrumentalizing Zionist ideology in politics, the education system, the media and film to construct its public image since even before the state's foundation in 1948. Jonathan Cummings (2016), too, provides a detailed account of what he terms the Israeli state's information apparatus in the early stages of its formation, and its concern with international legitimacy through constructing a positive and progressive image that contrasts with the negative and regressive image of Palestinians. For Cummings, the emergence of *Hasbara* before the formation of the state of Israel in 1948 is a reactive and defensive concept of political persuasion, rooted in Jewish culture. As such, *Hasbara* has often been used as referring to public diplomacy. However, Shaul R. Shenhav and others (2010) distinguish what they see as Israel's public diplomacy practices that incorporate media and public opinion into policymaking from *Hasbara* which, for them, 'assumes a tactical, rather than a strategic, approach aiming to explain actions and policy' (2010: 145). For them, public diplomacy incorporates reactive, proactive and relationship building, which applies to Israel's practices in the twenty-first century as well.

Some other scholars see the deliberate attempts of Israel to manage news narratives and media representations to construct its self-image as actions that are *in response* to what it claims to be an existential threat. This line of reasoning is sufficiently argued in Lisa-Maria Kretschmer's 2017 study of Israel's tweets in the 2012 Gaza war, in which she shows Israel's emphasis on the inevitable use of military for self-defence to legitimize its actions, and, as such, is a defensive action, rather than actively proposing political solutions or seeking to build relations with others. The study also demonstrates Israel's reliance on conventional pre-Cold War hard power, which Joseph Nye (2004) defines as the use of economic or military power to influence other actors, as opposed to the more benign soft power which relies on diplomacy, values and culture. What is more relevant to note, however, are the specific contexts under which Israel produces its self-image. Indeed, as Aouragh (2016) rightly notes, *Hasbara* has emerged within Israel's settler-colonial practices which, she argues, fundamentally contradict the concept and practice of public diplomacy because Israel 'attempts to construct consensus through persuasion about its right to occupy and repress Palestinians. Yet, it does so while executing military campaigns in the oPt (occupied Palestinian territories) and maintaining segregationist policies for Palestinians inside Israel' (2016: 9).

While many studies have considered Israel's long-standing and persistent efforts to manage its public image and achieve international legitimacy, few studies have discussed the PLO's efforts to manage its image over time and particularly since the signing of the Oslo agreements in 1993. A notable exception is Paul Chamberlin's book *The Global Offensive* (2016) which discussed the PLO's public diplomacy moves on the international stage between 1967 and 1975 and the US response to these moves. The lack of scholarship on this important aspect of the PLO's political communication practices can be attributed to the fact that the PLO had been seen and discussed in the mainstream international relations literature as a terrorist non-state actor up until the Oslo agreement in 1993, as well as the fact that since the signing of the accords, the PLO lost some of its roles, ceding some administrative responsibilities and control to the Palestinian Authority (PA). Since the peace agreement, the PLO, as an umbrella organization founded in 1964 to represent all Palestinians, has maintained some official duties and responsibilities particularly with regard to international relations and negotiations with Israel.

The PA, established in May 1994, discernibly overlapped, and in fact overshadowed, the shrunk PLO in terms of their respective executive powers and international support. While officially, the PLO has remained the top national institution, representing the Palestinian people at large, and perhaps in a nominal fashion, the PA's jurisdiction was confined to the occupied Palestinian territories and the Palestinian population assigned to it by consecutive agreements with Israel. However, Israeli-Palestinian negotiations and agreements were all conducted and signed by the PLO, not the PA. Both the PLO and the PA remained dominated by Fatah, despite attempts by both the late president Yasser Arafat and his successor Mahmoud Abbas to distance its senior members from key positions preferring to rely on the bureaucratic system, including the security services, elevating themselves above factional differences.

Despite the signing of the Oslo accords, the relationship between Israel and the PLO/PA continues to be defined by structural asymmetry at all levels, most starkly evident in Israel's highly advanced military apparatus and technologies of control that have impacted Palestinian lives, particularly Palestinians in Gaza. Despite the accords, there is no official Palestinian representation in Israel and there are limited opportunities for Palestinian diplomats to engage with Israeli citizens. It is against this backdrop of limited diplomatic recognition that the Palestinian government in the West Bank launched the Palestine in Hebrew Facebook page in 2015, which posts content solely in Hebrew and which is managed by the PLO's Committee for Interaction with Israeli Society (Manor and Holmes, 2018). Furthermore, the diplomatic isolation of Gaza since 2007 when Hamas took over the Gaza Strip following its rupture with the PA has been strengthened by Israel's maintenance of a strict blockade and restrictions on its population, rendering Gaza into an open prison and stripping its inhabitants of their rights. These restrictions have extended to the banning since 2014 of Hamas's Twitter account after Hamas's classification by the United States and Europe as a terrorist organization. In the attacks in May 2021, Israel completely or partially destroyed – as it has in previous assaults – some of Gaza's infrastructure including homes, schools, health facilities, businesses, factories, roads and government offices, resulting in significantly higher war victims and casualties than the Iron Dome-shielded Israel.

Israeli Twitter feeds: Seeking legitimacy

This chapter offers a comparative analysis of Israel's and the PLO's public diplomacy efforts during the May 2021 attacks. It focuses on forty tweets, purposely selected randomly, of each of the official Twitter accounts of the PLO (@nadplo) and Israel's PM (@IsraeliPM) posted from 7 May to 21 May 2021. In making the comparison, the content analysis of these tweets was conducted using the online All My Tweets platform (allmytweets.net), which helped display all the tweets posted on each of the accounts on one page. Certain repetitive phrases in the tweets were captured and tracked before using thematic analysis of the tweets which was conducted by grouping central recurrent narratives of both accounts under themes discussed in the analysis given later in the text. Although analysing the online engagement with these tweets was beyond the scope of this chapter, it was noticed that the tweets by the Israeli prime minister's office attracted more public engagement than the PLO's, underlining Israel's advanced internet use illustrated earlier and its ability to drive online activity. It was also noted that the official Israeli prime minister's account posted a significantly higher number of tweets than the less active Palestinian account during the war.

Based on the analysis, Israel's attempts to dominate and control the digital sphere during the attacks, this chapter suggests, are intended to suppress Palestinian voices and de-legitimize Palestinian narratives in diverse spaces, including digital platforms. Israel's use of the internet as a technology of power and a tool of occupation is well documented in several studies. For example, Helga Tawil-Souri (2012) uses the term digital occupation to suggest that Israel's control over Gaza, in particular, continues and increasingly includes the high-tech real, while Gil Hochberg (2015) argues that Israeli occupation of Palestine is driven by the unequal access to visual rights, or the right to control what can be seen, how and from which position. Israel maintains this unequal balance by erasing the history and denying the existence of Palestinians, and by carefully concealing its own militarization. Israeli surveillance of Palestinians, combined with the militarized gaze of Israeli soldiers at places like roadside checkpoints, also serve as tools of dominance.

As part of Israel's continuous quest to control what Palestinians say in order to control international public opinion and legitimize its image, the state has also started to target Arab audiences through the use of Arabic to communicate its ideology and self-constructed image to a wider audience in the Arab world where hostility to Israel's policies is pervasive. Along with Arabic language newspapers, radio and broadcasting, Israel has created several Arabic-language Twitter accounts, including the virtual Twitter embassy, @IsraelintheGulf dedicated to fostering dialogue with people in the Gulf and @IsraelArabic, which has almost 500,000 followers. Any analysis of Israel's public diplomacy as discursive practices that are intentional requires a detailed analysis of all its communicative practices, which is beyond the scope of this study. Given our focus in this chapter, we limit the analysis to addressing the Twitter feed of the Israeli prime minister's account @IsraeliPM, which tweets in English, during the May hostilities. A total of forty tweets were collected between 7 May and 21 May 2021, the period of the latest round of military attacks. Thematic analysis was used to address the main themes emerging from the tweets before relating them to the sociopolitical contexts.

The first finding in the analysis is that despite the constant use of Twitter, which invites dialogical and multi-flow communication, Israel's official tweets are unidirectional, suggesting a one-to-many mode of communication by elite and power sources. In fact, the tweets analysed mainly comprised quotes and video speeches by then prime minister Benjamin Netanyahu and other senior officials. The analysis also showed that the mode of delivery was formal rather than informal, with the tweets delivered in a format reminiscent of formal official TV addresses by state actors and elites who were popular before the digital age and specifically used to appeal to international audiences. Importantly, some of the tweets referred to Netanyahu in the third person, thus further hindering dialogic communication, interactivity and responses from the intended audiences, and, as such, appeared to be similar to communicative formats familiar in the 1990s when television was the main mass medium. The finding is interesting because it not only seeks to add credibility and legitimacy to the language used in the tweets, but also reflects Israel's bid to control the narrative through controlling the sources and the information provided and limiting criticism or challenging through dialogic communication.

In the thematic analysis, a key theme repeatedly emerging in the tweets communicated to about 950,000 followers was the discourse about Israel's power as the most advanced military force in the region and the use of this force for self-defence, thus repeating the defensive/reactive approach that has been at the core of Israel's *Hasbara* for years. The theme came across clearly in the repetition of words and categories associated with military power and with the use of this power against enemies, as in the reference to Hamas (63 times), security (38 times), attacks (37 times), IDF (36 times), rockets (35 times), terrorists (34 times) and defence (31 times), all of which convey an image of Israel as a powerful actor with military means (Hadari and Turgeman, 2018). For example, a tweet published on 14 May 2021 specifically emphasized Israel's military power and control of the battleground by repeating phrases such as Hamas was 'paying a heavy price for attacking the state', while accusing Hamas of using civilians as 'human shields', a term repeated six times (@IsraeliPM, 17 May). At the end of the war, Netanyahu was quoted saying that 'we regret every loss of life, but I can tell you categorically, there is no army in the world that acts in a more moral fashion than the army of Israel' (@IsraeliPM, 21 May). His language underscored Israel's use of strategic public diplomacy narratives to gain international support by linking 'military successes of counterterrorist operations' instead of 'the presentation of peace-oriented policies' (Kretschmer, 2017: 20).

In addition, in multiple tweets, Netanyahu deployed a strategic narrative justifying force as a form of self-defence and/or protection of its civilians from Hamas rockets, a narrative Israel has used repeatedly to present itself and its people as victims of violence. This is a narrative used by 'political actors to shape the behavior of domestic and international actors … . [They] are a tool for political actors to extend their influence, manage expectations and change the discursive environment in which they operate. They are narratives about both states and the system itself ... the point of strategic narratives is to influence the behavior of others" (Miskimmon, O'Loughlin and Roselle, 2013: 2). Indeed, the tweets communicated in English along with the videos of Netanyahu speaking in Hebrew with English subtitles sought to portray the war against Hamas as a war against terror, which neatly fit the Western narrative of the US-led global war against terrorism. Importantly, these tweets were largely aimed at Western elites, particularly those who have been supportive of the Jewish state, thus sidelining foreign publics with limited knowledge of the Israeli-Palestinian issue, as well as Jewish opponents of the state's military practices.

Israeli tweets also instrumentalized historical narratives that emphasized its inherent right to land, a dynamic made possible by world powers, including the Ottoman and European occupation and the British mandate, which facilitated Israel's occupation of Palestine in 1948 (Tawil-Souri, 2015). This was evident in Israel's first tweets about Al Aqsa clashes on 9 May, two days after violence began, portraying Israel as a democratic state with Jerusalem as its capital, and a state that had the right to defend and build itself 'just as every people builds its capital' (@IsraeliPM, 9 May). In another tweet, Netanyahu was quoted as saying 'Jerusalem has been the capital of the Jewish people for thousands of years. Our roots in Jerusalem go back to Biblical times' (@IsraeliPM, 9 May). In the same thread, Netanyahu adopted a threatening tone to 'terrorist organizations', vowing that 'Israel will respond powerfully to any act of aggression' (@IsraeliPM, 9 May), a threat that was repeated throughout the war. Reminding online users of Israel's historical roots and vowing aggressive responses against its enemies target Western states who support Israel's status as a democratic state in the Middle East., this narrative is established further by showcasing Western support in tweets that report phone calls with US and European leaders. By the end of the war, Netanyahu was shown hosting European foreign ministers, showing them a wing of an Iranian UAV that Israel shot down as proof that Iran supported Hamas (@IsraeliPM, 20 May).

Israel's militarized language was accompanied by indirect dehumanization of Palestinians who were injured or killed during the war. In fact, Netanyahu's occasional acknowledgement of loss of life in Gaza was mostly blamed on Hamas with the Jewish state repeatedly portraying the strikes in Gaza as part of the state's right to defend itself and restore calm, while the casualties were Hamas's doing. In a video, Israel portrayed a rocket misfired by Hamas into Gaza in a bid to attribute human casualties to Hamas who was committing a 'double war crime' by using its civilians as human shields (@IsraeliPM, 19 May 2021). Besides demonstrating a defensive approach, this narrative dehumanized Gaza's civilians, while the stories of Israeli casualties were repeatedly mentioned. In a tweet depicting Netanyahu's hospital visit to check on a wounded Israeli girl, he is quoted as saying: 'Next to her (the wounded girl) is a boy from Gaza being cared for', as an example of the 'difference between civilized people and the forces of darkness' (@IsraeliPM, 12 May 2021). The Palestinian boy, however, was not acknowledged in the image. Meanwhile, the word 'Palestinians' was mentioned only 5 times, compared to the words Israel or Israelis, which were highlighted 129 times. Palestinians are not given a name, let alone a face; in stark contrast, Netanyahu offers condolences to the family of a Jewish man killed in a riot, mentioning Yigal Yehoshua by name (@IsraeliPM, 17 May).

These narratives, however, were challenged by unmediated images and videos of civilian suffering circulating on social media platforms. Among the online videos that went viral is one that shows a ten-year-old child crying over his father's dead body (Aldroubi, 2021). Similarly, journalists posted videos of their arrests by Israeli officers directly challenging Israel's claims of being a democracy. For example, the UK Sky News's correspondent shared a viral video on his Twitter condemning Israeli forces for mistreating CNN crew and sharing similar experiences he faced while reporting the war on ground (@Stone_SkyNews). The bombing of a media building that hosts Al Jazeera and AP was widely shared online, drawing condemnations against Israel which failed to provide evidence that Hamas had operatives there (Federman, 2021).

Our analysis shows that despite a history of past failures in its *Hasbara* project, Israel's public diplomacy continues to follow the same reactive approach while ignoring criticism of its actions. This is evident in the acknowledgement of an expected backlash in Netanyahu's early tweets where he vows that the state will 'not be beholden to the keyboards of Twitter users' or by narratives 'being expressed erroneously and misleadingly in the global media. In the end, truth will win but we must constantly reiterate it' (@IsraeliPM, 10 May). The defensive tone persisted until the end of the war, when Netanyahu hosted foreign ambassadors and explicitly stated that criticizing Israel 'not only is absurd and unjust and untrue ... (but) it does enormous damage to democracies ... It says you cannot protect yourself' (@IsraeliPM, 19 May). Choosing to follow the same narratives despite expected shortcomings reflects Israel's stagnant approach that makes it fall short of winning the online war of ideas.

Palestinian tweets – culture and affect

Palestinians have been early and enthusiastic adopters of the internet in the early twenty-first century, particularly during and since the Second Intifada (uprising) in 2000. However, the PLO's digital diplomacy efforts have been inconsistent as evidenced by the meagre PLO digital presence in all countries where Palestinian representative offices are based (Manor, 2019). In addition, unlike Israel which employs numerous channels to bridge barriers with Arab counterparts, the PLO has only one virtual Facebook embassy, 'Palestine in Hebrew', through which it aims to foster dialogue with Israelis and promote the two-state solution (Manor and Holmes, 2018). The Palestinian official diplomatic Twitter pages, or pages produced by the PA's governing entities, use English as the main language, thus indicating the bid to reach elite international audiences. These pages include the PA's prime minister's account @PalestinePMO and the PLO's official Twitter account @nadplo, which is the focus of this study. Like the Israeli prime minister's account, most of the tweets communicated on this account reported updates on war events.

The findings in this study show a different picture from that discussed earlier in the analysis of the official Israeli prime minister's Twitter feed. In fact, in stark contrast, it is noticed that the PLO's Twitter feed relied on unofficial sources, including reports and postings by Palestinian activists and civil society actors as well as media reports and external sources. In addition, unlike Israel's official tweets, the PLO's Twitter feed used graphic images and stories uploaded by what might be called citizen journalists to highlight Israeli atrocities and discredit its narratives. Most of the forty tweets analysed were accompanied by images and videos, the majority of which were amateur videos provided by members of the public or citizen journalists, offering a stark contrast to Israel's use of highly sophisticated formats, such as the video displaying Israeli settlers' attacks on Palestinians in Sheikh Jarrah (@nadplo, 13 May). One video, for example, showed Palestinians banned from entering Al Aqsa Mosque compound, noting that the Israeli state 'continued to attack them with sonic bombs and rubber bullets' and that 'medics and journalists were removed from the gate area' (@nadplo, 10 May). Most tweets contained scenes of Israeli violence against Palestinians, primarily in the Gaza Strip and Sheikh Jarrah.

Such narratives and images are powerful representations of realities on the ground, posted by ordinary people affected by them. However, the PLO's Twitter feed's use of such images and narratives may have undermined its political credentials and its ability to influence the international elitist agenda, particularly because the Twitter feeds also reflected the lack of coordination (and continued infighting) with Hamas and with the PLO's diplomatic missions in global capitals. However, the use of ordinary people's reports of events on the ground also reflected that the PLO was targeting a different audience from that targeted by the Israeli prime minister's Twitter feed, namely global and regional publics (unfamiliar to the Palestinian cause) rather than power elites.

Interestingly, the PLO's Twitter feeds mostly appropriated affective and meaningful symbols and words to emphasize Palestinians' sense of identity as people living under occupation. Such symbols were evident in the repeated use of words such as: 'Palestine' and its derivatives (67 times); 'Gaza' (48 times); 'attack' (36 times), 'occupying', 'occupation' (30 times) and 'Israel' (29 times). In addition, the tweets incorporated affective hashtags to summon a global solidarity community to support Palestinians, such as #HereGaza, #SaveJerusalem #SaveSheikhJarrah and #GazaUnderAttack, underscoring the fact that Israel remains an occupying power, such as in the tweet that affirmed the PLO 'held the occupying power (Israel) fully responsible for the consequences of the dangerous developments in #Jerusalem' (@nadplo, 8 May 2021). Another tweet used a video circulating on social media platforms which showed a Palestinian girl repeatedly pleading with her mother and saying: 'I don't want to die' from the Israeli strikes (@nadplo, 16 May 2021). On the Nakba (catastrophe) anniversary on 15 May, a tweet declared 'Palestine: forever a land with a people', thus underlining the length of and the history of occupation (@nadplo, 15 May 2021), while another video was posted of residents in Sheikh Jarrah chanting a historical anthem called *Mawtini* (My Homeland), which the PLO used during its revolutionary phase in the 1960s and 1970s, to mark the occasion (@nadplo, 16 May 2021). The use of such affective symbols and images, the analysis suggests, is intended to bring together Palestinians as a collective identifying with the *Nakba* (catastrophe) and its effect as well as to elicit solidarity amongst pro-Palestinian groups, underlining the potential of digital platforms for promoting a Palestinian virtual resistance (Aouragh, 2011). The image and the language used helped define the war's reality as a conflict taking place between a powerful state and disempowered people, contradicting Israel's claims of it being a war on terror and a war to defend itself and underlining the inequalities between the two sides.

Realizing the potential threat to its image from Palestinian grassroots activism in digital spaces, Israel collaborated with social media platforms to censor pro-Palestinian content citing the need to halt hate speech and violence (Cook, 2021). However, despite social media's facilitation of government surveillance, the digital sphere paradoxically empowered online publics during the war who disclosed Facebook and Instagram's algorithmic censorship and shared ways of overcoming them (Abu Sneineh, 2021). Besides revealing increasing collaboration between social media platforms and governments, prompted by the commercial nature of digital companies, the 2021 war demonstrates that today's publics, well-informed and opinionated, require different diplomatic practices to meet their expectations.

Conclusion

This paper addressed the Twitter feeds communicated by the Israeli prime minister's office and the PLO during the May 2021 hostilities between Israel and Hamas in Gaza. The comparative analysis of the Twitter feeds showed different emphases and intentions in the two entities' public diplomacy campaigns during the conflict. In fact, the analysis showed that Israeli tweets were intended to reach foreign elites and maintain Israel's self-constructed image of itself as a nation seeking to defend itself. In contrast, the PLO's official tweet sought to reach regional and global publics to promote solidarity and empathy for Palestinians living under occupation. Furthermore, the comparative analysis demonstrated that Israel continued its military-driven approach that focuses on victory in the battlefield, confirming Ben D. Mor's argument that 'Israel may have won the "war" ... but in terms of the political consequences – especially world public opinion – it "lost the peace"' (2006: 171). Israel used the same narratives related to its need to defend itself against attacks, while the PLO relied on ordinary people and activists' digital activism to mobilize support, stir international empathy and encourage diasporic communities to share the Palestinian story. Although the 2021 war ended with both Israel and Hamas declaring victory, it was the Palestinian people and social media users who celebrated mobile phone images, videos and posts that gave voice to an oppressed population.

There is little doubt, however, that public diplomacy efforts by Israel, and to a lesser extent the PLO, were challenged by numerous narratives posted by ordinary people and citizen activists in 2021, further denting the self-image of the Jewish state which had been discussed in several studies. For example, in a study in 2020, Eytan Gilboa showed that younger Americans and liberal Jews are less supportive of Israel's military confrontations in Palestine than previous generations, attributing the diminishing support to anti-Israeli campaigns held in the wake of the Black Lives Matter movement protests that erupted after the brutal murder of George Floyd in the

United States. At the time, Palestinian activists used social media to compare racial injustice in the United States to Palestine, using the tweaked #PalestinianLivesMatter to raise awareness (Boxerman, 2020), presenting an additional challenge to Israel's diplomatic efforts in the United States where 'public opinion is a significant factor in the formulation and implementation of US foreign policy and in the US-Israel special relationship' (Gilboa, 2020: 106).

That said, while the digital arena allows publics (ordinary people and grassroots activists) to make their voices heard, it is important to avoid a determinist view of the power and potential of technologies in the Palestinian cause particularly given the lack of firm evidence about their effectiveness of grassroots activism in changing hearts and minds. As Papacharissi (2014) writes, there is a need to link online social movements with their offline impact as social media 'help[s] activate latent ties that may be crucial to the mobilization of networked publics' (2014: 3). Aouragh (2011) further suggests that while the internet may have expanded Palestinians' political involvement, it had not replaced offline mobilization. Moreover, if citizens and non-state actors use social media for their own purposes, so do governments. Israel, for example, has recruited tech-savvy university students to promote pro-Israeli sentiments online, especially in anti-Semitic groups (Cook, 2009). It also used algorithms to detect negative filter bubbles before pushing online users into disseminating pro-Israeli content to dismantle negative echo chambers (Manor, 2019). The algorithmic filter bubbles make it difficult for audiences to get exposed to information beyond their own activities and enable a swift spread of misinformation. With all its challenges, the digital sphere can empower ordinary citizens, presenting additional responsibilities for governments to focus on achieving success in the virtual world, in parallel with the offline world.

Like most modern conflicts, the protracted conflict between Israel and the Palestinians is fought on various battlefields and spaces, including the mediated 'image war', in digital platforms. A deeper understanding of the circumstances that allow political actors (both states and non-state actors) to transmit their messages through foreign media could help public diplomacy professionals to better prepare themselves to deal with the image war aspect of asymmetric conflicts and manage successful public diplomacy as a pivotal aspect of today's conflicts. This study, which has used a focused research to address the image war between Israel and the PLO, has some limitations in terms of its scope. However, it offers a microcosm through which to address public diplomacy in asymmetric conflicts and its limitations, particularly when one actor is a recognized state and the other remains a non-state actor seeking to form a state. Furthermore, the study has shown that despite its superior military power, Israel remains concerned with legitimizing its image and securing support, a concern that has been the cornerstone of its political communication strategies and marketing its image since its foundation in 1948. The PLO, on the other hand, remains reluctant or unable to make use of the mediation opportunities digital platforms offer, reflecting a rather inconsistent political communication strategy that has marked its international politics since the Oslo accords. Whether the PLO can harness popular activism to its full potential remains to be seen.

References

Abu Sneineh, M. (2021), 'Facebook Users Deploy Old Arabic Font to Bypass Algorithm, Support Palestinians', Middle East Eye, 23 May, www.middleeasteye.net/news/israel-palestine-facebook-algorithm-old-arabic-font (accessed 10 July 2021).

Al-Sharif, O. (2021), 'Palestinians Need Help Fighting Ethnic Cleansing in Jerusalem', Arab News, 6 July, https://www.arabnews.com/node/1889696 (accessed 1 July 2021).

Aldroubi, M. (2021), 'Palestinian Boy Mourns Father's Death after Israeli Strike on Gaza in Viral Video', The National, 12 May, www.thenationalnews.com/mena/palestin ian-boy-mourns-father-s-death-after-israeli-strike-on-gaza-in-viral-video-1.1221456 (accessed 10 August 2021).

Aouragh, M. (2011), *Palestine Online: Transnationalism, the Internet and Construction of Identity*, New York: I.B. Tauris.

Aouragh, M. (2016), 'Hasbara 2.0: Israel's Public Diplomacy in the Digital Age', *Middle East Critique*, 25 (3): 271–97.

Boxerman, A. (2020), ' "Palestinian Lives Matter": Activists Draw Parallels between Israel, US Killings', Times of Israel, 2 June, www.timesofisrael.com/palestinian-lives-matter-activists-draw-parallels-between-israel-us-killings (accessed 23 July 2021).

Chamberlin, P. T. (2016), *The Global Offensive: The United States, the Palestine Liberation Organization and the Making of the Post-Cold War Order*, Oxford: Oxford University Press.

Cook, J. (2009), 'Internet Users Paid to Spread Israeli Propaganda', The Electronic Intifada, 21 July, www.electronicintifada.net/content/internet-users-paid-spread-israeli-propaga nda/8355 (accessed 9 July 2021).

Cook, J. (2021), 'Tech Giants Help Israel Muzzle Palestinians', The Electronic Intifada, 5 June, www.electronicintifada.net/content/tech-giants-help-israel-muzzle-palestini ans/33336 (accessed 1 July 2021).

Cummings, J. (2016), *Israel's Public Diplomacy: The Problems of Hasbara*, 1996–75, Lanhan, MD: Rowman and Littlefield.

Federman, J. (2021), ' "Shocking and Horrifying": Israel Destroys AP Office in Gaza', AP News, 16 May, www.apnews.com/article/media-israel-middle-east-business-israel-pale stinian-conflict-fe452147166f55ba5a9d32e6ba8b53d7 (accessed 03 August 2021).

Gilboa, E. (2020), 'The American Public and Israel in the Twenty-First Century' [monograph], *Mideast Security and Policy Studies*, 181: 9–140.

Hadari, G., and A. Turgeman (2018), 'Public Diplomacy in Army Boots: The Chronic Failure of Israel's Hasbara', *Israel Affairs*, 24 (3): 482–99.

Hochberg, G. (2015), *Visual Occupations: Violence and Visibility in a Conflict Zone*, Syracuse, NY: Duke University Press.

Holtzhausen, D., and A. Zerfass (2013), 'Strategic Communication – Pillars and Perspectives of an Alternative Paradigm', In A. Zerfass, L. Rademacher and S. Wehmeier (eds), *Organisations kommunikation und public relations*, Wiesbaden, Germany: Springer, 73–94.

Hoskins, A., and B. O'Loughlin (2010), *War and Media: The Emergence of Diffused War*, Cambridge: Polity Press.

@IsraeliPM (PM of Israel), 'PM Netanyahu: "Just as every people builds its capital ..." ' Twitter, 09 May 2021, 5:02 pm, https://twitter.com/IsraeliPM/status/139137816214 4120835.

@IsraeliPM (PM of Israel), 'Jerusalem has been the capital of the Jewish people …' Twitter, 09 May 2021, 5:02 pm, https://twitter.com/IsraeliPM/status/1391378152153358337.

@IsraeliPM (PM of Israel), 'In the same breath, I say to the terrorist organizations: Israel will respond powerfully to any act of aggression from the Gaza Strip' Twitter, 09 May 2021, 5:02 pm, https://twitter.com/IsraeliPM/status/1391378150299406339.

@IsraeliPM (PM of Israel), 'We will not fall into the traps of our enemies …' Twitter, 10 May 2021, 10:39 pm, https://twitter.com/IsraeliPM/status/1391825331749806082.

@IsraeliPM (PM of Israel), 'Next to her a boy from Gaza is being cared for …' Twitter, 12 May 2021, 7:15 pm, https://twitter.com/IsraeliPM/status/1392498604162568201.

@IsraeliPM (PM of Israel), 'They attacked us on our holiday. They attacked our capital …' Twitter, 14 May 2021, 7:28 pm, https://twitter.com/IsraeliPM/status/1393226710955474949.

@Israeli PM (PM of Israel), 'We will settle the score with whomever …' Twitter, 17 May 2021, 10:42 pm, https://twitter.com/IsraeliPM/status/1394362799959252993.

@IsraeliPM (PM of Israel), 'Prime Minister Netanyahu emphasized that Hamas …' Twitter, 17 May 2021, 9:13 pm, https://twitter.com/IsraeliPM/status/1394340342284095488.

@IsraeliPM (PM of Israel), 'Not only is absurd and unjust and untrue, it does enormous damage to democracies that are fighting this kind of evil. It says you cannot protect yourself' Twitter, 19 May 2021, 6:23 pm, https://twitter.com/IsraeliPM/status/1395022288156778508.

@IsraeliPM (PM of Israel). 'Also presented were videos of firing at citizens of Israel and misfiring …' Twitter, 19 May 2021, 6:25 pm, https://twitter.com/IsraeliPM/status/1395022928555741193.

@IsraeliPM (PM of Israel), 'Prime Minister Benjamin Netanyahu met this afternoon' Twitter, 20 May 2021, 5:40 pm, https://twitter.com/IsraeliPM/status/1395373754113536008.

@IsraeliPM (PM of Israel), 'We regret every loss of life, but I can tell you categorically, there is no army in the world that acts in a more moral fashion than the army of Israel' Twitter, 21 May 2021, 4:38 pm, https://twitter.com/IsraeliPM/status/1395720685843095562.

Kaempf, S. (2013), 'The Mediatisation of War in a Transforming Global Media Landscape', *Australian Journal of International Affairs*, 67 (5): 586–604.

Khalidi, R. (2019), *The Hundred Years' War on Palestine; A History of Settler Colonialism and Resistance, 1917–2017*, New York: Metropolitan Books.

Kretschmer, L. (2017), 'Imagine There Is War and It Is Tweeted Live – An Analysis of Digital Diplomacy in the Israeli-Palestinian Conflict', *Global Media Journal*, 7 (1): 1–23.

Manor, I., and M. Holmes (2018), 'Palestine in Hebrew: A New Approach to Palestinian Digital Diplomacy', International Affairs Blog, 29 January, www.medium.com/international-affairs-blog/palestine-in-hebrew-a-new-approach-to-palestinian-digital-diplomacy-81870d523c25 (accessed 26 July 2021).

Manor, I. (2019), *The Digitization of Public Diplomacy*, Switzerland: Palgrave Macmillan.

Miskimmon. A., B. O'Loughlin and L. Roselle (2013), *Strategic Narratives: Communication Power and the New World Order*, London: Routledge.

Mor, B. D. (2006), 'Public Diplomacy in Grand Strategy', *Foreign Policy Analysis*, 2 (2): 157–76.

Nye, J. (2004), *Power in the Global Information Age: From Realism to Globalization*, New York: Routledge.

@nadplo (Palestine PLO-NAD), 'In Al-Aqsa Mosque Compound tonight and ongoing …' Twitter, 08 May 2021, 1:17 am, https://twitter.com/nadplo/status/139077783221 8021896.

@nadplo (Palestine PLO-NAD), 'Just before noon prayer at lions gate, the occupying Power's forces' Twitter, 10 May 2021, 2:45 pm, https://twitter.com/nadplo/status/1391 705937937944577.

@nadplo (Palestine PLO-NAD), 'Eyewitness video in #SheikhJarrah just before midnight …' Twitter, 13 May 2021, 1:09 am, https://twitter.com/nadplo/status/139258786536 9030660.

@nadplo (Palestine PLO-NAD), '#Palestine: Forever a land with a people. #Nakba73 #FreePalestine #GazaUnderAttack #PalestineUnderAttack' Twitter, 15 May 2021, 2:44 pm https://twitter.com/nadplo/status/1393517681056305154.

@nadplo (Palestine PLO-NAD), 'A video circulating on social media of a little girl in Gaza telling her mother: "I don't want to die" #HereGaza #GazaUnderAttak #Palestine' Twitter, 16 May 2021, 8:05 pm, https://twitter.com/nadplo/status/139396077288 8367111.

@nadplo (Palestine PLO-NAD), 'Marking #Nakba73 today in Sheikh Jarrah …' Twitter, 16 May 2021, 12:13 am, https://twitter.com/nadplo/status/1393660912263962626.

Papacharissi, Z., and M. Oliveira (2012), 'Affective News and Networked Publics: The Rhythms of News Storytelling on #Egypt', *Journal of Communication*, 62 (2): 266–82.

Papacharissi, Z. (2014), *Affective Publics: Sentiment, Technology, and Politics*, New York: Oxford University Press.

Pappe, I. (2016), *The Idea of Israel*, London: Verso.

Seib, P. (2012), *Real-Time Diplomacy: Politics and Power in the Social Media Era*, New York: Palgrave Macmillan.

Shenhav, S. R., and T. Sheafer (2010), 'Incoherent Narrator : Israeli Public Diplomacy during the Disengagement and the Elections in the Palestine Authority', *Israel Studies*, 15 (3): 143–62.

Tawil-Souri, H. (2015), 'Media, Globalization, and the (Un)Making of the Palestinian Cause', *Popular Communication*, 13 (2): 145–57.

Tawil-Souri, H. (2012), 'Digital Occupation: Gaza's High-Tech Enclosure', *Journal of Palestine Studies*, 41 (2) (Winter 2012): 27–43.

13

Platform necropolitics: Content moderation and censorship of pro-Palestinian voices on social media

Kelly Lewis

The violence of the May 2021 Israeli-Palestinian conflict played out on the ground and across social media as Palestinians shared imagery of brutalized bodies, collapsing buildings and armed conflict to global audiences. Yet, content posted to social media by Palestinians and pro-Palestinian voices was routinely removed from platforms through various forms of content moderation processes and platform policies that were opaque and controversial. This period put into sharp relief the significance of social media platforms for Palestinians as spaces to publicize instances of human rights violations, conflict and dispossession, particularly because Palestinian narratives are frequently underrepresented in international media. Platforms provide a critical space for Palestinians to report the unfolding of events in their own terms and free from long-standing practices of veiled journalism that have enabled the Israeli narrative to dominate mainstream media coverage. For Palestinians, social media evidence that speaks to instances of brutality and unjust violence can often be the only form of testimony with the power to make false narratives be held accountable to truth. If Palestinians' freedom of expression is taken away online, this risks further obscuring their struggle.

In this chapter, I develop the term *platform necropolitics* as an explicit vocabulary to articulate the struggle for the right to life and freedom of expression online. Platform necropolitics speaks to emergent and troubling developments of digitally mediated violence: when platforms exercise the power to effectively let digital subjects live or to kill contentious content and voices of dissent. It provides a critical lens to attend to and interrogate the consequences of interventions made by platforms, as well as the necessary theoretical and conceptual vocabulary for framing, engaging and holding accountable forms of systematic discrimination and automated injustice. Platform necropolitics adds to the existing terminologies of 'digital authoritarianism', 'digital apartheid' and 'digital colonialism' that speak to broad forces of domination and oppression facilitated by platforms and political actors. In the context of Palestine, such terms importantly situate the Palestinian struggle against the Israeli state and the quest for rights, dignity and liberation. However, I argue that we need to rethink and reconceptualize the broader and precarious implications of platforms as spaces that we live *with*, *in and through*, which operate as *political* and *material* actors to effectively condition the social, political and material (in)existence of digital subjects.

Platform necropolitics offers an interdisciplinary theory of information and power. It aligns with the extant body of literature that critically interrogates the politics of platforms as social and technical intermediaries that do not simply host user-generated content, but curate and mediate the contours of public discourse by policy and by design (Benjamin, 2019; Gillespie, 2018, 2010; Noble, 2018; Roberts, 2019; Suzor, 2019; York, 2021; Zuboff, 2015, 2019, among others). It intersects this interdisciplinarity scholarship with the theory of necropolitics, as developed by political theorist Achille Mbembe (2003; 2019), to comprehend and describe the implications of corporate platforms that are situated in sociopolitical contexts and embedded within geopolitical relations more fully. Platform necropolitics distinguishes itself from other critical approaches in digital media and platform studies through its attention to the specifics of necropolitics and necropower that enable the systematic and structural positioning of digital subjects towards death aided by technologies that enact 'power over the living' (Mbembe, 2019: 14). In doing so, it pushes against normative and dichotomous notions of the human subject in digital culture, along the human/nonhuman divide, to consider death as a social event that is not dislocated from the lived reality of flesh and blood precarious life.

I illustrate the originality and theoretical resourcefulness of platform necropolitics to analyse the censorship of pro-Palestinian voices during the May 2021 Israeli-Palestinian conflict as well as contentious and legitimate forms of political expression more generally. From this perspective, I create an alternative reading of platform politics to reorient a critical theorizing of platforms as technologies of necropolitical power to think and imagine the implications of their discursive, material and geospatial interventions. This also complicates conventional understandings of necropolitics as manifesting largely in states and spaces of exception – such as the plantation, the colony, refugee camps and the Occupied Palestinian Territories – by expanding the spaces of necropolitical violence to include ordinary social spaces like platforms that operate as lawless intermediaries when they (re)produce spaces of insecurity (Suzor, 2019: 90). By necropolitical violence, I mean the mediated violence of platforms that operate as sovereign actors through the violent policing of the boundaries of speech and space and that take as their object the digital subject and enact their 'right to kill'. Killing in this sense does not directly fall upon the flesh of the body. It is a digitally mediated killing that materially and discursively relegates digital subjects as undesirable 'others' and differentially distributes certain populations towards a perpetual state of vulnerability and finitude. It consigns othered digital subjects to spaces of non-existence and social death.

The chapter unfolds by mobilizing some necessary theoretical groundwork attending to platforms and their politics and the implications this presents for human rights. I then interface that literature with Mbembe's (2003; 2019) theory of necropolitics to illustrate the modes of necropolitical power that manifest in the contemporary present through the digital infrastructures and mediating logics of platforms. From this, I develop and elaborate my conceptualization of platform necropolitics before applying it as a framework to analyse the May 2021 Israeli-Palestinian conflict. This is an important lens of inquiry that incorporates Western understandings of digital technologies together with non-Western ways of knowing and experiencing the violent consequences of such technologies that act on bodies already at the margins and living within domains of excessive struggle. By bringing together conceptual and analytical tools grounded in critical platform studies, political theorizing and decolonial critique, the following discussion challenges and investigates conventional normativities, subjectivities and regimes of power. I conclude by reflecting on the implications of platform necropolitical power for freedom of expression and digital futures of social and political life.

Platforms and their politics

I apply the term platform to situate and interrogate social media as cultural, commercial and political intermediaries that operate as computational actors (Gillespie, 2010; Helmond, 2015), which cannot be examined in isolation from their social, political and ideological infrastructures (Dijck, Poell and Waal, 2018), as they comprise new centralizations of power that shape the way we live and how society is organized (Gehl, 2011), and define the boundaries and conditions for providing (and limiting) the material means of existence for digital publics (Jørgensen, 2019). Extant scholarly literature and critical commentary speak to the notion that platforms have politics, that is, from their ideological conventions, design, policies, corporate logics and practices. I position the politics of platforms within the larger context of threats posed to freedom of expression and human rights and, importantly, growing threats from oppressive state actors. This facilitates a deeper examination of how platforms exercise control to consider not only the power that platforms enact over digital rights, but to the real-world consequences of these actions for individuals, activists and organized groups as well.

Platforms habitually frame themselves as transparent, neutral and non-interventionist distributors of information – in part because of the ideology of their founders, and in part to circumvent moral obligation and legal liability (Gillespie, 2018: 7). In reality, platforms operate as arbiters of truth, mediators of norms, interpreters of laws, referees of disputes and enforcers of rules that serve to create the conditions for and access to digital spaces, often in conflicting ways and void of accountability mechanisms (Gillespie, 2018: 5; Roberts, 2019: 32). Platforms essentially function as 'the new governors' (Klonick, 2018: 1598) of online freedom of expression and democratic participation; they wield tremendous power over what can and cannot be said, who can and cannot speak and, as such, they become arbiters of human rights. York and Zuckerman (2019: 139) argue that under the current systems imposed by platforms, minority voices increasingly face the threat of being further silenced because platforms are ill equipped to protect contentious but lawful forms of freedom of expression.

Platforms enact their politics through content moderation processes that determine what content can appear, how it is curated, prioritized, monetized and what can be and does get removed and why. This includes compliance with platform-specific rules, cultural norms and legal obligations, which set and enforce regulatory decisions about content appropriateness (Witt, Suzor and Huggins, 2019: 558). Moderation is enforced through complex and opaque processes that take place through proactive processes of (machinic) preemptive filtering and automated detection and reactive processes of (human) post publication review (Suzor, 2019: 99). The increasing velocity of content faced with the problem of moderating at scale has progressively seen platforms almost entirely rely on automated processes. Automated content moderation is profoundly political because it functions through logics of 'operational surveillance' (Andrejevic, 2019: 74) by policing content as an invisible response to the detection of a potential threat and strategy of oppressive control. The vagueness surrounding automated moderation processes particularly makes it significantly harder to determine the dynamics of content takedowns and decreased visibility where human rights violations are concerned – where initial flagging mechanisms are made by automated systems and where the criteria for how and why those decisions were enacted remains unknown (Gorwa, Binns and Katzenbach, 2020: 11). This lack of transparency facilitates moderation processes that can render entire discourses and digital populations invisible while circumventing the appearance of censorship. Content moderation practices, therefore, should be viewed in the context of a digital landscape 'that is now more than ever fundamentally a site of control, surveillance, intervention, and circulation of information as a commodity' (Roberts, 2019: 6).

Gillespie (2018: 12) is convinced that most of the challenges platforms face in their content moderation processes are structural. There remains a need to move beyond the structural bounds of platforms. Critical comprehension of the ways platforms also accommodate national and international government and state actor requests to moderate content in ways that favour their own self-serving political interests is needed. As Suzor (2019: 82) emphasizes, foreign governments are becoming more advanced in exercising power over what citizens can access, share and ultimately do by pressuring platforms to moderate and block particular content that do not conform with local norms and legal criteria within their jurisdictions. The fact that platforms enjoy strategic relationships with Western governments as well as with authoritarian states and oppressive actors represents a troubling development: the expansion and expression of largely uncontested and new distributed forms of power (Roberts, 2019: 14; Zuboff, 2015: 75). As Benjamin (2019: 99) contends, 'who is seen and under what terms holds a mirror onto more far-reaching forms of power and inequality'. Contentious images that expose instances of political discontent and human rights violations have been some of the primary weapons that governments seek to censor. When platforms comply with takedown requests it can reinforce existing forms of violent oppression and restrict exposing human rights abuses and the potential for prosecution. Platforms are thus complex, ideologically and algorithmically managed visibility machines (Gillespie, 2018: 178) that differentially construct regimes of visibility for bodies considered as valuable enough and invisibility for those that are not (Bucher, 2012: 1171). These logics simultaneously orient already at-risk bodies towards oscillating modalities of surveillant observability and to the threat of endlessly disappearing. The risk of disappearing is particularly prevalent for user-generated content that is graphic, disturbing and controversial, especially when uploaded by voices critical of government and state actors.

Reimagining necropower through the digital machineries of platforms

The politics of platforms and necropolitics are mutually productive phenomena that operate in concert, facilitated through the digital machinery of platforms. This section develops an ontological understanding of necropolitics as exercised through digital technologies of necropower that produce the 'generalised instrumentalisation of human existence and the material destruction of human bodies and populations' (Mbembe, 2019: 68). Mbembe first developed his notion of necropolitics in a 2003 essay and expanded his critique in the book *Necropolitics*, which was translated into English in 2019.

In his conceptualization of necropolitics and necropower, Mbembe (2019) adopts a decolonized approach inspired by the work of Frantz Fanon, and he radicalizes Michel Foucault's notion of biopolitics and biopower. Mbembe argues that biopolitics and biopower cannot adequately describe or theorize the contemporary processes through which forms of political and social power subjugate 'life to the power of death' (necropolitics) (ibid.: 92). He traces how historic and emergent technologies of violence are deployed within society and accounts for the various ways digital technologies orient human existence towards a perpetual state of vulnerability and finitude.

Mbembe (2019: 13) argues, and we are in an era conceptualized through the 'ongoing redefinition of the human' as a 'digital subject' aided by the power and ubiquity of computational digital technologies. No separation exists between 'the screen and life', 'life now transpires on the screen, and the screen is now the plastic and simulated form of living that, in addition, can be grasped by code' (ibid.: 14). This is a key principle to hold onto throughout the chapter, as we review and critique the mediated nature of platforms as spaces that we live *with*, *in* and *through*.

For Mbembe, if we are to be serious about the fate of democracy in our societies, we need a critique of technology – and of machinic reasoning – that is up to the challenge posed by increasing forms of computational infrastructures and automated processes (ibid.: 112–13). He contends that reason, properly understood, cannot be reduced to mere calculation, computation and quantification. The project of reason then, in the age of surveillance capitalism (York, 2021; Zuboff, 2019), is to enable 'different modes of seeing and measuring to appear' (Mbembe, 2019: 113). That is, to work against the political power of platforms.

This means to understand that technologies of computational logics that commodify human subjects risk the total automation of sociality, and that present to us one vision of the social world among the 'many actual and possible worlds' that exist (ibid.: 113). Intelligible and just forms of reasoning, therefore, remain critically dependent on human consciousness and of critique. The interconnectedness of neoliberal capitalism, computational technologies and platforms has led to a different kind of human existence that is inseparable from digital technologies and infrastructures. So much so, that people's sense of self and modes of being are now 'constituted through and within digital technologies and new media forms' (ibid.: 114); where people are 'now embedded in increasingly complex technostructures' (ibid.: 95) that seek to optimize social life and, in doing so, redistribute power towards the transgressive and technological.

In what follows, I think on and reframe key issues posed by Mbembe (2019: 68) to articulate my conceptualization of platform necropolitics. My theorizing is guided by a critique of the conditions under which the power to kill or let the digital subject live is exercised. I interrogate what the subjugation of the digital subject to a state of inexistence reveals for contemporary corporate-political configurations of necropolitical power. And I examine how present configurations of necropolitical power reconfigure responsibility and accountability for or in the politics of a recalibrated form of killing (as in digitally mediated social death).

Platform necropolitics

Platform necropolitics designates the prevalent removal and suppression of contentious digital (social) media content by private corporations and in accordance with governments and oppressive political actors. Platform necropolitics manifests in various situations, especially when platforms work in coordination with governments to expedite the removal of content deemed 'offensive', 'graphic' or 'inciteful', particularly those which are legitimate forms of political expression and do not violate platform policies or community guidelines. This has specific consequences for freedom of expression and human rights as it governs the conditions for whose voices and what content are (or are not) given the right to life online. Platform necropolitics provides a prism through which to understand how unjust policies and content moderation processes are increasingly enacted by platforms in cooperation with state and government actors. It is a phenomenon that demonstrates not only the unequal imparting of power on often already oppressed and marginalized people, but which also governs the conditions under which we see, understand and remember conflict and revolt.

When platforms and political functionaries deploy violent techniques of power, they shape the way certain lives are rendered more (or less) important than others to reveal the politics of life and death struggles. The capacity of platforms to moderate and remove undesirable content is as significant as their capacity to make undesirable life unseeable and undiscoverable. Such differential renderings of forms of social life as apprehensible or inapprehensible are closer to what Butler (2009: 1) calls the precarious conditions of existence that are 'politically saturated [and] are themselves operations of power'. Thinking with Butler, I argue that the normative and obscure logics of the machinic and automated moderation processes of platforms, those that register, classify and mark forms of digitally mediated life, allocate forms of recognition differentially because they are bound up in sense-making and predicting, but in ways that operate outside of properly intelligent comprehension. Such logics, as Butler (ibid.: 3) argues, 'not only organise visual experience, but also generate specific ontologies of the subject'.

In this case, it creates an ontological rendering of the digital subject, where already oppressed and marginalized voices can be subjected to new forms of occupation and to the exercising of sovereignty itself. This form of contemporary oppression not only has the power to curtail freedom of expression and thwart political futures, but also poses an imminent existential threat to human life.

In her critique on sovereignty, and through the conceptualization of 'slow death' as the defining condition of social existence under contemporary regimes of capital, Berlant (2007) emphasizes the need to recast historical conceptualizations of sovereignty. Attending to the relationship between political and what she terms as practical sovereignty, Berlant reconsiders the taxonomies of causality and subjectivity towards the practical, structural and mediating conditions of zoning and governmentality that are enacted in spaces of ordinariness (ibid.: 758). Within these spaces of everydayness, Berlant argues the reproduction of social life and its destruction are coextensive (ibid.: 762), opening to a genealogy of contemporary existence that takes on specific forms for particular populations within the temporal and spatial 'regimes of exhausted practical sovereignty' (ibid.: 780). Such a recasting of sovereignty, as positioned within the temporality and spatiality of everyday social life, provides for an alternative reading of sovereignty as the ultimate expression of necropolitical power. Importantly, it offers a development in the ways we conceptualize the sovereign and capital logics of platforms to attend to the ways platforms enable the reproduction of ordinary desirable social existence while simultaneously enacting apartheid-like architectures that perpetually orient undesirable problematic forms of social existence towards spaces of irreproducibility. When platforms intervene in matters of the political with indifference to the endurance of the human right to freedom of expression, they move beyond the bounds of mere intermediaries to become hostile foreign powers and serve as active political actors in their own right.

This is what Mbembe (2019: 10) conceptualizes as the sovereign logics or 'commercial colonialism' of monopolizing powers, like platforms – that reaffirm the centrality of Western imperialism – and that extend outward their commercial logics by means of asymmetrical, inequitable relations, almost devoid of any meaningful local investment. Where platforms are perhaps most conceivable as sovereign actors is through the policing of imagined digital citizenship. Anderson (1991: 6) reminds us that a nation is 'an imagined political community – and imagined as both inherently limited and sovereign'. Within a digital landscape, citizenship is imagined through an awareness of the ephemerality of our common condition – platforms as spaces that we increasingly live *with*, *in* and *through*, to which our social worlds are hyperconnected, but to which access to citizenship can be re-borderized by platforms that boundary-make spaces as states of inclusion and exclusion. Platforms enact borderization by surveilling and policing digital subjects in the name of security and safety, through automated logics and algorithmically managed checkpoints that govern the speech and action of billions of users and that transform particular spaces into impassable zones for certain populations of people.

Theorizing platform necropolitics opens a space for critically rethinking how platforms operate as sovereign actors, not with the rule of international human rights law embedded in their logics, but lawlessly, as Suzor (2019: 90) describes through the architecture of their networks and through the enforcement of their own rules. The outward projection of platform necropolitical power simultaneously reframes and respatializes contemporary assemblages of social, political and economic power in ways that recast traditional geopolitical logics and practices. Not only does the borderization of platform spaces sever connections between citizens and non-citizens in ways that transform and proliferate new forms of the 'geopolitical social' (Cowen and Smith, 2009: 43), it configures new spaces of socio-spatial struggle.

This presents a remapping of traditional geopolitical conceptions of citizenship (ibid.: 36), where already at-risk and dissenting bodies are subjected to new forms of discrimination and domination on the basis of the threat they pose to the social order. The discriminatory logics of content moderation processes enact borderization as an alleged security solution that expels certain bodies from the platform and transposes them to 'dead spaces of non-connection which deny the very idea of a shared humanity' (Mbembe, 2019: 99). This is the entanglement of life and death struggles for digital subjects that manifest through platform necropolitics.

The enactment of platform necropolitics during the May 2021 Israel–Palestine conflict

In what follows, I examine the ways platform necropolitics manifest within the contemporary context of Israel's ongoing military occupation of the Palestinian territories and, specifically, as it materializes *with, in* and *through* the spaces of platforms. The case study mobilizes existing research and critical journalistic accounts that examine instances of unjust content moderation of pro-Palestinian content on social media platforms as documented during the eleven-day Israeli-Palestinian conflict between 7 and 21 May 2021. It attends to the implications of unjust content moderation processes in ways that demonstrate how platforms, chiefly Facebook and Instagram (owned by parent company Meta[1]), enact forms of necropolitical power over digital subjects though corporate and machinic logics and that simultaneously extend and reproduce the necropolitical power of the Israeli state.

The May 2021 Israeli-Palestinian conflict erupted following a series of mounting tensions since the beginning of Ramadan in April, and sharply escalated into brutal violence across the Occupied Palestinian Territories in May. The hostilities intensified following the violent repression of protests against the forced eviction procedures enacted against Palestinian refugee families living in the East Jerusalem neighbourhood of Sheikh Jarrah and worsened when Israeli police brutally stormed and blockaded the Al-Aqsa Mosque on 7 and 10 May, respectively. Israeli forces and Jewish Israeli settlers also waged brutal attacks against Palestinians across the occupied territories of Jerusalem, the West Bank and Gaza (Berger, 2021). In retaliation to the crackdown on protesters by Israeli forces at the Al-Aqsa Mosque and the ongoing occupation of Palestine by Israel, Hamas (which rules besieged Gaza) and the Palestinian Islamic Jihad armed group also launched attacks against Israel (Rasheed, Alsaafin and Siddiqui, 2021).

The aggression played out across social media as Palestinians and pro-Palestinian voices shared imagery of brutalized bodies, collapsing buildings and armed conflict to global audiences. The brutal violence was documented through images, videos and hashtags in both English and Arabic including #SaveSheikhJarrah, #GazaUnderAttack, #SavePalestine and #FreePalestine, among others. But activists, digital rights defenders, journalists and social media users repeatedly called out, namely, Facebook and Instagram, as well as Twitter, TikTok and YouTube for systematically removing, suspending or restricting Palestinian voices and pro-Palestinian content through various forms of content moderation processes and platform policies that were opaque and controversial.

7amleh – the Arab Center for Social Media Advancement (2021a), issued a report on 21 May documenting 500 cases of Palestinian digital rights violations between 6 and 19 May and the responses of platforms to the reports. A majority of the violations were reported on Instagram. A tweet by Instagram (2021) on 7 May claimed that a technical problem had caused the majority of violations. Yet, 7amleh (2021a) received numerous reports of violations after the fact with 68 per cent of the total reports occurring after 7 May. 7amleh (ibid.) reported violations including content takedowns, closing of accounts, hiding hashtags, reducing the reachability of specific content, deleting of archived content and restricting user access. The reported cases include 250 instances on Instagram (50 per cent), 179 on Facebook (35 per cent), 55 on Twitter (11 per cent) and 1 per cent on TikTok. In the majority of cases, 7amleh (ibid.) found users were not provided with an explanation for the deletion or suspension of accounts and censoring of content. Some accounts and content were restored after 7amleh's submission of the reports to platforms.

During this period, Sada Social Center for the Defense of Palestinian Digital Rights (2021a) recorded more than seven hundred violations of Palestinian social media content mostly related to the Sheikh Jarrah demonstrations in occupied East Jerusalem. In its February 2021 report, Sada Social Center (2021b) described such violations as 'arbitrary measures against Palestinian content, especially with the tendency to stigmatise criticism of Zionism with anti-Semitism'. Similarly, global digital rights organization Access Now (2021) reported it had received hundreds of reports that platforms were suppressing pro-Palestinian content. This included the removal of content and disabling of accounts on Facebook, Twitter, TikTok and Instagram or the blocking of features on Instagram, such as story highlights, liking, sharing or saving content, live video streaming, hashtags or restricting access to and engagement with Palestinian content. Middle East-based journalists and media organizations (Ibrahim, 2021) covering Palestine also reported that access to YouTube content had been restricted or listed as inappropriate.

In response to the platform suppression, Social Media Exchange (SMEX) (2021), in collaboration with Stanford University, launched a survey to track the extent of the censorship and to document violations of Palestinian rights. The online petition #SavePalestinianVoices was also launched by 7amleh (2021b), SMEX and Access Now, together with twenty-five other digital rights groups, which called on platforms to 'provide transparency on the decision-making processes involved in content takedowns related to Palestine' and to commit to transparent and accountable content moderation principles as set forth in the Santa Clara Principles (2018).

On Instagram, users documented myriad examples where the platform had removed innocuous posts for alleged hate speech and restricted access to and engagement with Palestinian content. Pro-Palestinian voices recurrently called out Instagram and Facebook for disproportionately removing or decreasing visibility of pro-Palestinian content, in English and Arabic, while criticizing the platform for not doing enough to remove content that insighted violence against Palestinians. Incitements to violence against Palestinians were present across Meta's portfolio of applications on Instagram, Facebook and the encrypted messaging service WhatsApp, as well as on Telegram, and a surge of activity by Jewish extremists escalated in this period. Analysis by the *New York Times* and FakeReporter, an Israeli watchdog group that studies misinformation, documented the formation of 100 new WhatsApp groups 'for the express purpose of committing violence against Palestinians' (Frenkel, 2021). This incitement extended to offline vigilantism and led to the killing of two Palestinians during this time. A WhatsApp spokeswoman told the *New York Times* that the content of WhatsApp encrypted messages cannot be read by the platform. Yet, they said WhatsApp had removed some accounts and acted when accounts were reported for violating its terms of service. Vice News also reported harmful content was shared to YouTube by the Israeli Ministry of Strategic Affairs that aimed to justify Israel's violent aggression in Gaza (Cox and Maiberg, 2021). The video circulated for five days and reached approximately 1.2 million views before it was finally removed by YouTube.

The May 2021 silencing of Palestinian digital activism and pro-Palestinian voices on social media gained widespread attention and attracted international condemnation, but the move to silence voices critical of Israel is not a new development. Access Now Middle Eastern Policy Manager, Marwa Fatafta, said that while she has been covering this topic for years, she had not seen anything of this scale: 'it's so brazen and so incredible, it's beyond censorship – it's digital repression. They are actively suppressing the narrative of Palestinians or those who are documenting these war crimes' (Ingram, 2021). The political creep of corporate platforms censoring Palestinian voices has been on the rise since 2015, a fact well documented by researchers (see Taha, 2020) and independent media (see Greenwald, 2017). Investigations by Adalah – The Legal Center for Arab Minority Rights in Israel revealed Israel's State Attorney's Office has maintained a Cyber Unit since 2015 that has been illegally surveilling and censoring pro-Palestinian social media content on the grounds of 'combatting incitement' in coordination with platforms, including Facebook and Twitter (Hanania, 2017). Longitudinal research by 7amleh also demonstrates increasing violations of Palestinian digital rights. In its annual #Hashtag Palestine report (7amleh, 2021c) published on 10 May it highlighted that 41.7 per cent of the survey participants were censored on Facebook, 25 per cent on Zoom and 16.7 per cent on WhatsApp. 7amleh established that Twitter suspended tens of accounts of Palestinian users based on information from the Israeli Ministry of Strategic Affairs, while TikTok and YouTube continued to allow videos that endorse Israeli military violence to circulate on the platform, respectively.

According to Meta's transparency report (Sonderby, 2021) for the reporting period between July and December 2020, Meta said it received 1,030 requests from Israel – supported by the Cyber Unit – to delete or block content. This is the highest number of requests from Israel since public reporting began in 2013. Of these requests,

81 per cent were accepted and carried out by Meta for which it did not provide a transparent explanation of how the requests were treated. In a 13 May meeting held between Israel's defence minister Benny Gantz and executives from Meta and TikTok, Gantz requested the private corporations to remove pro-Palestinian content considered as inciting by Israel (Akkad, 2021). In response, Sada Social Center (2021c) released a statement on 16 May calling out Israel for trying to 'impose its hegemony on social media platforms'. In the statement, Sada Social Center emphasized that social media users advocating for Palestine and its people had since reported numerous violations of their digital rights, with the closure of the Quds News Network account on TikTok being the most prominent. On 19 May former Facebook executive Ashraf Zeitoon spoke with Al Jazeera Plus (AJ+) about historic and ongoing pressure by the Israeli government to censor pro-Palestinian content saying that Facebook consistently complies with pro-Israeli allegations by systematically silencing Palestinian voices (Al Jazeera Plus, 2021).

A pronounced example of unfair and unjust content moderation processes occurred on 11 May when Instagram labelled the Al-Aqsa Mosque, one of Islam's holiest sites in Jerusalem, as a terrorist organization. This resulted in Instagram removing and blocking posts tagged with #AlAqsa or its Arabic counterparts #الاقصى or #الأقصى. Meta attributed the Instagram censorship to technical and human moderation issues and said it was updating its content moderation policies in response to the error (Mac, 2021). In a letter of intent to the Palestinian Mission to the United Kingdom, Meta said it would work to resolve these serious content moderation issues and investigate alleged campaigns to incite violence against Palestinians in Israel (Middle East Monitor, 2021). However, analysis reported by Access Now (Fatafta and Pirkova, 2021), on 2 March highlighted Meta's problematic history with content moderation though its hate speech policy, specifically through the moderation of the word 'Zionist' in a way that could further censor legitimate political speech. Internal Meta policies obtained by The Intercept (Biddle, 2021) in May also revealed that Facebook's moderating of the term 'Zionist' enabled the platform to suppress criticism against the state of Israel amid ongoing Israeli abuses and violence. According to The Intercept (ibid.) the moderation was enacted not only on Facebook but across Meta's subsidiary apps, including Instagram. This could plausibly be the cause for why social media users received notifications that their posts were removed from platforms because they violated platform policies related to hate speech or symbols.

On 19 May, in response to growing hate speech, calls for violence and spreading of misinformation about the Israeli-Palestinian conflict, Monika Bickert, Meta's vice president of content policy, said a 'special operations centre' had been established (Culliford, 2021). Meta has been regularly criticized for lacking local language expertise and resources in the region. The company said the new operations centre was staffed by experts who included native Arabic and Hebrew speakers. Meta, which has offices in Israel, has faced growing criticisms by digital rights defenders and activists over its business interests, as well as contentious platform policies and content moderation processes across its portfolio of applications. Facebook has a public policy director for Israel and the Jewish diaspora, Jordana Cutler, a former adviser to Israeli prime minister Benjamin Netanyahu. Yet, at the time of writing, Facebook did not have a dedicated public policy director for Palestinians. Rather; Palestinian matters fall under the remit of its Middle East and North Africa (MENA) policy chief, Azzam Alameddin, who is based in Dubai, an Arab Emirate that has normalized relations with Israel.

Meta established the Oversight Board in 2020 to redress growing criticisms about its role in suppressing online freedom of expression in recent years. The Oversight Board was assembled as an independent third party to appeal and make recommendations regarding content moderation decisions on Facebook and Instagram in accordance with stated platform policies. However, the legitimacy of the board was called into question after the controversial appointment of Emi Palmor, a former general director of the Israeli Ministry of Justice's Cyber Unit. Under Palmor's five-year administration thousands of Palestinian social media content were removed and her tenure imposed severe limitations on pro-Palestinian freedom of expression (Pulwer and Vidal, 2018). In protest to Palmor's appointment to the Oversight Board, the global campaign #FacebookCensorsPalestine was launched by Jewish Voice for Peace, in coalition with 7amleh and three other rights groups, to call for her removal and for Facebook to end its systemic silencing of pro-Palestinian voices. Palmor still remains on the board. Critics of Palmor's involvement with the Oversight Board say it is another example of Meta's close ties to the Israeli government and its inability to safeguard against Israeli government interference and conflicts of interest (Meyerson-Knox, 2020).

As the empirical discussion lays bare, we are witnessing a shift to outright, direct control and erasure of the pro-Palestinian narrative by hegemonic actors with substantial political and private power. Extant testimony tells that the tensions engendering this shift have been years in the making. Today, the gradually extending intertwinement of violent Israeli colonial occupation and the commercial logics of platforms reveal far-reaching and draconian implications for human rights. Not only do platforms govern the modes of political expression and participation in the Palestinian context, but they also redefine the boundaries of what constitutes the political for entire digital populations. The manifestation of platform necropolitics, therefore, must be treated as articulation between corporate–government power relations, social practices and historical trajectories.

These findings also expose contradictions to the democratic order where tensions fester between the quest for freedom, security and sovereignty. Today, democratic values and rights to freedom of expression are being overwritten by modes of governance and political interpretation where security matters more than freedom. Testimony to this fact is the revitalization of the (2016 originally conceived) Israeli social media censorship bill, dubbed the 'Facebook Bill', that is currently before the Israeli Knesset (the legislative branch of the Israeli government). The current configuration of the bill, if passed, would give unprecedented power to Israeli authorities to remove and block access to online content – extending beyond content hosted solely on social media platforms. Multiple countries, like Australia and Germany, have or are moving to introduce legislation for content removal from social media, but content removal in these contexts is limited to specific subjects and legal codes. According to Dr Asaf Wiener, head of regulation and policy at the Israel Internet Association, the current 'Facebook Bill' bill represents a 'level of intrusion that does not exist in any other country in the democratic world' (Ben-David, 2021: para 7). This is telling that the enactment of content moderation processes is itself geopolitical. It both manifests and enables the formation of new power relations through which economies of indifference and new cleavages of historic polarization between pro-Palestinian/pro-Israeli, sovereignty/ dispossession, self-determination/oppression are (re)produced and maintained. It respatializes and reconfigures traditional assemblages of geopolitics within digitally mediated territorial frameworks in ways that produce new power struggles and claims for sovereignty: between governments, corporations and people.

Beyond the politics of platforms

The case study of the May 2021 Israel–Palestine conflict demonstrates the myriad ways that platforms violated the right of Palestinians and pro-Palestinian voices to freedom of expression and denied people the ability to call out abuses of human rights. This transpired through the many failings of content moderation processes and platform policies that were deployed in ways that discriminated and reproduced forms of already existing injustice. Palestinians, physically excluded by the Israeli state from spaces of living through occupation and border controls, are increasingly subjected to the governing logics of platforms that enact borderization and force digital subjects to move through algorithmically managed checkpoints as part of an everyday operation. It brings into sharp relief the reality that, for Palestinians, spaces of violence duly proliferate through top-down power and panoptic formations that extend the technomilitarism of the Israeli state into platform spaces that function as optical mechanisms for extended surveillance, separation and the exercising of necropolitical power.

These contemporary assemblages of power necessitate new critical frameworks for conceptualizing the increasing role that platforms play as material and political actors in determining what people can and cannot access, share and say in emerging configurations of conflict and revolt. This is of particular importance for the Global South (York, 2021). Beyond Palestine and across the MENA region more broadly, digital authoritarianism has been on the rise in the wake of the 2010–11 Arab uprisings, and this has placed unprecedented strain on freedom of expression and human rights. In the MENA region, laws and regulations for freedom of expression and human rights vary from country to country and are habitually abused and enforced arbitrarily by oppressive actors (Gillespie, 2018: 191; Suzor, 2019: 81). In the current climate, a growing number of governments across the MENA region are asserting their authority over platforms to comply with social media censorship and surveillance resulting in a deepening repression of critical commentary, political dissent and marginalized populations (Shahbaz et al., 2021).

In this chapter, I proposed the concept of *platform necropolitics* to orient a focus that moves beyond considering the politics of platforms, through their infrastructure, commercial logics, policies and moderation processes, and towards interrogating the opaque relationships that platforms share with governments and oppressive state actors. We need much greater transparency into platforms' decision-making process, particularly where automated content moderation is concerned, and especially when platforms enjoy agreements with foreign governments and enact decisions at the behest of governments and political actors. But while transparency is necessary for looking inside the 'black box' and inner functioning of platforms' decision-making processes, transparency in and of itself is insufficient for explaining how alternative enforcement systems that are brokered though backdoor corporate–government agreements work, nor does it solve these problematics. Understanding the limits that transparency presents for addressing violations of human rights requires scrutiny of the ways that violence and repression are, as York argues (2021: 215) 'inextricably linked' through global networks of power, capitalism, militarism and platform censorship.

Platform necropolitics prescribes an actionable language that helps us rethink and reconceptualize the gravity of decision-making processes enacted by platforms that can operate as weapons that annihilate and systematically exclude certain digital subjects as well as entire digital populations. It also provides the necessary vocabulary required to comprehend the many consequences of private corporations that rule by their own decree and act in concert with oppressive governments and political actors to exert the ultimate expression of power over digital subjects: to let live or to kill. Future research should move beyond the interior politics of territorially bounded platform spaces to examine how this correlates with the exterior politics of nation states. Importantly, it should also interrogate the legitimacy of government and political actors that unjustly exert power to produce precarious conditions of (in)existence for digital subjects, which contradicts the state's obligation to protect the right to freedom of expression, particularly where exposing human rights violations are concerned.

Note

1. Note: Facebook changed its company name on 28 October 2021 to Meta. In this chapter, I use Meta to refer to the company, and Facebook to refer to the platform and policies and processes attached to the specific platform.

References

7amleh. (2021a), 'The Attacks on Palestinian Digital Rights', 7amleh, 21 May, https://7am leh.org/2021/05/21/7amleh-issues-report-documenting-the-attacks-on-palestinian-digital-rights (accessed 22 May 2021).

7amleh. (2021b), 'Sheikh Jarrah: Facebook and Twitter Systematically Silencing Protests, Deleting Evidence', 7amleh, 7 May, https://7amleh.org/2021/05/07/sheikh-jarrah-facebook-and-twitter-systematically-silencing-protests-deleting-evidence (accessed 9 May 2021).

7amleh. (2021c), '#Hashtag Palestine 2020: An Overview of Digital Rights Abuses of Palestinians during the Coronavirus Pandemic', 7amleh, 10 May, https://7amleh.org/2021/05/10/hashtag-palestine-2020-an-overview-of-digital-rights-abuses-of-pales tinians-during-the-coronavirus-pandemic (accessed 12 May 2021).

Access Now. (2021), 'Making matters worse, social media companies – like FB, Twitter, Instagram, and TikTok – are censoring Palestinians as they face military violence […]'

Twitter, 18 May, https://twitter.com/accessnow/status/1394373884170887175 (accessed 19 May 2021).

Akkad, D. (2021), 'Palestinian Journalists Accuse Facebook of Censorship', Middle East Eye, 19 May, https://www.middleeasteye.net/news/palestine-israel-facebook-censors hip-data-algorithms (accessed 20 May 2021).

Al Jazeera Plus (2021), 'Is Facebook Censoring Posts about Palestine?', Facebook, 19 May, https://www.facebook.com/watch/?v=180604827184597 (accessed 20 May 2021).

Anderson, B. R. O. (1991), *Imagined Communities: Reflections on the Origin and Spread of Nationalism*, revised and extended edition, London: Verso.

Andrejevic, M. (2019), *Automated Media*, New York: Routledge.

Ben-David, R. (2021), 'Proposed Online Censorship Bill More Intrusive than in Any Other Democracy – Expert', The Times of Israel, 28 December, https://www.timesofisr ael.com/proposed-censorship-bill-more-intrusive-than-in-any-other-democracy-say-researchers/ (accessed 9 February 2022).

Benjamin, R. (2019), *Race after Technology: Abolitionist Tools for the New Jim Code*, Cambridge: Polity.

Berger, M. (2021), 'In West Bank, Deadly Clashes between Palestinians and Israeli Forces Open New Flash Point', The Washington Post, 14 May, https://www.washingtonpost. com/world/middle_east/west-bank-palestinians-israel-violence/2021/05/14/4e5af 7a0-b4a9-11eb-bc96-fdf55de43bef_story.html (accessed 19 May 2021).

Berlant, L. (2007), 'Slow Death (Sovereignty, Obesity, Lateral Agency)', *Critical Inquiry*, 33 (4): 754–80.

Biddle, S. (2021), 'Facebook's Secret Rules about the Word "Zionist" Impede Criticism of Israel', The Intercept, 15 May, https://theintercept.com/2021/05/14/facebook-israel-zionist-moderation/ (accessed 18 May 2021).

Bucher, T. (2012), 'Want To Be on the Top? Algorithmic Power and the Threat of Invisibility on Facebook', *New Media & Society*, 14 (7): 1164–80.

Butler, J. (2009), *Frames of War: When Is Life Grievable?* London: Verso.

Cowen, D., and N. Smith (2009), 'After Geopolitics? From the Geopolitical Social to Geoeconomics', *Antipode*, 41 (1): 22–48.

Cox, J., and E. Maiberg (2021), 'YouTube Removes Israeli Government-Linked Ad that Justified Bombing of Gaza', Vice News, 19 May, https://www.vice.com/en/article/epn x3p/youtube-removes-israeli-government-ad-gaza (accessed 21 May 2021).

Culliford, E. (2021), 'Facebook Deploys Special Team as Israel-Gaza Conflict Spreads across Social Media', Reuters, 20 May, https://www.reuters.com/technology/facebook-running-special-center-respond-content-israeli-gaza-conflict-2021-05-19/ (accessed 21 May 2021).

Dijck, J. van, T. Poell and M. de. Waal (2018), *The Platform Society: Public Values in a Connective World*, New York: Oxford University Press.

Fatafta, M., and E. Pirkova (2021), 'Why Facebook's Proposed Hate Speech Policy on Zionism Would Only Add Fuel to the Fire', Access Now, 2 March, https://www.access now.org/facebook-hate-speech-policy-zionism/ (accessed 14 May 2021).

Frenkel, S. (2021), 'Mob Violence against Palestinians in Israel Is Fueled by Groups on WhatsApp', New York Times, 19 May, https://www.nytimes.com/2021/05/19/technol ogy/israeli-clashes-pro-violence-groups-whatsapp.html (accessed 21 May 2021).

Gehl, R. W. (2011), 'The Archive and the Processor: The Internal Logic of Web 2.0', *New Media & Society*, 13 (8): 1228–44.

Gillespie, T. (2018), *Custodians of the Internet: Platforms, Content Moderation, and the Hidden Decisions that Shape Social Media*, New Haven: Yale University Press.

Gillespie, T. (2010), 'The Politics of Platforms', *New Media & Society*, 12 (3): 347–64.

Gorwa, R., R. Binns and C. Katzenbach (2020), 'Algorithmic Content Moderation: Technical and Political Challenges in the Automation of Platform Governance', *Big Data and Society*, 7 (1): 1–15.

Greenwald, G. (2017), 'Facebook Says It Is Deleting Accounts at the Direction of the U.S. and Israeli Governments', The Intercept, 31 December, https://thein tercept.com/2017/12/30/facebook-says-it-is-deleting-accounts-at-the-direct ion-of-the-u-s-and-israeli-governments/ (accessed 19 May 2021).

Hanania, R. (2017), 'Israel's "Cyber Unit" Illegally Censors Social Media Posts', The Arab Daily News, 14 September, https://thearabdailynews.com/2017/09/14/isra els-cyber-unit-illegally-censors-social-media-posts/ (accessed 19 May 2021).

Helmond, A. (2015), 'The Platformization of the Web: Making Web Data Platform Ready', *Social Media + Society*, 1 (2): 1–11.

Ibrahim, A. (2021), 'Lots of people reporting that @YouTube is restricting access to @AJArabic channel, claiming that the content may be inappropriate [...]' Twitter, 19 May, https://twitter.com/arwaib/status/1394785519695974401 (accessed 19 May 2021).

Ingram, M. (2021), 'Social Networks Accused of Censoring Palestinian Content', Columbia Journalism Review, 19 May, https://www.cjr.org/the_media_today/social-networks-accused-of-censoring-palestinian-content.php (accessed 20 May 2021).

Instagram (2021), 'We know that some people are experiencing issues uploading and viewing stories. This is a widespread global technical issue not [...]' Twitter, 7 May, https://twitter.com/InstagramComms/status/1390376354332487681 (accessed 9 May 2021).

Jørgensen, R. F. (2019), 'Introduction'. In R. F. Jørgensen (ed.), *Human Rights in the Age of Platforms*, Cambridge, MA: MIT Press, 18–46.

Klonick, K. (2018), 'The New Governors: The People, Rules, and Processes Governing Online Speech', *Harvard Law Review*, 131 (6): 1598–669.

Mac, R. (2021), 'Instagram Censored Posts about One of Islam's Holiest Mosques, Drawing Employee Ire', Buzz Feed News, 12 May, https://www.buzzfeednews.com/arti cle/ryanmac/instagram-facebook-censored-al-aqsa-mosque (accessed 14 May 2021).

Mbembe, A. (2019), *Necropolitics*, Durham: Duke University Press.

Mbembe, A. (2003), 'Necropolitics', *Public Culture*, 15 (1): 11–40.

Meyerson-Knox, S. E. (2020), 'Thousands Call on Facebook to Stop Censoring Palestine', Jewish Voice for Peace, 24 September, https://jewishvoiceforpeace.org/2020/09/fb-stop-censoring-palestine/ (accessed 18 May 2021).

Middle East Monitor (2021), 'Facebook Apologises to PA after Restricting Palestinian Content', Middle East Monitor, 18 May, https://www.middleeastmonitor.com/20210 518-facebook-apologises-to-pa-after-restricting-palestinian-content/ (accessed 20 May 2021).

Noble, S. U. (2018), *Algorithms of Oppression: How Search Engines Reinforce Racism*, New York: New York University Press.

Pulwer, S., and E. Vidal (2018), 'Facebook Complying with 95% of Israeli Requests to Remove Inciting Content, Minister Says', Haaretz, 12 September, https://www.haar etz.com/israel-news/business/facebook-removes-inciting-content-at-israel-s-request-minister-says-1.5432959 (accessed 18 May 2021).

Rasheed, Z., L. Alsaafin and U. Siddiqui (2021), 'Celebrations in Gaza as Ceasefire Takes Hold', Al Jazeera English, 20 May, https://www.aljazeera.com/news/2021/5/20/death-destruction-in-gaza-as-israel-defies-truce-call-live (accessed 21 May 2021).

Roberts, S. T. (2019), *Behind the Screen: Content Moderation in the Shadows of Social Media*, New Haven: Yale University Press.

Sada Social Center (2021a), '770 Violations during May and the Center Sues Facebook', Sada Social Center, 2 June, https://sada.social/?p=1907 (accessed 2 June 2021).

Sada Social Center (2021b), 'Sada Social Documents 24 Violations during February 2021', Sada Social Center, 4 March, http://sada.social/sada-social-documents-24-violations-during-february-2021/ (accessed 18 May 2021).

Sada Social Center (2021c), 'Israel Imposes Its Dominance on Social Media', Sada Social Center, 16 May, https://sada.social/?p=1867 (accessed 17 May 2021).

Santa Clara Principles (2018), 'The Santa Clara Principles on Transparency and Accountability in Content Moderation', Santaclaraprinciples.org, 7 May, https://santaclaraprinciples.org/ (accessed 9 May 2021).

Shahbaz, A., A. Funk, A. Slipowitz, K. Vesteinsson, G. Baker, C. Grothe, M. Vepa and T. Weal (2021), 'Freedom on the Net 2021: The Global Drive to Control Big Tech', Freedom House, United States of America, 29 September, https://freedomhouse.org/report/freedom-net/2021/global-drive-control-big-tech (accessed 2 October 2021).

Social Media Exchange (2021), 'Have you noticed anything strange after posting about #Palestine? SMEX is collaborating with Stanford University to track unfair censorship [...]' Twitter, 18 May, https://twitter.com/SMEX/status/1394542446961381378 (accessed 18 May 2021).

Sonderby, C. (2021), 'Transparency Report', Facebook, 19 May, https://transparency.fb.com/data/government-data-requests/country/IL (accessed 21 May 2021).

Suzor, N. P. (2019), *Lawless: The Secret Rules that Govern Our Digital Lives*, Cambridge: Cambridge University Press.

Taha, S. (2020), 'The Cyber Occupation of Palestine; Suppressing Digital Activism and Shrinking the Virtual Sphere', Global Campus Arab World Policy Briefs, Global Campus of Human Rights, Italy, 10 July, https://repository.gchumanrights.org/handle/20.500.11825/1620?show=full (accessed 19 May 2021).

Witt, A., N. Suzor and A. Huggins (2019), 'The Rule of Law on Instagram: An Evaluation of the Moderation of Images Depicting Women's Bodies', *University of New South Wales Law Journal*, 42 (2): 557–96.

York, J. C. (2021), *Silicon Values: The Future of Free Speech under Surveillance Capitalism*, London: Verso.

York, J. C., and E. Zuckerman (2019), 'Moderating the Public Sphere'. In R. F. Jørgensen (ed.), *Human Rights in the Age of Platforms*, Cambridge, MA: MIT Press, 137–61.

Zuboff, S. (2019), *The Age of Surveillance Capitalism: The Fight for a Human Future at the New Frontier of Power*, New York: Public Affairs.

Zuboff, S. (2015), 'Big Other: Surveillance Capitalism and the Prospects of an Information Civilization', *Journal of Information Technology*, 30 (1): 75–89.

14

Pro-Palestinian activism: Resisting the digital occupation

Dounia Mahlouly and Zaina Erhaim

Introduction

In April 2021, Palestinian landowners from the neighbourhood of Sheikh Jarrah were expelled from their homes by Israeli forces, following a decision of the Israeli Supreme Court to reassign their properties to Israeli settlers. The Palestinian citizens of Sheikh Jarrah resorted to document their personal experiences of human rights abuses through social media. TikTok videos and Twitter posts were used in an attempt to relay Palestinian voices, with the hope that this user-generated content would reach out to a global and transnational audience. However short-lived, these grassroots campaigns were successfully launched in spite of a long history of surveillance, censorship and inequality of access to ICT infrastructures (Hussein, 2021; Kharoub, 2021; Matar and Harb, 2013). They contributed to circulate critical information to the Arab diaspora, eventually alerting a number of media outlets about a crisis, which – in the midst of the Covid-19 pandemic – ran the risk of being ignored or misreported by international observers. However, in the aftermath of the Sheikh Jarrah protests, communication with transnational pro-Palestinian networks was compromised by the content moderation policies regulating the largest social media platforms. Online posts and comments referring to the Israeli police raid – which took place in the surroundings of the Al Aqsa Mosque on the twenty-seventh night of Ramadan – were automatically flagged and removed from mainstream social media. The following week, Israel's military operations in the Gaza Strip continued to reduce opportunities for Palestinian interactions with foreign media outlets. Gaza was once again the target of air strikes, which the Israeli forces allegedly conducted to counter the missiles fired by Hamas towards the Israeli cities bordering the Gaza Strip. On 15 May, a warning was issued to the occupants of Gaza's Al Jalaa tower, which housed the offices of Al Jazeera and the Associated Press. The foreign media staff was asked to evacuate the premises. One hour later, the tower was instantly destroyed by Israeli Forces, who claimed they were targeting Hamas's military intelligence.

This succession of events reintroduced a debate on the impediments to Palestinian self-expression, drawing public attention to the multiple forms of censorship that hinder the inclusion of the Palestinian perspective in international news sources. The destruction of local media infrastructures reemphasized the structural challenges to inclusion and representation. Simultaneously, evidences of algorithmic bias revealed that digital occupation extends far beyond the region, limiting the echo of Palestinian voices in the international media sphere (Biddle and Speri, 2020; Eidelman and Walter-Johnson, 2021; Kharoub, 2021; Mac, 2021). This case study precisely illustrates the challenges faced by pro-Palestinian voices and the ways in which they navigate what has been described as a 'transnational "censorscape"' (Matar and Harb, 2013: 18). It brings us to re-examine the conditions in which content moderation reinforces hegemonic discourse while reproducing pre-existing systems of control and surveillance. Drawing on evidence from interviews with online pro-Palestinian activists and participant observation, we identify creative techniques of digital resistance. In light of these findings, we argue that users can successfully circumvent content moderation by continuously disrupting linguistic norms (Peteet, 2016) and traditional practices of content production.

History of 'digital occupation'

The recent engagement of transnational pro-Palestinian networks is part of a long struggle for the representation and inclusion of Palestinian voices. Historically, territorial control and military surveillance have continuously limited opportunities for the consolidation of Palestinian communication networks. Local activists have suffered violations of their right to freedom of movement in the form of travel bans and arrests. The security measures imposed by the Israeli state prevents human rights defenders from documenting military presence, in spite of its significance for those living in the occupied territory of the West Bank and the Gaza Strip (Taha, 2020; Tawil-Souri, 2012). Territorial occupation has, on the other hand, critical implications on the technological infrastructure available, when it comes to building communication networks that can be both independent and reliable. This process of control and exclusion has been commonly referred to as 'digital occupation'. Communication scholar Helga Tawil-Souri (2012) contributed to formulate this concept by drawing on the history of telecommunication networks in the Gaza Strip. Her work demonstrates that, over time, territorial control resulted in a monopoly over the development of ICT infrastructure. In spite of the Oslo II agreements – which state that Palestinians have the right to use independent communication networks – the local telecommunication market has been dominated by private Israeli cellular providers, which operate under the regulation of the Israeli Communications Ministry. These companies have relied on a centralized ICT network, which was originally installed as part of military infrastructure in the West Bank and have consistently delivered a lower signal in the Gaza Strip. Until January 2018, an Israeli ban was imposed upon all local 3G networks in the West Bank. Higher frequencies could only be delivered by cell towers located in Israel and Jewish settlements. The network operating in Gaza was relying on 2G, offering very limited data transmission (Sawafta, 2018). Besides the lack of independent ICT infrastructure, Palestinian internet users are expected to comply with the Israeli legal framework around 'hate speech', 'extremism' and incitement to violence, which determines how tech companies regulate and monitor user-generated content. Over time, these multiple forms of digital divide have created more obstacles to inclusion and self-representation, widening the gap between local Palestinian voices and the international media sphere.

Overcoming a dystopian form of technological determinism

Studying experiences of resistance to digital occupation brings us to rethink conventional assumptions about technology as a means of control and empowerment. In the early 2010s, research suggested that social media users would become in charge of *setting the agenda*, regaining agency over traditional mass media (Feezell, 2017; Weimann and Brosius, 2015). Yet these theories failed to consider inequalities of access to technologies. They often overlooked the pre-existing power structures upon which the market of digital media was originally founded. These early assumptions relied on a cyber-utopian form of technological determinism, which has been contested in light of the recent debate around privacy, freedom of speech and the commodification of big data. Today, the idea according to which social media users interfere in the *agenda setting* function of the mass media can still be refuted. For example, in the case of the May 2021 events, we argue that online pro-Palestinian engagement did not significantly alter the coverage and media frames of international news outlets. However, creative practices of online engagement were used to circulate information to the transnational pro-Palestinian community, while reaffirming a sense of belonging to the cause. Moreover, it contributed to document evidence of digital rights violations, eventually drawing public attention to the lack of transparency and accountability around automated content moderation.

In recent years, academic research has been increasingly preoccupied with the issue of algorithmic bias and its implications for online activism. In fact, one could argue that today's academic debate has shifted towards an understandably more sceptical and pessimistic view of digital technologies. The scale of state and corporate surveillance combined with the lack of diversity in the tech industry generate a number of legitimate concerns, with regard to the market of big data and the development of AI. However, some of the structural and systemic critiques of digital technologies still fail to overcome technological determinism by assuming that digital media systematically rules out creative experiences of political dissent. In many cases, a dystopian account of surveillance capitalism may divert our attention away from the social dynamics through which users manage to subvert these mechanisms of control.

In recent years, the academic literature on algorithmic bias and digital activism has already raised important issues about the systemic impediments to inclusion and representation. Amongst others, Leavy et al. (2020) and Siapera (2021) argue that content moderation relies on a logic of hierarchical categorization and pathological normalcy, which is guided by neoliberal incentives. This practice is, in her view, destined to reproduce the very same relationships of domination that online activists hope to tackle by using mainstream social media platforms to relay their message. As she contemplates on social media engagement in relation to the debate around race and representation, Siapera (2021) eventually quotes the words of the famous Black activist Audre Lorde: 'the master's tools will never dismantle the master's house' (Lorde: 1984). Tufekci (2013) formulates a similar argument with regard to 'microcelebrity' activism. Her research demonstrates that these practices of online campaigning can be counter-productive, because they divert attention away from the essence of one's political demands by focusing on *mass self-communication* (Castells, 2007; Fuchs, 2009). Most importantly, they abide by the rules of the attention economy, eventually serving the process by which user-generated content is increasingly regulated and commodified. This body of research (Leavy, Siapera and Sullivan, 2021; Siapera and Viejo-Otero, 2021) addresses the implications of content moderation by placing the emphasis on the limitations of online activism. However, it predominantly focuses on the structural and systemic issues that condition opportunities for political action in the realm of social media. Such approach implies that one can only fight for inclusion and representation by implementing legal and institutional reforms at a macro level. Most importantly, it tends to disregard alternative practices of digital activism, which have succeeded in circumventing surveillance and censorship. Yet these creative forms of online mobilizations occasionally prove to disrupt hegemonic structures as well as the legal frameworks that dictate the rules of content moderation. Arguably, this critique overlooks a broader range of social parameters that contribute to explain our interaction with technology. The discourse around content moderation is, in that sense, not much different from early (cyber-utopian) academic debates on the potential development of the internet in the Global South:

> While measuring the assumed impact of the Internet on developing societies has been a prominent area of focus, an account of the development of the Internet in Africa should not only focus on how technologies change societies, but also on how societies change technologies in the process of adoption, appropriation and adaptation. (Wasserman, 2017: 134)

Our case study precisely focuses on the second aspect of this dialectic process. It shows how online pro-Palestinian communities find creative ways to trick automated content moderation to subvert the normative framework of mainstream social media platforms. Our research is informed by interviews with pro-Palestinian activists, participant observation and a review of the literature on recent digital rights violations. By relying on these three empirical strands, we identify creative applications of the technology that enabled social media users to successfully circumvent censorship.

Algorithmic bias and content moderation

During the course of the Sheikh Jarrah mobilizations, pro-Palestinian activists from across the region and the Arab diaspora mobilized to document evidence of human rights abuses. Their reach and action however proved to be significantly diminished by the censorship policies regulating online content moderation (Smith, 2021). 7amleh, a Palestinian non-profit digital rights group, documented close to five hundred removals of online content between 6 May and 19 May 2021 (7amleh, 2021). The report stresses that individual accounts were blocked, and targeted posts and hashtags were automatically removed. The visibility of pro-Palestinian content considerably decreased as users reported a 50 per cent content removal on Instagram, 35 per cent on Facebook, 11 per cent on Twitter and 1 per cent on TikTok (7amleh, 2021: 3). Users were notified that their posts had been identified as 'incitement to violence' or included references to a dangerous organization. A media monitor and advisor to 7amleh, who was interviewed for this study, stated that the Israeli cyber unit had submitted hundreds of requests to social media platforms with the aim to put down online pro-Palestinian content since 2015. The interviewee maintained that a total of 1,242 requests were submitted by the unit to the largest tech companies in 2016 and that each request listed up to hundreds of content pieces. That number increased to 19,000 requests in 2019. Interviews also revealed that human rights advocates are particularly concerned about the lack of transparency around tech companies' decision-making process and the ways in which they have treated the requests submitted by the Israeli cyber unit. The scope of these censorship policies was widely noticed and reported when Palestinian worshippers in Al Aqsa Mosque were attacked by the Israeli forces (Knell, 2021) in the last days of Ramadan, around the second week of May 2021. Facebook-owned Instagram removed hundreds of posts and blocked hashtags (Gebeily, 2021; Levensen, 2021), 'because its content moderation system mistakenly associated the site with a designation the company reserves for terrorist organizations' (Mac, 2021a). Along with official Israeli requests to social media platforms, organized campaigns were launched to flag and report on Palestinian content on social media (Siddiqui and Suleymanova, 2021). A Facebook-led research documenting users' complaints at the time of the May 2021 events revealed that 'Israel, which had 5.8 million Facebook users, had been the top country in the world to report content under the company's rules for terrorism, with nearly 155,000 complaints over the preceding week' (Mac, 2021a). Commentators also highlighted that Israel was ranked third amongst the most proactive countries to flag and report content deemed as hateful or violent under the regulatory framework applied by the company. The volume of submitted complaints was much higher than in countries, where governments had formally expressed concerns about disinformation as well as in countries where dividing populist rhetoric was on the rise.

Algorithmic censorship specifically targeted online posts with mentions of the Al Aqsa Mosque (#AlAqsa; #الأقصى) (Eidelman, Lee and Walter-Johnson, 2021) due to an irrelevant analogy with the *Al-Aqsa Martyrs Brigades*. Other generic terms such as شهداء; شهيد (martyr) and مقاومة (resistance) were also filtered from Arabic posts. As per their own admission, Twitter and Facebook had blocked millions of pro-Palestinian posts, sometimes deactivating the accounts of prominent social media activists and influencers. The phenomenon extended to a broad range of platforms including YouTube, WhatsApp and mobile payment applications (Middle East Institute, 2021). Experiences of digital occupation were only exacerbated by the Covid-19 crisis, as social interactions became increasingly reliant on messaging apps and video conferencing. Prior to the events of May 2021, it was reported that video conferencing applications such as Zoom had blocked its access to a number of online public events and official webinars hosting local Palestinian activists and sympathizers of the Popular Front for the Liberation of Palestine (Biddle and Speri, 2020).

In comparison, pro-Israeli communications did not seem to be affected by algorithmic bias. On 17 May, the official Twitter account of the Israeli state repeatedly posted a series of tweets containing nothing but rocket emoticons. This was barely contextualized in a final tweet referring to the rockets shot at Israeli civilians. The official post stated these missiles were 'meant to kill', featuring the hashtag 'IsraelUnderAttack'. The Twitter thread did not engage with the particular context of the crisis. Instead, it applied an explicitly antagonizing imagery of warfare, while validating the duality of violence. Once we deconstruct these complex layers of meaning, it is arguably fair to consider whether this rhetoric qualifies as hate speech. However, technology fails to achieve this level of inference as it remains, in its current stage, blind to the context in which potentially controversial terms are being used. Digital rights experts like Marwa Fatafta raised the fact that automated content moderation is designed to treat specific linguistic terms as hate speech regardless of the intention behind the message (Middle East Institute, 2021). This level of algorithmic censorship not only annihilates public knowledge about the history of the conflict but also affects the way we shape collective memory and understand current events in relation to the past.

Media bias in the traditional media sphere

This is not to suggest that pro-Palestinian voices did not experience a certain sense of agency over the frames and narratives pertaining to the May 2021 crisis. Indeed, as we will see, systemic repression does not invalidate creative and inventive applications of social media by pro-Palestinian voices. On the contrary, one could argue that there has been a great sense of empowerment amongst those who have been actively engaged in disrupting and circumventing content moderation. However, this did not translate in a significant change with regard to the *agenda setting* and *framing* practices of international media outlets. The destruction of the Al Jalaa tower only increased the limitations to impartial media coverage, making it almost impossible for foreign journalists to report the conflict from the Gaza Strip. Over the course of the twenty-four hours following the attack, a number of media rights organizations and press freedom groups reacted publicly, interpreting the attack as a deliberate attempt to prevent all foreign media activities operating within Gaza occupied territory. These concerns however received limited public attention. Ironically, the questions of impartiality, inclusion and representation that international media outlets could have raised in reference to this event were hardly ever addressed (Uddin, 2021). Media monitoring later revealed that high-readership newspapers and mainstream news channels had produced a biased reporting of the crisis in favour of the narrative supported by the Israeli state. Non-profit media watchdog organizations and observers produced a comprehensive assessment of the framing delivered by some of the most established media outlets (Hamid et al. 2021; Shupak, 2021). They identified a number of consistent issues indicating a limited understanding of the context around the recent crisis. International media outlets such as the New York Times, the Washington Post, the Wall Street Journal, BBC News, the Sun, Sky News or the Daily Express applied a binary and highly connoted vocabulary combined with sensationalist headlines and representations. Biased media frames could be identified in the coverage of other prominent newspapers, including those, whose political alignment was more likely to resonate with the views of the pro-Palestinian left. Media monitors commented on misleading assumptions about the causality of the events and the fact that the language prevailing across the international media sphere gave a deceptive sense of power symmetry between all the actors involved in the crisis. They critiqued the 'TikTok Intifada' (Ball, 2021) media narrative, which invalidated pro-Palestinian campaigns, implicitly associating them with information warfare. Finally, monitors reemphasized the fact that international media outlets had, once again, applied a traditionally orientalist lens. Religious imagery and the theme of sectarianism were often associated with depictions of violence, reasserting common stereotypes about political unrest in the region. Such narrative thus inevitably failed to account for the historical and geopolitical complexity of the conflict, as it was often the case with regard to the mediatization of war in the Middle East (Melki, 2014). These misrepresentations are, on the one hand, consistent with a long history of orientalist discourse and media bias around the Israeli occupation of Palestine (Matar, 2016). On the other hand, they are evidence that the real and most significant achievement of the online pro-Palestinian community does not reside in its effect on mainstream media coverage.

Creative approaches to digital resistance

Tawil-Souri describes the struggle for Palestinian agency as an 'ongoing dialectic' and 'dynamic process', by which *the oppressed* continuously reinvents new practices of resistance to disrupt hegemonic media:

> A core contradiction arises against which to understand technology infrastructures: the confinement of Gazans in a narrowing and disconnected space occurs at the same time that high-tech globalization is posited as the route to openness and to overcoming confinement. Third, Gazans themselves 'occupy' digital spaces, even if with constraints and sometimes illegally: they reach out to friends and family, report abuses, and escape physical confinement in virtual ways. It is an ongoing dialectic. (Tawil-Souri, 2012: 28)

Acknowledging this phenomenon allows us to shift perspective away from the question of *what* type of communication tools should be used to consider *how* they may be used as a form of resistance. In other words, it shows how creative social practices can help marginalized audiences regain ownership of their narrative, in a globally competitive media environment that operates on the basis of normative and technologically deterministic regulations. A Palestinian activist interviewed for this study described this process in simple yet powerful terms:

> Israeli authorities and social media companies are trying to silence Palestinians online by preventing us from sharing our narrative and our own stories [about] Israeli violations. As a result, Palestinians [come to find] creative ways. (Salma, August 2021)

Following the events of May 2021, pro-Palestinian activists, who attempted to report on the crisis from around the world, came to experience digital oppression first-hand. This contributed to a broader realization within international networks of human rights advocates, who had witnessed similar forms of repression and exposure to online surveillance. Prominent voices from the Arab diaspora worked collaboratively to circumvent global automated censorship by thinking creatively about communicative practices on social media. They relayed the posts of local activists, whose social media accounts were blocked after they had covered civil mobilizations in Sheikh Jarrah. This was the case for the Palestinian-American writer Mariam Barghouti (Maiberg and Cox, 2021), who was then reporting on protests from the West Bank. Her profile had been temporarily locked along with hundreds of Palestinian Twitter accounts, because the tech company had allegedly 'mistakenly identified the rapid-firing tweeting as spam' (Dwoskin and De Vynck, 2021). After her account was reactivated, Barghouti posted[1]:

> Important point, my account was suspended then reinstated without me having to do much, because you all spoke up. For that, thank you all for being so quick, for refusing to just be shocked. Thank you for those that offered your own accounts for me to use.

Her followers had proved to be proactive and responsive, liaising with each other over multiple alternative platforms and messaging applications to relay her posts during the crackdown. Amongst those who were tweeting on Barghouti's behalf were influential activists like the Bahraini human rights defender Maryam Alkhawaja, who had consolidated an audience of more than one hundred thousand followers. This resulted in expanding Barghouti's Twitter reach once her account was reactivated.

Simultaneously, activists circumvented algorithmic censorship by avoiding standardized Arabic writing. Alternative writing systems ranged from the use of the Latin alphabet in Arabic language to sinistrodextral writing in Arabic. Pro-Palestinian activists, whose comments were subjected to censorship, also resorted to communicate in colloquial dialects, occasionally adding dots or commas between letters to confuse automated content moderation. They would sometimes distort the writing of a word by altering specific letters or substitute written statements for another type of visual cues, such as original photos. A Latin alphabet letter was for example inserted in the Arabic word 'شهيد' (martyr) to trick algorithmic censorship: شhيد.

Special characters were also used to distort the English spelling of the word 'Palestine': 'P@lestine'.

Online activists also substituted the Palestinian flag for a watermelon emoji (Berger, 2021). This practice was rooted in a long history of civil resistance over the symbolic representations of Palestine. After the Six-Day War in 1967, the Israeli government had banned all public displays of the Palestinian flag and its colours (Ahmed, 2021).

Any outward show of the flag, from publications to advertisements, including old photographs, could result in imprisonment. It is in this context that Palestinian voices referred to the image of the watermelon, whose colours are suggestive of the Palestinian flag. Palestinians had used this alternative symbol to express their sense of belonging, after being deprived of the right to consolidate and cultivate a shared identity. Over time, the Palestinian watermelon had become a public expression of cultural pride in artworks representing the struggle against Israeli censorship. In the aftermath of the May 2021 events, pro-Palestinian activists paid a tribute to this form of symbolic resistance by incorporating the image of the watermelon as part of a transnational mobilization against digital rights violations.

Pro-Palestinian activists also reverted to ancient Arabic writing, removing all dots (diacritics) from the modern alphabet. Diacritical points (dots above or below letters) were introduced to the Arabic script between the eighth and eleventh centuries. In a book retracing the history of Arabic language, Ibrahim Gooma (1947: 49) reminds us that the traditional writing system did not feature any dots or marks in the pre-Islamic era. These characters were institutionalized subsequently to standardize Arabic scriptures. According to the same source, the normalization of the Arabic writing was initiated by Abo Al Aswad Al Douali in 686 AD. Al Douali had borrowed these additional characters from the Syriac script to ensure a more accurate pronunciation of consonants. One thousand years later, this ancient writing system was reclaimed by hundreds of Pro-Palestine social media accounts to overcome another form of normalization, which imposed a rigid framework upon language, culture and self-expression. This realization inspired a number of independent media outlets, which had also been exposed to surveillance, censorship and political repression across the region. On 18 May 2021, the independent Egyptian news website Mada Masr applied the same technique to publish an article entitled 'Human Against God, The Arabic Dots Revolution'. In this short piece, activist Muhammad Hamameh described how he came up with the idea of reapplying pre-Islamic standards of writing, saying that he had previously considered using Morse code or replacing some letters with symbols: 'It's an easy technique … But it's much more challenging to the AI machine, which has a [binary] code for each letter' (Hamameh, 2021).

Websites and applications were created to convert Arabic text to the Dotless script such as Dotless[2], Tajawz[3] and Ektob.[4]. Among the most used terms were Palestine in Arabic فلسطين > ڡلسطس and the slogan «ڡلسطس عربىه وسطٮل عربىه» (Palestine is Arab and will remain Arab). It is worth noting that the word algorithm itself originates from Arabic, named after the ninth-century mathematician Abu Ja'far Muhammad ibn Musa, who was more commonly known as al-Khawarizmi. He was a member of the House of Wisdom, an academy of scientists in Baghdad.

The digital resistance techniques didn't stop at avoiding the restrictions, but also included social mobilizations designed to demand more transparency and accountability on the part of tech companies. Activists led coordinated campaigns to downgrade Facebook's app review ratings (Rappler, 2021). The campaign called on people to give Facebook a one-star review in the Apple and Google app stores. The average star rating of the social platform dropped from 4/5 to 1.8/5 on Apple's App Store and 2.4/5 on the Google Play store. A significant number of reviews addressed the fact that Facebook had silenced Palestinian voices, mentioning hashtags such as #FreePalestine or #GazaUnderAttack. The campaign impacted the company's brands, to the extent that some of its employees reached out to both Apple and Google, attempting to remove negative reviews. Mainstream media outlets covering the debate on digital rights violations reported negotiations involving Apple and Facebook, according to which the latter had allegedly requested the former to remove negative comments from the App Store (Solon, 2021). Regardless of the decisions made by the corporate actors involved in this crisis, the online civil mobilization had successfully raised awareness about the issue of media bias in content moderation. The scale of the censorship, which pro-Palestinian social media users had experienced, led to a broader realization of the oppression faced by Palestinians living in the occupied territories of Gaza and the West Bank. In response to digital rights violations, pro-Palestinian activists and members of the Arab diaspora developed short-lived yet relatively impactful communication practices. This allowed them to relay perspectives and frames which had been predominantly absent from the coverage of the traditional mass media.

Over the course of the May 2021 mobilizations, users' inventiveness was informed by a long history of cultural resistance and an ability to disrupt the codes of content moderation in a very literal sense. Pro-Palestinian networks did manage to challenge *the order of (algorithmic) discourse* (Foucault, 1970), in spite of the fact that they continued to apply mainstream social platforms. As much as a top-down structural take on technology would lead us to believe that we are fully subjected to media control, audiences are still proactively engaged in the process of *decoding* meaning (Hall, 1980). In contrast, content moderation is rather reactive as it only *encodes* language based on what it can identify as a widespread conventional practice. Users remain, in this regard, ahead of the curve and may find the opportunity to reinvent the rules of language as a vehicle for power. This is precisely where the relative success of pro-Palestinian activism (Hussein, 2021) lies in relation to the events of May 2021. The creative power of counter-hegemonic voices does not so much revolve around the communication tools per se, but around a shared media literacy that is informed by lived experiences of repression. And it is this media literacy that contributed to raise the issue of digital rights violations, ultimately drawing the attention of international observers. Over time, those who suffered digital occupation have demonstrated a greater awareness of the tool and its limitations. In this particular case, they carefully handled the double-edged sword of online activism by subverting conventional applications of the technology. However, this can only be achieved once we effectively overcome the assumption of technological determinism to consider the social and dynamic nature of language as a means of empowerment.

Conclusion

Our case study suggests that marginalized voices have proved to develop creative practices of communicative resistance. These practices involve social skills as well as an organic relationship with language. Most importantly, they rely on a complex, multidimensional and relatable understanding of the context. As such, they contrast with the normative framework of content moderation and contribute to successfully disrupt the standardized (automated) process, through which language is currently and increasingly normalized. That is not to say that social media platforms still act as a legitimate space for freedom of speech or political dissent. The debate around human rights violations against Palestinian voices only reemphasizes the challenges and limitations of online activism, insofar as it pertains to mainstream social media platforms. This perspective however invites us to shift focus away from the systemic power structure of digital media. Further, it highlights the resilience of counter-hegemonic voices as well as the political and sociocultural parameters that continue to condition our experience of technology. This shift of perspective is particularly useful when it comes to understanding the recent evolution of social media activism across the Middle East and North Africa region. One could argue that, in the aftermath of the 2011 Arab uprisings, the securitization of the online public space has considerably limited opportunities for freedom of expression. Along with the implementation of tighter media regulations, exposure to state surveillance, censorship and government-led smear campaigns increasingly constrain civil society. Yet, between 2019 and 2020, a second wave of civil movements took place in countries like Sudan, Algeria and Lebanon. During these mobilizations, activists documented the process through which protesters reclaimed ownership of the public space. Similar to the 2021 Palestinian mobilizations, the events were occasionally mediatized through social media in creative ways, so as to engage with the diaspora, circumvent censorship or interact in spite of a highly fragmented media environment. This suggests that, besides the need to advocate for long-term structural change, users may nevertheless find innovative ways to gain agency in the age of surveillance capitalism. It is therefore crucial to further investigate how these practices of digital resistance have evolved, now that the political discourse around social media appears to have shifted from a cyber-utopian to a rather dystopian form of technological determinism.

Notes

1. https://bit.ly/3zXFWDp.
2. https://www.dotless.app/.
3. https://tajawz.com/.
4. https://play.google.com/store/apps/details?id=com.soda.ekteb&hl=en&gl=US.

References

Ahmed, S. (2021), '1967: Israel Bans the National Colours of Palestine', Medium, 26 May, https://medium.com/the-crimes-of-israel/1967-israel-bans-the-national-colors-of-palestine-d1141162e374 (accessed 8 October 2021).

Aouragh, M. (2011), *Palestine Online. Transnationalism, the Internet and Construction of Identity*, London: I.B. Tauris.

Berger, M. (2021), 'Why Palestinians Are Uniting around Watermelon Emoji', The Washington Post, 9 July, https://www.washingtonpost.com/world/2021/07/09/palestin ian-watermelons/ (accessed 8 October 2021).

Ball, J. (2021), 'TikTok Intifada: The Role of New Media in Old Conflicts', The Spectator, 22 May, https://www.spectator.co.uk/article/tiktok-intifada-the-role-of-new-media-in-old-conflicts (accessed 8 October 2021).

Biddle, S., and A. Speri (2020), 'Zoom Censorship of Palestine Seminars Sparks Fight over Academic Freedom', The Intercept, 14 November, https://theintercept.com/2020/11/14/zoom-censorship-leila-khaled-palestine/ (accessed 8 October 2021).

Castells, M (2007), 'Communications, Power and Counter-Power in the Network Society', *International Journal of Communication*, 1: 238–66.

de Bruijn, M., F. Nyamnjoh and I. Brinkman (eds) (2009), 'Mobile Phones: The New Talking Drums of Everyday Africa'. *Australian Journal of Communication*, 37(2): 123–6.

Dwoskin, E., and G. De Vynck (2021), 'Facebook's AI Treats Palestinian Activists like It Treats American Black Activists. It Blocks Them', The Washington Post, 28 May, https://www.washingtonpost.com/technology/2021/05/28/facebook-palestinian-cen sorship/ (accessed 8 October 2021).

Eidelman, V., A. Lee and F. Walter-Johnson (2021), 'Time and Again, Social Media Giants Get Content Moderation Wrong: Silencing Speech about Al-Aqsa Mosque Is Just the Latest Example', ACLU, 17 May, https://www.aclu.org/news/free-speech/time-and-again-social-media-giants-get-content-moderation-wrong-silencing-spe ech-about-al-aqsa-mosque-is-just-the-latest-example/?initms_aff=nat&initms_c han=soc&utm_medium=soc&initms=210518_blog_tw&utm_source=tw&utm_campa ign=&utm_content=210518_freespeech_blog&ms_aff=nat&ms_chan=soc&ms=210 518_blog_tw (accessed 8 October 2021).

Feezell, J. T. (2017), 'Agenda Setting through Social Media: The Importance of Incidental News Exposure and Social Filtering in the Digital Era', *Political Research Quarterly*, 71 (2): 482–94.

Foucault, M. ([1970]1981), ' "The Order of Discourse", Inaugural Lecture at the Collège de France, 2 December'. In R. Young (ed.), *Untying the Text: A Post-Structuralist Reader*, London: Routledge, 51–78.

Fuchs, C. (2009), 'Some Reflections on Manuel Castells' Book *Communication Power*', *TripleC (Cognition, Communication, Co-operation)*, 7 (1): 94–108.

Gebeily, M. (2021), 'Instagram, Twitter Blame Glitches for Deleting Palestinian Posts', Reuters, 10 May, https://www.reuters.com/article/israel-palestinians-socialmedia/instagram-twitter-blame-glitches-for-deleting-palestinian-posts-idUSL8N2MU624 (accessed 8 October 2021).

Gooma, I. (1947), قصه الكتابه العربيه ابراهيم جمعه, The Story of Arabic Writing, Cairo: Dar Al Maaref.

Hall, S. (1980), 'Encoding/Decoding'. In S. Hall, D. Hobson, A. Lower and P. Willis (eds), *Culture, Media, Language: Working Papers in Cultural Studies, 1972–79*, London: Routledge, 117–27.

Hamameh, M. (2021), بوره النقاط العربيه: الاسان صد الاله. 'Human Against God, The Arabic Dots Revolution', Mada Masr, 18 May, https://mada31.appspot.com/www.madamasr.com/ar/2021/05/18/feature/%D8%B3%D9%8A%D8%A7%D8%B3%D8%A9/%D8%A 7%D9%84%D8%A7%D9%AE%D8%B3%D8%A7%DA%BA-%D8%B5%D8%AF-%D8%A7%D9%84%D8%A7%D9%84%D9%87-%D9%AE%D9%88%D8%B1%D9%87-%D8%A7%D9%84%D9%AE%D9%AF%D8%A7%D8%B7-%D8%A7%D9%84%D8 %B9%D8%B1%D9%AE%D9%89%D9%87/ (accessed 8 October 2021).

Hamid, R., and A. Morris (2021), 'Media Reporting on Palestine. Centre for Media Monitoring', The Muslim Council of Britain, https://cfmm.org.uk/wp-content/uplo ads/2021/05/MediaReportingOnPalestine-Report-and-Toolkit-Final.pdf (accessed 8 October 2021).

Hussein, M. (2021), 'States Can't Control the Narrative on Israel-Palestine Anymore', The Intercept, 12 May, https://theintercept.com/2021/05/12/israel-palestine-jerusalem-soc ial-media/ (accessed 8 October 2021).

Kharoub, T. (2021), 'Systematic Digital Repression: Social Media Censoring of Palestinian Voices', 8 June, Arab Center, Washington DC, https://arabcenterdc.org/resource/sys tematic-digital-repression-social-media-censoring-of-palestinian-voices/ (accessed 8 October 2021).

Knell, Y. (2021), 'Al-Aqsa Mosque: Dozens Hurt in Jerusalem Clashes', BBC News, 8 May, https://www.bbc.co.uk/news/world-middle-east-57034237 (accessed 8 October 2021).

Leavy, S., B. O'Sullivan and E. Siapera (2020), 'Data, Power and Bias in Artificial Intelligence', Insight Centre for Data Analytics, 28 July, Proceedings of the 'AI for Social Good' Harvard CRCS Online Workshop, 20–21 July 2020.

Leavy, S., E. Siapera and B. O'Sullivan (2021), 'Ethical Data Curation for AI: An Approach Based on Feminist Epistemology and Critical Theories of Race', Proceedings of the 2021 AAAI/ACM Conference on AI, Ethics, and Society, 695–703.

Levensen, M. (2021), 'Instagram Blocked Posts about the Aqsa Mosque in a Terrorism Screening Error', *The New York Times*, 13 May, https://www.nytimes.com/2021/05/13/ world/middleeast/instagram-aqsa-mosque.html (accessed 25 November 2021).

Lorde, A. (1984), 'The Master's Tools Will Never Dismantle the Master's House'. In A. Lorde (ed.), *Sister Outsider*, 110–13, New York: Crossing Press.

Mac, R. (2021a), 'Amid Israeli–Palestinian Violence, Facebook Employees Are Accusing Their Company of Bias against Arabs and Muslims', Buzz Feed News, 27 May, https:// www.buzzfeednews.com/article/ryanmac/facebook-employees-bias-arabs-muslims-palestine (accessed 8 October 2012).

Mac, R. (2021b), 'Instagram Censored Posts about One of Islam's Holiest Mosques, Drawing Employee', Buzz Feed News, 12 May, https://www.buzzfeednews.com/article/ ryanmac/instagram-facebook-censored-al-aqsa-mosque (accessed 8 October 2012).

Maiberg, E., and J. Cox (2021), 'Twitter Said It Restricted Palestinian Writer's Account by Accident', Vice, 11 May, https://www.vice.com/en/article/qj8b4x/twitter-said-it-restric ted-palestinian-writers-account-by-accident (accessed 8 October 2021).

Middle East Institute (2021), 'Digital Occupation: Content Moderation, Palestine, and the Role of Social Media', Webinar panel discussion (Washington, DC, 2 June 2021), https://www.mei.edu/events/digital-occupation-content-moderation-palest ine-and-role-social-media (accessed 5 February 2023).

Matar, D., and Z. Harb (2013), *Narrating Conflict in the Middle East. Discourse, Image and Communications Practices in Lebanon and Palestine*, London: I.B. Tauris.

Matar, D. (2016), *Gaza: Image Normalization in Gaza as Metaphor*, London: Hurst.

Melki, J. (2014), 'The Interplay of Politics, Economics and Culture in News Framing of Middle East Wars', *Media, War and Conflict*, 7 (2): 165–86.

Peteet, J. (2016), 'Language Matters: Talking about Palestine', *Journal of Palestine Studies*, 45: 24–40.

Rappler (2021), 'Pro-Palestinian Activists Hit Facebook with 1-Star App Store Reviews – Report', Rappler.com, 24 May, https://www.rappler.com/technology/apps/pro-palestin ian-activists-hit-facebook-app-store-reviews (accessed 8 October 2021).

Salma [Pseudonym] (2021), Pro-Palestinian digital rights advocate, Zoom personal interview, 25 October.

Sawafta, A. (2018), 'Palestinians Get 3G Mobile Services in West Bank', Reuters, 24 January, https://www.reuters.com/article/israel-palestinians-telecom-idUSL8N1PJ3FW (accessed 8 October 2021).

Smith, A. (2021), 'Palestinians' Digital Rights "Violated" by Censorship on Facebook, Twitter, and Instagram, New Report Claims', Independent, 21 May, https://www.inde pendent.co.uk/life-style/gadgets-and-tech/palestine-israel-censorship-facebook-twit ter-instagram-7amleh-b1851328.html (accessed 8 October 2021).

Siapera, E. (2021), 'AI Content Moderation, Racism and (de)Coloniality', *International Journal of Bullying Prevention*, 4 (1): 55–65, https://doi.org/10.1007/S42 380-021-00105-7 (accessed 5 February 2023).

Siapera, E., and P. Viejo-Otero (2021), 'Governing Hate: Facebook and Digital Racism', *Television and New Media*, 22 (2): 112–30.

Siddiqui, U., and R. Suleumanova (2021), 'Israel, Social Media Groups Cooperating against Palestinians: NGO', Al Jazeera, 21 May, https://www.aljazeera.com/ news/2021/5/21/close-cooperation-between-israel-and-social-media-companies-ngo (accessed 8 October 2021).

Shupak, G. (2021), 'Israel/Palestine Coverage Presents False Equivalency between Occupied and Occupier', Fair, 18 May, https://fair.org/home/israel-palestine-cover age-presents-false-equivalency-between-occupied-and-occupier/?utm_campaign=shar eaholic&utm_medium=facebook&utm_source=socialnetwork&fbclid=IwAR0ve0 R7xKWYQkwUsoufqw7VC-0aoNIP2MPeeKKp41kWi4uJ6Ta89PpwAxA (accessed 8 October 2021).

Solon, O. (2021), 'Pro-Palestinian Activists Target Facebook with 1-Star App Store Reviews', NBC News, 23 May, https://www.nbcnews.com/tech/social-media/pro-pale stinian-activists-target-facebook-1-star-app-store-reviews-n1268258 (accessed 8 October 2021).

Taha, S. (2020), 'The Cyber Occupation of Palestine; Suppressing Digital Activism and Shrinking the Virtual Sphere', EU Policy Brief, Global Campus Arab World, https:// repository.gchumanrights.org/bitstream/handle/20.500.11825/1620/6.GlobalCamp us2020_Arab%20world.pdf?sequence=1&isAllowed=y (accessed 8 October 2021).

Tawil-Souri, H. (2012), 'Digital Occupation: Gaza's High-Tech Enclosure', *Journal of Palestine Studies*, 41 (2): 27–43.

Tufekci, Z. (2013), 'Not This One: Social Movements, the Attention Economy, and Microcelebrity Networked Activism', *American Behavioural Scientist*, 57 (7): 848–70.

Uddin, R. (2021), 'Israel-Palestine: British Media Coverage "Skewed" and "Biased", Report Finds', Middle East Eye, 27 May, https://www.middleeasteye.net/news/british-media-biased-skewed-israel-palestine-report (accessed 8 October 2021).

Wasserman, H. (2017), 'African Histories of the Internet', *Internet Histories Digital Technology, Culture and Society*, 1 (1–2): 129–37.

Weimann, G., and H-B. Brosius (2015), 'A New Agenda for Agenda-Setting Research in the Digital Era'. In G. Voew and P. Henn (eds) *Political Communication in the Online World: Theoretical Approaches and Research Designs*, London: Routledge, 26–44.

7amleh – The Arab Center for the Advancement of Social Media (2021), 'The Attack on Palestinian Digital Rights', Progress report, 6–19 May, https://7amleh.org/stor age/The%20Attacks%20on%20Palestinian%20Digital%20Rights.pdf (accessed 8 October 2021).

15

The media war in the Palestinian-Israeli conflict

Examining interstate character assassination in international media

Aspriadis Neofytos

Introduction

The Israel–Palestine conflict may be the most long-lasting ongoing conflict of our times. International news coverage of the Israel–Palestine conflict is as complex and dynamic as the conflict itself (Ruigrock, van Atteveldt and Takes, 2013). Several studies cover and analyse the conflict from different perspectives, especially from a communication media point of view (Ackerman, 2001; Korn, 2004; Normand, 2016; Ruigrock van Atteveldt and Takes, 2013; Siapera, Hunt and Lynn, 2015; Zelizer, Park and Gudelunas, 2002). One basic problem posited by previous research on conflict coverage was the lack of explanations for the causes of the conflict in comparison to high presentations of drama, fighting and violence (Ackerman, 2001; Zelizer, Park and Gudelunas, 2002). The bias in the news coverage of the Israel–Palestine conflict is to be found in the presentation of the casualties (Korn, 2004), or the absence of wording for the cause of the conflict like the use of the word 'occupation' for Israel (Zelizer, Park and Gudelunas, 2002).

The problem with this selective presentation of news is the long-term character of the conflict. As generations pass, it is not clear to foreign audiences what is at stake and what is the problem that leads to a conflict between the two communities. In fact, for most of the population around the globe, news coverage is the only source they have about the Middle East (Ruigrock, van Atteveldt and Takes, 2013). In the long term, this kind of news coverage may lead to a memory erasure of the initial causes of the conflict, making it more difficult for its resolution.

This chapter aims to examine the eleven-day Israel–Palestine conflict in the May 2021 news coverage. Particularly, it examines the presence of character assassination in international media for the coverage of the conflict. This would expand the hypothesis of character assassination in international relations and show that such strategies could affect or be used by international news media. In addition, it would add to the existing literature on the Israel–Palestine conflict coverage proposing another explanation for the bias observed.

The chapter first elaborates on the theory of character assassination and its role in international relations and the media; it then discusses differences in the modus operandi of news media for the use of character assassination in interstate conflict, and the methodology and findings of the present study.

Character assassination in international relations and the media

Character assassination is the deliberate destruction of a person's reputation or credibility through character attacks (Icks et al., 2019; Icks and Shiraev, 2014; Samoilenko et al., 2020; Samoilenko et al., 2017). Its meaning is twofold: on the one hand, it can refer to the process of attacking someone's character and on the other, to the result of such attacks if they are successful (Shiraev et al. 2021). Character assassination is always deliberate, which means it is done with the intention to damage, it is always public in nature and is all about perception, meaning that the attacker's goal is to influence the way others see a particular person (Icks and Shiraev, 2014; Shiraev et al., 2021).

Character assassination contains the notion of 'character' and the notion of attack. The first means the characteristics, reputation or personality of an individual, although personality stands for stable features rather than the moral aspect of an individual's behaviour (Shiraev et al., 2021). Therefore, character assassination refers more to the reputational aspect of an individual's character rather than someone's personality.

The second, a character attack, according to Walton (2006), focuses on the bad character of the person. However, character assassination is a broader procedure that may include character attacks but aims at the destruction of someone's reputation or image. 'The ultimate aim of CA is to isolate an individual from its social network, by destroying his or her reputation and integrity' (Seiffert-Brockmann, Einwiller and Stranzl, 2018: 3).

Furthermore, character assassination is strongly related to rhetorical attacks against individuals (Shiraev et al., 2021) although it may also be used against collective entities (Icks and Shiraev, 2014). The attacker may use propagation of an enemy image that is usually directed against a group of people (Icks et al., 2019) or against a leader of a nation, affecting the image of the whole nation (Simons, 2020; Laruelle, 2020). According to Krebs and Holian's (2007) research, attacks on an individual from another group may be perceived as attacks on the entire group.

Rhetorical attacks are very common during international conflicts (Shiraev, 2014). Political leaders may use rhetorical attacks either to persuade the internal public by demonizing an enemy other (e.g. Goussios et al., 2014; Thussu and Freedman, 2003), or to marginalize a country in the international system by attacking/destroying its reputation to win diplomatic goals (Aspriadis, Takas and Samaras , 2020). In such cases, the state usually works as a person metaphor, attributing human characteristics to the state, and the ruler of the state stands for the state metonym, attributing his characteristics to the state (Rojo, 1995).

Consequently, rhetorical attacks in the form of character assassination against the leader of a country may lead to the delegitimization of the image of the nation and its depiction as a 'demonized enemy' (Laruelle, 2020; Simons, 2020). In effect, character assassination in international politics differs from that in domestic politics in terms of the scope and the outcome. The scope is to gain diplomatic or military advantages for the attacker, the outcome is the creation of a hated enemy image or the destruction of the image and defamation of the country. The process, however, may remain the same or may have very similar methods to that in domestic politics.

Character assassination in the news media: From campaign mode to media logic

Character assassination in international politics is not necessarily limited to the leadership rhetoric but can also come from the media. Nevertheless, there is a distinct differentiation between the functions of strategic communication in the political discourse and the functions of the news media. This may also affect the correlation between the character assassination procedure in the political and interstate political discourse and the media. This difference may be searched for in the strategic function of communication and the function of the news media logic.

Strategic communication in politics is driven by the function of campaign mode. According to Burton and Shea (2002: 4), the campaign mode is a state of mind that combines a visceral drive to win elections with a deep-seated habit of strategic thinking. The political actors operate under the 'campaign mode', which expresses their strategic thinking and is motivated by their will to prevail in the elections (Takas and Samaras, 2016). Ideally, strategic thinking in a campaign mode is based on an understanding of the political terrain that helps a professional choose the right campaign rules (Burton and Shea, 2002: 157). This means that politicians act in the political communication environment with a focus on constant campaigning and antagonism. The same goes for the international political communication environment, where the political, geopolitical and power politics dictate such rivalry behaviour.

The media, however, differ in terms of role and function in the political communication landscape. This differentiation lies in the two core concepts regarding the function of the media: the news media logic and the political logic. Altheide (2004: 294) defines media logic as

> the assumptions and processes for constructing messages within a particular medium. This includes rhythm, grammar, and format. Format, while a feature of media logic, is singularly important because it refers to the rules or 'codes' for defining, selecting, organizing, presenting, and recognizing information as one thing rather than another.

In other words, media logic refers to 'the news values and the storytelling techniques the media make use of to take advantage of their medium and its format, and to be competitive in the ongoing struggle to capture people's attention (Strömbäck,

2008: 233; Takens et al., 2013). Under the function of media logic, the media choose the presentation of the news according to the news-making process and economic necessities, which are guided by commercial rules to maximize their audience shares (Esser, 2013). The concept of media logic is also closely linked to issues of bias and frames in media content.

The opposite function is political logic. It refers to the 'self-presentational' side of politics, like strategies of political pseudo-events, image projections and symbolic politics (Esser, 2013). The main task of political parties from the perspective of political logic is to inform the public about their issue positions and solutions to societal problems (Takens et al., 2013). According to Strömbäck (2008: 234), 'the needs of the political system and political institutions—in particular, parties, but also governmental agencies as well as democracy as a set of norms and procedures—take center stage and shape how political communication is played out, covered, and understood'.

The rise of media logic affects news presentation, whereas political logic affects the parameters of media content (Samaras, 2004). The political logic may be the outcome of the function of the campaign mode, mentioned earlier. The campaign mode as a communication process of political actors may affect the news-making process and framing of events by the news media, according to the political logic assumption. On the contrary, when the media function under the media logic, it is the journalistic practice, the commercialization and other factors of mediatization that affect the news-making process (Asp, 2014; Esser, 2013; Samaras, 2004; Strömbäck, 2008).

Under these media functions, it can be understood how the media operates under the concept of media–state relations and may develop strategies, strategic framing, discourse and media agenda. According to the different circumstances of the political environment, the media functions in a different role. As Entman's (2003;2004) cascade model suggests, the governmental frames in times of crisis may affect the presentation of news by the media, leading to a hegemonic model of news making. On the contrary, the CNN effect theory (Bahador, 2007; Belknap, 2002; Gilboa, 2005) suggests that news media frames and presentation of news may affect governmental decision-making.

Consequently, it can be inferred that the media may use strategies and strategic framing independently of the purpose they serve (if they operate under the media logic or the political logic) because it is considered a part of their political communication function. The presentation of news and the inherent strategies the media may use may be the result of either a hegemonic function, meaning the result of the campaign mode of political elites for circumstances like crises or conflict situations, or the outcome of a media logic function that may lead to the CNN effect.

In the first case, the strategic function may enhance the campaign mode of the political elite and empower the pursuit of political leadership's goals, whereas, in the second, they may influence political decision-making and public opinion through the projection of specific images and news framing. This means that their strategic use of the presentation of events may play a role in the strategic communication process.

In the international political environment, the media usually play a part in the information war, taking the position of the home country. According to Samoilenko et al. (2017: 34), character assassination techniques represent an important part of information warfare. This leads to the hypothesis that the media in conflict situations may portray events differently according to their national identity. Samoilenko's (2014) research on mediated character assassination for the conflict in Ukraine in 2014 describes that Russian media outlets used the standard expressive clichés to label the Kyiv protesters as 'terrorists', 'fascists' or 'bandits' who brought 'democracy to its knees' in Ukraine. On the contrary, US and Western media have been actively cultivating the images of the Cold War and demonizing Russian president Vladimir Putin as the main threat to Europe and the rest of the civilized world.

In concluding the theoretical part of the study, three main research questions arise:

RQ1) Do international media use character assassination strategies in the presentation of news regarding the Israel–Palestine conflict?

RQ2) What can be inferred regarding the relationship between the country of origin of the media examined and the character assassination strategies used?

RQ3) What are the main character assassination strategies used by the media examined regarding the Israel–Palestine conflict?

RQ4) How are the images of the countries in conflict being presented by the different news media?

Research method

The methodology used is qualitative content analysis with elements from discourse analysis and frame analysis. Qualitative content analysis is more appropriate for a relatively small amount of textual matter (Krippendorff, 2004; Van Evera, 1997) and allows the liberty of viewing the case from inside out (Gillham, 2000).

Discourse analysis is considered a research method grounded in a more qualitative research logic (Carpentier, 2010) that can help exclude important conclusions with the use of language analysis, style, grammar, rhetoric, symbolism, word use and so on (Carpentier, 2010; Paul, 2011; van Dijk, 1997). The reason for using discourse analysis in a media study is because the use of words, their frequency and their context may highlight a strategic use or a strategic objective, providing useful insights into the media messages.

Moreover, a frame analysis may contribute to the identification of the side that is being highlighted in the presentation of the events by the news media networks. A general definition of frames can be Entman's (2003) 'Framing entails selecting and highlighting some facets of events or issues and making connections among them to promote a particular interpretation, evaluation, and/or solution.' Based on this definition, a news media frame analysis may highlight not only the position of a news media towards an issue but also strategic aspects of the use of the framing to influence the media's audience.

The analysis is being conducted on three major news media networks: CNN, The Times of Israel and Al Jazeera. The choice of these three media networks is because of their impact on their communities and at the same time their international standpoint. The study aims to examine character assassination in interstate conflicts and is based on the formation of images of the countries in conflict. This is mainly the reason for choosing international and English-speaking media networks. Times of Israel has been chosen for one additional reason. Although it cannot be characterized as international media, since it is mainly local, it was needed in the analysis as it was anticipated to be more biased towards Israel than the other two media networks. This would help establish the marginal tone of the analysis. At the same time, the fact that it had an English-speaking section makes it suitable according to the selection criteria for having some international or at least supranational impact.

The unit of analysis is the online articles of the news media examined, concerning the Israel-Palestine conflict of May 2021. The articles concerning the conflict were gathered from the websites of the three news media networks in a timeframe from the beginning of May until the beginning of June, slightly after the ceasefire agreement was implemented.

Presentation and discussion of the findings

CNN

The US-based CNN media network covered in twenty-four articles the eleven-day Israel–Gaza conflict in May 2021. The network seemed to maintain a balanced projection for both sides. The Palestinians were being depicted as just victims provoking the attacks, whilst the articles reporting Palestinian casualties usually followed a justification for the attacks by the Israeli side. The Palestinian stories and accusations about the Israeli attacks were being taken by witnesses, victims or other Palestinian citizens and were usually followed by an explanation from an official Israeli source like the government, the Israeli Defense Force (IDF) or a high-ranking official, explaining that the attack was an answer to a prior provocation from the Palestinian side. This was an indirect use of responsibility attribution and blame shifting towards the Palestinian side.

> In Gaza, which has few bomb shelters and no air defense system, several buildings and apartments were damaged by Israeli airstrikes. One of those strikes destroyed Al-Shorouk Tower, a 14-story building in the southern Gaza strip on Wednesday evening … . The IDF said the tower housed Hamas military intelligence offices, as well as the infrastructure used by 'the terror organizations to communicate tactical-military information'. (CNN, 2021a)

The sequence of presenting first the claims of the Palestinians and then the explanation of an official Israeli side, using usually accusations or demonization, works as a justification for the actions taken by the Israelis and a cancelling of the claims posed by the Palestinians.

Another pro-Israeli stance of CNN is seen through bolstering. The Israeli military was being depicted as a state-of-the-art force that undertakes high-precision attacks and used techniques that do not affect civilians.

> Earlier on Wednesday, the Israeli military said it had killed several key Hamas officials in a 'complex and first-of-its-kind operation' at two separate locations.

Among the dead, it said, was a Hamas Brigadier General and the head of the militant group's 'cyber and missile improvement system'. (CNN, 2021b)

The overall dispute was being framed as a defence operation by the Israeli military that was very successful.

> Israel has been 'able to strike a significant part if not the majority of the military leadership of Hamas' in the past three days of bombardment, IDF spokesman Lt. Col. Jonathan Conricus told reporters.
> The IDF has struck 'significant parts' of Hamas' and Islamic Jihad's rocket-firing capability, he added, 'but it is by no means degraded'. (CNN, 2021c)

By bolstering the image of the Israeli military in a nexus of 'good' and 'evil', the side of the Palestinians was being downgraded and depicted in a more negative context. It is noteworthy that CNN, especially compared to the other news media examined, differentiated between Hamas and the Palestinians. Usually, the Palestinians were depicted as the victims of the conflict, whereas Hamas was the perpetrator. However, the word 'Palestinian' was used 1,391 times in the articles examined in comparison to 'Hamas' which was used only 192 times. This difference shows that in most cases in the depiction of the conflict, the connection was made with the Palestinians and not with Hamas.

Finally, strategic blame and demonization strategies mainly included atrocities undertaken by Palestinians and the number of innocent victims caused by the Israeli attacks.

> Other parts of the region have seen violence, too. Protests and mob violence, including attempted lynchings, have been reported in Israel, Jerusalem, and the West Bank. (CNN, 2021d)

Demonization was not used very frequently and included mainly very negative actions that were attributed to either side. However, for the Israeli side, demonization was used only to show the victims produced by the air raids of the military and was usually connected with a blaming strategy by the Palestinian reports.

> Al-Quadra said Israel had deliberately targeted civilian homes and crowded residential neighborhoods, adding that 43% of the victims of strikes in Gaza were children and women. (CNN, 2021d)

The network did not use any hard demonization techniques for any side of the conflict, probably to maintain significant objectivity in the news reporting.

Al Jazeera network

The Al Jazeera news media network showed more support to the Palestinian side than CNN. In the presentation of events, this news media network used more witness stories that formed a melodramatic frame and the image of the innocent victim of the Palestinians. Titles like 'Victims of Aggression' or 'Everything Lost in an Eye Blink: Gaza Towers Targeted by Israel' constructed a narrative of victimhood for the Palestinians and an image of the perpetrator for Israel.

The innocent victim frame for the Palestinians and the 'weak vs strong' narrative served as an indirect accusation and blame for the Israeli attacks. The fact that Palestinians 'have no bomb shelters to take refuge, unlike the Israelis' framed the Palestinians as the weak side. The victimization strategy aimed to deconstruct the Just War narrative and deconstruct any positive images for Israel. In addition, it formed a brutal image for the attackers.

> 'How can we be silent when they (Israel) are killing children in Gaza. Every human on earth should stand up for them. This is about showing humanity and solidarity, but we are not even able to do that due to fear,' a 25-year-old resident Illyas, a resident of Srinagar, told Al Jazeera. (Al Jazeera, 2021a)

A frequent strategy recorded in Al Jazeera was demonization. The use of words and titles like 'war crimes', 'devastation from Israeli attacks pummel Gaza' and 'death and destruction' pointed in that direction. The emphasis was placed on the victims of the attacks and especially on the women and children.

> Israel continued to bombard the Gaza Strip with air raids and artillery shells on Saturday, killing several children and women at a refugee camp. (Al Jazeera, 2021a)

The demonization process was constructed through the syllogism that only evil people would kill children and women in refugee camps, thus the Israelis are evil. This forms a demonization process without directly attacking the other side.

Another strategy was strategic blame. The media network attributed blame to Israel for the attacks. Blame is attributed to Israel even in cases where it is on the defensive side.

> At least 65 Palestinians have been killed in Israeli strikes on Gaza since Monday after Hamas fired rockets toward Israel in response to a continuing Israeli crackdown on Palestinians in occupied East Jerusalem. (Al Jazeera, 2021b).

The presentation of the events was being placed in a causation circle. Israel killed 65 Palestinians with its strikes against Gaza in an answer to the Hamas rocket fires. Nevertheless, the cause for the Hamas strikes was the 'crackdown on Palestinians in occupied East Jerusalem'. This way, the blame returned to Israel, because it was depicted as the initiator of the whole conflict.

Israel was also accused of causing major destruction to buildings and neighbourhoods.

> For days now, Israeli fighter jets have targeted several landmark buildings in the heart of Gaza City, completely flattening at least two high-rise blocks. Hanadi,

a tower with a mix of residential apartments and commercial offices, including Qadada's Planet for Digital Solutions, was one of them. (Al Jazeera, 2021c).

The accusations strategy also enhanced the negative image of Israel. Allegations were being presented also through the opinions and public addresses of other countries and international organizations regarding the conflict.

Reactions from foreign countries like the United States, the United Kingdom, Turkey and Russia and organizations like the United Nations, the European Union and the ICC were being presented.

> United States: 'Halt the violence'
> Russia: Putin urges de-escalation, minister calls on Israel to stop settlement activities
> United Kingdom: Johnson urges sides to 'show restraint'
> Turkey: Israel must be taught a 'lesson'
> ICC: 'Crimes' may have been committed
> EU: 'Very worried' (Al Jazeera, 2021d)

The presentation of the remarks of other countries implied an indirect accusation towards the continuation of the conflict from Israel. Another type of allegation towards Israel was the ironic translation of an article in the case of the warning for the attack on the Al Jazeera offices.

> Israel warns of air attack on a media building
> Israel has given a 'warning' that it will bomb the building that houses the Al Jazeera offices and other international media outlets in Gaza City within the next hour.
> (Highlighted text) Translation: The Israeli occupation army gives one hour to evacuate a building that houses international press offices, including Al Jazeera. (Al Jazeera, 2021e)

This allegation aimed directly towards Israel's actions and the decision to attack media outlets in Gaza city, including the Al Jazeera network.

Finally, the last strategy used was association. The first use was the association of Israel with negative practices like war crimes, which prime other times of severe conflict.

> The United Nations last week urged Israel to call off the forced expulsions, warning such action could amount to war crimes. (Al Jazeera, 2021a)

> From calls for 'restraint' to worries about possible war crimes, political leaders and international courts weigh in on the latest escalation. (Al Jazeera, 2021d)

The second form was guilt by association as an indirect accusation of the United States and its support for Israel.

The United States, a major supporter of Israel that provides the country with $3.8bn in military aid annually, has faced calls to 'put the brakes on the Israelis' as violence escalates in the occupied Palestinian territories and inside Israel itself. (Al Jazeera, 2021a)

Associating Israel with the United States shows the power status of Israel and highlights the enmity towards the Arab world.

Times Of Israel

The Times of Israel differed significantly in comparison to the other two media networks. The news-media network is pro-Israeli. The outlet emphasized the casualties of the Israeli forces and citizens rather than the Palestinians. Furthermore, it referred directly to the opposing side not as Palestinians but as Hamas, calling it also a terrorist organization.

The overall presentation of the attacks here was softer than in the other news media examined. The IDF attacks were being presented as a very organized and precise plan with specific targets that affected only the terrorist leaders and operatives. No major civilian casualties were being recognized.

The operations were undertaken to counter the underground network of Hamas and destroy its attack capabilities. The casualties from the Palestinian side were being presented as just victims as they were considered, in their majority, members of Hamas.

The main strategy used was bolstering of the image of the Israeli forces. It was mainly used to highlight the effectiveness of the IDF's capability in fighting the attacks.

Several other rockets were intercepted by the Iron Dome missile defense system, while others landed in open areas. The Israel Fire and Rescue Services said firefighters were working to douse a number of blazes sparked by rocket fire. (Times of Israel, 2021a)

Another strategy was allegations. The allegations focused on the attacks held by the opposing sides like the Palestinians and the 'different terrorist groups' that were responsible for the attacks against Israel. The aim was to justify the attacks of the IDF as a defence.

In a statement Wednesday, the IDF said the overnight raids included an attack by fighter jets on three Hamas operatives in an 'operational safe house' in Gaza City that was part of the terror group's cyber-warfare apparatus. (Times of Israel, 2021a)

The Palestinian side was presented as responsible for the deaths. In some cases, the victims were terrorist operatives, in others, victims of friendly fire. Consequently, the blame was strategically shifted to the Palestinian side for the casualties, forming, at the same time, the just victim frame.

Israel says over half of those killed were terror operatives, and that others were killed by errant Palestinian rockets. (Times of Israel, 2021b)

This way, the side of Israel was being presented as effective and just, whereas the opposing side was being demonized through its identification with terrorist organizations. In addition, the cause of the conflict was attributed to the Palestinian side and the terrorist organizations operating within its territories. The blaming strategy aimed to show the causes of the conflict.

> The fighting began May 10, when Hamas terrorists in Gaza fired long-range rockets toward Jerusalem. Palestinian terror groups have tied rocket fire from Gaza to unrest in Jerusalem connected to both prayers on the Temple Mount during the Muslim holy month of Ramadan, as well as the pending eviction of several Palestinian families from the Sheikh Jarrah neighborhood. (Times of Israel, 2021c)

Moreover, the journal used a demonization strategy and name-calling for the Palestinians. It is noteworthy, that the term 'Hamas' was being used 267 times in comparison to the term 'Palestinians' used only 45 times. In addition, the journal used characterizations like 'terror groups' and 'Palestinian Terrorists'. Hamas was considered a terrorist organization and was implied to be identified with the Palestinian side.

This identification works twofold. On the one hand, the Palestinian side was being delegitimized and their demands or rights were being identified with the terrorists' demands. On the other hand, the delegitimization leaded to the construction of the just victim frame, meaning that the Palestinian casualties were being perceived as the elimination of enemy targets.

Throughout this process, the enemy image was being constructed in a way that legitimized the actions of the Israelis, at least for the domestic audience. Furthermore, the Palestinians were taking the blame for the attacks and the killings that happenned on both sides, and at the same time, the Israelis were presented on the defensive trying to free both sides from terrorist activities. The presentation of Hamas as the actual 'enemy' revealed the image Israel had for the Palestinian side. Consequently, the use of the enemy image and the other strategies constructed a narrative of 'good' Israelis and 'bad' Palestinians. It is noteworthy that the other two media did not directly use such a negative depiction of either side.

Conclusion

The study explored the character assassination strategies in international media for the representation of the eleven-day Israel–Palestine conflict in May 2021. The finding suggests that international media may use character assassination strategies to influence public opinion about the conflict and make negative depictions of participating countries. However, whether this is done strategically following a political position (RQ2) because of their country of origin (political logic) is partially supported by the findings. CNN may be considered as having followed its media logic and presented the events in as distanced a manner as possible, although some character assassination strategies were identified. Similarly, Al Jazeera was also driven by media logic to some extent but considering that the use of character assassination strategies was more frequent and targeted, it could be inferred that political logic drove some articles. In contrast, the Times of Israel used more severe character assassination strategies with a very focused target on the opposing side. This points to the direction of acting under the political logic.

The main character assassination strategies used (RQ3) were strategic blame, association, identification, name-calling and demonization. Except for demonization and name-calling, the other strategies may be characterized as softer character assassination strategies. In addition, the way they were implemented by the media points in that direction. This strengthens the findings that at least the two international media were more discrete than the local Israeli media.

The image formed through these strategies (RQ4) is related to the media stance. CNN implements a more distanced position towards the conflict and therefore depicts both sides as equally responsible. Israel is being depicted as a stable power with specific and focused objectives with an image of a just response. Al Jazeera forms the image of the weak for Palestine, presenting Israel as evil. This way, the image of innocent victims is being developed for Palestinians. Finally, the Times of Israel depicts Palestine in a very negative manner. It directly identifies it with terrorist organizations and does not differentiate the Palestinians from Hamas. On the contrary, Israel is being depicted in a very positive way, as an organized country with a strategic aim against specific targets that do not affect innocent victims but terrorists.

To sum up, as the study's key findings show, character assassination techniques may be used by the media during the representation of an interstate conflict. It is not clear, however, whether the aim of such use is intentional (for reasons of political logic) or based on the news-media-making process. Although this may be a limitation of the current study, follow-up studies may focus on the connection between the media and the state considering the use of Character Assassination strategies. Future studies may also focus on more media networks.

References

Ackerman, S. (2001), 'Al-Aqsa Intifada and the U.S. Media', *Journal of Palestine Studies*, 30 (2): 61–74, https://doi.org/10.1525/jps.2001.30.2.61.

Altheide, D. L. (2004), 'Media Logic and Political Communication', *Political Communication*, 21 (3): 293–6, https://doi.org/10.1080/10584600490481307.

Al Jazeera (2021a), 'Several Children Killed as Israel Pounds Gaza Refugee Camp: Live', 15 May, https://www.aljazeera.com/news/2021/5/14/israels-bombardment-of-gaza-contin ues-live (accessed 3 December 2021).

Al Jazeera (2021b), 'US again Urges "De-escalation" as Israel Strikes on Gaza Continue', 12 May, https://www.aljazeera.com/news/2021/5/12/us-again-urges-de-escalation-israel-strikes-gaza-continue (accessed 3 December 2021).

Al Jazeera (2021c), '"Everything Lost in an Eye Blink": Gaza Towers Targeted by Israel', 13 May, https://www.aljazeera.com/news/2021/5/13/lost-in-blink-of-an-eye-gaz a-high-rise-towers-targeted-by-israel (accessed 3 December 2021).

Al Jazeera (2021d), 'The Israel–Palestine Conflict Raises Alarm across the World', 12 May, https://www.aljazeera.com/news/2021/5/12/israel-palestine-conflict-raises-alarm-in-europe (accessed 3 December 2021).

Al Jazeera (2021e), ' "Give Us 10 Minutes": How Israel Bombed a Gaza Media Tower', 15 May, https://www.aljazeera.com/news/2021/5/15/give-us-10-minutes-how-israel-bom bed-gaza-media-tower (accessed 3 December 2021).

Asp, K. (2014), 'News Media Logic in a New Institutional Perspective', *Journalism Studies*, 15 (3): 256–70, https://doi.org/10.1080/1461670X.2014.889456.

Aspriadis, N., E. Takas and N. Samaras Ath (2020), 'Country Reputation Assassination during the Greek Memorandum Renegotiations'. In S. Samoilenko, M. Icks, J. Keohane and E. Shiraev (eds), *The Routledge Handbook of Character Assassination and Reputation Management*, New York: Routledge, 236–49.

Bahador, B. (2007), *The CNN Effect in Action; How the News Media Pushed the West Towards War in Kosovo*, New York: Palgrave Macmillan.

Belknap, M. (2002), 'The CNN Effect: Strategic Enabler or Operational Risk'?, *Parameters*, 32 (3): 100–25.

Burton, M. J., and D. M. Shea (2002), *Campaign Mode: Strategic Vision in Congressional Elections*, Lanham, MD: Rowman and Littlefield Publishers.

Carpentier, N. (2010), 'Deploying Discourse Theory: An Introduction to Discourse Theory and Discourse Theoretical Analysis'. In N. Carpentier (ed.), *Media and Communication Studies Intersections and Interventions*, Belgium: Tartu University Press, 251–66.

CNN (2021a), 'At Least 35 Killed in Gaza as Israel Ramps Up Airstrikes in Response to Rocket Attacks', At least 35 killed in Gaza as Israel ramps up airstrikes in response to rocket attacks – CNN, https://edition.cnn.com/2021/05/11/middleeast/israel-gaza-air strikes-rockets-intl/index.html (accessed 1 December 2021).

CNN (2021b), At Least 10 Palestinians Killed by Israeli Soldiers in Violent Confrontations in West Bank, as Gaza Rocket Fire Enters Fifth Day', 15 May, https://edition.cnn. com/2021/05/14/middleeast/israel-palestinian-clashes-intl/index.html (accessed 1 December 2021).

CNN (2021c), 'Heavy Artillery Fire on Gaza Escalates Violence as Clashes between Arabs and Jews Rock Israeli Cities', 14 May, Israel–Gaza conflict: Heavy artillery fire escalates violence as clashes between Arabs and Jews rock Israeli cities – CNN, https://edition. cnn.com/2021/05/13/middleeast/israel-palestinian-violence-intl/index.html (accessed 1 December 2021).

CNN (2021d), 'Supporters of Palestinian Rights Hold Protests across the United States', 23 May, https://edition.cnn.com/2021/05/22/us/pro-palestinian-protests-us/index.html (accessed 1 December 2021).

Entman, R. M. (2003), 'Cascading Activation: Contesting the White House's Frame after 9/11'. *Political Communication*, 20(4), 415–32.

Entman R. M. (2004), *Projections of Power, Framing News, Public Opinion and U.S. Foreign Policy*, Chicago: University Chicago Press.

Esser, F. (2013), 'Media Logic Versus Political Logic'. In M. B. Hanspeter and S. L. Kriesi, F. Esser and J. Matthes (eds), *Democracy in the Age of Globalization and Mediatization*, London: Palgrave Macmillan, 155–76.

Gilboa, E. (2005), 'The CNN Effect: The Search for a Communication Theory of International Relations', *Political Communication*, 22 (1): 27–44, https://doi.org/10.1080/10584600590908429.

Gillham, B. (2000), *Case Study Analysis*, London: Continuum.

Goussios, C., N. Aspriadis, Z. Tsirimiagou and M. Dogani (2014), 'Rhetorical Use of Fear in Presidential Speeches: The War on Terror Discourse', *Journal of Arab & Muslim Media Research*, 7 (2): 163–83.

Icks, M., and E. Shiraev (2014), *Character Assassination throughout the Ages*, New York: Palgrave Macmillan.

Icks, M., E. Shiraev, J. Keohane, and S. A. Samoilenko (2019), 'Character Assassination: Theoretical Framework'. In *Routledge Handbook of Character Assassination and Reputation Management*. Routledge, pp. 11–24.

Krebs, T. B., and D. B. Holian (2007), 'Competitive Positioning, Deracialization, and Attack Speech: A Study of Negative Campaigning in the 2001 Los Angeles Mayoral Election', *American Politics Research*, 35 (1): 123–49, https://doi.org/10.1177/15326 73X06292320.

Krippendorf, K. (2004), *Content Analysis: An Introduction to Its Methodology*, Thousand Oaks, CA: Sage Publications.

Korn, A. (2004), 'Reporting Palestinian Casualties in the Israeli Press: The Case of Haaretz and the Intifada', *Journalism Studies*, 5 (2): 247–62, https://doi.org/10.1080/14616700 42000211212.

Laruelle, M. (2020), 'Reductio ad Hitlerum Is a New Frame for Political and Geopolitical Conflicts'. In S. Samoilenko, M. Icks, J. Keohane and E. Shiraev (eds), *The Routledge Handbook of Character Assassination and Reputation Management*, New York: Routledge, 307–19.

Normand, L. (2016), *Demonization in International Politics*, 1st edition, Highlands Ranch, CO: Palgrave Macmillan, https://doi.org/10.1057/978-1-137-54581-7.

Paul, J. (2011), *An Introduction to Discourse Analysis: Theory and Method*, London: Routledge.

Rojo, L. (1995), 'Division and Rejection: From the Personification of the Gulf Conflict to the Demonization of Saddam Hussein', *Discourse and Society*, 6 (49): 49–80.

Ruigrok, N., W. van Atteveldt and J. Takes (2013), 'Shifting Frames in a Deadlocked Conflict? News Coverage of the Israel–Palestine Conflict'. In J. Seethaler, M. Karmasin, G. Melisscek and R. Woelert, *Selling War: The Role of the Mass Media in Hostile Conflict from World War 1 to the War on Terror*, Bristol: Intellect, 259–89.

Samaras, A.N. (2004), 'Home Front Management and Media Logic', *Defensor Pracis*: 67–84.

Samoilenko, S., M. Icks, J. Keohane and E. Shiraev (eds) (2020), *The Routledge Handbook of Character Assassination and Reputation Management*, New York: Routledge.

Samoilenko, S. A. (2014), 'The Situation in Ukraine: One or Many Realities?', *Russian Journal of Communication*, 6 (2): 193–8.

Samoilenko, S., A. E. Erzikova, S. Davydov and A. Laskin (2017), 'Different Media, Same Messages: Character Assassination in the Television News during the 2014 Ukrainian Crisis', *International Communication Research Journal*, 52 (2): 28–52.

Seiffert-Brockmann, J., S. Einwiller and J. Stranzl (2018), 'Character Assassination of CEOs in Crises – Questioning CEOs' Character and Values Incorporate Crises', *European Journal of Communication*, 33 (4): 413–29.

Shiraev, E. (2014), 'Character Assassination: How Political Psychologists Can Assist Historians'. In *Character Assassination throughout the Ages*. New York: Palgrave Macmillan, 15–33.

Shiraev E. B., J. Keohanne, M. Icks and S. A. Samoilenko (2021), *Character Assassination and Reputation Management: Theory and Applications*, New York: Routledge.

Siapera, E., G. Hunt and T. Lynn (2015), '#GazaUnderAttack: Twitter, Palestine, and Diffused War', *Information Communication and Society*, 18 (11): 1297–319, https://doi.org/10.1080/1369118X.2015.1070188.

Simons, G. (2020), 'The Role of Propaganda in the Character Assassination of World Leaders in International Affairs'. In S. Samoilenko, M. Icks, J. Keohane and E. Shiraev (eds), *The Routledge Handbook of Character Assassination and Reputation Management*, New York: Routledge, 163–79.

Strömbäck, J. (2008), 'Four Phases of Mediatization: An Analysis of the Mediatization of Politics', *International Journal of Press/Politics*, 13 (3): 228–46, https://doi.org/10.1177/1940161208319097.

Takas, E., and A. N. Samaras (2016), 'Legitimation and De-legitimation Processes of Memorandum II in Greece: Facets of Strategic Framing in Greek Parliamentary Discourse', *French Journal for Media Research*, 5 (3): 1–22.

Takens, J., W. van Atteveldt, A. van Hoof and J. Kleinnijenhuis (2013), 'Media Logic in Election Campaign Coverage', *European Journal of Communication*, 28 (3): 277–93, https://doi.org/10.1177/0267323113478522.

Times of Jerusalem (2021a), 'Hamas Pummels South, Central Israel with Rocket Salvos on 10th Day of Fighting', 19 May, https://www.timesofisrael.com/hamas-pumm els-south-central-israel-with-rocket-salvos-on-10th-day-of-fighting/ (accessed 3 December 2021).

Times of Jerusalem (2021b), 'Gaza Officials Say Israeli Strike Kills Disabled Man, His Wife and Child', 19 May, https://www.timesofisrael.com/liveblog_entry/gaza-officials-say-israeli-strike-kills-disabled-man-his-wife-and-child/ (accessed 3 December 2021).

Times of Jerusalem (2021c), 'Minister: From Now On, We'll Preemptively Strike Hamas Rocket Activity', 23 May, https://www.timesofisrael.com/minister-from-now-on-well-preemptively-strike-hamas-rocket-activity/ (accessed 3 December 2021).

Thussu, D. K., and D. Freedman (2003), *War and the Media: Reporting Conflict 24/7*, London: Sage Publications.

Van Dijk, T. A. (1997), *Discourse as Social Interaction (Vol. 2). Sage.*

Van Evera, S. (1997), *Guide to Methods for Students of Political Science*, Ithaca, NY: Cornell University Press.

Walton, D. (2006), *Character Evidence: An Abductive Theory*, Dordrecht, The Netherlands: Springer.

Zelizer, B., D. Park and D. Gudelunas (2002), 'How Bias Shapes the News', *Journalism*, 3 (3): 283–307, https://doi.org/10.1177/146488490200300305.

Index

www.ingramcontent.com/pod-product-compliance
Lightning Source LLC
Chambersburg PA
CBHW071844270326
41929CB00013B/2097